Collegiate Capitalism

The Battle for the Future of College Sports

Donald M. Remy

Networlding PUBLISHING

Contents

Preface: The End of Amateurism

A New Model for College Athletics

The call came on a Tuesday morning while I was standing in a high school gym, whistle around my neck, the familiar smell of old leather and floor wax all around me as I watched fourteen-year-olds fumble through a defensive drill I'd taught a thousand times before. The call was not from a client nor a court clerk, but from the NCAA. The NCAA. They wanted me, a trial lawyer and grassroots basketball coach who'd spent years rolling his eyes at their rulebooks, to become their chief legal counsel.

The irony was delicious. An organization I'd viewed as more interested in bureaucracy than young people was asking me to help navigate their legal battles. I almost laughed out loud. Almost. Instead, I found myself saying yes to a chance of a lifetime, and walking into a world that would soon explode around all of us.

That was years ago, back when college athletics still clung to the notion of amateurism. Back when "student-athlete" wasn't a punchline, and the NCAA could still believe that billion-dollar television contracts somehow coexisted with pure amateur competition. I'm afraid those days are gone forever, buried under an avalanche of court decisions, name image and likeness deals, transfer portals, revenue sharing, private equity investments, and the harsh reality that pretending something isn't big business doesn't make it so.

I first envisioned this project three years removed from my days at the NCAA and one year after government service. I started writing a year later, and today, as I complete this iteration, American college athletics at the highest levels stands in the rubble of its former self. The Supreme Court has spoken with devastating clarity. NIL deals have created a wild west of recruitment that makes the old under-the-table payments look quaint. Athletes transfer like free agents, chasing better deals and bigger stages. The coaching carousel has accelerated, with program and institutional loyalty often taking a back seat to market forces. Sanctioned revenue sharing is here to stay. Gambling permeates everything: politicians write contradictory laws from state to state; the United States Congress has failed to act; and private investors circle like sharks, sensing blood in the water. Even United States presidents have weighed in. The old model isn't just dying, it's already dead, and we're all just imagining we don't smell the corpse.

But here's what nobody is yet ready to see: transformation isn't a tragedy. It's an opportunity.

I learned early in my career that you could work within the system without becoming the system. I wore cowboy boots under my suit while other lawyers clicked across marble courtroom floors in polished oxfords. This quiet rebellion taught me that the most powerful transformations happen from the inside, by people willing to wear their boots in wing-tip corridors.

That philosophy guided me through my journey from skeptical coach to legal advocate to NCAA insider to college sports chief operating officer, as I watched the tectonic plates shift beneath an industry too proud or too stubborn to adapt. I've argued cases to victory and defeat that helped shape this new landscape, negotiated in boardrooms where billion-dollar decisions were made, and counseled everyone from Olympic hopefuls to administrators grappling with change they never saw coming.

What I learned will surprise you, maybe even shock you coming from me. The future for big-time college sports I envision, the one I call "Collegiate Capitalism," looks nothing like yesterday or even what we have today. Picture the Alabama Crimson Tide football team owned and controlled not by the University but by private investors. Imagine Olympic athletes training at specialized institutes, as they do in China or hybrid models like Germany's Olympic training centers, rather than on college campuses. Consider a world in which college athletes are unionized professional employees, not of the Universities but of private entities, while still maintaining access to education and many of the traditions fans hold dear.

Preface: The End of Amateurism

> This isn't science fiction. It's inevitability. And the sooner we embrace it, the sooner we can build something better than what we had, and way better than what we're losing.

The blueprint already exists. The NBA and NFL show us that American professional sports maintain competitive balance and fan loyalty. Japanese baseball demonstrates corporate ownership coexisting with community identity. European soccer proves professional athletics development can thrive outside traditional educational institutions. We don't need to reinvent the wheel. We just need to stop behaving like we're still riding horses in the age of electric automobiles.

This dilemma touches something deeper than sports. When I think about Jesse Owens running for The Ohio State University in the 1930s, or the Naval Academy rower I recently counseled to focus on academics and integrity, I'm reminded that college athletics has always been about more than the games. It's about dreams, development, and the uniquely American way we've chosen to cultivate excellence in both body and mind. However, it has also been about the erosion of principles that happens when money floods a system built for a different era and ideology, and when the infrastructure can't keep up with growth.

The questions we face aren't just about sports. These are questions that equally apply to the future of American institutions, especially those responsible for educating our young people.

How do we preserve what makes college athletics special, including its role in developing talent and maintaining Olympic excellence, while creating genuine fairness for athletes and building a model that can survive in a market-driven world?

The answer may require us to blow up everything at the highest levels and start over. I don't offer that lightly, nor revel in its reality. I passionately believe in the magic of American college athletics, and would enjoy nothing more than to find a way to preserve all the goodness it has offered to generations. Perhaps that remains a possibility with schools that opt out, lower divisions, and sports that don't generate revenue. Yet, through my years developing legal strategies, negotiating billion-dollar deals, and yes, engaging in quiet non-conformity with unconventional thinking, I've gained insights into both what must change and what can be preserved.

This book offers not only a cause-and-effect analysis but a roadmap for revolution, including a new model that could save big-time college athletics by admitting what it really is and building something honest from the ground up.

I'm not simply writing about the games here. I provide a look back at the history of sports within American Universities, a journey through recent events, including athletics, political, legal, and economic developments that have led us to today, and a futurist's perspective on what comes next. Originally, I drafted a series of essays about various issues in higher education athletics, which I have woven together here with a common thread. I recognize that sometimes I write about the details of legal cases, and while lawyers may love it, others may not. At times, I lean heavily into sports policy and governance, which I suspect may only be fascinating to college sports administrators. The history buffs will enjoy my documentary reflection. And the leadership and policy aficionados will find something interesting in my discussions about how things happened and where they are going. Everything may not be for everybody, but whether you're an athlete dreaming of greatness, a coach building young lives, an administrator managing impossible pressures, a lawyer trying to persuade the Court and the court of public opinion, a fan who bleeds your school colors, an investor sensing opportunity, a policymaker crafting legislation, or simply someone who cares about the future of American institutions, this story matters to you.

A word about what this book is not. In 1981, Jack Falla wrote *NCAA: The Voice of College Sports*, which chronicled the NCAA's first seventy-five years, and in 2006 Joe Crowley produced *In the Arena*, the definitive history of the Association's first century. As the NCAA approaches its quasquicentennial in 2031, someone will write the comprehensive account of those 125 years, especially since 2006. This is not that book. While I was inspired by their work and I weave the historical significance of certain events into the time continuum of change, this work is one participant's reckoning with a single, decisive era, with the part I played in defending a model under siege, and with what comes next.

Preface: The End of Amateurism

This book gives you a unique perspective on the rooms where it happened, from someone who was in many of them. I have written, reviewed, and revised it from the public record and my own reflection, and it discloses nothing that is privileged or confidential. You'll read about the strategy in groundbreaking court cases, including *O'Bannon*, *Alston, and House.* The reasons behind conference realignment, the transfer portal, and NIL adventures will become clearer. I'll help you understand how criminal prosecution and enforcement actions in the Southern District of New York, Penn State, Miami, North Carolina, to name a few, exposed weaknesses in the system. You'll learn how business, cultural, and political icons Ken Chenault, Jay-Z, Condi Rice, Will Smith, Vivek Murthy, and others influenced the trajectory of college sports. I'll explore how civil rights and gender equity movements have shaped our thinking about fairness and justice. We'll examine together the serious threat posed by sports gambling. The economic imperatives will be vividly evident as we crawl, walk, and run through history. And, there is so much more. In the end, you'll learn about me, some of my journey, my triumphs and failures, my leadership philosophies and analytical framework, and why I believe what I believe about what's next.

The stakes extend well beyond college football Saturdays or March Madness brackets. At its core, this is about how America develops talent, creates opportunities, and sustains excellence in the unique marriage of sports and education.

The end of amateurism is here. Are we ready? Are we brave enough to recognize the problems of the old system and build something better from what's left?

I'm Donald Remy, former Chief Legal Officer and Chief Operating Officer of the NCAA. Welcome to the age of Collegiate Capitalism. It's going to be a hell of a ride.

Chapter 1
The Historical Foundation for Collegiate Capitalism
The Template Was Set

The die was cast on a warm August day in 1852, though nobody at Lake Winnipesaukee could have imagined they were witnessing the birth of a multi-billion-dollar industry. When Harvard's crew pulled ahead of Yale's in that first intercollegiate athletics contest, more than just a boat race was decided; the very DNA of American college sports was being spawned.

It started as a publicity stunt. The Boston, Concord & Montreal Railroad Company had sponsored the whole spectacle, offering free transportation and lavish hospitality to draw crowds along their scenic route. By some accounts, thousands arrived by special trains, money changed hands through heavy gambling, and the commercial machinery hummed beneath the veneer of collegiate competition. The template was set. American college athletics would forever blend sport with commerce, student activity with public entertainment, amateur ideals with professional realities.

What began with rowing soon expanded to football and basketball, sports that would become the twin engines driving college athletics into the modern era. Early football contests bore little resemblance to today's choreographed spectacles. Versions of the game can be traced back to more violent and deadly forms from the 1600s, the British Middle Ages, the Ts'in and Han Dynasties of the third century, and even Ancient Greece and Rome. The style of the game we find familiar began to take shape in 1874. Even still, in the college environment, games were informal affairs with no standardized rules, played between regional universities before modest crowds. As popularity grew, so did the need for oversight, and by 1906, mounting concerns over player safety led to the formation of what would become the National Collegiate Athletic Association (NCAA).

Its primary aim, at the start, was to stop the killings. The sport had become notoriously brutal, claiming eighteen or more lives in 1905 alone, until United States President Theodore Roosevelt intervened, threatening to ban the game entirely unless colleges and universities implemented reforms. The NCAA, a membership-led organization, emerged as the solution. It was to be a regulatory body that would civilize college football while preserving its competitive spirit.

For the first half of the twentieth century, this arrangement worked reasonably well. The NCAA remained a modest governing body focused on safety and fair play, while college sports maintained their character as student activities with an educational purpose. Athletes were amateurs in the truest sense. They were students first, competitors second, and participants in what was fundamentally an extension of campus life.

Then came television, and everything changed.

The post-World War II boom brought prosperity and technology that transformed American culture, and college sports rode the wave. Major contests like the Rose Bowl began drawing massive television audiences, creating revenue streams that universities had never imagined. Broadcasting rights became valuable assets, and what had once been student activities suddenly generated serious money. By the 1960s, iconic programs like Penn State, Notre Dame, USC, Texas, and Alabama weren't just playing football; they were producing entertainment that captivated millions and filled university coffers.

The NCAA found itself managing more than safety and the rules of the game. Campuses, conferences, and the national office were steering a growing industry. The men's basketball tournament evolved into March Madness, a cultural phenomenon that mesmerized the nation for weeks. Television deals proliferated, ticket sales soared, and revenues grew exponentially. Through it all, the NCAA and its member schools clung to its amateur model, insisting that athletes were students who happened to play sports, not athlete-entertainers who helped to drive the economic engine.

This framework became increasingly difficult to sustain. In 1948, recognizing that the system was showing signs of stress fractures, the NCAA established its "Sanity Code," restricting athletes' compensation to need-based assistance covering tuition, fees, and living expenses, with no awards based on athletic ability. No salaries, no benefits beyond the basics, and the line between amateurism and professionalism would be firmly drawn and vigilantly defended.

But commercial cats, once released, rarely return to their cages voluntarily. The Sanity Code symbolized the NCAA's Maginot Line against commercialization. It was ambitious in design but ultimately could not contain the forces it sought to control. That failed regulatory effort was the first unavoidable step toward Collegiate Capitalism.

The 1960s and 70s also brought legal rulings that began chipping away at the NCAA's authority. Courts and legislators questioned the Association's power over increasingly lucrative enterprises, particularly regarding player and coach compensation, rule enforcement, racial integration, and gender equality. Each challenge revealed the growing incongruity in a system in which almost everyone profited except the performers themselves. While Chapter 10 will detail the legal landscape, some preliminary observations highlight the challenge.

The earthquake came in 1984 with *NCAA v. Board of Regents of the University of Oklahoma* (*"Board of Regents")*. The Supreme Court's decision shattered the NCAA's alleged price-fixing and output-limiting television plan, using the rule of reason to find that the Association's control over broadcasts violated antitrust laws. Suddenly, individual schools and conferences could negotiate their own television contracts, unleashing an explosion of broadcasting deals and revenues.

There is no doubt *Board of Regents* opened the floodgates, leading to today's rampant commercialization. With schools and conferences free to pursue their own television riches, major college sports morphed from campus activities into entertainment properties competing with professional leagues for viewer attention and advertiser dollars. The decision didn't just increase revenue possibilities. The Court's ruling altered the nature of college athletics, making it more visible, more valuable, and more removed from any genuine connection to historical views of amateurism.

Over the years, the NCAA won some battles even as it was losing the war. In the 1988 *NCAA v. Tarkanian* case, the Supreme Court ruled 5-4 that the NCAA was not a state actor subject to constitutional due process requirements, effectively shielding its enforcement and disciplinary proceedings from Fourteenth Amendment challenges. Importantly, however, coaches were fighting NCAA sanctions for competitive reasons *and* because significant compensation hung in the balance.

Throughout the 1990s and early 2000s, legal challenges progressively focused on the elephant in the room. Should college athletes receive greater benefits? Cases attacked the NCAA's scholarship restrictions as anticompetitive, arguing that while universities and conferences profited handsomely, athletes' scholarships and benefits failed to cover their full educational costs.

The handwriting was on the wall and in the legal briefs. By the time I arrived at the NCAA in 2011, notwithstanding our legitimate legal arguments, the practical contradictions were impossible to ignore. The Association was winning most cases, but each victory felt increasingly pyrrhic. While we continued to prevail in court, the broader landscape was shifting. The arguments challenging the traditional model were gaining traction in the courts, state legislatures, and public opinion, and the revenue gap between what athletes helped generate and what they received was becoming more glaring.

Then came *O'Bannon v. NCAA* in 2014, a direct assault on the Association's prohibition on athletes profiting from the use of their name, image, and likeness (NIL). The ruling in the case cracked open fundamental questions about athletes' rights and the NCAA's authority that couldn't be dismissed or deflected.

Under mounting pressure from state legislation and court decisions, the NCAA reluctantly changed its rules in 2021, adopting an interim policy that allowed athletes to profit from their NIL rights. This new approach marked the NCAA's appreciation that its traditional amateur model was significantly at risk. NIL deals proliferated rapidly, reshaping the financial dynamics of college athletics and accelerating the revolution that had been building for decades.

The final blow came in *NCAA v. Alston,* a case in which I was intimately involved in developing our legal strategy all the way to the United States Supreme Court. The Court's 9-0 ruling was more than another legal defeat. Justice Neil Gorsuch's majority opinion rejected the NCAA's attempt to shield its compensation rules from ordinary antitrust scrutiny, while Justice Brett Kavanaugh's concurrence went further, questioning whether any of the NCAA's remaining compensation restrictions could survive legal challenge. His harsh words mocked the very foundations of our position.

Alston set the stage for the *House v. NCAA* case. Rather than face treble damages in an increasingly hostile legal environment, the NCAA and major conferences chose surrender over potential annihilation, agreeing to a settlement that, for the first time in history, allowed schools to pay athletes directly.

And between these landmark legal battles, the system was battered by enforcement failures, policy missteps, safety crises, fraud, and corruption, all of which will be explored in the chapters ahead. Standing at this historical inflection point, the arc becomes clear.

> What began with a boat race sponsored by a railroad company has evolved into something entirely new. The NCAA, as we've known it, is being fundamentally reshaped, not only by external legal and market pressures but also by the accumulated weight of a model that could not adapt quickly enough to a changing world.

In its place, Collegiate Capitalism has emerged, and it will fundamentally transform how college sports operate.

The revolution is here, and there's no going back.

Chapter 2
The Architecture of Collegiate Capitalism
Money Talks

The future arrived faster than most expected and many desired. When NIL payments by collectives kicked off in 2021, and then the *House* settlement checks began passing the ball to college athletes in 2025, we crossed a threshold from which there can be no return. But those first payments, which can initially amount to more than $20 million distributed annually by participating schools, represent only the first quarter of a far more dramatic pivot in the game.

Collegiate Capitalism is not simply about paying athletes or allowing NIL deals. It is a complete restructuring of how college sports at the highest levels operate, are financed, and will be governed. This new model will fundamentally reshape the relationship among universities, athletes, investors, and fans, creating an industry that looks less like traditional college athletics and more like a marriage between professional sports and entertainment conglomerates on college campuses.

The architecture of this system rests on four foundational pillars: private investment supplementing and increasingly supplanting traditional university and donor funding; athletes treated as compensated employees or contracted labor of private entities rather than as traditional university students; intellectual property licensing that maximizes revenue streams; and facility leasing arrangements that separate ownership from operations. Together, these elements create an ecosystem in which financial performance, not the educational mission, drives decision-making.

So, what is Collegiate Capitalism in a nutshell? It is the market-driven system replacing amateurism in which major college athletics programs or teams either transform into professional commercial enterprises themselves or cede operational control to them, retaining collegiate branding while functioning on the economic principles of professional sports, compensating athletes, negotiating labor arrangements, and operating under market competition for both talent and revenue.

Understanding this concept, private equity firms and venture capitalists have already begun circling the college athletics space. They see what university administrators often miss. College sports are an undervalued entertainment property with massive growth potential. While universities have been content with television contracts and modest sponsorship deals, sophisticated investors recognize that college sports represent one of the last great untapped entertainment markets in America. We've been waiting for someone, anyone, to cross the threshold first with private equity. The University of Utah has given us a case study.

On December 9, 2025, Utah's Board of Trustees unanimously approved a deal with New York-based Otro Capital that creates Utah Brands & Entertainment LLC, a for-profit entity that will control the athletics department's major revenue streams while the university retains majority ownership.

It is easy to understand why Utah felt compelled to act. In fiscal year 2024, Utah athletics reported \$126.8 million in operating costs and \$109.8 million in revenue, resulting in a \$17 million deficit. Football generated more than \$26 million in profit, while men's basketball generated less than \$3 million, but the remaining 17 sports lost around \$21 million. The structural imbalance had become unsustainable, and the *House* settlement commitments only accelerated the bleeding.

Utah was first, but will not be last. The Big Ten seriously pursued a \$2.4 billion deal with UC Investments that would have given the California pension fund a 10% stake in the conference's media and sponsorship rights, but Michigan and USC objected to the proposal. The fact that it advanced so far, however, indicates how quickly financial pressures are normalizing the unthinkable. The Big 12 similarly considered but rejected a partnership with CVC Capital Partners, reportedly worth up to \$1 billion.

Utah's athletics director, Mark Harlan, has acknowledged publicly that the conference's revenue sits below the SEC and Big Ten. Private capital offers a path to competitiveness that traditional university financing and booster support cannot provide. Schools that embrace these arrangements will have resources to pay athletes, hire coaches, and build facilities that those relying solely on traditional funding can't match.

The implications extend far beyond Utah. Every athletics department running deficits, which is to say nearly all of them, will now consider whether private capital offers a solution. Every PE firm will examine whether college athletics represents the undervalued entertainment property that Utah's deal suggests it is. The floodgate has opened, and we will spend years discovering how much water flows through.

Consider the mathematics. The NFL in 2024 generated roughly $23 billion annually across 32 franchises, a number that has grown almost every year since 1920. Of the over 135 NCAA Division I Football Bowl Subdivision (FBS) programs, with arguably more passionate fan bases (not to mention the 129 FCS football schools), only a fraction produce that much. Think about this historical and present-day reality: the generated revenue exceeds expenses in fewer than two dozen FBS programs, and every single FCS program operates from a deficit. The inefficiency is staggering, and private investors are eager to "fix things." They'll bring the same analytical rigor and revenue optimization strategies that have defined professional sports, entertainment, and technology companies.

But these investors won't simply write checks and hope for championships as returns. They'll demand operational control, professional management, and measurable performance metrics. In the most extreme version of this transformation, University athletics departments, with their committees, bureaucracy, and competing academic priorities, will be replaced by streamlined operations focused exclusively on winning games and maximizing profits. The days of athletics directors juggling educational responsibilities with sports management will end, replaced by CEOs accountable to investor boards in place of faculty senates.

For the moment, as with Otro Capital and Utah, the university president and athletics director may retain majority control over decision-making.

But with PEs' operational expertise and management of ticketing, concessions, corporate sponsorships, merchandise, trademark licensing, and more, university leadership will soon become a passive participant in the new paradigm.

The change will be most visible in how athletes are compensated and protected. The characterization of all college athletes as simply students who happen to play sports has already evolved significantly, and will continue to change as the economic realities of the enterprise become more transparent. These young men and women contribute significantly to revenue generation, attract nationwide television audiences, and drive consumer behavior. As the financial dimensions of their participation become more visible, the traditional framework for categorizing and compensating them is undergoing a fundamental reexamination.

Unionization, which has a strong chance to take hold, would give athletes the collective bargaining power they have never had. Instead of accepting whatever scholarships and benefits universities deign to offer, athletes will negotiate compensation packages that reflect their actual market value. We are already witnessing the top quarterback at a major program earning more than some NFL backups. That circumstance will become common. At the same time, elite basketball players will secure guaranteed contracts and endorsement deals that rival those of NBA stars.

Compensation will extend far beyond salaries to include comprehensive healthcare that covers not only immediate injuries but also the long-term consequences for athletes' careers. Former players suffering from chronic conditions without adequate long-term medical support is a problem that the new model has an opportunity to solve. Professional-grade training facilities, nutritionists, mental health support, and career development programs will become standard benefits for all, not luxuries dependent on university generosity and limited by school finances.

Perhaps most importantly, intellectual property will become the engine of the new economy. Universities will license their marks, including names, logos, colors, slogans, trade dress, nicknames, etc., to third-party operators for substantial sums. Without marks the consumer recognizes, the product isn't the same and has much less value. Athletes, in turn, will license their own NIL and more, building multimedia empires that extend far beyond what today's NIL deals begin to suggest.

Facility leasing will reshape university economics. Instead of universities bearing the massive costs of maintaining stadiums, arenas, and training facilities, private entities will lease these assets from the schools, absorb all operating expenses, and pay the schools a hefty sum for this structure. This arrangement inverts the typical pro sports model, in which public owners often subsidize private teams, by positioning universities as landlords who actually capture premium value.

For universities, this shift removes enormous capital expenditures from their balance sheets while providing steady rental income. A top-tier program like Texas might lease its football stadium to a private operator for $50 million annually, funds that could be redirected toward academic programs, research, infrastructure, or even other sports. The private operator, meanwhile, maximizes revenue through enhanced concessions, premium seating, corporate partnerships, and year-round event hosting that universities typically handle poorly because it isn't their primary purpose.

These facility arrangements will enable the creation of purpose-built venues optimized for television production and fan experience rather than serving multiple university functions. Modern sports facilities will feature advanced broadcast capabilities, dynamic pricing systems, and integrated technology that enhance how fans consume games. Think about the environment created by Steve Ballmer in the new $2+ billion Intuit Dome, home of the LA Clippers. The sterile, multipurpose venues common on many campuses will give way to entertainment complexes designed to generate revenue from every available surface and season. Gone will be the days when the NCAA prohibited advertising of things like gambling, alcohol, performance enhancement and tobacco products, and enforced other "morality prohibitions" foreign to pure capitalism.

The governance structure will evolve to match this new economic reality. The NCAA, already weakened by legal defeats, marginalized by Congress and the White House, and facing impending member defections, will either morph into a dramatically different organization or become irrelevant in the new professional sports model. Or it may revert to its original role of managing the rules of play for sport, ensuring athlete safety, and maintaining contest conformity.

In place of what we currently have at the NCAA, we may see conference-based leagues operate with the autonomy and professionalization of major sports organizations. We are getting a glimpse of this new structure, with power conferences taking control of enforcing the financial components in the new paradigm.

A new league, or alternative leagues, will negotiate collective television contracts worth billions, manage officiating to professional standards, and coordinate schedules for fan engagement and television ratings, rather than academic calendars. The final chapter will be closed on the arbitrarily limited geographical conferences that made sense when travel was expensive and regional rivalries dominated. They will be replaced by competitively balanced leagues designed to maximize entertainment value and media revenue.

The restructuring I describe is no longer theoretical. Two concrete Super League proposals now circulate among power conference administrators, each backed by substantial capital and experienced operators.

"Project Rudy," named for the famous Notre Dame walk-on, would consolidate the 70 top programs from the four power conferences into a single structure. Former Disney executives Evan Richter, Kevin Mayer, and Tom Staggs, now at venture capital firm Smash Capital, have presented the concept to more than 25 power conference athletics directors and three of the four power conference commissioners. Their proposed model would infuse billions in private capital, with projections exceeding $15 billion in new revenues over 12 years, would expand the postseason, overhaul scheduling, and tier revenue distribution based on performance rather than equal shares.

The most striking aspect of Project Rudy is who has joined the effort. Jack Swarbrick, who spent more than a decade and a half as Notre Dame's athletics director and sat on the College Football Playoff governing committee, now works with Smash Capital on this proposal. I respect Jack tremendously, and his apparent move from the traditional power structure position to the private equity side signals that serious people believe the current model cannot endure.

A competing proposal from College Sports Tomorrow would create a 136-school football-only breakaway, organizing the top 72 programs into a "Power 12" conference with the remaining 64 in a "Group of Eight." This model emphasizes collective bargaining with athletes, geographic divisions, and consolidated media rights. Its backers include Texas Tech athletics director Kirby Hocutt, Cleveland Browns owner and Tennessee booster Jimmy Haslam, and university presidents Gordon Gee of West Virginia and Kent Syverud of Syracuse.

Both proposals would essentially end NCAA oversight of major college football. Both promise substantially higher revenues than current arrangements deliver. Both would exclude the bottom of FBS from the elite structure. And both face the same underlying obstacle: Greg Sankey and Tony Petitti, the SEC and Big Ten commissioners who control the 34 most valuable brands in college sports, have shown little interest in sharing power or revenue.

Sankey has been clear that the SEC views itself as a super league already and has no interest in diluting its brand by merging with 70 programs. His resistance reveals both the leverage the top conferences hold and the challenge any restructuring faces. The schools with the most to gain from consolidation are not the schools with the power to make it happen.

Yet the discussions continue because the status quo satisfies no one. Athletics directors at ACC and Big 12 schools, watching revenue gaps with the SEC and Big Ten widen each year, see super league proposals as their path to survival. Private investors see a fragmented, inefficient market ripe for consolidation. And even SEC and Big Ten administrators acknowledge that the current chaos of competing legal challenges, inconsistent NIL implementation, and enforcement failures can't persist indefinitely.

The question is not whether college football will reorganize but whether it will come from within or be imposed from outside. Indeed, President Trump has issued two executive orders and convened college sports leaders in a manner similar to that of President Roosevelt in 1905. Some fundamental restructuring is inescapable.

Revenue sharing, piloted by the *House* settlement, will eventually resemble professional sports models, in which national media and sponsorship revenue is distributed among programs through negotiated formulas, while individual athlete compensation is determined within those pools through a mix of school allocation decisions and market-driven NIL arrangements. Smaller programs may secure sustainable if modest revenue streams, while star players and marquee programs will command compensation reflecting their market appeal. The new prototype will also create different categories of sports entertainment. The highest level will feature fully professional athletes competing for championships with playoff systems designed for maximum drama. Below that, we might see semi-professional leagues in which athletes maintain a direct connection to educational institutions. At the core of higher education, in the end, traditional amateur sports may continue, but with sharply reduced visibility and resources.

An example is club sports. In the aftermath of COVID-19 and exacerbated by the *House* settlement, club sports have been on the rise on college campuses. An estimated two million college students now participate in competitive club sports nationwide, roughly four times the approximately 554,000 athletes competing in NCAA programs. When combined with intramural and recreational sports participants, approximately 5.5 million students flow through campus recreational programs. This participation base has expanded since 2020 as varsity sport eliminations pushed athletes toward club alternatives, while emerging sports like pickleball (which grew from 17 to over 130 college clubs between 2022 and 2024) and esports have added entirely new categories of club competition.

The economic implications extend far beyond athletics departments. Universities will need to restructure their entire relationship with sports, deciding whether they want to be entertainment companies that happen to offer education or educational institutions that host professional sports teams. Some will choose the former path, integrating athletics revenues into broader institutional strategies. Indeed, sports excursions into international markets may even open opportunities for a university's academic offerings. Others will largely separate their academic and athletics operations, licensing their names and leasing facilities, while shifting primary focus back to education and research.

Corporate partnerships will expand exponentially as sophisticated investors recognize opportunities that universities have consistently undervalued. Innovative broadcast deals, naming rights, sponsored content, integrated advertising, and branded experiences will generate revenue streams that dwarf current arrangements. The amateur model's restrictions on commercial partnerships will disappear, replaced by aggressive monetization strategies limited only by market demand and consumer tolerance.

International expansion will become truly viable for the first time, as privately operated college sports entities can pursue opportunities that traditional universities couldn't consider. Games in major international markets, partnerships with foreign media companies, and athlete exchange programs will create global revenue streams while building international audiences for American college sports.

The technology integration will accelerate rapidly under professional management. Advanced analytics, virtual reality training, performance monitoring, artificial intelligence, and fan engagement platforms will become standard rather than experimental. Private investors will drive innovation in ways that risk-averse university bureaucracies never could, creating competitive advantages for programs that embrace technological advancement.

Yet for all these changes to succeed, they must navigate the complex intersection of market forces, regulatory requirements, and cultural expectations. The transition from amateur to professional won't happen overnight, nor will it occur uniformly across all programs and regions. But don't ignore the signs. It may not be immediate, but the transition is coming sooner than you think. Some universities will resist change until they are forced; others will embrace it early, like Utah, gaining first-mover advantages that could prove decisive.

It is undeniable that the regulatory framework will need to be completely reconstructed. Current NCAA rules, state laws governing NIL rights, federal antitrust regulations, and employment and labor law will all require updates to accommodate this new reality. The legal system that struggled to address simple questions about athlete compensation and benefits will face far more complex challenges around union rights, revenue sharing, facility ownership, and interstate commerce.

Consumer acceptance will ultimately determine the pace of this shift. The generational divide is already visible: younger fans adapt readily, while traditional supporters resist changes they see as threats to the nostalgia that made college sports special. A perfect example is that some fans love unregulated NIL because they believe it has created competitive balance. In contrast, others hate it, viewing it as nothing more than buying talent and creating winners through bank account statements. The industry will need to balance innovation with tradition, professional quality with college atmosphere, and market efficiency with fan loyalty.

The stakes couldn't be higher. Done correctly, Collegiate Capitalism will create a sustainable, profitable, and fair system that properly compensates athletes and investors while providing consumers with entertainment that rivals any professional sport. Done poorly, it could destroy the unique culture and regional connections that make college sports special, creating a hollow imitation of professional leagues without their established fan bases or institutional stability.

The upheaval has begun, and the choices made over the next several months and years will determine whether college sports evolve into something greater than they have ever been or whether the pursuit of profit destroys what made them worth saving.

I do not celebrate this future. I am no more fond of it than I am of one in which machines quietly direct the rhythms of daily human life. But fondness is not the standard. Inevitability is. Collegiate Capitalism is not the system I would have designed. It is the system that has arrived, and the sooner we stop arguing about whether it should exist, the sooner we can turn to the harder and more useful question of what it should become.

Chapter 3
The Ripple Effects
Winners, Losers, and the Transformation of American Sports Culture

The architecture of Collegiate Capitalism will create winners and losers with a ruthlessness that the amateur system, for all its flaws, managed to avoid. As market forces replace tradition, the comfortable illusions that sustained college sports for over a century will shatter, revealing truths that many stakeholders would prefer to ignore.

The biggest winners will be the athletes themselves, particularly those in high-revenue sports. In this new model, a starting wide receiver at LSU or a lottery-pick basketball player at Duke will finally earn legitimate compensation reflecting their actual market value. These elite performers will build generational wealth during their college age playing days.

The benefits, however, will extend beyond superstars to athletes across the competitive spectrum. Role players who might never make professional rosters will earn meaningful compensation during their peak performance years. Of greater importance, all participating athletes will gain access to healthcare, legal representation, and career development resources previously reserved for pure professionals. The days of allegations of former college players suffering from chronic injuries with disparate medical support will end, replaced by comprehensive care achieved through collective bargaining that provides consistent care that extends throughout their lives.

Women's athletics may be the most intriguing opportunity. Contrary to conventional wisdom that suggests women's sports will suffer under pure market dynamics, I believe Collegiate Capitalism will actually accelerate their growth. The current system's artificial constraints and bureaucratic inertia have prevented women's sports from reaching their commercial potential. Under market-driven operations, successful women's programs will attract investment proportional to their revenue generation and growth prospects.

Consider the explosive popularity of women's basketball, soccer, and volleyball at both college and professional levels. These sports have demonstrated significant market demand, but artificial limitations and poor marketing have constrained their growth. Private investors, focused purely on return potential rather than traditional gender hierarchies, will recognize opportunities that university administrators have missed. I may not have unique insights, but I've put my money and time where my beliefs are, investing in professional women's soccer and volleyball precisely because I see the growth potential that others overlook.

Major conferences and elite universities will thrive, leveraging established brands, superior facilities, and large alumni bases to attract both top athletes and sophisticated investors. Participating programs from the SEC, Big Ten, Big Twelve, ACC, and future power conferences will become even more dominant, commanding premium television contracts and corporate partnerships that smaller programs can't match.

But this success will come at the expense of broad-based competitive balance, which some dispute completely existed in the first place. Indeed, the claim that all Division I programs compete on equal footing will finally end, replaced by honest acknowledgment of the economic realities that have perennially shaped college sports. The most successful schools and sports in the Power Four will separate so completely from their competitors that they'll essentially operate on different tiers. Where this leaves the Group of Five, Division I FCS and Division I non-football schools, as well as Division I FBS school non-revenue sports, is volatile, unpredictable, and obviously unsettled.

For universities, the outcomes will vary remarkably depending on their strategic choices and institutional capabilities. As I highlighted in Chapter 2, schools that embrace full professionalization and successfully attract private investment will see their athletics programs or certain sports become significant profit centers that can subsidize a range of institutional interests. Others that resist change or lack the resources to compete effectively will face difficult decisions about their athletics futures.

Some will discover that exiting high-level athletics entirely serves their interests better than struggling to maintain programs they can't adequately fund. These schools might redirect resources toward academic excellence, research initiatives, or other institutional priorities that better align with their missions and capabilities. The current system's pressure on every university to field competitive athletics programs, regardless of cost or institutional fit, will finally ease. Of course, I am most especially referring to football and men's basketball at the highest level.

The brutal reality is that Olympic and other non-revenue-generating sports will face existential challenges. Sports like wrestling, track and field, swimming, gymnastics, and others that rely heavily on institutional subsidies will find themselves competing for resources with revenue-generating programs that can demonstrate clear returns on investment, and an insatiable appetite for retaining the revenue generated by those programs.

Some Olympic sports will adapt by developing their own revenue streams through private sponsorships, media partnerships, and athlete-driven content creation. Athletes with strong personal brands and social media followings will build independent sources of financial support, reducing their dependence on university funding. The most successful will create new professional or semi-professional structures that operate parallel to whatever college programs remain.

Others will require outside intervention to survive. The federal government may need to step in with funding for Olympic sports development, similar to systems in other countries where national sporting success is considered a public good worth supporting. Private foundations focused on youth development and amateur athletics might also emerge to sustain programs that serve important social functions despite limited commercial appeal.

The harsh truth is that many Olympic sports programs simply may disappear from universities that can no longer justify their costs. This will force these sports to develop alternative structures (club programs, regional leagues, or private academies) that can operate more efficiently than university-based systems. While this represents a notable loss in the breadth of college athletics offerings on campus, it may eventually benefit these specific sports by removing them from institutional constraints that historically limited their growth and innovation.

Indeed, the threat I'm describing is quickly becoming a documented reality. Since the announcement of the *House* settlement, more than 40 Division I Olympic sports teams have been eliminated, with thousands more roster positions cut.

Washington State eliminated its throwing and jumping events from track and field "effective immediately," fired coaches in those disciplines, and informed athletes they could stay with "limited resources" or transfer. This is from a program that produced four track and field and seven total Olympians in 2024. Grand Canyon University cut its men's volleyball team despite a Final Four appearance, eliminating a program that carried 21 players. NC State and Virginia eliminated their diving programs. Georgia Tech reduced rosters across all 17 of its sports.

The scale of roster reductions defies easy comprehension. Estimates suggest that the 64 power conference schools alone will eliminate at least 4,000 roster positions (and possibly 15,000 across all of Division I) as they comply with new roster limits, while redirecting resources toward revenue-sharing payments. In football, where rosters were reduced from unlimited walk-ons to 105 players, approximately 1,500 walk-on positions disappeared across FBS.

The cuts disproportionately affect athletes in sports where rosters had grown beyond the new limits. Track and field, swimming, and cross-country, sports that traditionally carried large rosters to compete across multiple events, face the deepest reductions. A track program that once carried 60 or 70 athletes must now operate at 45. The math requires cutting 15 to 25 athletes, typically the specialists in less glamorous events, who contributed depth rather than championships.

Olympic sports coaching associations recognized the threat and responded by hiring the powerhouse government relations firm FGS Global to lobby Congress. Their statement following the settlement's approval was blunt: "Congress must intervene to address these pressing issues and ensure a balanced, equitable path forward for all student-athletes, including the protection of existing requirements of schools to maintain robust sport sponsorship and meaningful allocation of resources for non-football and non-basketball programs."

The tension is evident. The *House* settlement was designed to compensate athletes whose NIL opportunities were restricted under the prior model. Its implementation, however, has created concerns about unintended consequences for thousands of athletes in sports that generate no commercial revenue. The swimmers, divers, wrestlers, and runners who lose roster spots receive nothing from the settlement. They may be bearing the cost of a restructuring that primarily benefits athletes in football and men's basketball.

Under Max Siegel, Chief Executive Officer of USA Track & Field, the United States won 34 medals, the most in any non-boycotted Olympics since 1968, at the 2024 Paris Olympics, and the U.S. led the overall count for the ninth consecutive Summer Games. Approximately seventy-five percent of American Olympians were current or former collegiate athletes. The system that produced that dominance is now being restructured to redirect resources toward football and basketball players, creating genuine uncertainty about how Olympic sports development will be sustained.

Whether this trade-off serves national interests or undermines them will become clear only over time. If Olympic sports development can transition to alternative structures, club programs, private academies, or government-funded training centers, the losses may prove manageable. If those alternatives fail to materialize, American Olympic performance will suffer, and we will look back on this moment as the point at which short-term commercial interests overwhelmed long-term national capability.

Division II and Division III schools will face perhaps the most dramatic upheaval. These levels of college athletics, which have operated on the principle that sports should complement rather than dominate the educational experience, are finding their fundamental assumptions challenged by the new economic realities. These divisions are not parties to the *House* settlement. The $2.8 billion in damages and $20.5 million revenue-sharing apply only to Division I.

In theory, Division II and Division III could continue operating as they always have, maintaining traditional amateur models while Division I evolves around them.

In theory.

But Division II programs are caught between the future professional model of parts of Division I and the academic enrollment-enhancement approach of Division III. They will face impossible choices. They lack the resources to compete with newly professionalized Division I programs for top athletes, but they also can't retreat to the more simplistic model that has typically defined Division III. Many will be forced to drop athletics entirely or markedly reduce their scope. As capable a leader as NCAA Division II vice president Terri Steeb Gronau has proven to be over the years, both in Division II and at the Board of Governors, these difficulties will be the ultimate test of her team's governance acumen and creativity.

In practice, cultural expectations are shifting in ways that make isolation impossible. NIL opportunities are not enough. Athletes who see Division I peers receiving direct payments wonder why they receive nothing of the sort. Coaches who recruit against Division I programs must explain why their schools cannot match revenue-sharing offers. Parents now factor in potential payments their children might receive elsewhere when calculating the value of athletic scholarships.

The employment status question poses even more direct risk. The *Johnson v. NCAA* litigation, proceeding through federal court, could establish that Division I college athletes are employees under the Fair Labor Standards Act. Division II and III athletes are not parties to it. But the legal framework the Third Circuit established could have downstream implications for all divisions, depending on how courts apply the economic realities test in the future. If athletes at every level qualify as employees entitled to minimum wage and overtime, Division II and Division III schools would face compensation obligations they cannot afford. With more than 500,000 athletes across all NCAA divisions, aggregate employment costs could exceed the total athletics revenue generated by many smaller institutions.

The demographic challenge compounds these pressures. The "enrollment cliff," a 15% decline in college-age population beginning in 2026, will hit smaller institutions hardest. States like Illinois face projected drops of 32% in the number of high school graduates between 2023 and 2041. Schools dependent on tuition revenue will struggle to maintain academic programs, let alone athletics departments. For institutions where athletics serves as both a recruiting tool and a revenue source, the enrollment cliff threatens both functions simultaneously.

The merger and closure activity already underway suggests where this leads. Multiple small colleges have closed or merged in the past year, and their athletics programs have disappeared with their institutions. Others have dropped sports, conference affiliations, or entire athletics departments. The pattern will accelerate as enrollment pressures mount and employment status litigation progresses.

Division III will face what I can only describe as an existential crisis. Its model has historically depended on college athletics closer to the high school model, communities supporting sports played for the love of competition rather than financial reward. This philosophy made sense when all of college athletics seemed to operate under similar principles. In a world where Division I athletes receive millions while Division III athletes receive nothing, the philosophical foundation weakens. Why would a talented athlete choose pure amateurism when professional compensation is available? That economic question is real, even if the athlete will never see playing time.

Some Division III schools will seek to maintain their current model, creating a distinct tier focused solely on educational and personal development. They will attract athletes and their families who genuinely prioritize academics over athletics, who want the college experience rather than professional rewards. Whether there are enough such athletes to sustain viable programs remains an open question.

Others may propose development of hybrid approaches, perhaps allowing greater NIL activity or modified compensation structures that preserve some amateur characteristics while acknowledging changed expectations. Many will eliminate athletics programs entirely, concluding that they no longer serve their institutional missions effectively. The NCAA's divisional structure, if it continues at all, will need reconstruction to accommodate models that no longer fit neatly into existing categories.

The comfortable assumption that Division II and Division III would remain unchanged while Division I passes the baton is proving incorrect. The commercial forces reshaping Division I create ripple effects throughout the system. No level of college athletics can remain fully insulated from the Collegiate Capitalism that has emerged at the highest levels.

And rest assured, the cultural change will extend far beyond athletics departments, reshaping American sports culture more broadly.

Perhaps nowhere is this transformation more brutal than for the high school recruit navigating today's new landscape and a future driven by Collegiate Capitalism. Where once a scholarship offer represented a genuine commitment from a university willing to develop potential into performance and to educate you on and off the field, today's blue-chip prospect faces a significantly different calculation, shaped by NIL wealth and transfer portal dynamics. Major programs are increasingly prioritizing proven transfers over development projects. In early 2025, coaches like St. John's Rick Pitino openly declared they wouldn't take five-star high school recruits, preferring portal-tested college players who can contribute immediately, though even Pitino later acknowledged the need for some freshman talent. Tommy Reamon, Jr., offered in Sports Illustrated that this isn't just about fewer scholarships or smaller recruiting classes. He posited that it was, in fact, about the soul of high school football.

The question has shifted from "what could this athlete become in three years?" to "what can they deliver this fall or winter?" With over 31,000 athletes entering the transfer portal annually and roughly 25% of all FBS scholarship players, high school recruits find themselves competing not just against their prep peers but also against college athletes with proven performance at higher levels. Even elite recruits who secure commitments face uncertainty, knowing their positions can effectively be replaced by portal transfers if they don't produce immediately. The development pipeline that once characterized college athletics has largely disappeared at major programs.

Sure, smaller DI, II, & III schools initially benefit from this shift, landing higher-rated high school recruits who are passed over by power programs, chasing immediate impact through the portal and NIL inducements. But even then, those recruits will transfer as soon as they have the chance. And for the top prospect, the path has become treacherous in the current system and will be even more difficult under the future Collegiate Capitalism. Presently, an athlete can sign with a major program knowing they might be replaced before developing, or accept a smaller program offer that doesn't reflect their potential. In the future state, an athlete's professional status will be on full display, and they will be "recruited" and paid by an entity focused on the bottom line.

> Indeed, at the highest levels, the line between traditional professional and professional college sports will become so blurred as to be meaningless, creating a more coherent hierarchy based on skill level and market value rather than arbitrary distinctions.

This will force professional leagues to reconsider their current development systems. Why should the NFL rely on college programs to develop talent when they could create their own minor leagues with possibly better coaching, training, and compensation? The NBA's growing investment in the G League suggests this transition is already underway. College sports will need to compete directly with professional development systems for top athletes, ending their majority share of the path to professional careers. I propose, however, to maintain a clear product distinction defined by its tether to the brand of higher education, the new system will place age limits on competitors. I believe that the age range of 18-24 is reasonable. This will benefit by eliminating the absurdity of the current waiver system, which, in some instances, can extend Division I eligibility into an athlete's late 20's or even 30s.

The broader implications for higher education itself remain unclear, but potentially profound. Of course, the timeline for this conversion will vary significantly across different segments of college athletics. The transition will be messy, uneven, and often painful for institutions and individuals caught between the old and new systems.

The ultimate success of Collegiate Capitalism will depend on its ability to preserve what made college sports special, while eliminating the artificial constraints on athletes that have limited their potential. The passionate fan loyalty, regional rivalries, and cultural significance of college athletics represent valuable assets that purely professional leagues struggle to replicate. Destroying these elements in pursuit of economic efficiency or growth would represent a catastrophic failure of the new model.

Yet the status quo has become unviable. The pressures have grown too significant to manage within the existing framework, the legal challenges too numerous to win, and the economic opportunities too valuable to waste. The *House* settlement closed the debate about whether change was coming. Can the future fulfill its promise of creating a fairer, sustainable, and entertaining system, or will the pursuit of profit undermine the unique culture that made college sports special?

The blueprint is on the table. Whether it becomes a cathedral or a ruin depends entirely on the choices made in the days, weeks, months, and years to come.

Chapter 4
The Inevitable March
How a Century of Failed Reforms Paved the Road to Collegiate Capitalism

The blood on the grass told the real story of American college football's early years, long before anyone imagined billion-dollar television contracts or athlete unionization. In 1905 alone, eighteen young men, most of them at the high school and club level, died playing a game that barely resembled modern football. Their deaths were the inevitable result of "mass plays" including the "flying wedge" that launched bodies at each other in midair collisions that frequently proved fatal.

By October 1905, President Theodore Roosevelt had seen enough, including his own son's injuries at Harvard. Summoning representatives from Harvard, Yale, and Princeton to the White House, he delivered a simple ultimatum. The schools were to reform the game or watch it disappear entirely. When another player died just a month later, NYU Chancellor Henry MacCracken convened a broader reform conference that, in 1906, would birth the Intercollegiate Athletic Association of the United States, which would change its name to the NCAA in 1910. From its very inception, however, the Association faced an impossible task. It was charged with preserving the amateur ideal while managing a progressively violent and increasingly commercialized entertainment product. The pattern was established in those early meetings: crisis would drive reform, reform would create new opportunities for exploitation and recruiting creativity, and the cycle would begin anew.

The primitive football contests we touched on in Chapter 1, emerging after the Civil War, could not have been more dissimilar from today's choreographed spectacles. Yet, they already contained the seeds of modern commercialization. When Rutgers faced Princeton in 1869 with twenty-five players per side using a round ball, the game was essentially organized chaos. By 1876, the oval leather ball and eleven-player teams had appeared, marking football's separation from soccer toward the rugby-influenced sport that would captivate American audiences.

But even in these early contests, the amateur ideal proved fragile. Institutions routinely employed "ringers" who were non-student-athletes explicitly hired to play. Fielding Yost, who would later become Michigan's legendary coach and vocal in debates around strict academic standards, exemplified the era's casual approach to eligibility when he transferred mid-season from West Virginia to Lafayette solely to play one game against Penn before returning to his original school. At Yale, James Hogan, who entered school at age twenty-five, received not just tuition but luxury accommodations, free meals, free tuition, program sales profits, tobacco sales commissions, and a Cuban vacation... all for playing football.

The combined violence and commercialization crisis reached its peak in 1905, but Roosevelt's intervention merely treated the symptoms instead of the causes. The newly formed NCAA established rules to reduce deaths and injuries while promoting "a high standard of personal honor, eligibility and fair play." Recruiting players, offering inducements, and fielding non-students were explicitly prohibited. Yet enforcement responsibility rested with individual member institutions through a principle known as "home rule." Home rule proved to be a fateful choice that established the fundamental tension that has defined the organization's entire history.

Faculty dominance characterized the NCAA's early governance, with professors arguing that only their control could secure "generous, wholesome, honest, glorious rivalry" rather than programs that emphasized "coaches afflicted with professional notions, recruiting, inducing, falsifying" and treated "athletics as a business." The paradox was profound. Educators warned against treating athletics as a business, even as their institutions increasingly depended on athletics revenue to fund ambitious campus expansion and research projects.

Despite clear rules against recruiting and subsidizing players, violations remained widespread. Summer baseball presented unique issues, as college athletes often played for pay during vacation months. The NCAA's first president was Brigadier General Palmer Eddy Pierce, who served as

NCAA president from 1906 through approximately 1929, with interruptions for military service. He regularly condemned the summer baseball practice as causing moral degeneration among students who would deceive the college authorities to maintain eligibility. Yet his condemnations carried no enforcement mechanism. Home rule meant that institutions policed themselves, and schools routinely chose competitive advantage over compliance with the rules. While implementing home rule, Pierce learned the hard way that the honor code mastered at West Point was not transferable to the win-at-all-costs competition on college campuses. It was destined to fail.

Moreover, the 1920s brought unprecedented growth and commercialization that would have been unimaginable to those in the conference room with Chancellor MacCracken when the organization was established.

Sounds like the 2020s, but more on that later.

In the 1920s, large, expensive stadiums appeared on campuses nationwide, often financed through gate receipts rather than academic budgets. Radio broadcasts, beginning with Princeton against Chicago in 1922, dramatically expanded public interest and commercial potential. The decade's excesses were epitomized by Harold "Red" Grange, Illinois' "Galloping Ghost," who signed a professional contract with the Chicago Bears, earning approximately $12,000 for his first game alone and more than $100,000 in his rookie year, followed by a $300,000 movie deal.

The 1929 Carnegie Foundation study delivered a devastating assessment after visiting 105 American campuses. Faculty control existed "in name but scarcely in fact" and was "often a mere subterfuge." Player recruitment had "reached the proportions of nationwide commerce" with "profoundly deleterious" effects on character. About subsidized athletes, the report stated they "connive at disreputable and shameful practices for the sake of material returns and for honors falsely achieved."

Yet even this comprehensive indictment produced only cosmetic changes. The NCAA developed what can only be described as a dual personality. A personality rooted in maintaining amateur rhetoric while facing increasingly pressing enforcement challenges. The Sanity Code, which I briefly discussed in Chapter 1, symbolized the Association's most ambitious attempt at meaningful reform up to that point. It established five principles covering financial aid, recruitment, academic standards, institutional control, and amateurism, along with enforcement mechanisms including expulsion for violations.

The code's failure was swift and decisive.

In 1950, seven universities found in violation avoided expulsion when the vote fell short of the required two-thirds majority. After only three years in existence, the 1951 Convention repealed the Sanity Code in its entirety, though the enforcement concept survived. That October, Walter Byers became the NCAA's first full-time executive director, beginning a thirty-six-year tenure that would revolutionize the organization and, ultimately and sadly, create many of the contradictions that have made today's circumstances its destiny.

Byers inherited an organization ill-equipped to handle post-World War II challenges. Taking over amid gambling scandals and widespread rule violations, he built a regulatory powerhouse from what had been a voluntary association of educational institutions. Under his leadership, NCAA membership exploded, staff grew exponentially, championships expanded to include women's sports, and television contracts generated unprecedented revenue. It was reported that football deals increased from $1.1 million to $74.2 million, while basketball tournament rights soared from $550,000 to $36 million.

Enforcement became Byers' defining achievement and ultimate contradiction. As the "chief enforcer" and "only cop on the block," he developed a substantial regulatory apparatus that punished violators and deterred others, earning comparisons to J. Edgar Hoover and the Ayatollah Khomeini. At NCAA headquarters, he imposed strict protocols, including mandatory in-office work when not travelling, dress codes, Saturday work, and a ban on coffee breaks and eating at desks, among other measures, creating a professional environment that would earn the respect of member colleges.

The ultimate irony emerged after Byers' 1987 retirement to his cattle ranch outside Kansas City. The man who had passionately defended amateurism in a romantic era eventually condemned the system he built as a centralized bureaucracy with what was tantamount to overseers controlling plantation workers. His 1995 memoir was a stunning reversal that reflected both his disillusionment and prescient understanding of where college athletics were heading.

By the 1980s, when I arrived at LSU and eventually worked as a student tutor helping athletes, the NCAA was pushing a series of significant reforms through presidential control. The Presidents Commission, established in 1984 as a compromise after more aggressive proposals failed, quickly positioned itself as a reform force through special conventions and an ambitious legislative agenda. The 1985 "integrity convention" in my family's hometown of New Orleans produced eight major reforms, including the infamous "death penalty" for repeat violators. This penalty was first applied to Southern Methodist University's football program in 1987, following revelations of under-the-table payments involving coaches, boosters, and even the Texas Governor.

The Presidents Commission enhanced the presidential control movement in 1986 when Proposition 48 took effect. Initially adopted at the 1983 Convention, it established new academic eligibility standards requiring incoming first-year students to complete specific high school curricula and meet minimum GPA and standardized test score requirements. I remember vigorous campus debates at free speech alley about the measure's intent and impact, as well as athletes, coaches, faculty, and administrators arguing over whether academic standards or access and equity should take precedence. "Prop 48" was widely believed to serve as a racial barrier rather than a means to ensure academic integrity. The academic standards debate intensified in 1989 when the NCAA proposed Proposition 42, which would have further restricted financial aid for partial qualifiers. Legendary Georgetown coach John Thompson, the first Black coach to win an NCAA championship, sat out games in protest, arguing the measure served as institutional discrimination.

Between 1990 and 1992, the Presidents Commission achieved three consecutive years of substantial reform victories: reducing time demands on student-athletes, cutting scholarship numbers, limiting recruiting activities, phasing out athletics dormitories, and strengthening academic requirements. The 1993 Convention approved an athletics certification program requiring institutional self-study and external review. These would be what the Knight Foundation Commission on Intercollegiate Athletics coined the "one-plus-three" model of presidential control, which supports academic integrity, financial responsibility, and certification.

Yet as presidents consolidated power within the NCAA, the Supreme Court's *Board of Regents* decision accelerated the very commercialization that reform movements sought to control. The Justices in the majority believed their decision would benefit amateur athletics, but history proved otherwise.

And then, over a decade later, in 1996, the NCAA's governance structure underwent one of its most dramatic modifications when the Convention approved complete reorganization, establishing presidential control in all three divisions and giving each division substantial autonomy. This represented the culmination of the presidential control movement that began with the integrity convention and Proposition 48, yet the main weaknesses persisted. Between 1995 and 2003, the NCAA penalized 100 institutions for major violations. Between 2003 and 2015, 96 institutions. Those numbers are remarkably similar to the roughly 96 cases from 1975 to 1983, suggesting that structural reforms had little impact on policing underlying problems.

More concerning, findings of "lack of institutional control" increased to 51% of cases, while unethical conduct penalties rose from 33% to 56% by 2003. And more than half of the Power 5 conference institutions spent time on probation through 2015. This demonstrated that even under presidential leadership, competitive and financial pressures driving rules violations remained overwhelming.

Looking back from today's vantage point, the pattern becomes unmistakably clear. Each reform movement, from the NCAA's founding through presidential control, addressed symptoms while ignoring root causes.

The fundamental tension created when educational rhetoric met billion-dollar enterprises could be managed temporarily through new rules, enforcement mechanisms, or governance structures, but never permanently resolved. Every attempt to strengthen amateurism created new incentives for creative circumvention, while every commercial success made the amateur model more difficult to sustain.

In the end, the NCAA's own success became its undoing. Byers' television negotiations demonstrated college athletics' enormous commercial potential, creating unparalleled revenue streams. By the early 2000s, it became apparent that the membership had built the NCAA's regulatory framework on shaky foundations. The organization had evolved from a safety-focused group of faculty representatives into a massive bureaucracy attempting to preserve nineteenth-century amateur ideals in a twenty-first-century entertainment industry. Each generation of leaders discovered what their predecessors had learned. Simply put, the central contradictions could be managed, but not resolved.

The historical pattern reveals why Collegiate Capitalism became inevitable rather than merely possible. The NCAA's century-long struggle to close the gap between what we claimed and what we built created a system that satisfied no one. Athletes received no direct share of the revenue they helped generate; institutions faced constant compliance burdens while competing for commercial advantage; and fans witnessed increasing professionalization without corresponding improvements in product quality or competitive balance.

Significantly, each failed reform cycle weakened the intellectual and moral foundations supporting amateurism, while strengthening the case for market-based solutions. When the paladins tried to preserve amateur ideals through better rules and enforcement, they inadvertently demonstrated that the problem wasn't in implementation but in fundamental design. When presidents attempted to reassert educational values through governance reforms, they proved that even academic leaders couldn't resist commercial temptations when competitive pressures mounted.

The legal problems that attacked the amateur model, from *Board of Regents* through *O'Bannon* to *Alston* to *House*, succeeded not because they presented novel arguments, but because they finally forced courts to confront contradictions that a century of failed reforms had made impossible to ignore. The NCAA's elaborate regulatory structure, built over decades of well-intentioned efforts to preserve amateurism, had become evidence of the growing distance between the amateur ideal and the commercial reality.

Byers' late-career recasting from amateurism's greatest defender to its harshest critic captures this historical incongruity perfectly. The man who built the modern NCAA in the end recognized that his life's work had created an unsustainable system that oppressed the very athletes it claimed to protect. His memoir's call to "give back to students who play sports the freedoms they deserve" wasn't a betrayal of his earlier beliefs; it was their logical conclusion.

And neither is my acknowledgment and advocacy for Collegiate Capitalism a betrayal. Rather, it is an epiphany. The road to Collegiate Capitalism was paved not with evil intentions, but with good ones that failed. Every reform movement, every enforcement initiative, and every governance restructuring brought the current shift closer by demonstrating that the contradictions couldn't coexist indefinitely. The only question was whether the change would come through gradual evolution or dramatic rupture. The *House* settlement's nearly $2.8 billion price tag gave the answer. What happened when the dichotomy finally became too large to ignore? The system didn't adapt gradually; it was forced into a transformation it had spent decades trying to avoid.

The NCAA's founders couldn't have imagined billion-dollar television contracts, social media empires, or private equity investment in college athletics. But they would have recognized the fundamental dynamic that made these developments inevitable. When enormous amounts of money are at stake, market forces eventually overcome regulatory limitations, regardless of how well-intentioned or carefully crafted those constraints might be. The century-plus-long march from amateur ideals to Collegiate Capitalism wasn't a deviation from the NCAA's founding principles. Instead, it was their predictable conclusion. The NCAA had changed dramatically in structure and leadership, but many of the challenges Walter Byers had faced throughout his tenure continued to test his successors and the presidents who guided the Association's future.

Chapter 5
The Impossible Job
How Decades of Well-Intentioned Leadership Hastened the Revolution

The tragedy of NCAA leadership in the post-Byers era wasn't that his successors lacked vision, intelligence, or integrity. Indeed, it was quite the opposite. Dick Schultz, Cedric Dempsey, Myles Brand, and Mark Emmert each brought exceptional qualifications and genuine commitment to educational values. Their collective failure to prevent the system's ultimate unraveling reveals not personal inadequacy, but the impossible nature of their task. The task of managing an increasingly professional entertainment industry while preserving an amateur framework that was becoming progressively harder to sustain.

Each man inherited contradictions that had grown more acute during his predecessor's tenure, applied thoughtful reforms that addressed symptoms rather than causes, and ultimately passed along problems that were larger and more intractable than when he arrived. Their combined forty-year effort to save amateurism through better leadership, smarter policies, and more effective governance, instead illustrated why market forces would eventually overwhelm any regulatory framework, no matter how well-intentioned or skillfully implemented.

Dick Schultz was appointed in 1987 and arrived in 1988 as the human face the NCAA desperately needed after Walter Byers' ever more pronounced authoritarian final years. Where Byers had ruled through a perception of intimidation and bureaucratic control, Schultz offered collaboration and transparency. With ten varsity letters earned across three sports at Central College and successful athletics director tenures at Cornell and Virginia, he understood both competitive athletics and university administration in ways that made him uniquely qualified to bridge the growing divide between educational and commercial interests.

Schultz's philosophy represented everything the membership claimed to want. He epitomized grassroots engagement, open communication, and collaborative reform. It is reported that he spent over 200 days annually travelling to work directly with athletes, coaches, athletics directors, faculty, and presidents, building consensus for changes that the previous administration had attempted to impose by edict. His emphasis on integrity over enforcement appealed to university leaders who were tired of being treated like malefactors by their own Association.

Yet Schultz's greatest strength became his fatal weakness. His commitment to virtue made him uniquely vulnerable when irregularities from his Virginia tenure surfaced, creating an unmanageable conflict between his enforcement responsibilities and his personal situation. Despite maintaining his innocence and receiving strong membership support, Schultz courageously resigned in 1993, stating that remaining could damage the credibility of the NCAA. His sacrifice signified the very principles he championed, but it also exposed how the system's contradictions could destroy even its most principled leaders.

As I would later discover in my own career, the NCAA presidency demands moral clarity that becomes almost impossible to maintain when the fundamental system and membership behaviors undermine that very moral authority. Schultz's departure after approximately five years showed that personal conscientiousness, no matter how genuine, couldn't resolve institutional contradictions that were gradually becoming more obvious to courts, critics, and even the association's own members.

When Cedric Dempsey assumed leadership in 1994, I was completing my Army legal service and watching from a distance as he inherited an organization that Schultz's reformist approach had humanized, but not materially reformed. Dempsey brought nearly three decades of athletics administration experience, from coaching two sports at Albion College to building championship programs at Arizona, where his tenure produced five national team championships and thirty-nine individual NCAA titles.

Dempsey's "educator first, businessman second" philosophy seemed perfectly suited to the challenges he faced. The NCAA was an unwieldy governance structure that operated as a huge, chaotic organization, with annual town-hall meetings in which every college got a vote on almost every item. He was staring down congressional pressure over gambling, and the membership was accelerating commercialization that threatened educational missions. His approach emphasized collaborative consensus-building and democratic participation. Again, precisely what university presidents said they wanted from their Association at that time.

The governance reforms Dempsey implemented were masterful exercises in organizational development. By eliminating disorderly annual conventions and creating division-specific decision-making structures, he streamlined operations while preserving democratic participation. His orchestration of the NCAA's move from Kansas City to Indianapolis saved over $50 million while establishing a more professional headquarters. The landmark television contracts he and the team negotiated with CBS and ESPN generated $6.2 billion over eleven years, creating sustainable revenue streams that appeared to solve the association's perennial financial pressures.

Yet, these very successes accelerated commercialization, eventually helping to dismantle principles of amateurism. Dempsey's television deals highlighted college athletics' enormous commercial potential; while providing universities with revenue streams they couldn't resist maximizing. His governance reforms, while more efficient, couldn't address the core contradiction between the student-athlete “mythology” and professional-level revenue generation. The modern organizational infrastructure he created would become the vehicle through which, in time, market forces would overwhelm regulatory constraints.

Myles Brand's arrival in 2003 marked the first time a sitting university president assumed the NCAA presidency, bringing philosophical rigor and moral authority that seemed ideally suited for clearing the association's highest hurdles. His distinguished academic career, including a B.S. in philosophy from RPI and a Ph.D. from Rochester, and successful presidencies at Oregon and Indiana, provided intellectual foundations that previous leaders had lacked.

Brand's firing of Bobby Knight while Indiana president had already revealed his willingness to subordinate athletics success to educational values, even amid enormous pressure from influential supporters who viewed Knight as untouchable. This decision, while generating significant controversy, established Brand's credibility as someone who would prioritize principles over popular opinion. And again, exactly what the membership and critics said the NCAA needed in a leader.

The academic reforms Brand implemented were both comprehensive and innovative. The Graduation Success Rate ("GSR") provided more accurate graduation data, while the Academic Progress Rate ("APR") created real-time tracking with meaningful consequences for underperforming programs. His creation of student-athlete advisory committees and expansion of support funds addressed welfare concerns that previous administrations had largely ignored. The diversity and inclusion initiatives he championed laid the foundation for addressing systemic inequities that extended far beyond athletics.

Brand's "Collegiate Model" represented the most sophisticated intellectual framework any NCAA leader had developed for preserving amateurism in an increasingly commercial environment. His argument that student-athletes attended college "primarily to learn and graduate, not merely to entertain or generate revenue" afforded moral clarity that had been missing from previous reform efforts. His scholarly approach to leadership, including innovative communication strategies like the "Mondays with Myles" conversations, demonstrated that rigorous philosophical discourse could coexist with big-time athletics.

Yet Brand's reforms, despite their moral authority and cognitive refinement, ultimately strengthened the case against amateurism by making its contradictions more apparent. The APR system created elaborate bureaucratic structures to track academic progress, while ignoring that athletes in revenue sports were being asked to balance heavy athletics obligations with academic responsibilities. The improvements in graduation rates his reforms achieved sometimes came as a result of academic accommodations that further separated athlete education from genuine academic engagement.

Most ironically, Brand's success in establishing academic standards provided legal ammunition for future assaults on amateurism. Through subsequent demonstrations that universities could and would prioritize athletics success when properly incentivized, his reforms foreshadowed that the NCAA's claimed commitment to education was malleable rather than fundamental. His tragic death from pancreatic cancer in 2009 cut short a presidency that was already revealing the near impossibility of resolving the complexities of college sports through better policies and stronger leadership. And still, I wonder, what if Myles Brand had lived?

Mark Emmert's appointment in 2010 coincided with my deepening involvement in NCAA legal strategy, providing me with an insider's perspective on the impossible position he inherited. He had unassailable academic credentials and was among the most sought-after university presidents in the country. Having been on the faculty at the University of Colorado Boulder, provost and vice president for academic affairs at Montana State, provost and chancellor for academic affairs at UConn, chancellor of my alma mater, LSU, and president of his alma mater, Washington, he had experienced campus life from a myriad of angles which would enhance his ability to understand the NCAA membership. In his leadership roles at major research universities, he secured over $1 billion annually in research funding at Washington and, through his “Flagship Agenda,” significantly advanced LSU's academic standing and national profile. This background seemed to position him perfectly to address the challenges Brand had identified, but had run out of time to resolve.

Notwithstanding his impressive higher education background, which by the way included hiring Nick Saban as LSU's head football coach leading to a National Championship, the NCAA presidency job was... well, the job. Emmert often explained that his role was "more like the secretary-general of the United Nations" than that of the NFL or NBA commissioner. He was overseeing a representative democracy of more than 1,100 member schools rather than governing a centralized league with unified ownership. The public's fundamental misunderstanding of his actual authority versus perceived power created unrealistic expectations that no leader could have satisfied.

The legal challenges mounted during Emmert's tenure weren't accidents of timing; they were the inevitable result of incompatibilities that previous reforms had made impossible to ignore. The *O'Bannon* case attacked NIL restrictions that had become unsustainable in a social media age. The *Alston* case challenged academic benefit limitations that Brand's own reforms had shown to be sometimes subjective, rather than educationally necessary. The *House* case questioned compensation restrictions that were becoming untenable to defend as anything other than economic restraints.

Emmert's servant-leadership philosophy and commitment to student-athlete welfare were genuine, but they couldn't overcome the legal realities created by decades of well-intentioned reforms. His emphasis on collaboration and consensus-building worked within the association, but proved irrelevant in federal courtrooms where judges focused on economic evidence rather than educational rhetoric.

The revenue explosion during Emmert's tenure, with annual athletics scholarship aid growing from $250 million to $2.7 billion, exemplified both his success in advancing student welfare and the unsustainability of the amateur model he was trying to preserve. Each increase in benefits for athletes added complexity to the association's longstanding position on athlete compensation, as the distance between what athletes received and what the market might bear continued to grow.

Emmert's greatest achievement may have been preventing complete organizational collapse while preserving educational missions that distinguished college athletics from professional sports. His governance reforms, health and safety initiatives, and student welfare improvements created foundations that will benefit athletes regardless of how the industry evolves. Yet his tenure also laid bare that even the most principled and capable leadership couldn't overcome structural conflicts that had grown too large to manage through traditional reform approaches.

The pattern across these four decades reveals why Collegiate Capitalism became inevitable, rather than merely possible. Each leader identified real problems, implemented thoughtful solutions, and achieved measurable improvements in their areas of focus. Yet their collective success in making the NCAA more professional, more transparent, more student-focused, and more academically rigorous actually accelerated the system's unraveling. Indeed, these advancements made the remaining amateur elements appear somewhat arbitrary and capricious.

Schultz's emphasis on integrity created expectations for fairness that the amateur model couldn't satisfy. Dempsey's governance reforms and television contracts demonstrated organizational competence while generating revenue streams that made compensation restrictions appear potentially anti-competitive. Brand's academic initiatives established standards for student welfare that made broader athlete rights claims more compelling. Emmert's collaborative approach and benefit improvements showed that change was possible, while the pace of that change seemed insufficient to address apparent inequities.

None of these leaders failed because of personal inadequacy or misguided priorities. They fell short because they were trying to solve problems that couldn't be solved within the existing framework and timeframe, no matter how skillfully they worked or how much support they received from university presidents who shared their commitment to educational values.

The tragedy isn't that they couldn't preserve amateurism. The tragedy is that their very success in making college athletics more professional, more fair, and more responsive to student needs made the amateur model's ultimate collapse both more inevitable and more dramatic.

These four leaders unwittingly demonstrated why amateurism couldn't be saved. Their collective forty-year effort to make college athletics better succeeded so well that it made the amateur model's fundamental unfairness nearly impossible to ignore or defend. The revolution they tried to prevent through better leadership became inevitable because of how effectively they led. That twist captures both the tragedy of their tenures and the inevitability of the drastic changes now underway.

The revolution that Emmert's predecessors had inadvertently accelerated and that Emmert himself couldn't prevent finally arrived with stunning precision. When Charlie Baker assumed the NCAA presidency in March 2023, he inherited not the challenge of preserving amateurism but the task of managing its byproducts. Unlike his predecessors, who had struggled to maintain narratives that were becoming increasingly untenable, Baker arrived as the system's contradictions were resolving themselves through legal force and market pressure.

Baker's appointment represented a core shift in the NCAA's view of what it needed in a leader. Whereas previous presidents had been drawn from higher education, either as athletics directors, university presidents, or academic administrators who understood collegiate culture, Baker, a men's basketball player at Harvard in the 70s, came directly from the world of politics, practical governance, and business management. His eight years as Massachusetts Governor, during which he maintained approval ratings above 70% while governing as a Republican in one of America's most Democratic states, demonstrated an ability to navigate seemingly unworkable political situations through pragmatic compromise versus ideological purity.

His background as CEO of Harvard Pilgrim Health Care provided experience in managing complex regulatory environments and stakeholder relationships that more closely resembled the NCAA's current complexities than those of traditional academic administration. It was believed that Baker understood how to operate within systems where market forces, regulatory requirements, and competing constituencies created constantly shifting pressure points that required adaptive rather than principled responses.

The timing of Baker's arrival was both fortunate and revealing. The *House* settlement negotiations were already underway when he took office, allowing him to position himself as a leader managing change rather than resisting it. Unlike Emmert (and me), who had spent 12 years advancing the association's established positions through a series of increasingly adverse legal outcomes and public criticism, Baker arrived without the accumulated weight of those battles and could chart a new course without the perception of abandoning prior commitments or values.

Yet Baker's tenure has revealed both the opportunities and limitations of pragmatic leadership during revolutionary change. His embrace of NIL deals and support for revenue sharing and private equity investment represent a dramatic philosophical shift from the NCAA's previous positions, but they also raise questions about whether the Association retains any coherent principles beyond merely accommodating the market. His statements supporting athlete welfare and competitive balance sound remarkably similar to those of his predecessors, even though the mechanisms for achieving these goals have changed.

The governance struggles Baker faces dwarf those confronted by previous leaders. Conference realignment has accelerated beyond any rational connection to geography, tradition, or educational mission, driven purely by media-revenue optimization, making previous concerns about commercialization seem quaint. The transfer portal has eliminated any pretense that athletes have meaningful connections to the institutions they represent, creating a free agency system that operates without the salary caps or roster stability that make professional leagues manageable.

Perhaps most significantly, Baker may have to navigate the NCAA's relationship with emerging collective bargaining units as athletes organize to negotiate compensation and working conditions. Federal agencies and courts are now scrutinizing the regulatory framework his predecessors built to preserve amateurism to determine whether the athlete experience exhibits characteristics more commonly associated with employment relationships.

Baker's success will be measured not by his ability to preserve educational values or maintain broad-based competitive balance, both concepts that face unprecedented challenges in the current environment, but by his effectiveness in managing a transition that was already inevitable when he arrived. His challenge is creating sustainable structures for an industry that has seemingly abandoned its foundational principles without developing coherent replacements.

The early signs suggest Baker understands that his role is quite different from his predecessors'. Rather than blindly defending amateur ideals that have not endured, he's focused on practical questions about how to distribute revenue, manage athlete mobility, and maintain some connection between athletics and education in an environment where those relationships appear to have become voluntary.

Yet Baker's pragmatic approach may ultimately prove as inadequate as his predecessors' principled stands. The economic forces that destroy amateurism won't necessarily create stable or educationally beneficial replacements simply because they're allowed to operate freely. The same legal and economic pressures that made the old system untenable could easily make any new system equally unstable if they're not properly channeled through effective governance structures.

Baker's tenure represents the NCAA's acknowledgment that the forty-year effort to preserve amateurism through better leadership and more innovative policies did not work.

> His success or failure will determine whether the association plays a meaningful role in the Collegiate Capitalism era or becomes a historical artifact, remembered primarily for its inability to adapt to changes it had made inevitable through its own actions.

What's poignant is that Baker may prove to be the most effective NCAA president precisely because he's not trying to be an NCAA president in the traditional sense. By abandoning the impossible task of reconciling amateur ideals with business realities, he's free to focus on practical governance problems that previous leaders couldn't address without compromising principles they were committed to defending.

The future he's helping to create may be more honest than the system it's replacing, but honesty about the system's structural inequities doesn't necessarily make those inequities more acceptable or sustainable. Baker's presidency will be remembered either as the successful management of an inescapable transition or as the final chapter in the NCAA's long march toward irrelevance. The difference will depend not only on his leadership skills, which appear considerable, but on whether the market forces he's trying to channel can be made compatible with any meaningful connection between athletics and education. The early evidence suggests the question remains open, with implications that extend far beyond college sports to the broader relationship between American higher education and commercial entertainment.

Chapter 6
The Architects of Alteration
How Visionary Commissioners Hijacked College Sports

While NCAA presidents struggled to preserve amateurism through better policies and stronger governance, a different breed of leader was quietly engineering the most dramatic power shift in college sports history. Certain conference commissioners, figures whose names don't appear on stadium facades or in university mission statements, were systematically dismantling the NCAA's central authority and rebuilding college athletics according to market principles that would make today's Collegiate Capitalism inevitable. A handful of shrewd executives operating from conference headquarters scattered across the nation would exert influence that shapes every Saturday in the fall and every March Madness bracket.

The environment for the subtle accumulation of power was ripe. As NCAA leaders from Byers through Baker fought legal and policy battles to defend the system, conference commissioners were creating the commercial infrastructure that made those battles unwinnable. Every television contract they negotiated, every realignment move they orchestrated, every revenue stream they developed, and every decision that prioritized athletics revenue over educational considerations added layers of commercial complexity that made the amateur framework progressively more difficult to maintain. I am not maligning the commissioners or their intent: I'm simply reflecting on the realities of different missions.

The evolution began not with football, as many assume, but with basketball and a visionary named Dave Gavitt who understood something that escaped his contemporaries. Geographic proximity and historic tradition mattered far less than television ratings, revenue potential, and the ability to build new traditions. When Gavitt created the Big East in 1979, assembling basketball programs from across the Eastern seaboard based on competitive merit and media appeal, he didn't just start a conference; he wrote the playbook for how modern college sports would operate.

Gavitt's background as Providence College's basketball coach brought credibility with athletics departments. Still, his true genius lay in recognizing television's promise decades before most administrators understood what they were witnessing. While other conferences remained bound by hundred-year-old assumptions about regional rivalries and academic partnerships, Gavitt assembled Georgetown, St. John's, Syracuse, Connecticut, Providence, Seton Hall, Boston College, and later Villanova into a basketball-focused confederation that produced compelling television content.

The partnership with ESPN, then a fledgling cable network desperate for programming, established precedents that would reshape the entire industry. Gavitt understood that passionate fans would watch quality basketball notwithstanding geographic location, and that television executives would pay premium prices for content that reliably delivered engaged audiences. The Big East's early success, culminating in Georgetown's 1984 national championship and Villanova's stunning 1985 upset, validated his vision while demonstrating that conferences built around media strategy, and not solely academic tradition, could achieve both competitive success and financial prosperity.

The Midwest's answer to Gavitt came in the form of Jim Delany, who assumed Big Ten leadership in 1989 with a combination of student-athlete experience, enforcement expertise, and legal training that prepared him perfectly for the battles ahead. Whereas his predecessor, Wayne Duke, had been a steady caretaker during gentler times, Delany possessed something different. He mastered vision coupled with ruthless pragmatism about what college sports were becoming.

Delany's approach revealed a sophisticated understanding of how conferences could function as unique brands, not mere administrative conveniences. Throughout the 1990s, he methodically built infrastructure that would support his ultimate ambitions. He would negotiate television contracts that emphasized national rather than regional appeal, champion academic initiatives that provided legitimate cover for increasingly commercial operations, and live by a philosophy that would become orthodoxy among his peers.

> Conferences must act as profit-maximizing enterprises, and commissioners must function as CEOs accountable to revenue in equal measure, if not as a priority, to higher education traditions or mission.

The Big Ten Network's 2007 launch represented perhaps the most audacious gamble in conference history, requiring enormous upfront investment with no guarantee of success. Traditional broadcasters and many within the conference viewed Delany's decision as dangerous overreach, but he made a smart call, and time proved him right. His calculation was prescient. The network's eventual profitability vindicated his vision while establishing a revenue model that every major conference would attempt to replicate, fundamentally remodeling the economics of college sports in ways that made amateur compensation restrictions increasingly difficult to justify.

Yet Delany's masterpiece was his approach to expansion, which may have abandoned all pretense that conferences served purely educational purposes. When Nebraska's addition to the Big Ten was announced in 2010, with competition beginning in 2011, the move made no geographic sense and created no new academic partnerships. It did, however, add a passionate fan base and a nationally renowned football program, enhancing the conference's media rights value. This is undoubtedly the calculation that modern Collegiate Capitalism would eventually make explicit.

The South's contribution to this change came through Mike Slive, whose tenure at the SEC from 2002 to 2015 proved how legal training and strategic thinking could accelerate a conference's ascent to national dominance. Slive inherited Roy Kramer's foundation but perfected every element of the model, including aggressive expansion that prioritized competitive strength over academic compatibility, television contracts that positioned the SEC as a national rather than regional brand, and a relentless focus on football success that generated new and more lucrative revenue streams.

Slive's addition of Texas A&M and Missouri in 2012, just as I was settling into my role at the NCAA, illustrated how commissioners had assumed authority once held by university presidents and faculty committees. These moves weren't debated in academic senates or evaluated according to educational criteria. The NCAA had no rules governing the process nor role in the choices. They were business decisions made by a conference CEO according to market logic, with member institutions serving as shareholder board members who had a significant interest in return on investment.

Commissioners adroitly leveraged the presidents' secure role in NCAA governance to make the process appear more university-based than commercially driven. But the fawning over university CEOs by conference CEOs looked remarkably like the relationship between Hyman Roth and Michael Corleone in the motion picture, The Godfather Part II.

The SEC's subsequent dominance in both football championships and television revenue validated Slive's approach while creating pressures that forced other conferences to adopt similar strategies or risk competitive irrelevance. His success established the template that would define modern conference leadership: build a national brand around your strongest sport, negotiate media deals that reflect that brand's value, and expand strategically to strengthen both. Every major conference realignment decision of the next decade would follow Slive's playbook.

The contrast between successful and unsuccessful commissioner strategies became starkly apparent through the Pac-12's experience under Larry Scott. Scott's appointment in 2009 generated enormous optimism, as his professional sports background seemed to position him perfectly for the business-oriented direction college athletics were heading. His vision for the Pac-12 Networks was conceptually sound. Indeed, conferences that controlled their own media distribution could theoretically capture more value than those dependent on external partners.

However, Scott's execution proved catastrophically flawed, demonstrating that commissioner success required not just business acumen but also a sophisticated understanding of the college sports community's unique dynamics. The networks launched with inadequate distribution, especially in crucial West Coast markets where fans sometimes couldn't access games. Production costs exceeded revenue, creating financial burdens that undermined the conference's competitiveness in other areas. Most damaging, the networks' struggles coincided with declining football performance across the conference and apathy toward athletics, creating a vicious cycle that in the end probably cost Scott his job and left the Pac-12 struggling for relevance to this day.

Scott's tenure also revealed the limits of a commissioner's authority when the underlying strategy failed. Unlike successful commissioners who built consensus around winning strategies, Scott faced mounting criticism from member institutions whose presidents and athletics directors watched other conferences pull ahead in revenue and competitive success. His eventual departure in 2021 showed that even commissioners operated within constraints. They needed to deliver results that justified their strategic choices, and failure to do so could end their careers as quickly as success could enhance their influence.

The rise of women's leadership in conference administration reached its pinnacle with former WNBA president Val Ackerman's remarkable rebuilding of the Big East. Gavitt had handed the baton to his trusted lieutenant, Mike Tranghese, who had preserved the conference's core for most of his 19-year tenure before passing the baton to John Marinatto, a Big East lifer, just as the conference's stability started to crack. Mike Aresco, the executive vice president of CBS Sports, took the helm in 2012 and oversaw a conference split that created the American Athletic Conference, which he led, and the "new" Big East.

When Ackerman assumed the commissioner position in 2013, she inherited a conference devastated by tension between "football schools" and "basketball schools" and by instability perpetuated by football-driven realignment across the country. Traditional powers like Syracuse, Pittsburgh, and Louisville had departed for football-focused conferences, leaving behind a shadow of Gavitt's original vision.

Rather than attempting to compete directly with football-centric conferences or mourning departed programs, Ackerman embraced a basketball model that capitalized on the sport's growing media value and passionate fan engagement. Her strategic vision proved both pragmatic and revolutionary. Instead of replacing departed schools with similar institutions, she assembled the strongest possible collection of basketball-focused universities united by shared athletics excellence and institutional compatibility.

The results validated her approach spectacularly. Villanova's national championships in 2016 and 2018 under Jay Wright demonstrated that basketball-focused conferences could compete with anyone when effectively managed. The 2016 championship was especially memorable, as Kris Jenkins' buzzer-beating three-pointer against North Carolina provided one of the most dramatic finishes in tournament history while showcasing the Big East on its biggest stage against a Tobacco Road powerhouse.

Ackerman's success also proved that alternative models could thrive in the modern landscape without mimicking football's arms race. Her emphasis on collaborative decision-making and student welfare offered a counterpoint to the increasingly corporate culture of other conferences, while Villanova's championships demonstrated that basketball-focused conferences could compete with anyone when effectively led. The Big East's renaissance under Ackerman illustrated something the rest of college athletics was slow to appreciate: sophisticated leadership could build sustainable business models around basketball excellence and passionate fan engagement without the massive infrastructure investments and injury liabilities that football demanded. It was a proof of concept that the future did not require every conference to follow the same path.

The power accumulated by commissioners like Gavitt and Ackerman, Delany, and Slive didn't occur in a vacuum. It coincided with broader changes in American media and entertainment that created unprecedented opportunities for sports programming. Still, it also required these leaders to develop sophisticated relationships with television executives, corporate sponsors, and political figures who could facilitate or obstruct their ambitions.

The symbiotic relationship between media platforms like ESPN and conference commissioners enriched both entities while accelerating college sports' commercial evolution. ESPN's platforms and revenue enabled conferences to expand their ambitions, while commissioners provided content and compelling narratives that drove the network's growth. This partnership reached its zenith with conference-specific networks that effectively converted college athletics into subscription television services, reshaping the relationships among universities, fans, and the commercial marketplace.

Nonetheless, every television contract that generated hundreds of millions in revenue made it harder to justify restrictions on athlete compensation. Every realignment move that prioritized media markets over academic tradition weakened arguments about college sports' educational mission. Every conference network that treated universities as content providers rather than educational institutions strengthened the case for treating athletes as professionals rather than students.

Little did I know it, but by the time the NCAA hired me, the power shift appeared to be on a path to irreversibility. Commissioners had accumulated authority that allowed them to make decisions affecting hundreds of thousands of athletes and billions of dollars in revenue, often without meaningful direction from the educational institutions they ostensibly served. Already burdened with running complicated educational institutions in an ever-increasingly complex world, most presidents were more than happy to turn over the reins of athletics affairs to the new stars of collegiate sports management. Conference headquarters had evolved into corporate enterprises that operated according to business logic rather than academic tradition, employing sophisticated marketing strategies, lobbying operations, and legal departments that rivaled those of major corporations and professional sports leagues.

This new world created both opportunities and threats for the future of college athletics. The professionalization of conference leadership brought sophisticated business practices and strategic thinking to college sports, generating extraordinary revenue and exposure for participating institutions. Television contracts worth hundreds of millions of dollars offered resources that enabled schools to enhance facilities, expand programs, and improve services for student-athletes.

However, the emphasis on revenue maximization and competitive advantage also created pressures that frequently conflicted with the educational mission. Traditional rivalries were sacrificed for access to media markets. Academic considerations took a back seat to athletics and financial priorities. College athletics as a multi-billion-dollar entertainment industry raised new questions about the relationship between sports and education that commissioners were neither equipped nor eager to address.

Don't get me wrong. The commissioners who engineered this game plan deserve recognition not as villains who corrupted college athletics, but as visionaries who appreciated market realities that academic administrators preferred to ignore. Their success in building commercially viable entertainment enterprises from university athletics programs demonstrated both impressive business acumen and a sophisticated understanding of American sports culture.

Yet their achievements also solidified the current journey toward Collegiate Capitalism. The infrastructure they built to maximize conference revenue and gain a competitive advantage has become the foundation upon which true professionalization will be built.

In the end, the revolution these commissioners engineered exposed what college athletics had been beneath the surface of amateurism. Their legacy will be measured not by the specific deals they negotiated or the championships their conferences won, but by their role in creating an industry that is honest about its commercial nature and fair to the athletes who generate its value. Whether that industry retains any meaningful connection to higher education remains to be determined, but the commissioners who made its emergence possible have already secured their place in the history of American sports.

Chapter 7
The Modern Power Brokers
How Today's Commissioners Completed the Corporate Takeover

The commissioners who inherited the empire built by Gavitt, Delany, Slive, and their contemporaries faced a different breakline. They were handed the task of managing the final sprint from amateur athletics to professional entertainment while still maintaining the connections to higher education that provided their enterprises with political and legal standing. The leaders who assumed power in the 2010s and 2020s, such as commissioners Greg Sankey, Kevin Warren, Brett Yormark, Tony Petitti, Jim Phillips, and George Kliavkoff would oversee not the creation of Collegiate Capitalism but its inevitable implementation.

Greg Sankey's arrival at the SEC in 2015 coincided perfectly with the conference's emergence as college athletics' dominant force, but his tenure has revealed both the opportunities and costs of pursuing that dominance with single-minded determination. While Sankey inherited Mike Slive's foundation of football excellence and television revenue, he has pushed the SEC's competitive advantages to levels that have reshaped the landscape of college sports. That success has drawn pointed criticism from those who believe his pursuit of conference dominance has come at a cost to the broader ecosystem.

Sankey's background as a former Division III athlete, compliance officer, conference administrator, and NCAA Committee on Infractions member gave him a deep grounding in the regulatory and competitive dynamics of college sports. But his leadership style has been notably more assertive than his predecessor's. Where Slive built consensus around expansion and media strategy, Sankey has more often moved first and negotiated later, identifying opportunities to enhance SEC advantages even when doing so unsettled peer conferences.

The COVID-19 pandemic offered a revealing window into his priorities. While other commissioners wrestled with health concerns and financial pressures, Sankey positioned the SEC to keep competing through the disruption. His conference's decision to proceed with football and basketball seasons under its own protocols drew criticism from medical experts and rival commissioners who argued he was prioritizing revenue over athlete safety. The reality was more complicated. The country was divided over how to handle the pandemic, and Sankey was responsive to a Southern constituency that strongly believed the show should go on.

His defenders saw decisive leadership in a crisis. Critics saw a willingness to accept risk in exchange for competitive position. Whatever the motivation, the SEC's ability to complete full seasons while other conferences canceled or curtailed theirs produced advantages that extended well beyond the immediate financial picture, shaping recruiting, media coverage, and national perception in ways that benefited SEC programs.

The Texas and Oklahoma move to the SEC, initiated in 2021 and finalized in 2024, embodied both strategic vision and, in the eyes of some, predatory ambition. Big 12 Commissioner Bob Bowlsby, whose conference bore the brunt of the realignment, was as pragmatic about these things as a former high school and college wrestler with a Phys Ed degree, credentials he often proudly proclaimed. Bowlsby viewed the move as a personal betrayal, but he resolved the schools' early exit and rebuilt by adding BYU, UCF, Cincinnati, and Houston. The addition of two prestigious football programs and major media markets nonetheless reinforced the SEC's already dominant position and created competitive imbalances that many observers continue to watch closely.

Critics argue that Sankey operates with a zero-sum mindset that prioritizes SEC interests over the broader health of college athletics. The conference's aggressive pursuit of television revenue and competitive advantage has pushed others into defensive postures, accelerating the commercialization of college sports beyond what many believe is sustainable. The arms-race dynamic that defines modern conference competition can be traced in significant part to Sankey's relentless pursuit of SEC standing.

His approach to name, image, and likeness rights and the transfer portal has likewise been the subject of debate. To his critics, his public positioning sometimes reads as advocacy for policies that preserve SEC advantages while raising concerns about reforms that might level the playing field. His comments at the 2025 SEC spring meetings, suggesting the SEC had made sacrifices to participate in the CFP because it did not need the format the way others did, illustrated the pattern. Defenders see candor about competitive realities; skeptics see SEC interests presented as synonymous with what is best for college athletics generally.

Even those critics, however, must acknowledge his effectiveness within the system as it exists. His expansion strategy reflected a sophisticated reading of competitive dynamics and media economics. His handling of regulatory change has consistently positioned the SEC to benefit from, rather than be destabilized by evolving rules. And his stewardship of the conference's football preeminence, alongside its growing strength in other sports and broader national footprint, has delivered member institutions resources and opportunities that few peers can match.

The contrast between Sankey's approach and Kevin Warren's, who assumed Big Ten leadership in January 2020, illustrates different models of conference leadership adapted to the realities of modern college sports within the dynamics of the schools that comprise the conference. Warren's background as an NFL team executive brought professional sports experience to college athletics at precisely the moment when the operational similarities between the two were becoming increasingly apparent, but his leadership style has emphasized partnership and institutional building rather than aggressive competition.

Warren inherited a conference with strong traditions and substantial resources, but one that had fallen behind the SEC in both football success and media revenue generation. His challenge was to restore the conference's competitiveness without abandoning the academic values and institutional relationships that distinguished it. His approach displayed that effective conference leadership can pursue competitive success while maintaining broader commitments to educational mission and collegial relationships.

The early tests of Warren's leadership revealed both his strengths and the constraints facing even the most capable commissioners. His initial decision to postpone Big Ten football in response to COVID-19 concerns generated enormous controversy and criticism, particularly from coaches, players, and political figures who viewed the decision as overly cautious and competitively damaging. However, the conference's initial approach appeared to prioritize medical advice and risk assessment over financial and competitive considerations, suggesting a decision-making process that differed from the SEC's approach under Sankey. In truth, neither acted alone: both commissioners were executing on conversations with the university presidents on their boards.

Warren's reversal of the football postponement decision, while controversial, showed adaptability and responsiveness to changing circumstances and stakeholder pressure. More importantly, his management of the crisis demonstrated a sophisticated understanding of the multiple constituencies that conference commissioners must satisfy, from university presidents and medical officials to coaches, athletes, fans, and political figures whose support or opposition can determine policy success. Critics noted, however, that Warren's communication during the COVID crisis revealed gaps in stakeholder management that remained a point of contention throughout his tenure.

His orchestration of USC and UCLA's addition to the Big Ten reflected perhaps the most audacious expansion move in conference history, creating a coast-to-coast footprint that abandoned all traditional assumptions about geographic proximity and regional rivalry. The move demonstrated Warren's understanding that modern college sports operate according to calculated media market logic in addition to academic tradition. He provided the Big Ten with access to the nation's second-largest media market and two prestigious university brands.

Warren's expansion strategy, while assuredly in part about media markets, was notably more thoughtful and institution-focused than a purely competitive approach. His emphasis on academic compatibility and institutional culture, while not determining his decisions, provided frameworks for evaluating potential additions that extend beyond immediate competitive and financial considerations. This approach has enabled the Big Ten to maintain its identity as a collection of major research universities while pursuing the commercial success necessary to compete with other major conferences.

The success of Warren's media strategy is clear, as the Big Ten's television contracts generated revenue that matches or exceeds those of its primary competitors. Critically, the strategy also maintained programming relationships that enhanced, rather than limited, institutional autonomy. His background in professional sports appears to have enabled him to negotiate with media executives and corporate partners in a manner that aligned with their expectations and priorities. Simultaneously, his understanding of higher education helped him preserve relationships and values that distinguish college athletics from purely professional enterprises.

Also of importance was Warren's approach to athlete compensation and rights issues. It differed markedly from that of others who view such changes primarily as threats to established advantages. His recognition that enhanced athlete rights and compensation are inevitable enabled him to work actively on implementation strategies that benefited Big Ten institutions and athletes while avoiding the reactive approach that characterized other conferences' responses to regulatory changes. Warren's return to the NFL in 2023 as the president and CEO of the Chicago Bears left a gap in the ranks of conference commissioners who genuinely understood how to effectively professionalize college athletics within the Collegiate Capitalism paradigm.

That gap was filled quickly. Along came Tony Petitti, the MLB chief operating officer and former CEO of the MLB Network, whose big law and inhouse legal background would serve him well as the next commissioner of the Big Ten. Petitti, with superior business acumen, would continue to run Warren's playbook and further expand the Big Ten by adding Washington and Oregon. The die-cast for Collegiate Capitalism was hardening.

To be clear, the leadership tests these commissioners inherited extend far beyond traditional conference administration into areas that would have been unimaginable for earlier generations of commissioners. Modern conference leaders must navigate federal antitrust litigation, congressional oversight, state legislation affecting athletes' rights, international expansion opportunities, and rapidly evolving media technologies that create both new opportunities and threats with bewildering speed.

The legal complexity of modern conference operations has created dependence on sophisticated counsel. Conference decisions about expansion, media contracts, athlete compensation, and regulatory compliance all require expert legal analysis that accounts for antitrust law, employment regulation, tax policy, and constitutional considerations that extend far beyond traditional college sports administration.

Similarly, the political dimensions of conference leadership have expanded exponentially as college athletics has become a subject of intense federal and state policy attention. Commissioners now employ lobbying firms and political consultants who monitor legislative developments, manage relationships with key political figures, and develop advocacy strategies that protect conference interests from adverse regulatory changes.

The implementation of name, image, and likeness rights revealed the extent to which conferences had become independent policy-making entities capable of developing their own approaches to athlete compensation. And, the transfer portal's impact created another area where conference leadership proved crucial, as commissioners needed to help member institutions adapt recruiting and roster management strategies to account for unprecedented player mobility.

These regulatory changes have accelerated discussions about athlete unionization and employment rights, posing existential challenges to the old and even current model of conference leadership. As athletes attempt to organize and negotiate compensation and working conditions through collective bargaining, conferences may face the possibility of dealing with organized labor rather than individual athletes or even individual institutions. This development would require significant changes in conference operations and potentially convert commissioners from athletics administrators or even league CEOs into labor relations managers.

The recent wave of conference realignment, culminating in moves that have created coast-to-coast conferences with no meaningful geographic logic, represents both the apotheosis of commissioner power and evidence of its ultimate limits. While commissioners like Sankey, Warren, and Petitti successfully orchestrated moves that enhance their conferences' competitive and financial positions, they have also created a system that may be untenable in its current form.

The travel costs, scheduling complexities, and competitive imbalances created by recent realignment moves have generated criticism from athletes, coaches, university administrators, fans, and politicians who argue that the pursuit of television revenue has undermined the educational and competitive values that justified college athletics in the first place. Some observers believe that the current system of mega-conferences spanning entire continents may collapse under its own weight, requiring new approaches to conference organization and leadership.

This environment has also created pressure for further consolidation that could ultimately result in a relatively small number of institutions controlling the majority of college athletics revenue and competitive opportunities. This development would reflect far more than an incremental shift from college sports as an educational activity to a pure entertainment enterprise, with implications that extend far beyond athletics into the broader missions of American higher education.

Indeed, the fragility of conference structures became most apparent through litigation that threatened to tear apart one of college athletics' oldest leagues. In December 2023, Florida State filed a lawsuit against the ACC, challenging the legal foundations of conference membership and media rights agreements.

Florida State's grievance had been building for years. The ACC's media rights deal with ESPN, negotiated in 2012 and extended through 2036, paid member schools significantly less than what Big Ten and SEC schools received. The gap widened as those conferences signed increasingly lucrative agreements. By 2023, Florida State was receiving roughly two-thirds of what comparable SEC programs earned from media rights, a gap of nearly $20 million annually. Given Florida State's football tradition and fan base, the disparity seemed unjust.

The immediate trigger was the CFP selection committee's decision to exclude undefeated Florida State from the four-team playoff in December 2023. The Seminoles had won the ACC Championship despite losing their starting quarterback to injury, yet the committee determined that a one-loss team, Alabama from the SEC, was more deserving. Jim Phillips, the ACC Commissioner who had a storied career as an athletics administrator and was known as a calm, steady leader, called the decision "unfathomable!" Notwithstanding Phillips' empathy for the school's slight, Florida State's board of trustees met on December 22 and voted unanimously to sue the ACC. They wanted to leave the ACC because it was not seen as powerful enough to protect their interests, nor rich enough to pay their worth.

The lawsuit challenged what Florida State called "draconian" withdrawal penalties that effectively trapped schools in the conference regardless of changing circumstances. The ACC's Grant of Rights agreement, signed by all members, transferred each school's media rights to the conference through 2036. If Florida State attempted to leave, it would forfeit media revenue worth at least $442 million. The exit fee on top of that was approximately $130 million.

Florida State argued that the ACC had "negotiated itself into a self-described existential crisis, rendered itself fiscally unstable, and substantially undermined its members' capacity to compete at the elite level." The conference had violated contractual, fiduciary, and legal duties owed to its members, Florida State contended.

In March 2024, Clemson filed its own lawsuit in South Carolina making similar arguments. The two schools, which together had won seven of the ACC's nine CFP appearances, were now in open legal warfare against their own conference.

The litigation threatened conference stability far beyond Florida State and Clemson. If the Grant of Rights could be successfully challenged, other conferences would face similar risks. The legal framework that had enabled long-term media deals and conference stability could unravel.

The ACC countered with its own legal strategy, filing suit in North Carolina before Florida State's action became public, in an attempt to secure favorable jurisdiction. Phillips publicly criticized the schools for "extremely damaging, disruptive, and incredibly harmful" behavior and committed to fight "as long as it takes." What had been private tensions about revenue distribution became a public battle that consumed the conference.

The resolution came in March 2025, after more than a year of litigation and negotiation. The settlement restructured ACC economics in ways that would have seemed improbable before the lawsuits forced the issue.

The new revenue distribution model allocated 40% of media revenue equally among legacy members, with 60% distributed based on a five-year rolling average of television ratings. Schools that generated more viewership, primarily Florida State and Clemson, would receive proportionally more revenue. The conference also created additional "success initiatives" rewarding performance in football, men's basketball, and women's basketball.

Critically, the exit fee structure changed dramatically. In place of what Florida State characterized as a potential $700 million-plus penalty that had trapped schools, the exit fee would start at $165 million in 2026 and decline to $75 million by 2030-31. Schools now had a realistic path to departure if circumstances warranted.

Both Florida State and Clemson remained in the ACC, their leverage having extracted concessions that years of internal advocacy had failed to achieve. The message was clear: litigation worked. Schools that wanted better terms could sue their way to them rather than accepting whatever the conference offered. And while Florida State and Clemson were the combatants, Miami would reap the spoils with its 2025 football performance.

The ACC settlement illustrated broader truths about modern college athletics governance. Traditional assumptions about conference loyalty and collective action had given way to naked self-interest enforced through legal combat. Schools would remain in conferences only as long as membership served their individual interests, and they would use every available tool to maximize their returns.

This was Collegiate Capitalism hatching in its purest form. The romantic notions of conference fellowship, regional identity, and collective purpose had been replaced by financial calculations and legal strategies. Schools were not family members bound by tradition; they were business partners bound by contracts, and contracts could be renegotiated or litigated.

And while the ACC fought to hold itself together through litigation, the Pac-12 experienced what happens when a major conference fails to quickly adapt to the new economics of college athletics. The Conference of Champions, as the Pac-12 had styled itself, effectively ceased to exist as a significant force in college sports, its members scattered across the country in a vast diaspora.

The collapse began in June 2022, when Commissioner Warren acquired USC and UCLA for the Big Ten. The move made no geographic sense by traditional measures. From Los Angeles to New Jersey, to Maryland, to Wisconsin, the travel requirements for Big Ten competition would be enormous. But the move made perfect sense by the only measure that now mattered: media revenue. The Big Ten's television contracts would deliver USC and UCLA far more money than the Pac-12 could offer.

Commissioner George Kliavkoff, a lawyer and media executive who succeeded Commissioner Scott in 2021, worked desperately to save the conference. He negotiated with Apple TV and other potential partners for a media deal that could match or approach what the Big Ten offered to its members. He explored expansion, approached schools from other conferences, and tried to convince remaining members that the Pac-12 could survive and thrive.

None of it worked.

The dominoes fell throughout 2023. Colorado, Arizona, Arizona State, and Utah announced moves to the Big 12. Oregon and Washington followed USC and UCLA to the Big Ten. Stanford and California, two of the Pac-12's founding members, departed for the ACC on the opposite coast.

By August 2024, only Washington State and Oregon State remained from what had been a 12-school conference. The Pac-12 as we had known it, the conference of John Wooden's UCLA basketball dynasty, of USC's football excellence, of Stanford's Olympic tradition, was finished. The underlying causes of the collapse, detailed in the preceding chapter, included the Pac-12 Networks' revenue shortfalls and the conference's structural disadvantages in media markets.

But the deeper cause was structural. The Pac-12's footprint in western states with smaller populations, and less interest in college sports, could not compete with the Big Ten and SEC's access to larger, more valuable media markets. Los Angeles alone could not compensate for the absence of the massive population centers that anchored other conferences. When the streaming revolution promised to make geographic distribution obsolete, it also meant that traditional regional advantages disappeared.

Kliavkoff inherited an impossible situation and proved unable to reverse the momentum toward dissolution. His negotiations dragged on too long while other conferences acted decisively. Schools that might have waited for a better Pac-12 media deal chose to go with certainty in other conferences instead.

The Pac-12's survivors, Washington State and Oregon State, filed lawsuits seeking damages from departed members and attempting to retain conference assets. They began recruiting new members from the Mountain West and elsewhere, planning to reconstitute some version of the conference by 2026. Whether this rebuilt Pac-12, under long-time athletics administrator and Pac-12 staffer, commissioner Teresa Gould's leadership, can become a meaningful competitive force remains deeply uncertain.

What died with the original Pac-12 was more than a conference. It was a vision of college athletics that valued tradition, academic prestige, and regional identity alongside competitive success. The schools that departed chose money over history, media markets over geographic logic, and individual advantage over collective identity.

I understood these choices even as I mourned them. I spent years working with schools and conferences to preserve the connections between athletics and the educational mission while managing growing commercial pressures. The Pac-12's dissolution illustrated how difficult that balance had become. When the revenue disparities grew large enough, institutional loyalty proved insufficient to hold traditional structures together.

Looking toward the future, the power accumulated by conference commissioners seems likely to continue growing rather than diminishing, if for no other reason than the weariness and wariness of institutional presidents to remain in the fray. The NCAA president now operates less as an authority over conferences than as a coordinator whose influence depends on his ability to provide value to commissioners who could increasingly operate entirely independent of NCAA membership. The commissioners who engineered this transformation have refashioned not just college athletics but American higher education itself, building multi-billion-dollar entertainment enterprises from university athletics programs and creating pressures that have forced institutions to reconsider their basic missions and priorities.

The revolution is almost complete, but its ultimate consequences remain to be determined. The commissioners who built this new world have created possibilities for athlete empowerment and professional-quality entertainment.

> Whether we've lost something valuable in the process, the unique connection between athletics and education that distinguished American college sports from all other forms of entertainment remains the central question facing the industry that commissioners have remade in their own image.

Chapter 8
When One Door Closes
Capitol Hill to Circle City

I wasn't thinking about NCAA headquarters, membership boardrooms, or conference offices. Collegiate Capitalism had not yet been conceived in my mind as I sat in the Dirksen Senate Office Building, surrounded by mahogany walls, where my own ambitions lay dying. But this day would teach me lessons that would prove essential when I later found myself defending a system that, as I would come to understand, was already under pressures that would fundamentally reshape it.

By 2009, all the forces we've examined thus far in this book were converging with mathematical precision. Conference commissioners were amassing unprecedented power while NCAA presidents struggled to uphold the system's original tenets that market forces undermined. Legal challenges were mounting, television revenues were exploding, and the tensions between educational mission and commercial growth were becoming increasingly difficult to reconcile. Yet none of that mattered to me personally. I was seated at a Senate witness table that spring morning, watching my nomination to serve as the Army's General Counsel unravel in real time.

The paradox was almost perfect. While the NCAA was struggling to defend amateurism in the courts of public opinion and justice, I was experiencing firsthand how political processes could destroy even well-intentioned public servants. I found myself caught between competing narratives about my character and my competence. The skills I would need to navigate the NCAA's challenging legal position, including analytical thinking under pressure, resilience in the face of unfair criticism, and the wisdom to know when tactical withdrawal serves larger purposes, were being forged in that confirmation hearing's crucible.

President Barack Obama issued his intent to nominate me on March 26, 2009, ironically, just over a week after Selection Sunday and a little more than a week before the University of North Carolina was crowned the men's basketball National Champion for the fifth time in what would be the last NCAA tournament game broadcast on analog television. I was not focused on basketball, but rather on an honor that should have reflected the crown jewel of a career dedicated to public service. In a strange twist of fate, my testimony before the Senate Armed Services Committee a month later was marked by controversy. Yet, I did my best to professionally describe my qualifications and commitment to serving our nation's soldiers. But Washington's political machinery operates according to its own brutal logic, and by June, I had learned that lesson in the most painful way possible.

The hullabaloo that ended my nomination seems almost quaint in retrospect. A generic biography that referred to Fannie Mae as a "major U.S. company" rather than explicitly identifying it as my former employer was the unforced error. In the context of the 2008 financial crisis, when mortgage giants like Fannie Mae and Freddie Mac were being blamed for the economic collapse, this omission became political ammunition for senators seeking to demonstrate their vigilance on financial-sector accountability.

I remember the moment everything changed with crystalline clarity. Immediately before my testimony, Senator John McCain approached me in the hearing room with barely controlled anger. "I'm going to pin the 2008 collapse of the financial system on you," he told me, his words hitting like physical blows. Then, in what I can only describe as a "Bruce Lee move," he pivoted from confrontation to warmth, embracing my two sons and posing for photographs with them. In that instant, my heart and mind fell into his hands, and I believed that the hearing was already over before it had truly begun.

As I took my seat alongside other nominees, Governor Ray Mabus for Secretary of the Navy, Bob Work for Under Secretary of the Navy, and Elizabeth King for Assistant Secretary of Defense for Legislative Affairs, I might as well have been sitting alone. Two of my closest friends in attendance, Michael Powell, who had served as chair of the Federal Communications Commission, and Phil Bartz, a fellow Deputy from the Justice

Department, could see the concern etched on my face. When I explained McCain's comments, Powell, who knew the Senator personally, offered profound but straightforward advice: "You, me, and many others are proud of the work you did at Fannie Mae. Help the Committee understand that, notwithstanding the omission, you stand by your work, which should be celebrated."

But it felt like I was in the fourth quarter of a basketball game, down by 10, and 30 seconds left on the clock. Senator Mel Martinez, who had previously served as HUD Secretary, joined McCain in expressing concerns about my candor, Fannie Mae, and my service from 2000-2006: indeed, a steal and a score. The closed meeting with members of the Senate Armed Services Committee on June 11 confirmed my fears, as I recall that only Chairman Carl Levin was present from the Democratic side. I interpreted this as a lack of support from the president's own party. I returned to the Pentagon and was granted time with the Department of Defense General Counsel, Jeh Johnson, to ask for advice on next steps. While he adroitly declined to tell me what to do, our conversation led me to conclude that I had only one path.

That evening, after conversations with my family and trusted advisors, including William James “Jim” Haynes II, the former Army General Counsel who had hired me during the administration of President George H.W. Bush and later served as Defense Department General Counsel under President George W. Bush, I made one of the most difficult decisions of my life. Having experienced his own brutal confirmation battle for the Fourth Circuit, Jim understood the political calculus better than most. His insights, combined with my own analysis, confirmed my inescapable decision.

I withdrew my name from consideration, writing to President Obama with a heavy heart: "As a veteran and someone who has dedicated much of his life to public service, including in the Army General Counsel's office, I am honored by your confidence in my ability to deal with the critical issues that face our soldiers and their families. Regretfully, I have decided to remove my name from consideration for this position." When I privately described my decision to the president, his response was both gracious and empathetic: "Donald, I understand."

The personal cost was devastating. For the first time in my life, anxiety and depression overwhelmed my usual resilience. This wasn't just another professional setback; it was a public humiliation that challenged everything I thought I knew about myself and my place in the world. I sought mental health counseling, something that required considerable courage in 2009, when such treatment carried stigma that could damage career prospects. I remember getting a referral for a therapist who specialized in discretion for athletes, entertainers, politicians, and other public figures. Embarrassed to receive treatment, I would schedule late evening appointments to avoid being seen, worried that knowledge of my struggles would impact future opportunities. Sounds silly in 2026… not so much 16 years ago.

I hid my struggle from my partners, associates, and clients, seeking a way to recalibrate in my profession. Every day I was masking my cries with smiles while grappling with what felt like a personal and professional disaster. I also poured myself further into coaching youth basketball across the DMV (DC, Maryland, Virginia), working with boys from ages 9 to 16 across competitive circuits from CYA through AAU and EYBL. The intensity of coaching provided both distraction and purpose, and the championship runs we achieved reminded me that I still knew how to compete and win.

Notwithstanding the distraction of coaching and my law practice, the confirmation experience was a stark reminder of how quickly things can change in Washington. One day you're on top, the next day, well… you're not. It was a blow. The experience taught me lessons that would prove invaluable during my NCAA tenure. I learned never to read the comments. That is advice I now give to anyone facing public criticism in our social media age. My incident was long before social media had grown to what it is today, and I can only imagine the emotions of people who try to read and respond to everything that's said about them. I believe experts who say that today's mental health crisis is exacerbated by social media. People can be unforgiving and downright nasty when they live in the anonymity of commenting on a page, article, or circumstance.

I also discovered something about my own resolve and ability to handle conflict and unfairness, even when the criticism seemed widespread and personally devastating. More importantly, I developed what I came to think of as my analytical framework, which was validated a couple of years later by the television series Person of Interest.

The show's premise fascinated me. A reclusive genius had created an artificial intelligence capable of predicting violent crimes by analyzing surveillance data from cameras and communications systems across the country. The system would identify potential victims and perpetrators and provide their identities so that an operative could intervene. But the computer would run situational simulations to determine the best possible action for the optimal outcome, even when that action required sacrifice.

I recognized myself in that analytical process. Depending on the situation, I could run those calculations in days, minutes, hours, or seconds, weighing facts and circumstances to determine the action most likely to produce the best possible outcome. Unlike people whose decisions begin and end with what they personally want, I work through the available information to determine the right course of action, even when the answer requires personal sacrifice.

The confirmation experience was my first truly public letdown, and it taught me that sometimes strategic retreat serves larger purposes better than prolonged battle. Live to fight another day. I believed that continuing to pursue confirmation would create ongoing controversy that could distract from the president's agenda and the Army's important work. My decision was about service rather than self-interest. I would step aside so the administration could move forward with someone who wouldn't carry perceived baggage.

American politics, like college sports, is in uncharted territory. In 2024, U.S. President Joe Biden stepped aside as the Democratic Party's presumptive presidential nominee. I don't for a minute liken my plight to holding and then not pursuing the American presidency. But I do understand the state of mind of the president when he decided to end his quest to remain the most powerful person on the planet, in his words, "in the best interest of my party and the country... to stand down and to focus solely on fulfilling my duties as President for the remainder of my term." Certainly, such a decision is not easy. It's difficult to "give all this up for the greater good." For me, on a much, much, much smaller scale, that's what I was doing. It was the beginning of the Obama presidency. Of course, I would have loved this position for a myriad of reasons. It was a historic Presidency. It was a perfect progression to my professional journey. It was a full-circle moment. But I would not push forward in this environment because it may harm the greater good.

We live in different times. In the second Trump term, we are witnessing an altogether atypical approach. I don't know if I would have done anything differently, but maybe I would have. Perhaps I would have decided to fight longer, ignore the noise, and push on. If the president wanted to move on past me, I'd let him make that decision, not me. Based on today's standards, it would be difficult not to push forward regardless of distractions and noise.

Yet, I knew in 2009 that many blamed the collapse of the financial markets on the housing crisis. It was intentional that the Presidential Personnel Office (PPO) wasn't selecting many people who had worked in the industry to be confirmed by the Senate as part of the president's administration. At the time, I was one of the very few, maybe even the only person nominated for Senate confirmation who had worked anywhere in the financial services industry, including companies like Fannie Mae, Freddie Mac, Lehman Brothers, Washington Mutual, Goldman Sachs, Morgan Stanley, Bank of America, and others. Thinking about what Sen. McCain said to me before the hearing and America's perspective on the financial crisis, my situational analysis kicked in and spit out what seemed to be the right and just decision.

This decision-making framework, which includes analyzing all available information, considering stakeholder impacts, and choosing the course of action most likely to serve the greater good, would define my approach to every major challenge I would face at the NCAA and beyond. Whether defending amateurism in federal court, navigating the membership governance labyrinth, or managing the seemingly weekly crises, I would consistently apply the same analytical rigor that led me to make those early career decisions.

The experience also provided crucial insight into how quickly circumstances can change in high-stakes environments, how unfair criticism can distort public perception, and how personal resilience becomes essential when serving institutions under pressure. These lessons would prove invaluable when I found myself defending an organization facing existential challenges from multiple directions at once.

I couldn't have known in 2009 that my nomination withdrawal was preparing me for a role that would place me at the center of college athletics' metamorphosis from amateur competition to professional entertainment. The analytical skills, emotional resilience, and strategic thinking that emerged from that difficult period would be tested repeatedly in legal battles, media controversies, and policy debates that would ultimately reshape American higher education and college sports.

The door to the Obama administration had closed, but as I would learn, sometimes when one door closes, another opens in a direction you never expected.

> The skills forged in my confirmation process: analytical thinking under pressure, resilience in the face of unfair criticism, and wisdom about when strategic retreat serves larger purposes, were precisely the tools I would need to navigate the most challenging legal and political environment in NCAA history.

The revolution was coming whether I participated or not. The same market forces that made my Fannie Mae experience politically toxic were putting pressure on the traditional model of amateur athletics, which would prove increasingly difficult to manage. The contradictions I had witnessed in government were playing out on an even larger scale in college sports. Importantly, the denial of athlete compensation was becoming a constantly hammered sore thumb of intercollegiate athletics that would not heal. My personal setback had prepared me for institutional challenges that would prove far more consequential than any individual career encumbrance.

Chapter 9
Finding Purpose in the Heart of a Revolution
You're Exactly What We Need

The opportunity arrived when I least expected it, offering an opportunity placing me at the epicenter of the very transformation we will examine throughout this book. Rick Bernthal, my partner at Latham & Watkins, and Abe Frank, who headed government relations for the NCAA, convinced me to explore the General Counsel position because of my romantic views on the value of higher education and my commitment to young athletes and their families' needs. Rick's words resonated profoundly: "This is a chance to combine your life's work with your avocation. Rarely are we offered such opportunities." This advice fueled my passion, and I pursued the position.

By 2010, the forces driving college athletics toward Collegiate Capitalism were escalating. The *Board of Regents* decision was already twenty-six years old, the balance among presidential, commissioner, and athletics director power was shifting, and legal assaults on amateurism were mounting with increasing sophistication. From my perspective as a big law partner chairing Latham's global aerospace and defense industry group, the NCAA seemed like a relic from another era. To be sure, it was an organization that used historically sound legal strategies and practical arguments to defend amateur ideals. Yet I wondered whether those rationales could hold in the modern sports and entertainment landscape.

My skepticism wasn't theoretical. As a grassroots basketball coach working with teams across the DMV, I witnessed firsthand how NCAA rules could derail young athletes' aspirations. Many of my players came from modest backgrounds without the financial resources or family support to navigate the complex requirements of college recruiting. When others stepped in to assist, and I was undoubtedly guilty of helping, it often led to NCAA violations that jeopardized their eligibility. Not knowing or perhaps willfully blind of whether it violated NCAA rules, I regularly paid for players' meals, bought shoes and uniforms, rented hotel rooms, and purchased plane tickets for parents and grandparents who could not afford to travel to watch their sons compete in distant tournaments.

From my coaching perspective, the system appeared to create significant value from athletes' participation, while the rules governing their compensation and support had not kept pace with the commercial growth of college sports, particularly for athletes from disadvantaged backgrounds who viewed professional sports as pathways to better lives. These issues fueled the reform movement that was already gaining momentum when I was approached about the General Counsel position.

The interview process was lengthy and rigorous, involving dozens of conversations with NCAA staff, member institution representatives, and athletics administrators who helped me understand the organization's complexity in ways that my legal and coaching experience hadn't revealed.

The final dinner meeting with Emmert and NCAA Chief Operating Officer Jim Isch took place at a steakhouse near Dulles Airport in northern Virginia. I remember being honored with selecting the wine, a 2009 Napa Valley Cabernet Sauvignon, which seemed perfect for the business meeting. I'm still not sure, however, whether Mark, a wine connoisseur himself, was impressed by the choice. The dinner went well, so I've always presumed he was.

After polite conversation, we began our discussion. Their explanations of the Association's complex legal and policy challenges revealed an organization grappling with forces far more serpentine than my own college mentoring or grassroots coaching experiences had suggested. Mark's comment, "You are exactly what we need to help lead us through the problems," proved prescient in ways none of us could have anticipated.

The NCAA announced my selection as its new General Counsel on January 3, 2011, seven days before an undefeated SEC Auburn Tigers team faced an undefeated Pac-10 Oregon team in the BCS National Championship Game. The Tigers, led by Heisman Trophy winner Cam Newton, won the game when Wes Byrum kicked a 19-yard field goal as time expired, capping a dramatic final drive. I watched the game on television, thrilled about my new position and the prospect of being part of this exciting industry. I was to start on March 14, one day after March Madness Selection Sunday, positioning me to witness the men's basketball tournament drama from an entirely new perspective.

Less than two weeks after my start, in my family's hometown of New Orleans, I watched Butler University's improbable run through the tournament brackets. The Bulldogs, led by Shelvin Mack and Matt Howard under coach Brad Stevens, outlasted the SEC powerhouse Florida Gators in overtime to advance to the Final Four. I then traveled to my 1st Final Four as an NCAA staff member. It was at Reliant Stadium in Houston, and I witnessed the magic of underdog Butler competing for a national championship against Connecticut's talented lineup featuring future four-time NBA All-Star Kemba Walker, Shabazz Napier, and Jeremy Lamb.

Butler's Cinderella run ended in the championship game, but I was exposed to the true meaning of "one shining moment." The experience provided insights that would prove invaluable throughout my tenure. Watching the games and engaging with college administrators, coaches, and players' families opened my eyes to new dimensions of college athletics. The passion, dedication, and genuine educational opportunities the system provided for hundreds of thousands of athletes began to balance out my previous views about the organization's motives.

My selection had garnered public interest, as everything in college sports inevitably does. Building on conversations with senior athletics executives, I commented to the media upon my hiring that I was excited to provide the NCAA with seasoned legal counsel and strategic advice to enhance the environments in which student-athletes could thrive academically and athletically. "I believe that practical solutions to difficult legal issues should be applied to protect the best interests of the student-athlete," I said, words that would be tested repeatedly over the following decade. "I look forward to working closely with the many professionals on the NCAA staff and in membership to advance the mission of the Association."

Mark added, "Donald's selection resulted from an extensive national search, and I found his formidable legal talents, coupled with his long-standing commitment to amateur athletics, make him the ideal candidate for serving on my team and leading the NCAA's legal department. Indeed, Donald has made a significant impact throughout his distinguished 20-year legal career, and I am confident that he will be a valuable asset to the NCAA and its members. We are excited he is joining us and look forward to the wealth of experience, leadership, and energy he brings to the job."

Mark's words touched me. And reminded me of that dinner meeting at Dulles airport. I recall that Jim placed an employment contract on the table. For a moment, it appeared he expected me to sign on the spot. I was sold on the job, but, as I told Jim and Mark, any good lawyer would take time to review the document and discuss the opportunity with those close to him. So, before formally accepting the position, I consulted family, friends, coaches, parents, and players, consistently receiving only lukewarm reactions.

I remember a particularly telling conversation with Boo Williams, the "Godfather of youth basketball," at the Hampton, Virginia Sportsplex bearing his name. When I mentioned joining the NCAA, his bewildered expression said everything. My basketball contacts and my own instincts were telling me to walk away from an organization viewed as directly opposed to the athlete's interests.

This skepticism reflected broader community attitudes that would shape almost every major challenge I would face as General Counsel. The grass-roots basketball community, including coaches, parents, AAU administrators, and the players themselves, viewed the NCAA with deep suspicion, seeing it as an obstacle to young athletes' dreams rather than an enabler of educational opportunity. Charles Pittman, a brother with an infectious enthusiasm for coaching young men, whom I coached alongside for years and greatly admired, said it best, "Rem, just go make a difference. These boys need you to do that." I kept a note on my desk that read, "Make A Difference," to remind me of that conversation every day. Indeed, understanding these perspectives proved crucial as I developed legal strategies that had to account for public opinion and legal precedent.

My decade as a grassroots coach also exposed me to the full spectrum of young athletes' backgrounds and circumstances. Some came from wealthy two-parent families with every advantage. In contrast, others lived in communities plagued by drugs and violence, raised by grandparents because their parents were incarcerated, or were recent immigrants, essentially raising themselves. This diversity helped me understand that NCAA rules affected different populations very differently, and that rules designed to preserve competitive balance could have devastating impacts on individual athletes who were simply trying to access educational opportunities.

I witnessed how strict NCAA rules, despite good intentions, could impede young athletes' ambitions, especially those aiming for professional careers in basketball and football. This situation was particularly acute for athletes from disadvantaged backgrounds, for whom professional sports represented not only career opportunities but pathways to improve their families' circumstances. My experience coaching these athletes prompted me to echo the common belief that the NCAA and its member schools prioritize financial interests over athletes' well-being and dreams.

Yet much of the information gleaned through the "listening tour" I did after I accepted the job, but before I started, revealed a different and refreshing perspective on the organization's goals and operations. I quickly learned the reasons behind the rules and better understood the recruiting system and the goals of competitive balance, equity, and fairness. I gained direct insight into why the Association's different components operated as they did. I came to understand that the schools themselves were the rulemakers and first-line enforcers, rather than a "Wizard behind the curtain" in Indianapolis issuing arbitrary edicts. Discussions with NCAA staff members, including Mike Racy, Bernard Franklin, Wally Renfro, Bob Williams, David Berst, Julie Roe Lach, and Kevin Lennon, awakened me to the value of the national office's work. Conversations with Emmert, Executive Committee Chair President Ed Ray of Oregon State University, Committee on Infractions Chair Dennis Thomas who served as MEAC Commissioner, SEC Commissioner Mike Slive, Big Ten Commissioner Jim Delany, Notre Dame Athletics Director Jack Swarbrick, and Dr. Walter "Walt" Harrison, President of the University of Hartford and chair of the committee on academic performance, convinced me that the organization was far more intricate and well-intentioned than I previously believed.

Walt Harrison, in particular, provided me with crucial information about the NCAA's commitment to academic success and how the national office collaborated with member schools to improve graduation rates. His measured, reflective, and persuasive manner helped me understand the delicate balance between athletics and academics in the college environment. I already held firm beliefs about the value of higher education, but conversations with Walt and others exposed me to a sophisticated network of policies and programs designed to ensure that athletics participation enhanced rather than undermined educational opportunity.

I was keeping an open mind despite my prior cynicism: something about the opportunity intrigued me. Perhaps it was the analytical framework I had developed during my confirmation experience or the advice I had received from mentors. I was able to look beyond surface impressions to understand deeper intrinsic dynamics.

I'd mastered this power years prior, after a discussion with acclaimed author James Baldwin. It proved particularly relevant as I considered the NCAA opportunity. In 1986, Baldwin visited LSU at the invitation of the Black Culture Committee, which I chaired. At dinner, he offered advice that has shaped my thinking ever since: to understand any issue honestly, I must not simply accept what I think I know, but endeavor to comprehend what others believe and why. This perspective has benefited me throughout my professional and personal life, and it would prove essential as I grappled with the NCAA's complex mission.

My initial perspective on the organization was shaped by my college experience, grassroots coaching, and engagement with communities that viewed the NCAA with cynicism. However, joining the organization and examining its governance legal challenges revealed true complexity that my external perspective had missed. The system was far more challenging and multifaceted than I had imagined, with competing constituencies, conflicting priorities, and regulatory requirements that created impossible tensions regardless of leadership intentions.

> By understanding what the NCAA sought to accomplish, I gained deeper insight into the higher education ecosystem and the role of athletics within it. I recognized this as a critical system worth defending because of the genuine opportunities it provided for hundreds of thousands of young people. Despite its imperfections and

occasional unfairness, the collegiate athletics system offered pathways to educational advancement that simply didn't exist elsewhere in American society.

As I prepared to assume my new role, studying the daunting array of issues facing the NCAA, I was struck not only by their complexity but also by their public visibility. Former General Counsel Elsa Cole had warned that every NCAA action, from litigating cases, negotiating deals, enforcing rules, suspending players, sanctioning universities, or punishing coaches, all faced intense scrutiny from television, radio, print, and internet outlets. Having managed high-profile cases at the Department of Justice involving incidents at Waco and Ruby Ridge, which we coined "litigation in a parallel universe," I understood exactly what she meant.

I was prepared to defend the system based on my evolving thinking, informed by knowledge and a deeper understanding. Yes, I questioned whether we could preserve everything good about college athletics while simultaneously advancing it toward greater fairness. And, I understood the inherent tension in that challenge would define my entire tenure. But I was fired up and ready to go.

Reflecting on arguments we would make and those advanced by our opponents, I frequently heard lawyers and pundits reason: "This is just a professional system that you're trying to treat like an amateur system. Why don't you pay the players and move on?" My response was that such an approach was too simplistic and would undermine the system's fundamental educational purpose. Now, watching the implementation of the *House* settlement and the emergence of Collegiate Capitalism, I find myself reflecting on what alternative paths might have preserved more of the educational mission while still addressing athletes' legitimate economic interests.

When I joined the NCAA in 2011, I couldn't predict today's developments. Still, I learned that changes were necessary to create fairer environments for athletes, or the weight of criticism would become too heavy for the system to sustain. The analytical framework I had developed during my confirmation experience, weighing all available information, considering stakeholder impacts, and choosing actions most likely to serve the greater good, would guide me.

And I was joining an organization at a crucial and historic moment. The amateur model was showing stress fractures that could lead to complete structural failure. My role would be to defend a system that was already evolving beyond recognition, using legal arguments that required increasing sophistication and adaptation as the landscape evolved.

My ultimate decision to accept the position was motivated by the opportunity to impact more than 15 local players annually through coaching, but to potentially affect more than 450,000 athletes across three divisions. I wanted to be part of solutions that would benefit young people broadly while preserving the unique connection between athletics and education that distinguished American college sports from all other forms of entertainment.

Yet I also understood that I was joining the revolution already in progress. The forces driving college athletics toward Collegiate Capitalism were already beyond any one individual's ability to control or redirect. My challenge would be to influence that transformation in ways that preserved the most significant benefit for athletes, while maintaining whatever connection to the educational mission remained viable.

The journey ahead would test every skill I had developed, challenge every assumption I held, and place me at the center of the most significant shift in the history of American college sports.

The door that had closed on my government service had opened into something far more consequential than I could have imagined.

Chapter 10
Inheriting the Whirlwind
The Legal Battlefield That Made Collegiate Capitalism Inevitable

My analytical framework would face its ultimate test in the legal environment I inherited at the NCAA. What I discovered upon arrival was an organization under legal siege from multiple directions, defending positions that were being tested with increasing frequency and sophistication as market forces undermined arguments for amateurism.

The days from Palmer Pierce's modest 25-page pamphlet to divisional manuals totaling well over 1500 pages by 2011 reflected far more than organizational growth. It revealed the NCAA's Sisyphean pursuit of that elusive "level playing field" while American ingenuity consistently found new ways to gain competitive advantages. This regulatory expansion invited greater scrutiny from governmental entities at every level, creating what I came to think of as the NCAA's own "law of litigative physics." As the NCAA's legislation and responsibility multiplied, so did litigation, positioning the association at the treacherous intersection of athletics, education, money, and federal and state law.

During my first weeks in Indianapolis, as I reviewed the legal files that would define my tenure, I made a startling discovery. The NCAA had faced virtually no judicial scrutiny during its first seven decades. From 1905 through 1970, there were remarkably few reported federal or state court cases involving the organization. This absence wasn't accidental but reflected historical reality. The NCAA functioned primarily as a voluntary rules-making body with minimal enforcement capacity until the 1950s, and the massive commercialization of college sports that drives modern litigation simply didn't exist in that era.

But beginning in the early 1970s, as the NCAA's enforcement powers expanded and college sports commercialized rapidly, litigation exploded with a ferocity that would have shocked the organization's founders. The cases traced a clear evolutionary arc from constitutional challenges focused on due process and equal protection, through the antitrust revolution that shattered the television stronghold, to increasingly sophisticated civil rights claims, and then to compensation challenges that were already pointing toward the old system's inevitable unraveling.

In 1973, two key cases established fundamental principles, while revealing deeper contradictions. In *Buckton v. NCAA*, two Boston University ice hockey players, both Canadian nationals, challenged NCAA bylaws that declared them ineligible to receive room and board compensation while playing for Canadian hockey teams before college. The federal district court found that the NCAA was operating as an extension of the government ("state action") and struck down the foreign-student rule, concluding that it created an unjustifiable classification of non-citizens that denied them equal protection of the laws.

That same year, my future law school alma mater, Howard University, challenged NCAA sanctions after the school's soccer team won the 1970 and 1971 championships with allegedly ineligible foreign players. The Washington, D.C. district court found state action based on the pervasive participation of state and federal institutions in the NCAA, upheld most rules under rational basis review, but struck down the foreign-student rule as alienage discrimination. When the D.C. Circuit affirmed in 1975, Judge Tamm's opinion extensively analyzed the state action doctrine, finding government institutions' involvement in NCAA governance was "pervasive." This was a conclusion that would haunt the organization until the Supreme Court's *Tarkanian* decision over a decade later.

These early cases established that courts would find the NCAA to ostensibly be a government agent when its membership was composed of public universities regulating other public universities, but they also uncovered the organization's vulnerability to equal protection complications when rules created classifications that legitimate educational or competitive purposes couldn't justify. The foreign-student rule fell not because courts generally rejected amateurism, but because the NCAA couldn't adequately explain why Canadian players receiving room and board presented different concerns than American players receiving similar benefits, or why Guinean athletes lose a year of eligibility every year after their nineteenth birthday, and Americans do not. Similar issues have arisen in present-day discussions about international and NBA players who have received benefits and want to play in the NCAA.

The distinctions among different types of NCAA activities became even clearer in the Third Circuit's 1974 decision in *College Athletic Placement Service v. NCAA*, where a company helping young athletes find college scholarships challenged NCAA bylaws that prevented high school students from paying for scholarship placement services. The court held that the NCAA bylaws governing educational standards served *non-commercial* purposes and were not subject to antitrust scrutiny. That distinction would prove crucial in subsequent litigation. It would also create the very framework that plaintiffs would eventually use to attack compensation restrictions as impermissible commercial restraints under the antitrust laws.

Perhaps the most significant constitutional decision of this era came in *Parish v. NCAA*, when, in 1975, the Fifth Circuit established a principle that would shape NCAA litigation for many years to come. The court found that student-athletes have no constitutionally protected property or liberty interest in participating in intercollegiate athletics. Five Centenary College basketball players, led by future nine-time NBA All-Star and Naismith Hall of Famer Robert Parish, challenged the NCAA's 1.6 rule, which required athletics scholarship recipients to have a minimum grade point average and test scores. Still, the court held that, without a protected interest, the NCAA's eligibility rules were subject to minimal constitutional scrutiny.

By establishing that athletics participation wasn't a constitutional right, the courts unconsciously channeled allegations into antitrust and statutory civil rights claims. Unfortunately, these were precisely the areas where the NCAA would prove most vulnerable. Let's also not forget the tragic human cost of the court's ruling. Parish became an "invisible man" in college. Although he averaged 21.6 points and 16.9 rebounds per game during his 4-year college career at the same school, and his team spent 14 weeks in the AP Top 20 poll, the NCAA would not recognize his statistical achievements in its official Record Book. It was not until 2018, during my tenure, that a formal appeal from Centenary College was approved, and Parish's and the school's records would be officially recognized.

The pattern of NCAA legal victories, containing the seeds of future defeats, became paradoxically plain in the eligibility cases from the late 1970s. In *Jones v. NCAA* (1975), a Northeastern University hockey player challenged his ineligibility based on prior compensation received from participation on Canadian and American "amateur" hockey teams. The Massachusetts federal court distinguished his case from *Buckton* and rejected both his equal protection and antitrust challenges. In *Colorado Seminary v. NCAA* in 1976, when the University of Denver challenged sanctions imposed for allegedly ineligible Canadian hockey players, the Colorado federal court found no due process violations. It upheld the sanctions under rational basis review.

These were victories for the NCAA, certainly, and many more would follow. But they established the framework under which courts would analyze future challenges. By distinguishing among categories of rules, accepting some NCAA justifications while rejecting others, and applying varying levels of scrutiny depending on the nature of the challenged regulation, courts created analytical tools that future plaintiffs' counsel would use to attack the amateur model's commercial restrictions.

As I briefly mentioned in prior chapters, the upheaval that would revolutionize everything came on June 27, 1984, when the Supreme Court decided *Board of Regents*. With the advent of television in 1951, a new world opened for the sports community, and the organization assumed control of college football television rights, implementing a plan that limited the number of nationally broadcast games and restricted individual schools' television appearances. This television domination faced little legal challenge for over three decades, partly because the Department of Justice had reviewed and taken "under study" the NCAA's television plans from 1951 to 1953 without declaring them unlawful.

But the growing financial stakes of college football television rights eventually created irresistible pressure for legal action. The landmark case emerged from a conflict between NCAA leadership and major football-playing schools that had formed the College Football Association to negotiate an independent contract with NBC. When the NCAA, under Executive Director Walter Byers, announced that any CFA member honoring the NBC contract would face sanctions extending across all sports, the

Universities of Oklahoma and Georgia filed what became *Board of Regents*.

The District Court in the Western District of Oklahoma found that the NCAA violated the Sherman Act and rejected its stated justifications for the rule: preserving in-person attendance, amateurism, and competitive balance. The Court of Appeals affirmed, holding that the television broadcast restrictions were *per se* illegal.

Justice John Paul Stevens delivered a majority opinion that did not find the rules *per se* illegal. Finding an antitrust violation under the Rule of Reason, he acknowledged the NCAA sought to market "a particular brand of football" differentiated by its "academic tradition," but this did not provide blanket protection from antitrust law. The decision's immediate effect was to democratize college football television rights, leading to the explosion of televised games and massive revenue streams that characterize modern college athletics.

But the long-term significance extended far beyond television contracts. By establishing that the NCAA's commercial activities were subject to federal antitrust law using a Rule of Reason analysis, the Court created an interpretive battleground that would define almost every major legal challenge I would face during my NCAA tenure. The Court's language noting that "most of the regulatory controls of the NCAA are justifiable means of fostering competition" and emphasizing that the organization "plays a critical role in the maintenance of a revered tradition of amateurism," provided the foundation for many of our defenses.

Most crucially, the Court stated that "[i]n order to preserve the character and quality of the 'product,' athletes must not be paid, must be required to attend class, and the like." This language, although later characterized as *dicta*, would be cited consistently in NCAA briefs defending compensation restrictions over the following decades. Yet, it also contained a contradiction that could eventually destroy amateurism. By acknowledging that the NCAA was marketing a commercial "product," the Court implicitly invited questions about why the essential producers of that product should be excluded from sharing in its financial success.

But even still, the *Board of Regents* dissenting opinion contained ominous warnings. Justice White's dissent, joined by Justice Rehnquist, argued that the majority had misapplied antitrust principles to college athletics and that the television plan's restrictions were reasonable and necessary to preserve the unique character of college football.

Justice Byron “Whizzer” White was not only speaking as a Phi Beta Kappa class valedictorian, Rhodes Scholar, and learned jurist, he was writing from the vantage point of a consensus All-American halfback for the University of Colorado Buffaloes, a runner up for the 1937 Heisman Trophy, and a NFL running back who led the league in rushing his rookie year and later attended Yale Law School. Needless to say, he knew what he was talking about. In 1996, several years after his retirement, I had the honor and privilege of interviewing with Justice White for a Supreme Court clerkship (to be shared with Justice Stevens). If only I had known what my future as a lawyer would include, I would have spent part of my interview gathering insight into the *Board of Regents* case.

In his dissent, Justice White warned that the majority's approach would subject virtually all NCAA rules to antitrust scrutiny, potentially destabilizing the entire amateur system. His dissent proved prophetic: "The NCAA's actions here are plainly designed to serve the NCAA's legitimate interest in preserving amateurism and in preventing the exploitation of college athletes by professional teams." Justice White knew that once commercial logic was fully applied to college athletics, the amateur model would become increasingly difficult to defend. Reading Justice White's dissent decades later, I was struck by how accurately he predicted the trajectory of NCAA litigation. Courts would go on to subject more and more NCAA rules to antitrust scrutiny, using the very framework established by the *Board of Regents* majority.

The *Board of Regents* Supreme Court decision may have opened the channels to antitrust challenges, but around that time, the NCAA's legal standing as a legitimate rules-making body also received crucial support from an unexpected source. In December 1988, the Supreme Court decided *NCAA v. Tarkanian*, holding 5-4 that the NCAA was not a "state actor" subject to constitutional due process requirements, even when dealing with public universities, settling a dispute arising in some of the early NCAA cases I discussed. Justice Stevens this time found that the NCAA was sufficiently independent of state control and that UNLV, rather than the NCAA, was the entity actually implementing coach Jerry Tarkanian's suspension.

The narrow 5-4 margin revealed deep divisions on the Court about the NCAA's true nature. Justice White dissented again, this time joined by Justices Brennan, Marshall, and O'Connor. He opined that the NCAA and UNLV had acted jointly in suspending Tarkanian, making the NCAA's conduct attributable to the government. White contended that when a state university agrees to enforce NCAA sanctions against its own employees, the NCAA exercises governmental power that should trigger constitutional protections. His dissent highlighted the uncomfortable suggestion that the NCAA wielded quasi-governmental authority over public institutions while enjoying immunity from constitutional constraints. This peculiarity, which confers power without accountability, would fuel future challenges to NCAA authority through statutory and antitrust channels, in contrast to traditional constitutional claims.

From a narrow legal perspective, *Tarkanian* was a victory that insulated the NCAA from this line of constitutional scrutiny. But I came to recognize its more profound significance. By establishing the NCAA as a private actor, the decision effectively confirmed that the organization operated as a commercial entity subject to commercial law. The shield against state actor constitutional claims became a sword supporting commercial status, which appeared likely to strengthen antitrust challenges.

The post-*Tarkanian* landscape forced creative lawyering by those challenging NCAA authority and provided strong defenses for the organization. In 1990, when University of Southern California soccer player Steve Tanaka challenged the NCAA's year-in-residence transfer requirement as an unreasonable restraint on trade, the Ninth Circuit found his antitrust claim inadequate, ruling that "Tanaka simply has no antitrust cause of action." The court held that eligibility rules designed to preserve amateurism and competitive balance were not the type of commercial restraints subject to scrutiny under the Sherman Act. This distinction between commercial and non-commercial NCAA activities seemed to provide a workable framework. It appeared appropriate that television contracts and other business operations be subject to antitrust review, while eligibility rules are given deference as necessary to preserve the amateur product.

Similar reasoning emerged in *Smith v. NCAA,* a case that was decided by the Supreme Court in 1999 and established important precedents on multiple fronts. Renee Smith, a volleyball player who wanted to continue competing as a postgraduate student, sued under both antitrust law and Title IX. The lower courts distinguished the types of NCAA activities. While "the Sherman Act applies to the NCAA with respect to those actions related to its commercial or business activities," eligibility rules would fall outside this scope. Importantly, the case also addressed whether the NCAA was subject to Title IX as a recipient of federal financial assistance or as a result of receiving dues from federally funded members. The district court ruled no. The Third Circuit said yes.

Future Supreme Court Chief Justice John Roberts, then an attorney with Hogan & Hartson (now Hogan Lovells), represented the NCAA. He argued that the NCAA was not subject to Title IX because it did not directly receive federal funding, and that the nature of its members' funding was too attenuated to trigger Title IX. Not only did Roberts have to contend with Carter G. Phillips arguing the case for Smith, but the United States also weighed in on her side in a brief filed by Solicitor General Seth Waxman, who would later come to represent the NCAA as well. I was a Deputy Assistant Attorney General at the Justice Department at the time. While I had nothing to do with the *Smith* case, I had known Seth and Ed Kneedler (who actually argued the case) to be formidable Supreme Court advocates.

When the Supreme Court ruled unanimously that the NCAA's receipt of membership dues from federally funded institutions didn't subject it to Title IX, the decision appeared to be another victory for the NCAA. But Justice Ginsburg's opinion explicitly left open alternative pathways for Title IX jurisdiction, noting the Court wasn't deciding whether the NCAA directly received federal assistance through other programs or whether entities exercising controlling authority over federally funded programs might be covered irrespective of direct receipt. These unresolved questions would spawn future litigation that would test NCAA authority under federal civil rights laws.

The late 1980s and early 1990s brought a new wave of litigation testing the boundaries established by *Board of Regent*s and *Tarkanian.* In 1990, Vanderbilt football player Bradford Gaines challenged NCAA eligibility rules under the Sherman Act after being declared ineligible for declaring for the NFL draft. The Tennessee court applied the now-familiar commercial/ non-commercial distinction and denied Gaines's request for a preliminary injunction.

In this new framework, commercial activities like television contracts would face full antitrust scrutiny, while eligibility rules would receive deference as necessary to preserve the amateur product. Yet even this apparently favorable decision revealed vulnerabilities. By accepting that some NCAA activities were clearly commercial while others weren't, courts implicitly invited litigation that would test whether specific rules fell into commercial or non-commercial categories.

The restricted earnings coach litigation of the 1990s surfaced how quickly the ground could shift beneath the NCAA's defenses. What began as a well-intentioned effort to address inequities in entry-level coaching positions resulted in one of the most expensive legal expeditions in NCAA history. That is, until *House*. In 1995, the Kansas federal district court in *Law v. NCAA* granted summary judgment for coaches challenging the rule capping their compensation at $16,000 annually, finding the salary cap violated the Sherman Act through explicit price-fixing in the coaching labor market.

I've often wondered why the NCAA chose to create a rule with those exact words, "restricted earnings coach," which seemed almost like an invitation, or dare, for an antitrust lawsuit. I understand the original proposal was brought to the NCAA Convention to eliminate the second assistant coach position. Indiana coach Bobby Knight, however, moved to restrict their compensation as a compromise instead of abolishing the position. Still, the name? Did the lawyers review that?

When the Tenth Circuit affirmed in 1998, and the Supreme Court declined review, the NCAA settled for $54.5 million. The mockery was unambiguous. Here was a measure designed to reduce institutional athletics expenditures that ended up costing those same institutions tens of millions of dollars, with the 1,636 coaches who received payments averaging just $19,912 each after attorneys' fees exceeding $18.2 million.

The case demonstrated how good intentions could create catastrophic legal exposure when implemented without sufficient attention to antitrust implications, but it also established a principle that would haunt future litigation. The NCAA couldn't justify price-fixing in one labor market (coaches) by claiming benefits in another market (consumer demand for college sports). This principle would eventually be applied to restrictions on athlete compensation.

Throughout the end of the decade and into the 2000s, civil rights litigation around eligibility criteria emerged as another front in the legal battle over NCAA authority. The 1998 consent decree with the Justice Department, which addressed whether initial eligibility requirements discriminated against students with learning disabilities under the Americans with Disabilities Act, required the NCAA to certify academic offerings designed for students with disabilities as "core courses." The membership was also required to permit freshmen who didn't meet initial eligibility criteria to earn a fourth year of eligibility if they were academically successful.

In 1999, the Eastern District of Pennsylvania in *Cureton v. NCAA* found that Proposition 16's minimum standardized test score requirement had an unjustified disparate impact on African-American student-athletes, violating Title VI, with 27% of Black student-athletes failing to meet the cut score, compared with 6% of white student-athletes. Although the Third Circuit reversed on narrow jurisdictional grounds, holding the NCAA wasn't a direct recipient of federal funds, the NCAA subsequently dropped the minimum test score requirement, effectively adopting the plaintiffs' position even after winning in court.

The new millennium brought Jeremy Bloom's high-profile challenge to the boundaries between Olympic opportunity and college eligibility, demonstrating how the NCAA's amateur restrictions could produce absurd results in an increasingly professionalized sports world. Bloom, a world-class moguls skier and University of Colorado football player, sought to maintain college eligibility while accepting endorsement income to fund his Olympic training. The NCAA denied his request, forcing Bloom to choose between his Olympic career and college football.

Though Bloom lost his 2003 case in Colorado federal court, the litigation highlighted the arbitrary nature of amateurism rules. Bloom could accept funding from his sport's governing body and the U.S. Olympic Committee, but not from commercial sponsors, even though the money served identical purposes. The case generated enormous public sympathy for an athlete caught between Olympic dreams and college opportunities, eroding public support for NCAA restrictions that seemed designed more to punish success than preserve educational values. Bloom's experience foreshadowed future challenges to name, image, and likeness restrictions, demonstrating that rules preventing athletes from monetizing their talents would become increasingly difficult to defend as professional opportunities expanded.

Throughout this period, I was peripherally aware, from various professional legal roles, that the NCAA faced mounting questions that revealed the fundamental instability of the amateur model. A pattern of NCAA victories in court followed by policy changes that gave plaintiffs something similar to what they sought was repeated often. I found it a familiar practice with some of my other clients and one that we similarly would deploy during my time with the Association; typically, because the membership was considering the changes long before the lawsuit was filed.

For example, in *Worldwide Basketball and Sport Tours Inc. v. NCAA* (2004), the Sixth Circuit reversed a district court ruling against the NCAA's "two-in-four" rule limiting basketball tournament participation, holding that the plaintiff failed to define the relevant market. Despite winning, the NCAA changed the rule to allow annual tournament participation. These strategic retreats after legal victories confirmed an organizational understanding that court decisions weren't the only battlefield. Fairness, public opinion, and institutional pressure mattered as much as judicial precedent.

The *White v. NCAA* settlement, approved in 2008, showed that challenges to amateurism rules regarding athlete compensation were becoming more sophisticated and harder to defeat. Former Stanford football player Jason White and other athletes filed a class action challenging the NCAA's cap on athletics scholarships as illegal price-fixing. The cap limited scholarships to tuition, mandatory fees, room, board, and required books. This amounted to less than the full cost of attendance. It appears that rather than risk a trial after Central District of California Judge R. Gary Klausner certified the class, the NCAA settled, reorganizing funds into the more flexible Student-Athlete Opportunity Fund with $218 million available through 2012-13, permitting schools to purchase health insurance for athletes, and creating a $10 million fund for former athletes.

State courts also posed problems for the NCAA during this period. The California Supreme Court's 1994 decision in *Hill v. NCAA* rejected a dispute over the NCAA's drug testing program under the California Constitution's privacy protections, finding that the organization's interests in fair competition and athletes' health justified the testing. This was a victory, but it came after years of litigation and required the NCAA to defend its testing protocols in extensive detail.

Nevada courts provided the longest-running saga, with Jerry Tarkanian's battles spanning from 1977 through the late 1990s and involving multiple state court decisions. Even after the U.S. Supreme Court's 1988 ruling that the NCAA wasn't a state actor, Nevada courts continued to adjudicate attorneys' fees, costs, venue changes, and related matters. In 1994, the Nevada Supreme Court required UNLV to pay Tarkanian's attorneys' fees of $150,725.58 plus interest despite the NCAA's Supreme Court victory, demonstrating that winning the legal war didn't necessarily mean avoiding all financial consequences.

The growing regulatory complexity also attracted Congressional scrutiny, especially when influential constituents faced sanctions. The 1978-79 House subcommittee hearings exemplified this dynamic, with Tarkanian's case serving as a catalyst for dramatic testimony from former NCAA investigator J. Brent Clark turned Congressional Hill staffer, who alleged vendettas, coercion, and "flesh-peddling" by fellow investigators. Although Clark's testimony was later characterized as "deficient," "derelict," and "misleading," the hearings established a pattern of Congressional intervention that would intensify over subsequent decades.

State legislatures joined the assault on NCAA authority following the Supreme Court's *Tarkanian* ruling. By spring 1992, fourteen states had proposed legislation requiring the NCAA to adhere to state-specific procedural requirements in enforcement cases. Nevada led this charge after the NCAA announced a postseason ban on UNLV basketball in 1990, passing a bill requiring the Association to follow Nevada's civil rules of evidence in enforcement proceedings involving Nevada institutions.

The NCAA successfully challenged Nevada's law in federal court, with the judge ruling that the statute imposed a "direct burden on interstate commerce" and violated the First Amendment's associational rights. This decision effectively invalidated similar legislation in other states, affirming that no national regulatory body could function when required to observe different procedural requirements across multiple jurisdictions.

Facing mounting pressure from courts, legislatures, and public opinion, the NCAA undertook considerable reforms under Dick Schultz's leadership. The 1991 Special Committee to Review the Enforcement and Infractions Process, chaired by former U.S. Solicitor General Rex Lee and including former Supreme Court Chief Justice Warren Burger and former Attorney General Benjamin Civiletti, produced eleven recommendations that strengthened procedural safeguards and added distinguished public members to the Committee on Infractions.

The Association also established a permanent Washington presence in 1995 under Cedric Dempsey's leadership, initially led by Doris Dixon and later by Abe Frank, whom I had known from his time as a vice president at Citigroup. Abe became a critical voice navigating an extremely complicated congressional atmosphere, building relationships with other higher education organizations while protecting NCAA interests from adverse regulatory changes.

When I arrived in March 2011, I began reviewing these opinions, legislative records, new accounts, and the like, from my new office in Indianapolis, weighing all available information and considering stakeholder impacts that revealed uncomfortable truths about the legal position I was hired to defend.

The same Supreme Court decision in *Board of Regents* that provided our most vigorous defense of amateurism also established the antitrust framework that would eventually make it difficult to preserve amateurism. The same state legislative challenges that we successfully defeated revealed the limits of federal preemption when public opinion demanded athlete rights. It seemed that every successful defense had created new vulnerabilities. Almost every precedent protecting NCAA authority included language that could be weaponized against that authority under different circumstances.

What struck me most profoundly during those early months was recognizing that I hadn't inherited a stable legal framework requiring maintenance and occasional repairs. I had inherited a legal landscape of extraordinary complexity in which arguments that provided strong defenses in one context could create exposure in another. Many arguments supporting the amateur framework relied on distinctions that required increasingly enlightened justification as college sports' commercial profile expanded.

And waiting in the wings, filed approximately two years before my arrival, was *O'Bannon v. NCAA*, Ed O'Bannon's challenge to NCAA rules prohibiting compensation for use of athletes' names, images, and likenesses in video games and broadcasts.

The legal landscape was not a storm to weather but the permanent climate in which college sports would operate going forward. The whirlwind would only intensify in the years ahead, but studying this history taught me a crucial lesson: we weren't fighting against the future. We were fighting against the logical consequences of our own past decisions.

> Do not get me wrong. I did not have crystal clarity on day 1, or even day 3652. But my growing awareness of these dynamics shaped every strategic decision that followed and proved essential as we faced obstacles that made the previous four decades of litigation seem like mere practice sessions for the main event already underway. My challenge would be to hold the line or influence how fast and furious the spin-out would be.

My responsibility, as I saw it, was to ensure we properly served the young people whose dreams had brought me to college athletics in the first place.

Chapter 11
The Video Game That Changed Everything
How My Sons' Christmas Present Produced a Legal Uprising

Christmas morning 2002, my sons came rushing downstairs with the unbridled excitement that only eight-year-olds and five-year-olds can muster. They attacked the presents under the tree with systematic efficiency, and one of the first packages my younger son unwrapped revealed EA Sports' NCAA March Madness 2003 with Kansas' Drew Gooden on the cover. My older son grabbed the game immediately, and they both sprinted to the PlayStation 2 we'd bought them a couple of years before.

For hours, they played, ignoring other gifts still wrapped beneath the tree, reliving the Final Four featuring Kansas, Oklahoma, Indiana, and the champion Maryland Terrapins. They mixed and matched players for custom games, creating matchups that had never occurred in real life, controlling avatars that looked, moved, and played remarkably like the actual college athletes whose jerseys they wore. This scene was replicated in households across America that Christmas with families enjoying a video game that seemed harmless, entertaining, and perfectly legal.

I gave no thought to the cover, the avatars' characteristics, or name, image, and likeness law. My sons were simply having fun with a game I had no reason to expect I would have a hand in ending eight years later. The analytical framework I developed during my confirmation ordeal couldn't have predicted that this Christmas morning would connect to the legal revolution I would help defend against. A revolution that would transform college athletics and vindicate criticisms of the amateur model I heard during my grassroots coaching years.

Among the cases I was charged with defending upon arriving at the NCAA in March 2011 was one filed eighteen months earlier but that hadn't yet revealed its full destructive potential. *O'Bannon v. NCAA* would become the most significant legal challenge to amateurism in the organization's history. It would demonstrate that the legal environment established by *Board of Regents, Tarkanian*, and *Law* had created the very framework that would eventually destroy the system those cases seemed to protect.

The case's genesis traced back to 2008, when Ed O'Bannon, the 1995 NCAA Tournament Most Outstanding Player who led UCLA to the national championship, discovered what he believed was his likeness in Electronic Arts' NCAA Basketball video game. While visiting a friend's house, he saw an avatar representing the classic 1995 UCLA team, complete with his jersey number, similar physical characteristics, and familiar playing style. The game didn't use his name, but the representation seemed unmistakably him.

O'Bannon later reflected: "I thought it was strange EA or the NCAA hadn't contacted my teammates or me." This discovery prompted inquiry revealing that game maker Electronic Arts, Collegiate Licensing Company (CLC), and the NCAA membership had been profiting from video games featuring realistic depictions of college athletes for years. At the same time, NCAA amateurism rules prohibited that very practice and prevented those athletes from receiving compensation from it. The nature of this apparent misappropriation, combined with revenues generated but not shared, led O'Bannon to conclude that legal action was necessary.

Yet what appeared to be a straightforward right-of-publicity case would turn out to be far more consequential. The attorney who took O'Bannon's case, Michael Hausfeld, had built a career on high-stakes class action litigation challenging institutional arrangements that allegedly harmed consumers or workers. Hausfeld's firm had successfully litigated against Swiss banks over Holocaust-era accounts, challenged the vitamin industry's price-fixing conspiracy, and pursued claims against major corporations across multiple industries. I suspected that we were litigating against a firm unlikely to settle for modest victories on video game licensing principles. We were in a battle with a lawyer who specialized in dismantling systems.

When O'Bannon filed suit on July 21, 2009, in the U.S. District Court for the Northern District of California against the NCAA, Electronic Arts, and the Collegiate Licensing Company, the complaint alleged violations of the Sherman Antitrust Act and unjust enrichment. The case was soon consolidated with similar lawsuits filed earlier by Steve Berman on behalf of former Arizona State & Nebraska quarterback Sam Keller, and by Timothy McIlwain and Eugene Egdorf representing Rutgers football player Ryan Hart, claiming violations of California's right of publicity law. These lawsuits by Keller and Hart challenged EA's alleged use of likenesses in its NCAA Football video games. The consolidated litigation became a class action on behalf of current and former Division I football and men's basketball players, with notable additions including NBA legends Oscar Robertson and Bill Russell.

The assignment of the case to Judge Claudia Wilken was, in retrospect, either remarkably fortunate for the plaintiffs or remarkably ill-fated for the NCAA, depending on one's perspective. Wilken was educated at Stanford in the early 1970s, when the university wasn't known for intercollegiate athletics, and earned her law degree from UC Berkeley's Boalt Hall in 1975. Her educational foundation at two prestigious institutions provided a deep understanding of higher education's culture and academic environment, but without the emotional attachment to big-time college sports that might have colored her judgment.

More significantly, Wilken had been appointed as a magistrate judge in 1983, right as the *Board of Regents* case was proceeding through the courts, and elevated to the district court by President Clinton in 1993. By 2009, she had developed a reputation as a careful, scholarly jurist with particular experience in institutional litigation and class actions. She wasn't known as an antitrust specialist, sports law expert, or higher education jurist, but her analytical approach and institutional litigation experience would prove ideally suited for dissecting the NCAA's economic arrangements.

One of my first priorities upon arriving at the NCAA was to resolve the case before it metastasized into something more dangerous. Mark Emmert and I both appreciated the potential impact, and we wanted to eliminate the threat before trial. I attended mediation with our trusted, longtime antitrust counsel, Greg Curtner of Schiff Hardin, and sat down with plaintiffs' attorneys Michael Hausfeld and Steve Berman, as well as co-defendants' counsel Bruce Siegel of CLC and Joel Linzner of EA Sports.

Over several sessions, Magistrate Judge Nathanael Cousins worked zealously to broker an agreement. He pressed both sides hard and searched, with real persistence, for any path that might lead us to a resolution. But despite sustained effort on all sides, the sessions produced no agreement, and the case would now proceed toward trial. We left without a deal.

Looking back now, I realize that whether or not we settled that day, the future of college sports had been and would continue to be defined in courtrooms. Hausfeld and Berman weren't seeking modest compensation for video game appearances. They were engineering the dismantlement of amateurism itself, using video games as vehicles to challenge the entire system's economic foundations.

After the mediation failed, we faced critical strategic decisions about trial counsel. For years, we'd been successfully represented in antitrust cases by Curtner's mid-sized firm, Schiff Hardin. Conference counsel, however, especially the lawyers representing SEC schools and Big Ten Schools, strongly encouraged us to expand our defense team to include "big law" trial lawyers with extensive class action and antitrust experience. We did not have the in-house legal resources to litigate major cases, but, having been one myself, I knew quite a few "big law" trial lawyers. The membership was willing to incur additional costs if it meant mounting the strongest possible defense.

After a nationwide search assessing skills and strategic fit, we selected Munger Tolles & Olson, with trial lawyer Glenn Pomerantz leading the team. He impressed everyone, particularly SEC counsel Robert Fuller, who carried enormous influence as a proxy for his conference commissioner. I also engaged internationally acclaimed trial lawyer Beth Wilkinson and her team at Paul Weiss to assist with trial preparation. I had known Beth since our Army lawyer days together, and she later started her own firm, Wilkinson Stekloff, with an amazing team of attorneys who continue to represent the NCAA. Knowing the case wouldn't end at the district court level, I attached former U.S. Solicitor General Seth Waxman to the trial team along with his partner Randy Moss, who would later become a district court judge himself. If we were going to war, we needed lawyers who could prepare and present the case with formidable skill, and take it all the way to the Supreme Court.

As the case progressed through discovery and pretrial motions, Judge Wilken allowed it to evolve far beyond its origins as a video game antitrust and right-of-publicity dispute. The plaintiffs' lawyers argued that FBS football and Division I basketball schools were the only suppliers in a "college education market" and used their collective power through the NCAA to fix prices. They contended that this price-fixing agreement constituted an unreasonable restraint of trade under the Sherman Act because schools could offer recruits only athletics scholarships and education in exchange for athletic services and the use of their name, image, and likeness.

This argument went well beyond the case initially filed and signaled that the strategy wasn't simply adjudicating a video game lawsuit. The strategy appeared to be dismantling amateurism's entire structure. The closest connection to the original video game issue came when Hausfeld's team presented evidence attempting to show genuine market demand for group licensing of college athletes. EA executive Joel Linzner, with whom I'd chatted at lunch during mediation to understand his company's position, was prepared to testify that EA wanted to pay college athletes for use of their NILs in video games and was willing to pay substantial sums for those rights, demonstrating apparent market demand for athlete NIL. Not helpful.

Given the morphed case we were handed, we mounted a vigorous defense based on four primary justifications for our restrictions: that amateurism preserved the unique consumer demand for college sports; that compensation restrictions maintained competitive balance among institutions; that the restrictions ensured athletics remained integrated with academics; and that our rules actually increased the total output of college sports by growing the number of schools, athletes, and games and creating a distinctive product.

As I explained to the press: "We frequently hear from student-athletes, across all sports, that they participate to enhance their overall college experience and for the love of their sport, not to be paid." We were protecting the essential character of college sports against commercialization, I thought.

A crucial aspect of the case involved defining the relevant market for antitrust analysis. The plaintiffs argued that the market consisted of services provided by elite college football and basketball players. At the same time, we contended that the broader market for all college educational services was the appropriate frame of reference. This market definition question proved complex, with extensive testimony from economic experts on both sides. The plaintiffs' expert, economist Roger Noll, submitted reports arguing the NCAA exercised monopsony power as the sole buyer of elite college athlete services. Our expert, Daniel Rubinfeld, argued that amateurism was a consumer demand driver, that competitive balance is harmed by paying athletes, and that the broader educational market provided sufficient competition to prevent anticompetitive effects.

The battle of the experts proceeded through a winding three-week bench trial before Judge Wilken in Oakland, California, beginning in June 2014. We presented testimony from Nobel laureate economist James Heckman, who attacked Roger Noll's arguments on NIL valuation and defended amateurism by showing that college athletes receive substantial, non-monetary "human capital" benefits, including education and training, that far outweigh the value of their publicity rights. In addition to the economic experts, the trial featured extensive testimony from current and former athletes and NCAA officials. O'Bannon himself testified, though his testimony included inconsistencies with earlier depositions that our attorney Pomerantz highlighted during cross-examination.

Specifically, Pomerantz pointed out that O'Bannon had stated in 2011 that he didn't think college athletes should be paid, contradicting his 2014 trial testimony. O'Bannon acknowledged the inconsistency, which clearly was an awkward moment, by remarking that he had expected it, which elicited laughter in the courtroom. The truth was that the case had mutated from O'Bannon's stated original aim: compensation for NIL misappropriation in video games. The case had become about what I believed the plaintiff's lawyers really intended from the start: establishing pay-for-play. Of course, we maintained that we had strong arguments against that broader claim, and we were prepared to defend the system's mission at every level.

On August 8, 2014, Judge Wilken issued her landmark 99-page decision finding that NCAA amateurism rules prohibiting compensation violated federal antitrust law. The opinion stated that the court was applying Rule of Reason analysis required for antitrust cases. However, it appeared to me that she was actually deploying a least restrictive alternative test that placed an enormous burden on the NCAA to justify every aspect of its restrictions.

Judge Wilken found that the NCAA possessed significant market power in the relevant markets (the college education market and the group licensing market) and that its rules constituted an unreasonable restraint of trade. Notably, she rejected our argument that amateurism rules deserved special deference, noting that "the NCAA is not above the antitrust laws, and courts cannot and must not shy away from requiring the NCAA to play by the Sherman Act's rules." I found that phrasing interesting since we'd never argued we were above antitrust laws. Instead, we'd argued that *Board of Regents* had established appropriate legal deference to rules necessary to preserve the amateur product.

Wilken identified specific less restrictive alternatives that she believed could achieve the NCAA's legitimate objectives. She offered that schools could provide scholarships covering the full cost of attendance, including expenses beyond tuition, room, and board, and hold licensing revenue in trust for athletes to receive after leaving college, with payments capped at $5,000 per year per athlete.

The decision represented only a partial victory for plaintiffs, as Judge Wilken rejected their broader request for unlimited athlete compensation. She found that maintaining some limits on athlete pay was necessary to preserve consumer demand for college sports as distinct from professional athletics. Wilken may have believed she was carefully limiting her remedy to avoid completely dismantling amateurism, and for the moment, she was correct. But we knew this ruling threatened to eventually upend the entire system.

Having embedded appellate counsel with the trial team from the beginning, we immediately explored our appellate options. On the one hand, the court's decision set limits on compensation. On the other hand, applying tests we believed were legally wrong, Wilken found the NCAA violated the antitrust laws. The trial team, appellate team, in-house team, and some conference lawyers spent hours in meeting rooms and on conference calls studying the ruling and the options it left open to us. I brought my final recommendation to President Emmert, the senior leadership team, and the Executive Committee.

On August 21, 2014, I announced we were appealing "because we do not believe the NCAA has violated the antitrust laws" and that "changes to the rules that govern college athletics would be better achieved outside the courtroom." "The Association and its members are best positioned to evolve its rules and processes to better serve student-athletes," I concluded. Notwithstanding the legal defeats and the history I had studied, I still had hope that the reform efforts underway would demonstrate our ability to self-govern.

On appeal to the Ninth Circuit, we argued that the district court had misapplied antitrust law and failed to give proper deference to the NCAA's amateurism model. We emphasized that the Supreme Court's 1984 *Board of Regents* decision had endorsed the organization's compensation restrictions as procompetitive, and that subsequent cases, such as *Tanaka, Smith, and Gaines,* had established appropriate deference to eligibility rules. We also took aim at the analysis Judge Wilken applied, believing it went beyond traditional Rule of Reason analysis and amounted to a least restrictive alternative test that resulted in an unreasonable remedy.

On September 30, 2015, a three-judge panel issued a decision that both affirmed and reversed portions of Judge Wilken's ruling. The appeals court upheld the finding that NCAA compensation restrictions violated antitrust law and affirmed the injunction allowing schools to provide scholarships up to the full cost of attendance.

However, the Ninth Circuit reversed the portion of the ruling that permitted schools to pay athletes up to $5,000 annually in deferred compensation. The court concluded that such payments, even if modest, would reorient the nature of college sports by crossing the line from amateurism to professionalism. As the panel explained, paying student-athletes "even a modest sum for the use of their NILs" could not be considered "virtually as effective" for maintaining amateurism as having them remain unpaid. The court characterized the distinction between education-related expenses and cash payments as a "quantum leap" that would likely lead to incremental increases and to the "eventual evisceration of the rule of amateurism altogether."

Was that observation prescient or simply common sense? Reading it now, after witnessing the *House* settlement and emergence of Collegiate Capitalism, the answer seems obvious.

Chief Judge Sidney Thomas filed a partial dissent, writing that the majority had erred in reversing the deferred compensation remedy. Judge Thomas found that the district court's decision was supported by "ample expert testimony" and that modest deferred payments wouldn't significantly harm the NCAA's amateurism objectives. His dissent, not the majority opinion, is what proved prophetic. Judge Thomas's reasoning would later be vindicated by the Supreme Court's unanimous decision in *Alston*, which adopted a far more skeptical view of the NCAA's amateurism justifications.

Both sides petitioned the Supreme Court for review. We challenged the entire antitrust ruling, while the *O'Bannon* plaintiffs requested reinstatement of the deferred compensation remedy. The competing petitions presented the Supreme Court with an opportunity to provide definitive guidance on the application of antitrust law to college sports.

I had long advocated to leadership and membership that a Supreme Court ruling could provide finality and clarity, whether we won or lost. In this case, I believed we had the perfect opportunity to have the Court set the landscape for the future. But on October 3, 2016, the Supreme Court denied both requests for review, allowing the Ninth Circuit's decision to stand as final.

Michael Hausfeld, with whom I had dueling courthouse steps press conferences during trial, stated: "While we would have liked the Supreme Court's review, we remain pleased with our trial victory and the 9th Circuit's decision upholding the finding that the NCAA violated the antitrust laws and affirming a permanent injunction to remedy that violation..."

I expressed disappointment while emphasizing the need to preserve amateurism: "While we are disappointed with this decision not to review this case, we remain pleased that the 9th Circuit agreed with us that amateurism is an essential component of college sports and that NCAA members should not be forced by the courts to provide benefits untethered to education...." The trial and appeal were over, and the Supreme Court declined to get involved.

But much was going on behind the scenes between the first mediation before Magistrate Cousins in 2011 and October 2016 that affected the circumstances as much as the legal opinions.

While the *O'Bannon* case proceeded against the NCAA, Electronic Arts and the Collegiate Licensing Company ("CLC") pursued separate negotiations with the plaintiffs to resolve their roles in the consolidated case. The agreement in principle, reached in September 2013, would add another layer of complexity to the litigation. In the end, in May 2014, before trial, EA and CLC finalized the $40 million settlement covering current and former athletes who appeared in EA Sports' NCAA Basketball and NCAA Football video games since 2003. The settlement offered payments to as many as 100,000 athletes, though individual amounts varied widely based on participation rates and years of appearance.

Individual payouts ranged from as little as $48 per year on a roster to $951 for each year an athlete's image was used in a video game. The named plaintiffs, O'Bannon, Keller, Hart, and others, received between $2,500 and $15,000. A little over 29,000 athletes filed claims, receiving an average payout of approximately $1,200. To facilitate settlement and avoid harming the athletes, the NCAA made clear that receiving payments would not affect athletes' eligibility.

Legal fees consumed approximately one-third of the settlement funds, including $13.2 million plus up to $2.5 million in additional costs. The plaintiffs' lawyers argued this was "particularly reasonable in light of the advanced stage of this case," noting that their collective legal services exceeded $30 million in value plus $4 million in expenses. The fee arrangement demonstrated the economic reality that, whatever its broader social purposes, class action litigation also serves as a profitable business for the attorneys who pursue it.

The EA/CLC settlement marked Electronic Arts' exit from the production of college sports video games. Mark Lewis, the NCAA's executive vice president for championships and lead business executive, made clear we would no longer tolerate EA's half-hearted compliance with NCAA rules. A straight shooter, Mark defended the value of amateurism at trial. I think he, like others, saw EA's claim that the characters in the video games were mere avatars, not meant to represent actual players, as specious. What EA did when producing the video games violated NCAA rules and its agreement with the NCAA, thereby creating a legal quagmire for us.

Mark's predecessor, Greg Shaheen, had inked the original EA deal during the Brand era, when the NCAA viewed the video game market as an important way to stay relevant to young people. But the NCAA wasn't making significant revenue from video games, and the litigation costs weren't worth the headache. With the game shut down and EA and CLC having previously settled, we resolved the *Keller* case on the first day of the *O'Bannon* trial in June 2014 for $20 million. NCAA Basketball 10 (2009) became the final game in that series, while NCAA Football 14 (2013) was the last college football game published before EA and the NCAA terminated their licensing agreement. The company concluded that the legal risks and licensing complications made the business untenable under existing NCAA rules, and the NCAA refused to allow EA to continue its practices, which it believed violated those rules and contracts.

Most college football and basketball players didn't like that result. Put simply, they wanted to continue playing video games featuring avatars of themselves and their teams. But the NCAA and EA had no choice, and ironically, the players who brought the suit were the ones who had the greatest hand in ending the games they enjoyed.

It's worth pausing here to reflect on how the changes I am discussing in this book reached back to the future to undo this video game cancellation decision. After an eleven-year hiatus, EA Sports College Football 25 was released in July 2024, featuring Quinn Ewers, Travis Hunter, and Donovan Edwards on the cover and including all 134 FBS teams. Each player who allowed his name to be used in the game received $600 and a copy in exchange for his NIL rights. College Football 26 was released in July 2025, featuring wide receivers Ryan Williams and Jeremiah Smith on the cover and including Delaware and Missouri State, recent FBS additions. EA, however, has decided not to produce a college basketball game, seemingly leaving its future in the hands of its competitor, 2K Games.

The *O'Bannon* case had immediate practical effects beyond the video games. In 2015, the membership passed legislation allowing schools to provide scholarships covering the full cost of attendance, including federally regulated expenses for travel, clothing, and food. This rule change explicitly implemented Judge Wilken's remedy and represented the first expansion of permissible athlete compensation in decades.

The cost-of-attendance scholarships afforded athletes with additional stipends typically ranging from $2,000 to $6,000 annually, depending on the institution and geographic location. While modest compared to revenues generated by major college sports programs, these payments represented a radical departure from traditional NCAA policy.

Predictably, many schools began recalculating their cost-of-attendance figures once payments to athletes were distributed. This activity was widespread, even though recalculation would impose higher costs to the schools for all students, not just athletes. Why would they do such a thing? It's simple. As we have witnessed throughout the history of college sports, universities' interests in athletics are sometimes paramount to anything else on campus.

The personal dimension of the case hit me particularly hard through my relationship with Oscar Robertson. I first met "the Big O" at a reception hosted by Judge Nathaniel R. Jones at his Cincinnati home in summer 1995. The Judge, Robertson, and I are all members of Kappa Alpha Psi fraternity, and I believe developed a genuine friendship over the years.

Before he joined the case with O'Bannon, we had a conversation I'll never forget. He called me D Rem and said it wasn't about me, it was about what was fair: it wasn't fair NCAA rules barred these young players from getting paid while everybody else was. His words captured the fundamental moral challenge we faced. How could we defend a system in which everyone profited except the athletes whose performances helped generate the value?

I tried to explain our position about preserving the educational model and maintaining competitive balance, but Oscar's simple question haunted me: when had fairness become complicated? The analytical framework I'd developed for making difficult decisions, which involved weighing all available information, considering stakeholder impacts, and choosing actions most likely to serve the greater good, struggled with that question.

Was defending the amateur model really serving the greater good, or did we need to find ways to ensure athletes shared more meaningfully in the value their participation helped create?

All in all, the *O'Bannon* case established crucial legal foundations that proved essential to subsequent developments. The case's emphasis on athletes' right of publicity and the economic value of their NIL rights provided the conceptual framework for later NIL policy reforms. When state legislatures began passing NIL legislation in the late 2010s, they frequently cited *O'Bannon* as demonstrating the injustice of denying college athletes compensation for their publicity rights.

O'Bannon also provided a precedential foundation for the Supreme Court's unanimous 2021 decision in *Alston,* which I will discuss in Chapter 25. That ruling further restricted the NCAA's ability to limit education-related benefits provided to athletes. Justice Neil Gorsuch's opinion in *Alston* explicitly built upon the antitrust analysis established in *Board of Regents* relied upon by the Ninth Circuit in *O'Bannon*, noting that the NCAA's restrictions must be justified by procompetitive effects rather than simply assumed to be reasonable.

When the NCAA finally allowed NIL access in July 2021, permitting athletes to profit from endorsements and other commercial opportunities, the policy change represented the ultimate fulfillment of what I believe the *O'Bannon* lawyers had envisioned. The interim NIL policy implicitly acknowledged that athletes possessed publicity rights that the antitrust laws would not allow NCAA amateurism rules to suppress indefinitely.

The modern NIL landscape, where college athletes routinely earn substantial sums from endorsement deals and social media partnerships, would have been inconceivable without the legal foundation established by *O'Bannon*. The emphasis on fundamental fairness and human dignity in controlling one's image had become the dominant framework for thinking about athlete rights.

Looking back at that Christmas morning in 2002, watching my sons play NCAA March Madness with pure joy and excitement, I couldn't have imagined that the game in their hands represented more than entertainment. Courts found it reflected violations of individual rights of publicity and antitrust laws. The avatars they controlled weren't just digital creations. They, in fact, were representations of real young men whose images were being used to generate profits that they would never share.

Michael Hausfeld's and Steve Berman's litigation strategy, combining sophisticated antitrust analysis with compelling narratives of fundamental fairness, provided a roadmap for challenging institutional arrangements that suppressed individual rights. My defensive efforts, while unsuccessful in preserving the NCAA's preferred status quo, demonstrated the organization's awareness that its legal frameworks would need to evolve alongside the industry.

Today's college sports landscape, where athletes routinely profit from their NIL rights, transfer freely between institutions, receive substantial education-related benefits, and share in revenue through the *House* settlement, was inconceivable when I arrived at the NCAA in 2011 to witness Butler's magical Final Four run. The *O'Bannon* case stands as a testament to the power of strategic litigation to challenge institutional arrangements and establish new frameworks for individual rights and dignity, and to the reality that arguments around simple fairness are ultimately difficult to combat. Unfortunately, the consequence of this court decision and its progeny has been as we foreshadowed: chaos. I will discuss in later Chapters how we navigate these new turbulent waters.

For now, I close the Chapter with this: The video game that brought my sons joy that Christmas morning clearly helped bring down a system that had endured for over a century. Sometimes the revolution begins not with grand gestures but with small discoveries. Like, a former athlete seeing his likeness in a video game and asking a simple question: "Why wasn't I asked? Why wasn't I paid?" Those questions, once asked, could never be satisfactorily answered within the framework of amateurism we were defending.

Chapter 12
Whipping Votes Should Not Be This Hard
When Reform Meets Reality

"Whipping votes should not be this hard," I said to President Emmert, frustration evident in my voice.

The words carried more weight than I realized at the time. I had been on the job for a mere five months, still learning the Byzantine political landscape of NCAA governance while simultaneously preparing our defense in *O'Bannon* and managing a dozen other crises that seemed to erupt weekly, sometimes daily. Someone had suggested when I first arrived that because we were part of American higher education, things would be "slower in the summertime" when administrators, faculty, staff, and athletes dispersed from campus. I'd envisioned family visits, maybe international vacations with my sons.

That proved to be wishful thinking at best. The summer of 2011 became a crucible that tested every skill I'd developed through two decades of legal and political work. I was pulling on experiences from the Justice Department, my confirmation battle, years of practice at Latham & Watkins, and even my grassroots basketball coaching. I would need to use persuasion, strategy, and sheer persistence to get stakeholders to vote for modest immediate change in hopes of preserving a future that was already slipping away.

The parallels were not lost on me. I'd spent years in Washington, D.C., watching the machinery of American government churn, observing legislative battles where billions of dollars and basic rights hung in the balance. In Congress, whipping votes on controversial legislation was expected to be difficult. That's why entire offices existed solely to count votes and pressure wavering members. Yet here I was, struggling to convince college administrators to approve a $2,000 annual stipend for athletes: a sum so modest it barely covered laundry, transportation home for holidays, and other basic expenses that non-athlete students could easily afford through part-time jobs that did not interfere with training schedules.

The comparison to Washington became even starker during those phone calls. On Capitol Hill, at least the arguments against legislation usually involve genuine policy disagreements or constituent concerns. Here, I encountered resistance that appeared divorced from any coherent principle beyond protecting institutional interests and maintaining competitive advantages. One athletics director told me flatly that his school couldn't afford the stipend, then, in the same conversation, mentioned plans for a $15 million renovation of the football facility. Another president expressed concern about creating a "slippery slope" toward paying athletes, apparently oblivious to the fact that we were already defending against lawsuits demanding exactly that.

If we couldn't secure university administrators' support for something this reasonable and I believe legally defensible, how could we maintain the amateur model in the face of the sophisticated challenges already mounting in federal courts?

The crisis that precipitated my comment had been building throughout that summer, with a parade of scandals dominating sports headlines and raising serious questions about the character of college athletics. Ohio State football coach Jim Tressel resigned in May amid revelations that players had traded memorabilia for tattoos and cash, and that Tressel had known about the violations for months without reporting them. North Carolina's football program was embroiled in an academic fraud scandal involving tutors writing papers for players. Auburn faced allegations about payments to quarterback Cam Newton's father during his recruitment. USC was serving sanctions for violations involving Reggie Bush and basketball player O.J. Mayo.

The scandals kept coming with numbing regularity. Scandals at Miami, Oregon, and Tennessee, each new revelation undermining public confidence in college sports and our ability to govern effectively. Against this backdrop of institutional failure, President Emmert made a bold decision as he walked through the doors of the NCAA. He would convene the most significant gathering of higher education leaders in decades to confront the existential environment facing Division I athletics.

The August 9-10, 2011, Presidential Retreat in Indianapolis represented something the NCAA had never before attempted. It was, in many ways, a direct acknowledgment by the membership's highest-ranking officials that the current system was unsustainable and required dramatic intervention. "I don't want to be melodramatic, but this meeting is very important," Emmert told ESPN.com on the eve of the retreat. "We do have serious challenges, and we do need to make some serious reforms. I don't think there is any debate about that."

Penn State President Graham Spanier, who would be an essential leader at the retreat, captured the accumulating frustration: "There are episodes every year like the ones we've seen this year. But it becomes almost an accumulation of frustrations. There have always been several of us who have had this level of frustration, but now I believe it's a majority of university presidents."

Spanier's words carried particular weight given Penn State's prominence as both an academic institution and an athletics powerhouse. None of us could have known that within three months, just as we'd be fighting the override battles over our retreat proposals, Spanier would be forced to resign amid the Jerry Sandusky child sex abuse scandal that would expose catastrophic failures of institutional oversight. The subsequent mockery was unabated. Here was a president calling for better governance and accountability in college athletics while his own institution was harboring horrors that would eventually lead to his criminal prosecution for child endangerment. The timing served as a brutal reminder that the problems facing college athletics extended far beyond recruiting violations and academic fraud into failures of basic human decency and institutional responsibility. More on that in the next Chapter.

Unlike previous gatherings that often devolved into political maneuvering and slow incremental adjustments, this retreat was designed with a different philosophy. I joined Emmert, Jim Isch, Bob Williams, Wally Renfro, David Berst, and other senior leaders in identifying which college athletics leaders would be active participants and, above all, not afraid to speak their minds and offer bold solutions.

As the newest member of this experienced team, I watched with admiration as leaders with over 100 years of collective experience in higher education and college sports assembled an attendee list representative of the entire Division I landscape and created a genuinely transformative agenda. Renfro, who had advised multiple NCAA presidents, proved particularly invaluable with his encyclopedic knowledge of college sports history and clear vision of necessary reforms. Watching him work was like observing a master craftsman. Wally knew precisely which presidents and other leaders needed to be in the room, which voices would move the conversation forward, and how to structure discussions to maximize the chance of productive outcomes.

When fifty-four university presidents gathered with athletics administrators and conference commissioners that Tuesday and Wednesday, the agenda focused on three interconnected pillars: academic standards, integrity, and financial sustainability. The academic components, raising the required GPA for incoming freshmen from 2.0 to 2.5 and reconsidering elements of Proposition 48, were relatively straightforward proposals that could be implemented through administrative action. The challenge was to achieve academic rigor without creating an unfair disparate impact on the student-athlete population, particularly given the concerns raised in earlier cases, such as *Cureton*, about racial discrimination in academic eligibility standards.

The integrity pillar proved more complex and politically fraught. Jo Potuto, Nebraska's faculty athletics representative and former chair of the Division I Committee on Infractions, captured the core challenge perfectly: "We have a group of violations that are somewhere in the middle; they aren't secondary and they aren't really putting anyone at a competitive advantage. Yet we shoot ourselves in the foot because a lot of them have to be reported as major violations. We need to talk about what really matters. The NCAA should be a leaner, meaner machine."

But financial sustainability emerged as the most contentious element, as the growing chasm between massive revenues generated by major college sports and the rewards and security provided to athletes who created that value became apparent. The tension had been simmering throughout my grassroots coaching years, but recent scandals had brought it to a boiling point. The retreat would produce two landmark proposals aimed at addressing this inequity. First, a miscellaneous expense allowance, then multi-year scholarships.

The $2,000 miscellaneous expense allowance carried revolutionary implications despite its modest sum. Based on federal cost-of-attendance calculations showing the gap between full scholarship packages and actual student expenses, this amount would acknowledge, for the first time in decades, that our traditional scholarship package had not kept pace with the real financial pressures college athletes faced. Tuition, room, board, books, and fees simply did not cut it. There was fierce debate over the appropriate dollar amount, with some presidents advocating higher amounts and others insisting that any payment beyond the traditional scholarship violated amateurism principles. But a strong consensus emerged that something had to be done.

Emmert later explained in an NPR interview: "The $2,000 issue is one that I felt very strongly about, and it was highly supported by our presidents because it does recognize that the full cost of going to school is greater than just tuition fees, books and supplies, room and board. And the current model's been in place for more than 40 years, and it was time that we made an adjustment to it."

The allowance addressed a genuine hardship that my coaching experience had shown me firsthand. Student-athletes on full scholarships often struggled to afford basic necessities like clothing, laundry, transportation home, and incidental expenses that their non-athlete peers could easily cover through part-time employment. That option generally was unavailable to athletes due to their training and competition commitments, creating real financial strain for young people who were dedicating this time in their lives to their institutions. I'd heard stories of players who were trying to follow the rules, skipping meals to save money, wearing threadbare clothes because they couldn't afford replacements, and missing family events because they lacked funds for travel home.

The proposal represented a carefully calibrated attempt to provide meaningful assistance while maintaining what we viewed as essential amateur structure for our legal and cultural legitimacy. It passed the Division I Board unanimously in October, generating optimism that we'd finally achieved modest but meaningful progress on athlete welfare.

Then reality crashed into idealism with devastating force.

Within weeks of the Board's action, we began hearing concerns from the broader membership. As many on the leadership team started calling schools around the country to understand and address those concerns, I found myself in conversation after conversation that ranged from genuinely thoughtful to bewilderingly resistant to what seemed obviously reasonable.

One call with a mid-major athletics director stands out in memory. After I explained how the $2,000 would help athletes cover basic living expenses, he asked: "But won't this just make them lazy? Right now, they're hungry, literally hungry at times, and that motivates them. If we give them spending money, what's their incentive to work hard?"

I was momentarily speechless. This was a senior administrator at a Division I university arguing that financial hardship was a feature, not a bug, of the system. I tried explaining that motivation shouldn't come from struggling to afford "laundry detergent," that we could expect excellence without requiring poverty, but I could hear in his voice that I wasn't getting through to him.

Another conversation involved an FCS conference commissioner whom I would later come to consider a friend. He acknowledged the merits but worried about competitive implications. "Look, I get it," he said. "But my smaller schools can't afford this. They're already struggling with Title IX compliance and facility upgrades. If the big boys can offer an extra $2,000 and we can't, we're done competing for recruits."

That argument had superficial appeal, but it unearthed a troubling mindset. The concern wasn't athlete welfare but institutional competitive positioning. I pointed out that if an extra $2,000 destroyed competitive balance, then our entire amateur model was in question, since schools were already spending wildly different amounts on facilities, coaching salaries, and support services. The $2,000 was a rounding error compared to those disparities.

I was astounded after one particularly frustrating afternoon of phone calls. I'd spent hours explaining basic fairness principles to people who should have understood them instinctively, and I was genuinely bewildered by the resistance.

Having watched congressional vote-counting on issues involving national defense, billions of dollars, and self-evident rights, I couldn't comprehend why we faced such difficulty building support for a $2,000 annual payment that would merely help athletes cover basic living expenses. I viewed it as a small step to right a historic wrong, but I clearly had much to learn about NCAA politics.

Under NCAA governance procedures, if enough schools requested it, they could override legislation passed by the Board. When 125 institutions, nearly forty percent of the Division I membership, called for an override, the legislation was automatically suspended under our bylaws, pending a membership vote. The opposition came primarily from smaller schools and mid-major conferences that viewed the allowance as a competitive disadvantage they couldn't afford to match.

"We are a 'have-not,'" I recall someone at Southeastern Louisiana wrote in the school's override request, a phrase that would be repeated in various forms across dozens of override petitions. These institutions feared the allowance would create a two-tiered system within Division I, where wealthy programs could offer an additional $2,000 per athlete. At the same time, resource-constrained schools would be unable to compete for top recruits.

Little did they understand how prescient their fears would prove, though not in the way they imagined. The $2,000 wasn't going to destroy competitive balance. Still, it would acknowledge a gap between the value of scholarship and living costs that had existed since the elimination of $15 laundry money stipends in the early 1970s. Once that gap was addressed, the association would face ongoing questions about how best to support athletes in an evolving environment.

Today, after witnessing schools distribute millions through NIL collectives and making *House* settlement payments exceeding $20 million annually per institution, $2,000 seems like pocket lint. But in 2011, it represented a philosophical shift that threatened to expose difficult contradictions in the amateur model. The schools opposing it recognized that any change to the traditional scholarship framework, however modest, would generate expectations for further changes, a dynamic that concerned institutions across the membership.

I now understand the debate over the miscellaneous expense allowance revealed tensions within the NCAA's structure and philosophy, which I hadn't fully appreciated during my first months on the job. While leadership was committed to student-athlete welfare, actual implementation depended on voluntary compliance by member institutions, which had vastly different resources and priorities. The suspension of the allowance in December 2011 and subsequent failed efforts to revive it by Middle Tennessee State President Sidney McPhee and the Student-Athlete Well-Being Working Group highlighted the reality that good intentions at the presidential level could be easily thwarted by collective action from schools that seemed more concerned with competitive balance and financial constraints than with student welfare.

I often wonder what could have been had the membership embraced this small gesture? Would *O'Bannon* have morphed into a case that forced payment of the cost of attendance anyway?

The multiyear scholarship proposal proved even more revealing of these underlying contradictions. Under existing rules at that time, athletics scholarships were renewable annually, giving coaches and administrators substantial leverage over student-athletes, who could lose their financial aid for injury, poor performance, or simply due to coaching changes. The retreat participants recognized this as unfair and inconsistent with educational values, and proposed instead that schools be permitted to offer guaranteed multiyear awards that provide genuine security.

The legal vulnerability of one-year scholarships had become starkly apparent through concurrent federal antitrust lawsuits. In October 2010, just months before my arrival, former Rice University football player Joseph Agnew filed a class action after losing his scholarship before his senior year. Agnew, who had played in all thirteen games as a freshman before suffering shoulder and ankle injuries, found himself facing a new coaching staff in his sophomore year that questioned his commitment. His scholarship wasn't renewed, leaving him to pay thousands out of pocket to complete his political science degree.

The *Agnew* lawsuit argued that prohibiting multiyear scholarships, combined with limits on the total number of scholarships per team, constituted illegal price-fixing under the Sherman Act that drove up education costs for athletes who lost their aid. The complaint painted a damning picture. Schools, it alleged, collectively agreed not to offer multiyear guarantees, leaving injured or underperforming athletes with no alternatives. They either accepted one-year renewable deals or gave up college athletics entirely.

A similar case emerged with former Gardner-Webb University quarterback John Rock, whose scholarship was revoked in July 2011 despite purported promises from his original coach that aid would continue as long as he remained academically eligible. Rock, who had served as team captain and starting quarterback, allegedly was told by the new coaching staff that they questioned his commitment after he arranged an internship with the North Carolina General Assembly, which had already been approved.

When Rock arrived at the team's spring game, he claimed his locker was empty and that his nameplate had been removed. The new coach's alleged dismissive response, "I don't know where you go but I'm going to watch film," epitomized the callous treatment that the retreat sought to address. Rock's case was specifically galling because he'd done exactly what universities claimed to encourage. He sought real-world professional experience that would prepare him for life after athletics. His reward was losing his scholarship and his place on the team.

We had strong arguments for the rule, and both lawsuits faced mixed results in federal court, with judges initially dismissing some claims while allowing others to proceed under traditional antitrust scrutiny. The legal challenges, however, intensified pressure on the NCAA to reform scholarship policies, particularly as the Justice Department began investigating our practices. A year or so before the retreat, Justice Department officials had met with NCAA representatives to discuss scholarship policies. Upon my arrival, I spoke briefly with Assistant Attorney General for the Antitrust Division Christine Varney, whom I had known through years of law practice in Washington, DC, and through my service in the Clinton administration. Ours remained a cordial professional rapport.

The antitrust risk here was real and hard to deny. The one-year scholarship system created legal exposure that voluntary reform might mitigate. The specter of federal antitrust action provided additional urgency to the reform agenda, and voluntary change was preferable to court-mandated or DOJ solutions that might sweep away far more than just scholarship duration rules. The NCAA's scholarship rules had to change. Interestingly, I had conversations in 2019 with President Trump's Assistant Attorney General for Antitrust, Makan Delrahim, about NIL, by which time the antitrust scrutiny of the NCAA had only grown sharper and more insistent. No matter the political party in power, the NCAA was in the antitrust chief's crosshairs.

There was a cautious tactical argument to be made that changing policies while lawsuits were pending would compromise our legal position. It might be considered an admission that our previous policies were flawed. My view was that our legal position was defensible whether we had one-year or multiyear scholarships, and that doing the right thing shouldn't be held hostage to litigation strategy. Besides, as I was simultaneously learning through *O'Bannon* preparation, our legal challenges extended beyond any specific policy to fundamental questions about how the framework of amateurism would be evaluated under modern antitrust analysis, and tactical litigation positioning alone could not eliminate that exposure.

The convergence of legal pressure, presidential frustration, and student-athlete advocacy created a unique moment for reform that the retreat was designed to capture. Once the Board passed multiyear scholarship legislation in October 2011, some schools began implementing it, but we faced override attempts again. I joined Emmert, Isch, Berst, and others staffing phones, calling across the membership to help schools understand the legislation and its rationale.

Like the $2000 stipend, the calls were illuminating and frustrating in equal measure. Many administrators genuinely didn't understand the proposal's implications. They worried that multiyear scholarships meant they'd be stuck paying for injured athletes who couldn't contribute, not realizing that the legislation permitted schools to not renew scholarships for a variety of specified reasons, just not arbitrarily. We were providing a framework for fairness, not eliminating institutional discretion.

Others understood perfectly well but opposed it because it reduced their leverage over athletes. One coach told me bluntly that if a kid doesn't buy into the program, I can encourage him to look elsewhere by not renewing his scholarship. With multiyear deals, I'm stuck with malcontents for four years.

I tried explaining that "malcontent" in practice meant "injured player the coach no longer values" or "athlete who questions coaching decisions," but again, I could hear I wasn't making progress. For some administrators, the institutional discretion that one-year scholarships provided was a feature they were reluctant to surrender, even when the resulting power dynamic raised legitimate fairness concerns. Of 330 institutions voting in February 2012, 62.12% voted to override the legislation. A 62.5% majority was required to override. The multiyear scholarship proposal survived by the narrowest imaginable margin of 0.38 percentage points, or roughly one vote.

This razor-thin victory highlighted deep philosophical polarization within Division I college athletics about the proper relationship between institutions and athletes. "I am pleased that student-athletes will continue to benefit from the ability of institutions to offer athletics aid for more than one year, but it's clear that there are significant portions of the membership with legitimate concerns," Emmert stated diplomatically. Privately, we were stunned that something so obviously fair had nearly failed.

The opposition also exposed troubling attitudes toward student-athlete welfare. Tennessee coach Derek Dooley articulated to the press the power imbalance with remarkable clarity: "We forget this is a contract, a two-way street. I think it's humorous that the academic institution can give an academic scholarship and take it away when a student doesn't perform at a certain GPA level, but it’s absolutely the worst thing you can do as a coach. It's so wrong what you do to these young people… when he doesn’t do what he’s supposed to do.”

Dooley's perspective was not isolated and displayed deep hypocrisy and candor. Coaches wanted absolute control over scholarship decisions while portraying themselves as victims when criticized for exercising that power.

The satire in Dooley's opposition became even richer the following season when Tennessee fired him in November 2012 after posting a 15-21 record over three years. The coach who opposed "job security" for his players enjoyed no such security himself, yet apparently failed to appreciate the parallel. Dooley's release for "poor performance" came with a $5 million buyout, demonstrating that coaches themselves benefited from guaranteed contracts even as they argued that athletes shouldn't receive similar protections.

Even more revealing was Indiana State's position in its override filing: "If it isn't broke, don't fix it." This stance ignored the power imbalance between eighteen-year-old recruits and major university athletics departments. At age eighteen, an athlete signs a National Letter of Intent, which prevents other schools from recruiting him, thereby eliminating his leverage in the relationship. In return for surrendering his leverage and his options, the athlete receives practically no security. In some instances, one-year renewable scholarships provided no meaningful guarantee beyond the immediate academic year if a coach decided to take a different direction.

The comparison to academic scholarships was especially galling. Academic scholarship recipients could lose funding for poor grades, but they maintained the scholarship as long as they met clear, measurable academic standards. Athletics scholarship recipients could lose funding for injury, coaching changes, "lack of commitment," or any number of subjective reasons that gave coaches nearly unlimited discretion. The comparison between academic and athletics scholarships, while frequently invoked, obscured fundamental differences in how discretion was exercised and the subjective criteria that gave coaches and administrators disproportionate control over scholarship decisions.

The Student Athlete Advisory Committee's response to multiyear scholarships proved equally instructive, though in different ways. SAAC issued a statement noting that "while student-athletes providing comment recognized the security a multiyear athletics aid agreement would provide, a majority of those student-athletes expressed concerns with possible complacency amongst their teammates and believe that an annual renewal of athletics aid is warranted to ensure individuals are putting forth every effort to maintain their athletics aid." Wow!

This response revealed how deeply student-athletes had internalized the competitive pressure and insecurity that defined their experience. Rather than embracing the security that multiyear scholarships would provide, many expressed concern that guaranteed aid might reduce motivation among their peers. This reaction suggested that years of operating within a highly competitive system governed by strict rules had shaped their expectations in ways that perpetuated their embrace of the power imbalance.

Like Brand and Emmert, I was a major advocate of including student perspectives in all debates. "No decisions about me, without me" is the athlete's motto I adopted, borrowing from disability rights advocacy. Yet the SAAC response presented the complexity of genuinely empowering young people who had been conditioned to accept their subordinate position within the system.

True empowerment would require not only soliciting their opinions but also helping them recognize how the existing structure had distorted their understanding of fair treatment. When athletes themselves argued that insecurity was necessary for motivation, it revealed how effectively the system had convinced its most vulnerable participants that their treatment actually was in their best interests. I refuse to make the comparisons here. I'll leave that to you.

The retreat's outcomes extended far beyond these two specific proposals. In response to reform momentum, the presidents established working groups with ambitious mandates. The Rules Working Group would simplify the NCAA manual and reduce the number of unenforceable Bylaws. The Enforcement Working Group would modernize the infractions process. And, specialized committees would focus on student-athlete well-being and resource allocation.

The Rules Working Group embarked on the most ambitious regulatory review in NCAA history, examining every bylaw to determine which served legitimate educational or competitive purposes and which merely created a bureaucratic burden. Clemson President James Barker led this effort with characteristic thoroughness, and the group recommended eliminating or simplifying hundreds of rules that had accumulated over decades without clear justification.

The Enforcement Working Group tackled equally complex challenges under the Executive Committee Chair, Oregon State President Ed Ray's leadership, seeking to create more efficient systems for investigating and punishing violations. The existing enforcement structure had proven inadequate for addressing major scandals like those at Miami and Ohio State while simultaneously overwhelming smaller schools with minor infractions that had little competitive impact. "We were damn mad and not going to take it anymore," Ray said.

The actual implementation of retreat recommendations, however, proved mixed, revealing both the potential and the limitations of reform within the existing governance structure. The multiyear scholarship proposal survived membership opposition and became available to schools that chose to offer such arrangements, though adoption remained voluntary and uneven across Division I. Some programs immediately implemented multiyear deals, recognizing them as recruiting advantages and moral imperatives. Others continued to offer one-year renewable scholarships, maintaining maximum leverage over their athletes.

After the membership rejected it, the miscellaneous expense allowance concept encountered continued resistance and required multiple revisions before evolving into cost-of-attendance stipends. Notably, that change ultimately resulted only from court pressure rather than voluntary membership action. Indeed, the $2,000 stipend the membership fought against in 2011 did not become a reality until Judge Wilken's 2014 *O'Bannon* ruling required us to permit cost-of-attendance scholarships, which, in many instances, far exceeded $2,000.

Academic reform components proved more successful. We raised the Academic Progress Rate standards and implemented new penalties for schools that failed to meet graduation and retention benchmarks. These changes represented genuine progress in aligning athletics and academic priorities. Critics argued, however, that they primarily affected marginal programs while allowing major violators to game the system through academic clustering and other strategies. We would later see those abuses exposed at the University of North Carolina, where for nearly two decades the African and Afro-American Studies department offered fraudulent "paper classes" that existed seemingly to help keep athletes eligible. We will discuss that in Chapter 24.

Enforcement reforms proved most challenging to implement, requiring changes to NCAA culture and procedures that had developed over decades. While we modernized some aspects of the infractions process, the basic structure remained largely intact. High-profile cases, such as the University of Miami matter, would continue to reveal considerable limitations of investigative tools, problems with investigative procedures, and shortcomings in penalty assessments.

Looking back now from the vantage point of 2026, with athletes receiving NIL payments, schools providing *House* settlement distributions, and the entire amateur model in disrepair, the 2011 retreat appears almost quaint in its modest ambitions. We were fighting tooth and nail for a $2,000 annual payment that today represents less than what many athletes receive for a single Instagram post. Some college athletes earn seven figures annually through NIL deals.

The multiyear scholarship battle that consumed enormous political capital has been rendered largely moot by the transfer portal, which has created free agency, making scholarship duration almost irrelevant. Athletes can now leave schools annually, regardless of scholarship terms, thereby reconstructing the power dynamic in ways our modest 2011 reforms could never have achieved and honestly didn't contemplate. Furthermore, post-COVID eligibility waivers now permit competition for seven years or more.

Yet the retreat's longer-term impact extended far beyond its immediate policy outcomes. It established reform as a permanent fixture of NCAA discourse and created expectations for ongoing change that subsequent leadership in the membership couldn't ignore. The emphasis on student-athlete welfare became a central organizing principle for future reform efforts, even when specific proposals failed to gain immediate adoption.

More significantly, the retreat's results acknowledged that college athletics had reached a crisis point requiring more than incremental adjustment. The frank discussions about amateurism, compensation, and institutional responsibility that took place in Indianapolis helped legitimize debates that had previously been relegated to the margins of NCAA discourse. While immediate outcomes were mixed, the retreat created intellectual and political space for more dramatic changes that would emerge in subsequent years.

The narrow margins on multiyear scholarships, the suspension of the miscellaneous expense allowance, and the resistance to even modest increases in athlete support showed that the NCAA couldn't reform itself voluntarily. Too many institutions had too much invested in maintaining the status quo, or feared competitive disadvantages that might result from change, to permit the kind of transformation that justice demanded.

This reality would become progressively apparent in the years that followed. Modest reform proposals would face similar resistance; attempts to improve athlete welfare would be portrayed as threatening competitive balance or institutional survival; and acknowledgments that athletes deserved fair treatment would be met with dire warnings about the destruction of the amateur model. The retreat taught me that voluntary membership action, while essential, would need to be supplemented by other forces to drive the pace of change the environment demanded.

"Whipping votes should not be this hard," I had said to President Emmert that summer, frustrated by the political challenges of securing support for obviously reasonable reforms. But I came to understand that it was hard precisely because we were trying to reform a system that wouldn't be reformed from the inside. A system built on contradictions that no amount of good-faith effort could resolve. Untreated symptoms in a system that would lead us to Collegiate Capitalism.

The votes were difficult to secure because we were asking institutions to voluntarily relinquish advantages they'd enjoyed for a century and to acknowledge that their athletes deserved fairer treatment, even when that acknowledgment might lead to demands for further change. We were asking schools to accept reality, knowing that once they acknowledged the obvious unfairness of denying athletes $2,000 for basic expenses, they'd have difficulty explaining why those same athletes shouldn't receive much more.

The August 2011 Presidential Retreat marked a crucial turning point in my understanding of the NCAA's challenges and limitations. I arrived in March believing that smart leadership, sound arguments, and appeals to institutional values could generate reforms necessary to preserve the unique educational character of college athletics while treating athletes more fairly. The retreat taught me otherwise. It revealed that the membership could resist even modest changes that threatened competitive advantages or required additional expenditures, regardless of how compelling the moral or legal arguments might be.

That lesson also proved invaluable as we faced mounting legal challenges in federal courts. Understanding the political impossibility of voluntary reform helped me see why legal pressure from *O'Bannon*, later *Alston*, and ultimately *House* might be necessary to force changes the membership would not adopt on its own. The retreat didn't fail because we lacked good ideas or committed leaders. Instead, it revealed that the system itself was broken, due to internal action or inaction.

Those frustrating summer and fall months in 2011, making phone calls to recalcitrant administrators, explaining basic fairness principles to people who should have understood them instinctively, watching narrow margins determine whether student-athletes would receive modest benefits they desperately needed, prepared me for the battles ahead with eyes wide open. The political education I received that year proved as valuable as any prior legal or lobbying training or experience.

It taught me that sometimes the most challenging part of fighting for justice isn't making the arguments or assembling the evidence. The hardest part is accepting that some systems can't be reformed from within, no matter how dedicated the reformers or how compelling their case. Some systems must be replaced, and sometimes that replacement requires external pressure that overcomes internal resistance.

To understand this reality, we had to go through that process. We had to attempt reform, watch it flounder on the rocks of institutional self-interest, and learn that voluntary change wouldn't be sufficient before courts and legislatures forced the transformation that the 2011 retreat had recognized as necessary but had proven unable to achieve.

The retreat was both a partial defeat and a necessary step toward eventual change. We couldn't skip directly to revolution; we first had to demonstrate that evolution wouldn't work.

Chapter 13
When Football Became More Important Than Children
The Penn State Scandal and NCAA's Credibility Crisis

September 2011 in Hawaii should have been straightforward. We were defending the NCAA in a jury trial involving the defunct Aloha Bowl, and Penn State athletics director Tim Curley had flown to Honolulu to testify regarding his role as chair of the Postseason Football Certification Committee. Outside counsel Greg Curtner and I spent hours preparing him, and by the end he was about as ready as a witness gets to be. Curley knew this material cold. Nobody understood bowl certification procedures better than Tim.

Then he took the stand and everything felt wrong.

Curley raised his right hand, swore to tell the truth, and began answering opposing counsel's questions with surprising ineffectiveness. He was unclear, confused, and hesitant in ways that made no sense given his expertise. One of the first questions was simple enough: "How's Joe Paterno?" Curley's response came quickly: "He's doing well." But something in his demeanor shifted after that exchange, and his testimony never recovered its footing.

I remember looking at Greg during a break, both of us puzzled. This was the chair of a major NCAA committee, testifying about procedures he'd overseen for years, yet he seemed distracted in ways we couldn't understand. His testimony wasn't inappropriate or untruthful, just oddly disjointed, as if his mind were elsewhere while his mouth formed words about bowl certification standards.

We couldn't have known that Curley was living through his own nightmare. As he sat in that Honolulu courtroom answering questions about bowl games, he was already under investigation for testimony he'd given to a Pennsylvania grand jury. He knew that, at worst, criminal prosecution loomed and, at best, termination, for his role in the most devastating scandal in college sports history. He was caught in a gathering storm about which we knew nothing.

That foreshadowing would haunt me two months later, when everything exploded into public view.

The timing of what was about to unfold was especially striking given what else was happening at the NCAA. We were simultaneously defending the *O'Bannon* case, fighting to get university presidents to approve a modest $2,000 stipend for athletes, and trying to pass multi-year scholarship protections. And now we were about to discover that while we fought these battles over the details of amateurism, one of our most prominent member institutions had been protecting a child predator because doing otherwise might damage the football program's reputation. The juxtaposition was obscene.

The Jerry Sandusky scandal at Penn State University represents one of the most devastating institutional failures in the history of American higher education. What began as criminal charges against a single individual evolved into a complex web that challenged everything I thought I understood about the NCAA's role, exposed the perilous power of football culture, and ultimately contributed to the erosion of the organization's authority that continues to this day. More than that, it would reveal the economic and cultural forces that would eventually transform college athletics from an ostensibly amateur educational enterprise into the professional Collegiate Capitalism system emerging today.

Jerry Sandusky, longtime assistant football coach under legendary Joe Paterno, was charged by the Commonwealth of Pennsylvania on November 4, 2011, on forty counts of child sexual abuse, with additional charges later bringing the total to fifty-two counts, spanning at least fifteen years. The grand jury investigation revealed a pattern of predatory behavior perpetrated against vulnerable children through The Second Mile, a charity Sandusky founded in 1977 ostensibly to help at-risk youth.

The charity, which at its peak had an annual budget of approximately $2.5 million and served thousands of children, became a hunting ground where Sandusky identified and groomed victims. He specifically targeted boys from disadvantaged backgrounds, often from single-parent homes, offering them access to Penn State football as a lure.

The grand jury presentment was stomach-turning in its details. Sandusky had sexually assaulted boys in Penn State football facilities, including the team showers. He brought boys to his office in the football building. He took them into the weight room and the coaches' locker rooms. He had taken children on the team plane to bowl games, invited them to his home, and used the prestige of Penn State football as currency to gain trust and access. The abuse wasn't hidden in dark corners or secret locations. It happened in the heart of State College, in facilities that thousands of people used regularly, enabled by an institutional culture that valued football success above children's safety.

But the scandal's true magnitude lay not just in Sandusky's crimes but in the institutional response, or lack thereof, by Penn State officials. A 1998 investigation by Penn State police into Sandusky showering with a young boy had been dropped without charges despite concerns raised by the boy's mother. That investigation actually involved interviews with Sandusky, surveillance of the locker room, and consultation with local prosecutors and child welfare authorities. Yet somehow, despite all this official attention, Sandusky was “cleared” and allowed to continue his unfettered access to Penn State facilities and children.

Then came the 2001 incident that would become central to the entire scandal. Graduate assistant Mike McQueary reported seeing Sandusky sexually assaulting a young boy, estimated to be about ten years old, in the football facility showers on a Friday night.

McQueary, a former Penn State quarterback who was twenty-eight at the time and hoping to build a coaching career, faced an impossible situation. Here was a young graduate assistant with no power evaluating how to confront a well-known defensive coordinator of a storied Penn State football program.

What he witnessed that night in the Lasch Building showers would haunt him for the next decade. McQueary testified that he saw Sandusky, naked, standing directly behind a naked boy who appeared to be about ten years old in the shower, with the boy's hands against the wall and Sandusky's arms around the boy's midsection. McQueary testified he believed he was witnessing sexual abuse. He reported what he had seen to head coach Joe Paterno the next morning at Paterno's home.

According to McQueary's testimony, Paterno asked a few questions and told McQueary he had done the right thing by reporting it and that Paterno would handle it from there. Paterno reported the matter to athletics director Tim Curley the next day. Approximately a week and a half later, McQueary was summoned to meet with Curley and senior vice president Gary Schultz. No law enforcement notification followed. According to internal Penn State communications later disclosed, Curley and Schultz initially considered reporting the matter to the Pennsylvania Department of Public Welfare, but Curley reversed course after speaking with Paterno. The university's ultimate response was to tell Sandusky not to bring children to Penn State athletic facilities, to confiscate his locker room keys, and to report the incident to The Second Mile.

Think about that response for a moment. A graduate assistant witnesses what he believes to be the rape of a child by a prominent coach in university facilities. He reports it up the chain of command to the university's most powerful figures. And their solution is to ask the perpetrator to please not bring his victims to campus anymore. Not to call law enforcement. Not to investigate who the child was or whether he was safe. Not to examine whether there were other victims. Just a request: please don't use Penn State facilities for future abuse.

McQueary's career and life were destroyed by what he witnessed and reported. Initially hailed as a whistleblower, he later faced death threats from Penn State supporters who viewed him as a traitor who had brought down Joe Paterno. He was placed on administrative leave and never coached another game at Penn State. His subsequent lawsuit against Penn State for retaliation was settled in 2016, though the terms were not disclosed. University Park treated the man who reported a child being raped as the villain, while the institution that enabled the rapist was defended.

The institutional reckoning began swiftly after Sandusky's November 2011 indictment. On November 9, the board of trustees forced President Graham Spanier to resign and fired Joe Paterno after forty-six years leading the football program. Paterno had become more than just Penn

State's coach. He was an institution himself, the winningest coach in major college football history, a figure whose statue stood outside the stadium and whose name adorned the university library. Paterno had won 409 games, two national championships, and five undefeated seasons. He'd sent hundreds of players to the NFL. His program had generated hundreds of millions of dollars for the university. He was Penn State football, and Penn State football was, in many respects, the identity of the entire region.

His firing sparked riots in State College, with students overturning a news van and clashing with police in the streets. The riots revealed the depth of football's grip on the community's identity. Students who should have been horrified by revelations of child rape were instead angry that their football coach had been fired. The image of young people rioting to defend a coach who had, at minimum, failed to do enough to stop a child predator captured the moral decay at the heart of big-time college football.

Board chair Kenneth Frazier, CEO of Merck & Co., played a pivotal role in these decisions. I was familiar with Ken from his prior work, and he was exactly the kind of leader an institution needed during a crisis. Frazier's experience was particularly relevant. As Merck's general counsel and later CEO, he had navigated the Vioxx litigation, where the company faced tens of thousands of lawsuits over a painkiller linked to heart attacks and strokes.

That experience, managing a crisis involving serious harm, intense public scrutiny, massive litigation exposure, and the need to preserve institutional honor, had prepared him for high-stakes decision-making under extraordinary pressure. Frazier later testified that Paterno's removal was based on "public perception of the University's values" rather than specific knowledge of wrongdoing. That framing was careful and legally sound, but it also revealed the calculations being made. Paterno had to go not necessarily because he'd committed a crime, but because his continued presence was incompatible with the university's survival.

The board appointed provost Rodney Erickson as interim president, tasking him with navigating the university through its darkest period. Erickson, a career academic who had served as provost since 2000, faced monumental challenges. He would have to solve criminal investigations, mounting civil litigation, media siege, and the task of preserving the institution's reputation while cooperating with multiple external investigations and potentially unprecedented NCAA enforcement.

Days after the indictments, Frazier announced that Penn State had hired former FBI Director Louis Freeh to conduct an independent investigation into the university's handling of the Sandusky allegations. Frazier, chairing the board's special investigative committee, emphasized Freeh's independence and authority to investigate all university employees, including the board itself. The investigation reportedly would cost Penn State over $8.1 million and was positioned as "full, fair, and completely independent."

I'd worked with Louis Freeh during my Justice Department days when he served as FBI Director. I'd led DOJ representation in the Idaho criminal trial of Lon Horiuchi, the FBI sharpshooter involved in the Ruby Ridge incident, and in civil cases arising from the Branch Davidian siege at Waco. Freeh was always well-respected, extraordinarily competent, and someone who would get to the bottom of complex situations. His reputation for thoroughness and integrity was exactly what Penn State needed if it genuinely wanted answers.

As Freeh commenced his work and more details emerged about the scandal's scope and the institutional failures that enabled it, we faced increasingly urgent questions about NCAA responsibility and authority to act. Based on my legal experience at Justice and elsewhere, I believed the best course was to let the criminal process run its course without interference. However, we closely monitored developments and began internal discussions and board consultations on possible next steps.

The challenge was unprecedented in NCAA history. We had not faced circumstances in which serious criminal conduct had occurred within an athletics program, enabled by athletics personnel who failed to intervene, but where the crimes themselves had nothing directly to do with competitive advantage, recruiting violations, or academic fraud. This was about child rape occurring in athletics facilities while athletics department officials looked the other way. Did we have jurisdiction? Should we exercise it even if we did? What would the appropriate response look like?

After extensive internal debate, the NCAA decided to approach Penn State directly as a member institution and request information to help us analyze potential responses. We sent a letter asking for specific data about the events. Simultaneously, we would monitor Freeh's investigation, which was gathering evidence with resources and authority that far exceeded anything the NCAA could deploy.

On June 22, 2012, Jerry Sandusky was convicted on forty-five counts of child sexual abuse. The jury had deliberated for about twenty hours over two days before reaching its verdict. Eight young men, now adults, had testified during the trial about abuse they suffered as children. Their testimony was devastating. One victim, known as Victim 1, described being groomed over months before Sandusky began touching him inappropriately during what were supposed to be workout sessions. Another, Victim 4, testified about being raped in the Penn State showers in 2001, likely the same incident McQueary had witnessed. The victims' impact statements painted a picture of lives destroyed by abuse and compounded by institutional indifference. Sandusky was sentenced to thirty to sixty years in prison, essentially a life sentence for the then sixty-eight-year-old.

One month after the convictions, in July 2012, the Freeh Group released its report after an eight-month investigation. The report was damning in ways that exceeded even the grand jury presentment's stark details. Freeh's team had conducted more than 430 interviews and reviewed approximately 3.5 million documents, creating a factual record unprecedented in scope for anything the NCAA had ever dealt with in enforcement investigations.

University President Rod Erickson and the Penn State Board of Trustees quickly adopted the Freeh Report's findings, giving the NCAA answers to our questions about what happened and providing a basis for determining what, if anything, we should do about it.

The Freeh Report delivered conclusions that were difficult to read and impossible to ignore. The investigation found that four key officials—Joe Paterno, Graham Spanier, Tim Curley, and Gary Schultz—had demonstrated "total and consistent disregard" for child sexual abuse victims while covering up Sandusky's attacks. The report concluded that these leaders had "empowered Sandusky to attract potential victims to the campus" by allowing him continued access to university facilities despite knowledge of the 1998 investigation and the 2001 McQueary report.

The report's most controversial finding involved Joe Paterno's knowledge and role. Freeh's investigation alleged that Paterno had known about Sandusky's behavior as early as 1998, contradicting the coach's testimony that he first learned of concerns in 2001. The report pointed to emails among Spanier, Curley, and Schultz discussing how to handle the 2001 incident. In one particularly damning exchange, after initially planning to report Sandusky to authorities, Curley wrote that after speaking with Paterno, he had changed his mind and wanted to manage it differently. The report claimed the four officials had concealed facts and violated federal law by failing to properly alert law enforcement.

Perhaps most troubling was the report's conclusion about motivation. According to Freeh, these officials had prioritized avoiding bad publicity for the football program over protecting children from a known predator. The report offered that the most saddening finding by the Special Investigative Counsel is the total and consistent disregard by the most senior leaders at Penn State for the safety and welfare of Sandusky's child victims. "The avoidance of the consequences of bad publicity is the most significant, but not the only, cause for this failure to protect child victims and report to authorities," it added.

Reading the Freeh Report was one of the more difficult professional experiences of my career. The details of Sandusky's abuse were sickening. The institutional response was enraging. But what struck me most forcefully was recognizing how the very things that made college football special, things like intense loyalty, tight-knit communities, institutional pride, the sense that the program was bigger than any individual, had been twisted into enabling mechanisms for unspeakable crimes.

The report made clear that Penn State football had become too big to fail in the eyes of its leadership. The program generated over $60 million annually in direct revenue and was estimated to contribute over $200 million to the local economy. It was the identity of an entire region, the pride of a state, and an economic engine that employed thousands. The choice to protect the enterprise over the children foreshadowed, more than anything else, the Collegiate Capitalism that was emerging, a system where football's economic value had grown so large that normal rules, normal morality, and normal institutional priorities no longer applied.

Over the next three weeks, we developed a course of action and negotiated what we termed a "consent decree" with Penn State, which included penalties and corrective actions to which they would agree. The concept of a consent decree came from my experience with government enforcement and private practice clients, but the terms Penn State would accept were familiar to everyone in college sports: fines, scholarship reductions, post-season bans, probation.

The negotiations were intense and involved some of the most notable figures in college sports regulation. David Berst, who had joined the NCAA in 1972 and spent forty years in enforcement and governance, served as our principal advisor. Berst had been involved in virtually every major NCAA enforcement case since the 1970s, from SMU's death penalty in 1987 to countless high-profile infractions cases. His institutional knowledge was unmatched, and his judgment on enforcement matters was trusted throughout the membership. Gene Marsh, former chair of the Committee on Infractions and a law professor at the University of Alabama who had been involved in NCAA enforcement for nearly as long as Berst, represented Penn State. Marsh had served on the Committee on Infractions from 1989 to 2010, including as chair from 2003 to 2007. He'd overseen some of the most complex infractions cases in NCAA history and knew every nuance of NCAA enforcement procedures. These were two men who knew NCAA enforcement inside and out, who understood both the formal rules and the informal norms that governed how the organization operated.

Despite allegations that would later emerge in litigation and political forums, the NCAA did not exert undue influence over the Freeh investigation or coerce Penn State into accepting penalties. We met with Freeh to understand the scope of his investigation, which would help us determine whether we needed to conduct a separate enforcement investigation. We provided the Freeh Group with background on the NCAA's constitution, bylaws, and rules. This was expected minimal cooperation, nothing more. Indeed, the Freeh Group was extraordinarily careful to keep the NCAA at arm's length from its processes and analyses, specifically to avoid later challenges to its independence.

It was clear to us that the egregious behavior recounted in Sandusky's indictment and conviction, and detailed in the Freeh Report, amounted to failures of institutional and individual integrity "far exceeding a lack of institutional control or individual unethical conduct." This wasn't about improper benefits to athletes or academic fraud or recruiting violations. This was about an institution choosing to protect a football program's reputation while children were being raped in its facilities.

On July 23, 2012, President Emmert announced sanctions against Penn State. Understanding that the Sandusky scandal represented institutional failure warranting immediate action, the university agreed to a consent decree that included a $60 million fine equivalent to one year of the football program's gross revenue, payable over five years for programs preventing child sexual abuse; a four-year postseason ban for the football team covering the 2012 through 2015 seasons; reduction of football scholarships from twenty-five to fifteen annually for four years; five years of probation; vacation of all Penn State football wins from 1998 to 2011, officially removing 112 victories from the record books; allowance for football players to transfer immediately without penalty; adoption of recommendations from the Freeh Report; and appointment of an independent athletics integrity monitor for five years.

No, reaching the consent decree did not involve the NCAA's traditional investigative process, primarily because of the Freeh Report's thoroughness. As I explained at the time, any traditional NCAA investigation would have been "duplicative and unnecessary." Why spend months or years investigating when we had access to the results of the review of 3.5 million documents and 430 interviews conducted by one of America's most respected investigators?

Initially, this creative approach received praise from almost every corner. Even many Penn State supporters acknowledged that the university needed to be held accountable for institutional failures that had enabled Sandusky's crimes. But in the end, Happy Valley was not happy with these penalties and corrective actions. Over the following months, public pressure, litigation, and political maneuvering would force the NCAA to rescind much of the agreement. The internal and public fights about this case would come to define the Emmert administration and serve as a stark reminder of football's power over institutional behavior.

As the sanctions took shape, their speed and severity reflected intense pressure within the NCAA membership leadership structure. The Executive Committee, which included 22 university presidents, seriously weighed the so-called death penalty, which would have shut down Penn State's football program for four years. As the Corman litigation and later press coverage would make this plain, the debate was extraordinary. To some, if any situation in NCAA history warranted the death penalty, this was it. To others, the precedent and the economic devastation to the State College community counseled restraint. And there was the central question, later litigated in the courts, of whether the NCAA had jurisdiction over criminal conduct that didn't directly relate to competitive advantage. These divisions over the NCAA's role and authority would only widen in the years that followed.

Penn State's legal counsel Gene Marsh negotiated fiercely to avoid that outcome. Gene, Berst, and I had several conversations about how to resolve the crisis appropriately. The negotiations were tense and strenuous, but respectful. Marsh would later describe the process as a "cram down," comparing it to federal bankruptcy proceedings where creditors must accept whatever deal is offered. There was no question that the possibility of the death penalty created enormous pressure on Penn State officials to accept the consent decree.

President Rod Erickson later revealed that he believed he had no choice but to accept the sanctions, stating that the university had its "backs to the wall." Yet, the penalties ultimately imposed were developed through negotiation, with some provisions even suggested by the university itself. Berst made it clear that we should support Erickson's actions. If we had not concluded the consent decree with Penn State's agreement, the NCAA would have been forced to use the traditional enforcement process, which might have resulted in the death penalty, among other consequences. Erickson's decision to agree, while controversial, likely saved Penn State from a long, drawn-out process and potentially harsher penalties.

But the fans in Pennsylvania, including politicians, were not fond of the agreed-upon penalties. I believe that if the sanctions had not included the vacation of Joe Paterno's wins achieved while Penn State football and administration looked the other way as children were being abused, much of the backlash might have been avoided. But taking away those 112 victories, which had made Paterno the winningest coach in major college football history, was a step too far for many Penn State supporters. The wins meant more than the children who had been victimized. That realization was profoundly depressing.

> The public reaction revealed the commodification of college football, which may eventually lead to its full professionalization. Penn State fans didn't riot because children had been abused. They rioted because their coach was fired and their wins were vacated. The economic and cultural investment in football success had become so complete that even horrific child abuse was viewed primarily through the lens of how it affected the football program's legacy. This was Collegiate Capitalism unfolding in its rawest form. Football as a commodity was so valuable that all other values became secondary.

Pennsylvania Governor Tom Corbett, who had been attorney general during the early stages of the Sandusky investigation, announced on January 1, 2013, that he was filing a federal antitrust lawsuit against the NCAA. Corbett's suit challenged the entire consent decree, arguing that the NCAA had exceeded its authority and violated antitrust law by imposing sanctions outside its normal enforcement process.

The lawsuit represented a dramatic reversal for Corbett, who had initially endorsed the NCAA settlement as "part of the corrective process." However, growing criticism from Penn State supporters and concerns about the $60 million fine for combating child sexual abuse being spent outside Pennsylvania rationalized his legal challenge. Corbett's handling of the original criminal investigation as attorney general had become a subject of intense scrutiny, particularly regarding the length of time between the investigation's initiation in early 2009 and Sandusky's arrest in November 2011. Some critics suggested that Corbett, as attorney general with gubernatorial ambitions, had slow-walked the investigation to avoid political damage from attacking Penn State football during his 2010 election campaign. Whether or not those allegations were fair, they highlighted the political calculations surrounding Penn State football that even investigating child rape was seen through the lens of electoral politics.

U.S. District Judge Yvette Kane dismissed Corbett's lawsuit in June 2013, ruling that the case lacked "any factual allegations" to support the antitrust claims. Kane characterized the suit as "a Hail Mary pass" that warranted dismissal, effectively ending Corbett's challenge to NCAA sanctions.

But State Senator Jake Corman, whose district included Penn State's main campus, pursued a more targeted legal strategy. Initially focusing on ensuring the $60 million fine remained in Pennsylvania rather than being spent nationally on child abuse prevention programs, Corman's lawsuit gradually expanded to challenge the entire consent decree process.

Corman's legal team centered its argument on claims that the consent decree was flawed due to alleged improper cooperation between the Freeh Group and the NCAA, and coercion of Penn State. The senator argued that the NCAA had orchestrated Freeh's conclusions to justify unprecedented sanctions exceeding the organization's authority. This conspiracy theory was precisely that: a conspiracy *theory*. Louis Freeh's incorruptibility was beyond reproach, and the consent decree was reached through arm's-length negotiations, in which Penn State was represented by one of the country's most capable attorneys, Gene Marsh.

Yet the lawsuit gained momentum when internal NCAA emails, including emails the NCAA had sought to keep out of the public records, surfaced during discovery, showing officials discussing negotiation strategy. The emails included discussions about whether Penn State could be "bluffed" into accepting the consent decree, given uncertainty about how the Committee on Infractions would ultimately rule, and whether the NCAA actually had authority to impose sanctions for conduct not related to competitive advantage. One email from an NCAA executive characterized the approach to Penn State as a "bluff," acknowledging that asserting jurisdiction would be "a stretch." Another conceded the NCAA was "banking on the fact the school is so embarrassed they will do anything," while admitting there was no good answer to the jurisdictional issue. These communications, while typical of candid internal deliberations in any organization weighing a difficult call, looked terrible when exposed in litigation.

They were used to suggest cynical manipulation rather than principled enforcement. It should have surprised no one that a legal team would weigh the relative strength of its position, the basis for its authority to act, the power to impose the death penalty, and whether the sanctions would survive legal scrutiny. These are precisely the kinds of strategic discussions that any competent legal team conducts when negotiating a significant settlement.

There were peripheral questions floated about whether Penn State, at that point in its history, was of such character in the operation of its athletics program that it should be considered on the same ethical plane as other institutions that were members of the NCAA. Simply put, the question in some minds was whether Penn State could be expelled from membership. While not part of the legal or governance strategy, it illustrated that some in the membership and public had even stronger ideas of what to do about the situation.

But the legal and governance debates that did happen provided potent ammunition for Corman's challenge to the consent decree's legitimacy.

Corman emerged as Penn State's most effective legal advocate, using his position as a state senator to challenge the NCAA's authority while his public platform sowed doubt about the consent decree process. His lawsuit strategy proved more successful than Corbett's broader antitrust challenge, ultimately leading to a settlement that would restore Paterno's victories and keep the $60 million fine in Pennsylvania.

By late 2014, the NCAA faced mounting legal challenges from multiple directions. Corman's lawsuit alleged improper collaboration between Freeh's investigators and NCAA officials. At the same time, the Paterno family had filed a separate defamation lawsuit challenging the Freeh Report's conclusions about Joe's knowledge and role. Internal NCAA emails suggesting we had "bluffed" Penn State into accepting sanctions were undermining the consent decree's legitimacy in the court of public opinion, if not in actual courts.

The legal pressure intensified when Commonwealth Court Judge Anne Covey refused to dismiss Corman's lawsuit and instead expanded it to examine the entire consent decree process. And after our motion was denied, the Pennsylvania's Supreme Court declined to reverse her decision, setting the stage for a January 2015 trial.

Judge Covey was an interesting jurist. As an elected state court judge, she would not only express her opinions and issue rulings in the courtroom but also take them to the campaign trail and engage in public dialogue on the NCAA and Penn State. Elected judges in Pennsylvania must run for retention, and Judge Covey represented a district where Penn State football was deeply important to voters.

She approached the case with perspectives that reflected the community's strong feelings about the NCAA's actions, and her rulings and public statements reflected that political reality. In many ways, Judge Covey's behavior opened my eyes to the lengths a community would go to support its local school's football program. The judicial system itself, which should have been insulated from such pressures, appeared to be captured by football culture. It was an early lesson about the power of football economics that would be replicated many times as the NCAA attempted to manage a myriad of issues.

Our outside counsel, my former Latham & Watkins partner Kip Johnson, clearly understood where things were headed if we didn't resolve the case short of trial. He had appeared before Judge Covey many times and experienced firsthand her determination to right what she perceived as a grave wrong inflicted upon the school and the community.

I recall vividly a call Kip made to me as President Emmert and I were about to enter a Board meeting at the NCAA Convention. The conversation was heated, and, as former partners and, more importantly, friends, neither of us wanted to budge. I was on earbuds; Kip was in a conference room with other attorneys from the firm. The discussion got louder and more intense. People around me could perhaps hear what I was saying, but not Kip's words. Attorneys in his conference room listened to the whole exchange.

Judge Covey had made clear through her rulings and comments that she viewed the NCAA's actions as an overreach that had unjustly harmed Penn State. Those internal emails about negotiation strategy were going to be admitted. Reported polling suggested that many Centre County residents, where Penn State football was practically a religion, believed the NCAA sanctions had been unfair to Penn State. We were going to face a hostile judge and a community that viewed defending Penn State football as a moral imperative. The reputational and practical exposure of a loss was material.

Deep down, I believed that we needed to stand our ground, that retreating would set a terrible precedent, that the underlying facts about institutional failure to protect children should carry the day regardless of procedural criticisms. But I was being naive about Pennsylvania politics and Penn State football culture. Given the perceived procedural irregularities, however, it was likely that no jury or, in this case, judge in State College would rule against Penn State, regardless of the evidence of institutional failures.

I understood what we had to do, but I didn't like it. The real risk was ultimately about institutional survival. If we went to trial and lost badly, it wouldn't just affect this case; it could undermine every enforcement action the NCAA had pending or might pursue in the future. A major legal defeat in one of our highest-profile cases would embolden every school facing sanctions to pursue aggressive litigation. We were already fighting *O'Bannon* in federal court, already facing questions about our authority to restrict athlete compensation, and already struggling with the contradictions in our amateurism model. Adding a devastating loss in Pennsylvania state court might be the blow that destroyed what remained of our credibility.

Facing the prospect of a potentially damaging trial outcome, the NCAA agreed to settle with Corman and State Treasurer Rob McCord in January 2015. The settlement included several provisions that essentially reversed much of what we'd accomplished in the original consent decree: restoration of all 112 vacated wins to Penn State's football program; restoration of Joe Paterno's status as the winningest coach in major college football history; agreement to spend the $60 million fine entirely within Pennsylvania rather than nationally; and replacement of the original consent decree with a new agreement that significantly softened the terms.

The settlement represented a significant victory for Penn State supporters, though I believe it came at the expense of the greater good. In the end, we maintained that Penn State acknowledged our "legitimate and good faith interest and concern regarding the Jerry Sandusky matter." That language was carefully negotiated to preserve some fig leaf of NCAA authority while essentially capitulating to political and legal pressure.

The financial implications of the scandal extended far beyond the NCAA sanctions. Penn State ultimately paid more than $109 million in settlements to Sandusky's victims, with individual settlements reportedly ranging from hundreds of thousands to over $7 million. The university's insurance carriers initially balked at coverage, leading to additional litigation. Donations to Penn State dropped significantly in the immediate aftermath, with the university reporting a $30 million decline in contributions in fiscal year 2012. However, the football program's revenue remained remarkably stable, demonstrating the economic resilience of major college football even in the face of catastrophic scandal. Season ticket sales dropped only slightly and within a few years had recovered to pre-scandal levels. The message was clear: nothing, not even enabling child rape, could seriously damage the economic machine that college football had become.

The truth was that these circumstances represented tragedies of Shakespearean proportions. The criminal cases against Penn State's former officials proved more complex than initially anticipated. Former President Graham Spanier, Athletics Director Tim Curley, and Vice President Gary Schultz were charged with conspiracy and child endangerment for their alleged roles in covering up Sandusky's crimes.

Curley and Schultz pleaded guilty, and Spanier was found guilty of misdemeanor child endangerment charges. However, all conspiracy charges, which had been central to the Freeh Report's allegations of a cover-up, were dropped against Curley and Schultz, while Spanier was acquitted of conspiracy. The convictions on reduced charges suggested that while these officials had failed in their responsibilities, prosecutors couldn't prove the more serious allegations of active conspiracy to conceal Sandusky's crimes. Curley received a sentence of seven to twenty-three months, with the first three months in jail. Schultz received six to twenty-three months, with the first two months in jail. Spanier received four to twelve months, with the first two served in jail, though his sentence was delayed for years and ultimately reversed on appeal. These relatively light sentences for officials whose failures allegedly enabled years of child sexual abuse struck many as inadequate justice.

The heartbreak of Graham Spanier's trajectory haunted me. At the August 2011 Presidential Retreat, just three months before the scandal broke, Spanier had been among the university presidents calling for greater accountability, speaking eloquently about institutional integrity and the need for the very values he had failed to uphold. Within months, he would be forced to resign and eventually convicted of child endangerment for his failures to respond properly to reports about Sandusky. The man calling for accountability had failed the most basic test of institutional leadership. The hypocrisy was staggering, but it also revealed something more profound. Even presidents who genuinely believed in reform couldn't overcome the structural imperatives of protecting football programs at all costs.

Jerry Sandusky remains imprisoned, serving his thirty- to sixty-year sentence for forty-five counts of child sexual abuse. Multiple appeals have been unsuccessful, and the Pennsylvania Supreme Court denied his appeal to it in April 2014. Sandusky maintains his innocence to this day, and as of this writing, he recently filed a new appeal seeking to reverse his conviction on prosecutorial misconduct grounds. He has never expressed remorse nor taken responsibility for his crimes. That failure of accountability mirrors the institutional failure of accountability at Penn State itself.

The scandal exposed fundamental weaknesses in university governance, particularly regarding the reporting and handling of sexual abuse allegations. The tragedy highlighted the need for clear reporting protocols, independent oversight, and cultural change within higher education institutions, not just at Penn State, but across the country. In the scandal's aftermath, many universities revised their policies on reporting suspected child abuse and other serious misconduct. The federal government strengthened enforcement of the Clery Act, which requires colleges to report crimes on campus. Pennsylvania passed stricter mandatory reporting laws.

The NCAA's handling of the Penn State case revealed limitations in our enforcement philosophy and procedures. Our decision to bypass traditional investigative processes and rely on an external report raised questions about due process and fairness that would come back to haunt us. While initially celebrated, our decision to get involved at all was eventually challenged as *ultra vires*, beyond our authority. We maintained that institutional failures enabling criminal conduct in athletics facilities fell within our constitutional mandate to ensure institutional integrity. But many came to believe the NCAA had no business involving itself in what was perceived as a criminal matter, even though a coach was molesting young boys in athletics facilities while leadership ignored the evidence.

The scandal also highlighted the complex and often toxic relationship between athletics and academics at major universities, where successful sports programs can foster cultures that prioritize winning over fundamental institutional values. Penn State was hardly unique in this regard. The economic model in which football programs generate massive revenues that fund other sports, subsidize athletics departments, and contribute to institutional prestige invariably creates tangible pressures to protect the football program at all costs. Penn State's failures were more extreme than most, but the underlying incentive structure exists at every major football school. When your football program generates $60 million annually and contributes $200 million to the local economy, protecting that revenue stream becomes the de facto priority regardless of official institutional values.

I believe the biggest tragedy was that the Penn State case marked a critical inflection point in the NCAA's authority over member institutions, catalyzing the gradual unraveling of the organization's regulatory power. The scandal exposed weaknesses and limitations in our enforcement philosophy and procedures that would reverberate through subsequent cases and ultimately shape the current environment, driving further the professionalization of college football and the development of the new power-conference enforcement system.

The settlement established a dangerous precedent that aggressive legal challenges could force the NCAA to reverse even its most high-profile enforcement actions. Observers believed that the NCAA would fold when faced with determined opposition backed by sufficient resources and political support. That lesson would be applied repeatedly in subsequent years, from basketball corruption to NIL litigation to gambling to the *House* settlement and, in the future, I predict athlete employment status.

The Penn State case emboldened other institutions and stakeholders to challenge NCAA authority more aggressively. It marked the beginning of more aggressive governmental intervention in the governance of college athletics. Governor Corbett's federal lawsuit, while ultimately unsuccessful, established a precedent for state-level challenges to NCAA authority that would be refined in subsequent cases. Senator Corman's more targeted approach proved that state officials could effectively constrain NCAA action through strategic litigation and legislative pressure.

This lesson was not lost on other state politicians and university leaders who began viewing the NCAA as a vulnerable target rather than an unassailable authority or, better yet, a partner in shared governance. This governmental intervention accelerated during the NIL debates of the late 2010s and early 2020s. States began passing legislation that directly contradicted NCAA rules, creating a patchwork of conflicting regulations that undermined our ability to maintain uniform standards. California's Fair Pay to Play Act, signed in September 2019, was the direct descendant of Pennsylvania's successful challenge to NCAA sanctions. Both demonstrated that states could and would intervene in college athletics when they perceived NCAA actions as harmful to in-state institutions.

These events unfolded during a period of mounting scrutiny of the NCAA's amateurism model, and the Penn State fiasco further undermined the moral authority needed to restrict athlete compensation. Critics argued that the scale of the Penn State fine highlighted tensions in the NCAA's regulatory philosophy. If the NCAA could impose financial penalties of this magnitude, they contended, it was implicitly acknowledging that college athletics operated as a commercial enterprise, which complicated the organization's position in *O'Bannon* that athletes should not receive compensation beyond scholarships. Judge Wilken essentially adopted this reasoning in her 2014 *O'Bannon* ruling, and Justice Kavanaugh echoed it in his *Alston* concurrence.

The financial dimensions of the Penn State matter also revealed something else: the sheer scale of money flowing through college athletics. The fact that Penn State could absorb a $60 million penalty without seriously damaging its football program demonstrated just how much revenue was at stake.

If Penn State football could survive child rape scandals and massive penalties, what couldn't it survive? The answer was nothing. Football was too big to fail. And if it was too big to fail, then maybe it was also too big to be amateur. The seeds of Collegiate Capitalism were planted in that aftermath.

The ultimate resolution satisfied few stakeholders. Criminal convictions came on reduced charges. NCAA sanctions were essentially reversed. Civil settlements compensated victims while institutional accountability was largely evaded. Penn State supporters celebrated the restoration of Paterno's victories as the university continued to grapple with governance reforms. And the NCAA's credibility was permanently damaged, setting in motion forces that would eventually dismantle the amateurism model at the highest levels of sport.

In recent years, Penn State added a plaque honoring Paterno to a new 'Wall of Honor' inside the stadium listing all former head coaches, while the statue itself remained in an undisclosed secure location. The university was trying to have it both ways. It sought to acknowledge that Paterno's failures were real while also celebrating his legacy. That ambivalence perfectly captured the cognitive dissonance at the heart of big-time college football.

> The hubris of all involved in the Penn State scandal, those attempting to secure accountability and those rejecting anything that interferes with a winning athletics team, illustrates why college sports is diving headfirst into an uncertain future. When football becomes more important than children, when 112 victories matter more than the boys who were victimized in facilities used to achieve them, when a community mobilizes to defend a coach's legacy rather than demanding justice for abuse victims, we've lost sight of what higher education should represent.

That's the real tragedy of Penn State, beyond even Sandusky's horrific crimes. The institutional response, the community's reaction, and the ultimate outcome revealed that for too many people in Happy Valley and beyond, football success trumps basic human decency. That calculus explains why the current system was destined to collapse into something new. You can't build a sustainable model on a foundation that values wins over children.

You can't maintain amateurism when the economic stakes are so high that institutions will protect predators to preserve revenue streams. You can't profess football is an educational activity when communities riot over a fired coach but remain silent about raped children. Penn State exposed all these contradictions at once, and in doing so, helped accelerate the transition to Collegiate Capitalism, a system that at least has the virtue of honesty about what college football has become. It is a commercial enterprise where money matters more than mission, where winning matters more than welfare, and where the amateur ideal died long before anyone dared to admit it.

Chapter 14
Baylor and Michigan State
The Limited Power of The NCAA Exposed

Sadly, Penn State was not an isolated failure. While we were still processing the implications of the Sandusky case and debating whether we had overreached in our response, another institution was demonstrating that the same toxic intersection of football culture and institutional negligence could occur elsewhere. And this time, we would respond very differently.

The Baylor University sexual assault scandal unfolded over several years before exploding into public view in 2016. What emerged was a pattern strikingly similar to Penn State in its essential elements. Multiple women alleged that Baylor football players had sexually assaulted them between 2011 and 2014, and university officials had allegedly failed to investigate their complaints adequately or protect them from further harm. A later lawsuit would allege that 31 football players committed 52 rapes during that period. Two players were convicted of sexual assault, with Tevin Elliott sentenced to 20 years in prison and Sam Ukwuachu convicted in 2015.

In September 2015, Baylor hired the Philadelphia law firm Pepper Hamilton to conduct an independent review of how the university had handled sexual violence allegations. The resulting report, delivered in May 2016, found what Pepper Hamilton called a "fundamental failure" to implement Title IX and the Violence Against Women Act. The findings described actions by university administrators that "directly discouraged some complainants from reporting or participating in student conduct processes" and, in one instance, "constituted retaliation against a complainant for reporting sexual assault."

The institutional response came swiftly. Head football coach Art Briles was fired on May 26, 2016. University President Kenneth Starr, the same

Ken Starr who had led the investigation that resulted in President Clinton's impeachment, was demoted and eventually resigned. Athletics director Ian McCaw resigned. Title IX coordinator Patty Crawford resigned, later alleging that the university had set her up to fail and retaliated against her efforts to help victims.

The parallels to Penn State were unmistakable. A powerful football program had allegedly created a culture where winning took precedence over young people's safety. University administrators had allegedly failed to act on complaints or actively discouraged reporting. A legendary coach and a prominent university president lost their positions. The investigations revealed systemic failures rather than isolated incidents.

But the NCAA's response could not have been more different.

At Penn State, we had acted with unprecedented speed and severity, imposing sanctions outside our normal enforcement process based on our determination that the Sandusky case represented a threat to the fundamental values of the collegiate model. We had justified our intervention by arguing that when football becomes more important than protecting children, the NCAA has an obligation to act regardless of whether specific bylaw violations occurred.

At Baylor, we took no comparable action. The university self-reported to the NCAA as part of the Pepper Hamilton process, and we opened an inquiry. But unlike Penn State, we did not invoke emergency powers or impose sanctions outside the normal infractions process. There would be no presidential letter, no special committee review, no immediate scholarship reductions or postseason bans.

The distinction was difficult to explain to those who expected consistency. Both cases involved alleged cover-ups of sexual misconduct. Both involved football programs whose success appeared to have contributed to institutional blindness. Both involved university presidents who were removed from office. Why had Penn State warranted extraordinary intervention while Baylor proceeded through normal channels?

Part of the answer lay in the criticism we had received for the Penn State approach. The consent decree, the vacated wins later restored, and the legal challenges to our authority all demonstrated the risks of acting outside established procedures. But part of the answer was also simpler and more troubling. Sandusky was a coach. The Baylor perpetrators were players. Our rules addressed coach conduct far more clearly than player misconduct outside athletic activities.

The Baylor case exposed another gap in our enforcement framework that we had not adequately addressed. We could punish institutions for violations of recruiting rules, academic fraud, improper benefits, and coach misconduct. But sexual assault by players, even when institutional failures enabled it, did not fit neatly into our bylaw structure. The NCAA was not designed to be a law enforcement agency or a Title IX enforcement body. We were a membership organization governing athletic competition.

Yet the public did not see these distinctions as meaningful. They saw two universities where football culture had allegedly contributed to institutional failures that harmed vulnerable people. They saw the NCAA act aggressively in one case and passively in another. They drew conclusions about our priorities and consistency that damaged our credibility, regardless of the legal and structural explanations we could offer.

Baylor ultimately faced no major sanctions comparable to Penn State's. The NCAA placed the program on probation but imposed no postseason ban, scholarship reductions, or vacated wins. The program self-imposed scholarship reductions and recruiting restrictions during the 2016 season. New head coach Jim Grobe, brought in as an interim replacement for Briles, tried to rebuild the program's culture while navigating unprecedented scrutiny. Matt Rhule followed Grobe and restored competitive success. By 2019, Baylor was playing in a Big 12 Championship Game as if the scandal had never happened.

Art Briles, despite being fired for cause, received $15.1 million in severance. Ken Starr received over $4.5 million. The financial consequences for the individuals deemed responsible were golden parachutes rather than punishment.

The contrast with Penn State was troubling. We had stripped Joe Paterno's wins, imposed crushing scholarship penalties, and banned the program from postseason play. Whatever one thought of our Penn State response, it had sent an unmistakable message that the NCAA would not tolerate institutional cultures that endangered children. Our Baylor response sent a different message, suggesting that our willingness to act depended on factors beyond the severity of institutional failures.

Some argued that our Penn State approach was wrong and that the Baylor approach was correct. The NCAA should stay in its lane, enforcing competitive rules rather than trying to regulate institutional culture or serve as a shadow Title IX enforcement agency. If universities failed to protect students from sexual violence, the appropriate remedies were criminal prosecution, civil litigation, and Department of Education enforcement, not NCAA sanctions.

I understood this argument intellectually. But I had supported the difficult decision that Penn State's failures warranted extraordinary action. I had believed then that some institutional failures were so severe they required a response beyond our normal processes. Baylor's failures seemed equally severe. The distinction in our responses reflected not a consistent philosophy but rather our uncertainty about what role the NCAA could play in addressing the darkest aspects of big-time college athletics.

When Larry Nassar's crimes at Michigan State University came to light, revealing sexual abuse of hundreds of young women over decades, the question arose again. The Michigan State case proved even more striking in its implications for NCAA enforcement and institutional accountability.

Larry Nassar was a team physician at Michigan State University from 1997 to 2016, serving simultaneously as the national team doctor for USA Gymnastics. Over more than two decades, he sexually assaulted at least 265 young women and girls under the guise of medical treatment, making it the largest sexual abuse scandal in American sports history. The survivors included Olympic gymnasts Simone Biles, Aly Raisman, and McKayla Maroney, along with countless young athletes who had trusted him with their care.

The scope of institutional failure was staggering. Female athletes had complained about Nassar's behavior to Michigan State officials as early as 1997, but the university took no effective action for nearly two decades. A 2014 Title IX investigation into complaints against Nassar somehow cleared him and allowed him to continue treating patients. Multiple MSU employees across multiple departments had received warnings about Nassar over the years, yet the abuse continued.

When the full extent of Nassar's crimes finally became public in 2016 and 2017, the institutional consequences were severe. Michigan State President Lou Anna Simon resigned. The same Lou Anna Simon who was a member of the NCAA Executive Committee during the Penn State scandal. The same Lou Anna Simon who had criticized Penn State's missteps as "purposeful and premeditated" and "pretty pervasive," offering that "the right thing is saying something when you see something and doing something after you said something. It's really that simple," Athletics Director Mark Hollis resigned. The university ultimately agreed to a $500 million settlement with Nassar's victims, one of the largest settlements in higher education history. The Department of Education fined MSU $4.5 million for violations of the Clery Act. Criminal prosecutions resulted in prison sentences for Nassar and several MSU employees who had failed to act on complaints.

In January 2018, while Nassar's sentencing hearings were generating national attention as victim after victim delivered impact statements detailing his abuse, the NCAA enforcement staff sent a letter of inquiry to Michigan State. We were investigating whether the university had violated NCAA rules in its handling of the Nassar case.

Many wondered, given our Penn State precedent, would the NCAA act against Michigan State for institutional failures that had enabled two decades of sexual abuse? Would we assert the same authority we had claimed when Jerry Sandusky's crimes became known?

In August 2018, we announced our conclusion: no violations of NCAA legislation had occurred. The enforcement staff wrote to Michigan State that the investigation "has not substantiated violations of NCAA legislation" and "it does not appear there is a need for further inquiry."

The reaction was fierce. Rachael Denhollander, one of the first women to publicly accuse Nassar, tweeted that the NCAA "needs to revisit their own legislation" if it did not prohibit coaches from threatening consequences for reporting abuse or asking athletes to sign sympathy cards for someone jailed on child sex abuse charges.

"If the world's worst pedophile in history working at MSU and getting away with abuse for 20 years isn't considered a violation, then what is the point?" asked Lindsey Lemke, a former captain of the Michigan State gymnastics team.

Our explanation was straightforward and legally defensible. Our rules governed athletics-related conduct: recruiting, eligibility, competition, benefits, and academic support. Sexual abuse by a team physician, while horrific, was not the type of misconduct our bylaws were designed to address. We were not a law enforcement agency or a Title IX enforcement body. Criminal prosecution and civil litigation were the appropriate mechanisms for addressing Nassar's crimes and Michigan State's failures.

Moreover, the Penn State precedent had demonstrated the risks of acting outside our standard enforcement framework. We had faced intense criticism and legal challenges for our approach there. Critics argued we had exceeded our authority and imposed penalties inconsistent with our own rules. The consent decree was controversial from the moment it was signed.

But to those outside our regulatory apparatus, the distinction was impossible to understand or accept. We had acted with overwhelming force against Penn State for institutional failures that enabled child sexual abuse. We had declined to act against Michigan State for institutional failures that enabled child sexual abuse on a far larger scale. The only coherent explanation seemed to be that our willingness to enforce depended on factors other than the severity of harm to young people.

The Nassar and Baylor cases revealed a fundamental truth about NCAA enforcement that the Penn State intervention had obscured. We were not actually in the business of holding institutions accountable for these failures. We were in the business of regulating athletics competition: who was eligible to play, how they could be recruited, and what benefits they could receive. When institutional misconduct fell outside those categories, our enforcement apparatus was powerless.

Penn State had been an exception, a moment when the severity of institutional failure led us to act outside our standard enforcement processes. The legal challenges that followed demonstrated the risks of that approach. Whether we should have done it differently remains debatable, but the practical effect was clear: the organization became more cautious about asserting authority in areas where our jurisdictional footing was uncertain. Baylor and Michigan State would proceed through normal channels, which meant they would face no NCAA consequences for failures that had devastated hundreds of lives.

This was the uncomfortable truth that the Nassar case laid bare. Our enforcement system had been built primarily around competition-related rules, and when institutional failures fell outside those categories, the association's tools were inadequate to address them. We could investigate whether a recruit received free gear or whether a tutor wrote a paper for an athlete. We could not meaningfully address the institutional cultures that allowed sexual predators to operate unchecked for decades.

The implications for the emerging Collegiate Capitalism would be significant. If the NCAA could not protect athletes from the most basic forms of harm, what legitimacy did we have to restrict their economic opportunities? If our enforcement power stopped at the boundary of competition-related Bylaws and rules, why should athletes trust us to have their overall best interests at heart?

The contrast between Penn State and Michigan State, between action and inaction, between our aspirational claims about protecting student welfare and our actual enforcement record, contributed to the erosion of trust that would make later reforms inevitable. Athletes, advocates, and observers concluded that the NCAA was better at restricting compensation than protecting safety. That conclusion oversimplified the distinction between what our rules could address and what they couldn't, but it captured a genuine frustration that we had never adequately answered. Whether fair or not, it accelerated the transformation toward the market-driven system emerging today.

Chapter 15
Culture Wars
Jay Z and When Uncle Luke Met Little Luke and the NCAA Lost Its Way

March 2014, NCAA Men's Basketball Tournament, a regional game. I saw Shawn Carter, better known to the world as Jay Z, in the arena. Seeing him there reminded me that Roc Nation Sports had launched only a year earlier, in early 2013, and that his new agency had recently secured a favorable resolution with South Carolina enforcement officials over its contacts with Jadeveon Clowney. I thought too of his line on *Magna Carta Holy Grail,* needling the NFL over its investigations into his move into representation. Was he there just to take in some college hoops, I wondered, or was he there on Roc Nation Sports business?

I had no idea that a month later, on April 29, DJ Khaled would release a single entitled "They Don't Love You No More" featuring Jay Z, Meek Mill, Rick Ross, and French Montana. Jay Z's verse stopped me cold. Without ever naming names, he saluted the people clever enough to find the loopholes, boasted that he had as many options as a college team, stiff-armed his imitators like a Heisman pose, and then, in language every bit as profane as it was pointed, cursed the NCAA outright, and demanded, in the plainest terms, that a young brother finally be allowed to receive compensation.

The very notion of loopholes and the demand to pay athletes echoed in my head long after the track had faded out. What I knew for certain was that one of the most iconic figures in all of hip-hop had aimed his enormous platform directly at the NCAA, its policies, and its executives. This was no fringe critic firing a cheap shot. This was Jay Z, a global artist whose words reached millions, maybe billions, and shaped culture the world over. Once again the message could not have been clearer. The NCAA had become a symbol of exploitation, and our own conduct kept handing critics the ammunition to demand change or our dismantling.

That cultural moment captured everything that had gone wrong with the Miami investigation and enforcement generally. We had become the villains in a story that should have been about holding rule-breakers accountable. How had this happened?

The University of Miami has long occupied a unique position in college athletics, embodying both the promise and peril of big-time collegiate sports. For decades, the Hurricanes football program served as a cultural phenomenon that transcended traditional academic boundaries, drawing its identity from the vibrant, rebellious energy of South Florida. Especially Miami in the 1980s and early 1990s, when the Hurricanes won four national championships while cultivating an outlaw image that was both magnetic and polarizing. Players celebrated touchdowns with choreographed routines that resembled NFL end zones more than college ones. They talked trash with a swagger that seemed more professional than amateur. They wore camouflage fatigues and combat boots in team photos. This was college football's bad boys, and they loved it. This identity attracted recruits who might have been uncomfortable at more traditional programs, but it also created an environment in which rule-breaking seemed normalized as part of the Miami mystique.

This cultural milieu gave birth to everything from the boundary-pushing musical stylings of 2 Live Crew to the swagger that defined Miami's championship teams. Luther "Uncle Luke" Campbell, leader of 2 Live Crew and Liberty City icon, became infamous for his association with the program. In 1994, the Miami Herald reported that Campbell and several NFL players operated a pay-for-play system from 1986 through 1992, offering cash rewards for touchdowns and big hits. The NCAA investigation verified these allegations and found that Miami's head football coach and associate director of athletics for compliance were aware of the payments. The resulting sanctions in 1995 were severe: a one-year postseason ban and thirty-one scholarship reductions.

But the precedent had been firmly established. In the Miami matter, it appeared that external financial support for players wasn't an aberration; it was tradition. The question wasn't whether boosters would take care of players, but who would step up to do it.

While Miami had been in the NCAA's crosshairs before, the story of what I believe was Miami's most damaging investigation during my tenure began not with violations on campus, but with the spectacular financial collapse of Nevin Shapiro. News stories, civil lawsuits, and criminal prosecutions described an astonishing story.

Shapiro was a diminutive figure at 5 feet 5 inches. But he had an outsized personality and an insatiable desire for recognition within Miami's athletics circles. Born in Brooklyn in 1969 and raised in Miami Beach, Shapiro claimed to operate Capitol Investments USA, a grocery distribution business that supposedly bought wholesale and sold to upmarket customers. In reality, Capitol had virtually no operations. Shapiro was running a Ponzi scheme.

Between 2005 and November 2009, Shapiro orchestrated a $930 million fraud, promising investors monthly returns of 10 to 26 percent. He used investor funds for everything except groceries. He misappropriated at least $38 million to finance outside business ventures, including a 30% stake in a sports agency called Axcess Sports, which signed Miami players like Vince Wilfork. He funded his lavish lifestyle, charging more than $640,000 in personal expenses to Capitol's credit card, including $116,000 spent by his girlfriend. He showered Miami athletes with benefits. And he bought his way into the inner circle of Hurricanes football, becoming exactly what he wanted to be: somebody important in Happy Valley South.

What distinguished Shapiro from typical white-collar criminals was his deep integration into Miami's athletics culture. Rather than simply stealing money and disappearing, he used ill-gotten gains to purchase influence and access. He reportedly spent approximately $2 million of his investors' money on what he characterized as "taking care of players," providing improper benefits to at least seventy-two current and former Miami athletes. Cash payments, luxury dinners, yacht parties, strip club outings, prostitutes, and abortions were some of the benefits. The allegations were staggering in scope and depravity, creating a web of NCAA violations that would have been shocking in scope even by Miami's historically permissive standards.

Shapiro viewed himself as the natural successor to Uncle Luke. He told Yahoo! Sports explicitly: "Here's the thing: Luther Campbell was the first uncle who took care of players before I got going. His role was diminished by the NCAA and the school, and someone needed to pick up that mantle. That someone was me. He was 'Uncle Luke', and I became 'Little Luke'." This statement revealed not just Shapiro's personal motivations but the institutional memory that persisted within Miami's athletics culture. Despite previous sanctions and serious reform efforts by administrators, the fundamental expectation that wealthy boosters would provide extra benefits remained embedded in the program's DNA.

When Shapiro's Ponzi scheme collapsed and he was arrested in April 2010, his relationship with Miami athletics transformed from generous benefactor to vengeful informant. Feeling abandoned by players he'd supported financially, Shapiro decided to take everyone down with him. "Once the players turned pro, they turned their back on me," he told The Herald in August 2010. "It made me feel like a used friend." He began cooperating with federal investigators as part of his plea agreement. More significantly for college athletics, he began compiling a detailed account of his interactions with Miami players and coaches. In June 2011, he was sentenced to twenty years in federal prison. From his cell, he conducted over 100 hours of jailhouse interviews with Yahoo! Sports reporter Charles Robinson.

The resulting exposé, published on August 16, 2011, just months after I arrived at the NCAA, sent shockwaves through college sports. Robinson's article was damning, detailing rule-breaking involving dozens of players across multiple sports spanning nearly a decade. The breadth and salacious nature of Shapiro's claims appeared to represent exactly the type of rule-breaking that demanded a forceful response.

The timing of Shapiro's revelations could not have been worse. President Emmert assumed the presidency with a promise to bring more aggressive enforcement and meaningful reform. We already were dealing with high-profile scandals at USC, Ohio State, and other major programs. The shadow of the "death penalty" imposed on Southern Methodist University in 1987, when the NCAA canceled an entire season due to massive booster pay-for-play violations for at least 10 years involving stars like Eric Dickerson, loomed over many discussions about major infractions. If any case since SMU warranted the death penalty, many argued, this was it. This story broke three months before Penn State, which we discussed in Chapter 13, where the spectre of the death penalty was also raised.

Unfortunately, our investigation of Miami would reveal as much about our own institutional failures as about the violations in Coral Gables. In October 2010, Emmert promoted veteran enforcement investigator Julie Roe Lach to replace David Price as vice president for enforcement. Lach was an Academic All-American Hall of Fame basketball player at Millikin University, an attorney, and an expert in NCAA policies with fifteen years at the association. She was the quintessential success story of someone forging her way to the top through hard work, determination, and results. When I arrived in March 2011, I agreed with Emmert's assessment that she was the right person for the job. I'd worked with investigators and enforcement officials at all levels in both civil and criminal matters, and I placed her among the best.

Yet from the outset, her enforcement staff struggled to corroborate Shapiro's allegations through traditional investigative methods. Many former players refused to cooperate, either denying Shapiro's claims or simply declining to grant interviews. Without subpoena power or other legal enforcement mechanisms, we found ourselves dependent on voluntary cooperation from individuals who had strong incentives to remain silent. This was the recurring nightmare of NCAA enforcement. We believed violations occurred but were unable to prove them because witnesses wouldn't talk.

This investigative challenge led to the case's most harmful aspect: the enforcement staff's decision to work with Shapiro's bankruptcy attorney, Maria Elena Perez. Without OGC's knowledge, Lach's staff approved the arrangement despite known objections from Naima Stevenson-Starks, a Harvard Law-educated, Arnold and Porter-trained senior attorney on the legal team. The scheme involved paying Perez to use her subpoena power in bankruptcy proceedings to depose witnesses who had refused to cooperate with the investigation. When I learned of it, similar to Naima's concerns, I suspected this scheme represented a fundamental violation of our own ethical standards, essentially allowing enforcement staff to circumvent our lack of legal authority by piggybacking on unrelated legal proceedings.

The details, laid bare in an independent investigation President Emmert commissioned, were stunning. I hired former FBI General Counsel and Assistant Attorney General for National Security, Ken Wainstein, of Cadwalader, Wickersham & Taft, to conduct the review. He reported several irregularities with the enforcement investigation. Enforcement investigator Ameen Najjar had approached Perez with what Wainstein's report described as a "way around" the roadblock created by our legal team's rejection of the payment scheme. Najjar assured his superiors, including Lach and managing director Tom Hosty, that legal approval had been obtained when it had not. This deception allowed the NCAA to pay Perez four times the expected price, including the costs of deposing two key witnesses whose testimony could have been crucial to our case.

The ethical implications extended far beyond procedural violations. By hiring Shapiro's attorney to conduct depositions on our behalf, the enforcement staff created a financial relationship with the accuser in our own investigation. This relationship raised questions about objectivity and justice, particularly since Perez had strong economic incentives to produce testimony supporting Shapiro's allegations. Miami alleged the arrangement violated basic due process principles by denying the university and its personnel the opportunity to confront their accusers in a neutral forum.

When these improprieties were discovered in January 2013, they triggered another credibility crisis. We had built our moral authority on demands that membership maintain ethical standards and institutional integrity. The revelation was undermining: it appeared that some in our organization were willing to violate our own ethical standards in pursuit of high-profile enforcement victories. We immediately publicly acknowledged that we had discovered "a very severe issue of improper conduct" and commissioned the Wainstein investigation to examine the enforcement staff's actions.

The resulting 52-page investigative report revealed other questionable tactics. Enforcement staff had purchased prepaid cellphones to facilitate communication with Shapiro and spent approximately $8,200 on his prison phone calls, including $4,500 deposited into his commissary account. While we intended to disclose these payments to evaluate Shapiro's credibility as a witness, the optics were terrible. We were funding a convicted felon's lifestyle while he provided allegations against a member institution.

As the leader of enforcement, Julie Roe Lach bore responsibility for these failures. However, the Wainstein report noted that subordinates had misled her, and that she was under unprecedented pressure while managing "significant cases." Lach was dealing with what the report called "a daunting workload," including efforts to restructure the enforcement staff and to coordinate new penalty structures following the August 2011 presidential retreat, which had produced calls for more aggressive enforcement.

We parted ways with Lach in February 2013, primarily to stabilize after the damage caused by the botched investigation. Her departure was particularly difficult given her talent and potential, especially since she had obtained the green light for the financing from Isch, who himself left the NCAA in 2014. But as Eisenhower said, "leadership consists of nothing but taking responsibility for everything that goes wrong and giving your subordinates credit for everything that goes well." In the end, Julie did what leadership requires. She took the responsibility as her own.

I reached out to Jonathan Duncan, a highly effective private attorney with extensive NCAA experience, to serve as interim vice president of enforcement. I recall the conversation with Jon, who always maintained steady calm and decorum. He expressed part surprise, part excitement, part fear. Duncan inherited an enforcement team in turmoil and a Miami case irreparably compromised by his predecessors' teams' misconduct, including some still on his staff. He was tasked with salvaging what remained while attempting to restore confidence in the enforcement process. But the damage had already been done, both to the specific case and to our broader credibility as an effective regulatory body.

The crisis created an opening for University of Miami President Donna Shalala to mount a public challenge to our authority and competence. I knew Secretary Shalala from our Clinton administration days. She had been Secretary of HHS while I was at DOJ. Shalala was an experienced political operator who understood how to use public pressure to achieve institutional objectives. She initially maintained a cooperative posture throughout the investigation, encouraging full cooperation and implementing self-imposed sanctions designed to demonstrate institutional responsibility. The revelation of enforcement misconduct prompted Shalala to shift her approach and gave her powerful ammunition to challenge the entire process.

Shalala's response was swift, forceful, and strategically calculated. In a statement released February 18, 2013, she characterized the NCAA's investigation as "unprofessional and unethical" and declared that our conduct had wronged Miami. She wrote: "Sadly, the NCAA has not lived up to their own core principles. The lengthy and already flawed investigation has demonstrated a disappointing pattern of unprofessional and unethical behavior. By the NCAA leadership's own admission, the University of Miami has suffered from inappropriate practices by NCAA staff."

More significantly, Shalala took the unprecedented step of demanding that the case be dismissed entirely, arguing that Miami had already "suffered enough" through self-imposed sanctions and that no additional penalties should be imposed based on an investigation fatally compromised by misconduct. She concluded: "We believe that this process must come to a swift resolution, which includes no additional punitive measures beyond those already self-imposed. We have suffered enough."

This public confrontation between Shalala and the NCAA went beyond a dispute over enforcement procedures. It reflected a shift in power dynamics between the NCAA and its most prominent member institutions. Historically, universities accused of major violations had little choice but to accept whatever penalties we imposed. The combination of obvious misconduct and Shalala's political sophistication created an opportunity to challenge traditional deference and expose our institutional weaknesses to public pressure.

Shalala's strategy proved remarkably effective in turning public opinion against us and generating pressure for a favorable resolution. Her background as a respected academic leader and former Cabinet official gave her statements credibility that transcended typical university-NCAA disputes. The fact that she had participated in the 2011 Presidential Retreat only added to the complexity. Here was a president who had been part of reform discussions now publicly challenging our competence and honesty. The Penn State debacle was still fresh. Now, Miami demonstrated that even when violations were real and egregious, botched enforcement made it nearly impossible to hold members accountable.

The Committee on Infractions hearing, which eventually took place in June 2013, occurred amid a cloud of controversy and mutual suspicion, making a fair resolution nearly impossible. Following President Shalala's public demand, Miami's legal team sent a letter requesting dismissal based on the enforcement staff's misconduct. Our staff, however, was determined to salvage something from an investigation that had consumed enormous resources and generated massive public attention. The hearing was complicated by questions about which evidence could be properly considered, given that portions of our case had been obtained through the improper Perez arrangement.

The final resolution, announced by Committee on Infractions Chair Britton Banowsky in October 2013, reflected the arduous position we found ourselves in. The Committee imposed penalties that many believed were remarkably light given Shapiro's initial allegations. They included three years of probation, nine lost football scholarships over three years, three lost basketball scholarships, and recruiting largely symbolic restrictions. Most significantly, the Committee accepted Miami's self-imposed bowl bans and did not add additional postseason restrictions that many had expected.

This resolution was widely interpreted as an acknowledgment that enforcement misconduct had fatally undermined the case, regardless of the violations that may have actually occurred. The apparent inability to impose meaningful penalties on a program that allegedly broke the rules for nearly a decade sent a powerful message about the consequences of procedural failures and the limits of NCAA authority when confronted by determined resistance backed by legitimate grievances.

The broader implications extended far beyond specific penalties. The case exposed weaknesses in our governance structure and investigative processes that continue to plague enforcement to this day. More concerning, Miami demonstrated that when economic and cultural stakes are high enough, even obvious rule-breaking becomes impossible to punish if procedural missteps give institutions grounds to challenge legitimacy. It's as simple as it is in the criminal justice system. Failure to follow the required process can result in the unavailability of evidence, a mistrial, or even an acquittal. Rules matter.

The Miami case also demonstrated the importance of institutional culture in shaping both rule-breaking and enforcement decisions. Miami's unique position within college athletics, as a private institution with strong ties to professional sports culture and a limited traditional alumni base, had always made it an outlier. The program's historical association with controversial figures like Uncle Luke and its celebration of an outlaw image had created an environment where rule-breaking wasn't just tolerated but actively encouraged as part of the Miami brand.

Looking back, it's clear the case represented a turning point in the relationship between the NCAA and its most powerful member institutions. Donna Shalala's successful challenge demonstrated that determined resistance could be effective, particularly when our own misconduct provided grounds for challenging the legitimacy of our system. The same rebellious spirit that had made Uncle Luke and 2 Live Crew cultural icons animated the university's response to NCAA overreach, creating a narrative of institutional resistance that resonated far beyond the boundaries of college sports.

> The cultural significance couldn't be overstated. The NCAA had become, in the eyes of many, synonymous with a system that generated enormous revenue from athletes while the amateurism framework limited their ability to share in that wealth. Uncle Luke had challenged that system in the 1980s by paying players directly for performance. Nevin Shapiro continued the tradition, however perversely. And now one of hip-hop's biggest names was using his platform to channel decades of frustration within the Black community about college athletics' mistreatment of athletes.

The Miami case concluded in the fall of 2013, and the very next spring, I heard those lyrics from Jay Z, which not only served as a reminder of what had happened in Coral Gables but also forced a reckoning with the arguments being advanced in *O'Bannon*. The song echoed in my mind long after. What had inspired him to record those blunt bars, I'll never know. But the timing felt significant. The NCAA had become a cultural symbol of exploitation, and our botched Miami investigation had reinforced that perception.

Penn State had shown that political and legal pressure could force us to back down on sanctions. Miami showed that even when violations were real, procedural failures meant no accountability. Together, these cases demonstrated that the association's enforcement framework faced challenges that would require a fundamental rethink to remain credible. The only path forward was acknowledging reality. College athletics had evolved into an environment where the economic stakes often made traditional enforcement mechanisms insufficient, a reality that the Miami case made impossible to deny.

That's what Jay Z understood and what Uncle Luke had known decades earlier. The loopholes weren't bugs in the system. They *were* the system. And the NCAA's attempt to maintain the principles of amateurism while everyone profited except the athletes was becoming increasingly difficult to sustain. And then, in 2018, we would empower the Commission on College Basketball, led by former Secretary of State Condoleezza Rice, to tackle the remnants of this tragic case.

Chapter 16
When the FBI Arrested College Basketball
The Worst Kept Secret Was Out

I was in my office at NCAA headquarters in Indianapolis on September 26, 2017, when my associate director, Kim Fort, interrupted a meeting. "Turn on the television," she said. "The U.S. Attorney for the Southern District of New York is holding a press conference. You need to see this right now."

The TV was on, so I reached for the remote and flipped from whatever NCAA Championship rerun was on the tube to one of the news channels. Acting U.S. Attorney Joon Kim stood at a podium in Manhattan, flanked by FBI officials and stacks of documents. What he said next would shake college basketball to its foundation.

He started by describing that, earlier in the day the FBI arrested ten people, including four Division I college basketball coaches, on various fraud and corruption charges. "The picture of college basketball painted by the charges is not a pretty one. Coaches at some of the nation's top programs soliciting and accepting cash bribes, managers and financial advisers circling blue-chip prospects like coyotes, and employees of one of the world's largest sportswear companies funneling cash to families of high school recruits."

FBI Assistant Director William F. Sweeney Jr. stepped to the microphone. His message was blunt: "All of those charged today played a role in creating a pay-to-play culture that has no place in college basketball."

I sat transfixed as names and faces flashed across the screen. Chuck Person from Auburn. Emanuel "Book" Richardson from Arizona. Tony Bland from USC. Lamont Evans from Oklahoma State. James Gatto, Adidas' director of global sports marketing. Christian Dawkins, an aspiring sports agent. Munish Sood, a financial adviser. Rashan Michel, a former NBA and SEC referee turned suit salesman.

These weren't minor programs or obscure assistants. Auburn, Arizona, USC, and Oklahoma State were major conference schools with significant basketball operations and multimillion-dollar budgets. And the investigation, we quickly learned, had been ongoing since 2015 with sophisticated surveillance, including wiretaps, undercover agents posing as investors, and financial tracking that documented every dollar changing hands.

The NCAA leadership had known nothing about it until this moment.

My phone started ringing immediately. Board members wanted to know what we were going to do. Media outlets wanted statements. University presidents whose programs weren't named were nervous about whether more shoes would drop. Those whose programs were named wanted to know what penalties they might face. Conference commissioners and their lawyers wanted guidance on how to respond.

And all I could think was that the FBI accomplished in two years, with tools we never had, what our enforcement system had been struggling to achieve for decades. Subpoena power, wiretaps, and the threat of prison changed the calculus for witnesses in ways our voluntary compliance model never could.

As we'd said countless times in our enforcement discussions, give us subpoena power and wiretaps and we could change college athletics. The FBI had exactly those tools, and what they found confirmed much of what critics had long suspected about the corruption in elite college basketball.

But I also knew, sitting there watching that press conference, that even this bombshell would face an uphill challenge in changing the fundamentals of the game around the game. Why? Simply put, because the corruption wasn't aberrational. It was structural, the inevitable result of a system where billions of dollars flowed through college basketball while those around the sport, like athletes, agents, apparel companies, schools, and families, wanted a piece, or a bigger piece, of the largess.

The story of how the FBI ended up investigating college basketball began not with sports but with financial fraud. In May 2016, the SEC—not the

Southeastern Conference, but the Securities and Exchange Commission—charged Louis Martin "Marty" Blazer III, a Pittsburgh financial adviser, with wire fraud. Blazer had founded Blazer Capital Management as a concierge firm targeting professional athletes and other high-net-worth individuals. But instead of managing their money responsibly, he had siphoned approximately $2.35 million from client accounts to invest in movie and music projects and finance Ponzi-style payments to other clients.

When SEC examiners uncovered the unauthorized withdrawals and asked Blazer to explain them, he lied and produced falsified documents attempting to hide his misconduct. He was caught, charged, and faced a potentially lengthy prison sentence. Blazer had embezzled from the very athletes he was supposed to protect, using their money to fund his own failed entertainment ventures.

But during the SEC investigation, Blazer made an admission that piqued the interest of federal prosecutors. He had a years-long history of paying college athletes while they were still in school to induce them to retain him as their financial adviser when they turned professional. This admission opened a door to a much larger investigation. Faced with charges that could have resulted in nearly 70 years in prison, Blazer chose another option: he became a cooperating witness for the FBI.

"I was an insider who spoke the language," Blazer told author Guy Lawson for his book, "*Hot Dog Money: Inside the Biggest Scandal in the History of College Sports*. Blazer knew how the underground economy worked because he had been part of it. He understood the networks of financial advisers, agents, coaches, and shoe company representatives who steered players toward particular schools and particular business relationships through cash payments and other inducements.

The FBI assigned the case to Special Agent Scott Carpenter, and together they launched what would become known internally as Operation Ballerz. Blazer would wear a wire, allow his phone to be tapped, and help undercover FBI agents pose as investors who wanted to fund a scheme to sign elite basketball players as clients. For nearly two years, from late 2014 through 2017, Blazer played his role while the FBI documented the methodical corruption that characterized elite college basketball recruiting.

According to court documents, Blazer's cooperation led to payments being made to or on behalf of assistant basketball coaches at Auburn, Alabama, Arizona, Louisville, Creighton, TCU, USC, and Oklahoma State. He also made payments to third parties to benefit athletes who attended other universities. In testimony during subsequent trials, Blazer described sending Western Union funds to players' girlfriends, friends, or family members who would pick up the cash while he confirmed receipt. The amounts varied, but his admitted payments to college athletes totaled at least $70,000 spread across schools including Pittsburgh, Northwestern, Alabama, North Carolina, Michigan, Notre Dame, and Penn State.

In one particularly striking example from his testimony, Blazer described how, in 2008-09, an unnamed Penn State assistant coach, concerned that a star defensive end was considering declaring for the NFL draft, connected Blazer with the player's father. The coach wanted the player to stay for another season and believed that money would help eliminate some of the financial motivations to turn pro. Blazer gave the father a $10,000 check. The player entered the draft anyway, was selected eleventh overall by the Buffalo Bills, and his father paid back the $10,000. The eleventh pick in 2009 was Aaron Maybin. Later, the coach was identified as Larry Johnson Sr., who vehemently denied the allegation.

Sometime in fall 2016, a mutual friend introduced Blazer to Rashan Michel, a former NBA and SEC referee who had left his officiating role in 2001 to open Thompson Bespoke Clothiers in Atlanta. This high-end custom suit business catered to professional athletes. Michel became a crucial connection, introducing Blazer to college coaches who might be interested in receiving cash to steer prospects toward specific financial advisers and schools.

On November 29, 2016, Blazer attended a meeting that would become central to the entire investigation. Chuck Person, Auburn's associate head coach and a former NBA star who had played fourteen seasons professionally, met with Blazer and Michel at a restaurant near Auburn's campus. Blazer wore a miniature video camera and recording device while FBI agents monitored the meeting from nearby.

During that meeting, Person agreed to accept $50,000 in bribe payments from Blazer. According to the complaint, Michel explained that Person would receive $5,000 in cash that day, followed by three additional payments of $15,000. Person signed a promissory note. Then he asked if he could receive $10,000 up front instead of $5,000. Blazer agreed to wire him an additional $5,000. Michel sent Blazer the information needed to wire money to Person's bank account, and the money was transferred the next day.

The scheme was simple. Person would steer Auburn players who were headed to the NBA toward Blazer and his associates as their financial advisers and business managers. In return, Person would receive cash payments. When bragging about his connections and ability to deliver players, Person said on one recording: "When you've coached Kobe Bryant, played with Phil Jackson, it goes a long way."

Less than two weeks later, on December 12, 2016, Person, Michel, and Blazer met with an unidentified Auburn player at a Manhattan hotel room. Auburn was in New York to play Boston College in the Under Armour Reunion at Madison Square Garden. The meeting was about steering the player toward Blazer's services when he eventually reached the NBA.

But Person wasn't just taking bribes to steer players toward financial advisers. He was also using that money to pay the families of recruits. According to the FBI, Person paid nearly $20,000 to the families of two active Auburn players, essentially laundering bribe money into recruiting inducements.

Throughout 2017, the FBI's investigation expanded. In February 2017, Munish Sood and Christian Dawkins began funneling money to other coaches. Dawkins was an aspiring business manager and agent who worked for ASM Sports, an agency headed by Andy Miller. Sood was a financial adviser connected to the network of people seeking access to elite basketball talent.

Emanuel "Book" Richardson, an Arizona assistant since 2009, met with Dawkins and others in June 2017. According to the charges, Richardson agreed to accept a $5,000 bribe to steer Arizona players to Dawkins' sports management company. He was also charged with accepting an additional $15,000 in bribes, with plans to use that money to pay at least one recruit to commit to Arizona.

In one taped conversation that was played during the trial, Richardson told an undercover FBI agent about his approach to managing relationships between players and potential business managers: "I used to let kids talk to three or four guys, but I was like, why would you do that? You know that's like taking a kid to a BMW dealer, a Benz dealer, and a Porsche dealer. They like them all. You have to pick for them."

> The statement revealed coaches treating elite players as commodities to be sold to the highest bidder rather than young people whose interests they were supposed to protect.

Lamont Evans at Oklahoma State was accused of taking at least $22,000 in bribes from two financial advisers, one of whom was Blazer working as an FBI informant. The alleged bribes were offered over a five-year period that included Evans' former tenure as an assistant at South Carolina, suggesting the corruption followed him from program to program.

Tony Bland at USC was charged with accepting $4,100 in cash to influence players toward certain financial advisers and business managers. While the amount was smaller than that received by other coaches, the principle was the same. Selling access to players in exchange for personal financial gain was a familiar practice.

But the FBI investigation revealed something even more problematic than individual coaches taking bribes. It exposed the central role of major athletics apparel companies, particularly Adidas, in funding schemes designed to steer top recruits toward schools sponsored by those companies.

The investigation documented how James Gatto, Adidas' director of global sports marketing, along with Adidas consultants Merl Code and T.J. Gassnola, worked together to funnel payments to the families of elite recruits. The goal was to create player loyalty to Adidas that would carry over from college into professional careers, effectively turning college programs into farm systems for the shoe company's marketing strategies.

The most high-profile case involved Brian Bowen II, a five-star recruit whose surprise commitment to Louisville in June 2017 had raised eyebrows throughout recruiting circles. I had watched "Tugs" play while in high school at La Lumiere Prep in LaPorte, IN and in Nike EYBL tournaments. Speaking as a former grassroots coach, he was one of the best players I'd ever seen on the circuit. According to FBI evidence presented at trial, Adidas agreed to pay Bowen's family $100,000 to secure his commitment to Louisville, a school with a lucrative Adidas sponsorship deal.

Court documents and wiretapped phone calls revealed how these payments were negotiated and disguised. In one intercepted call, Gatto asked Code whether payments to a Miami recruit could be pushed to 2018, as he wasn't sure he could make it work in 2017. "I just don't know if I can do anything in '17, that's what I'm saying," Gatto told Code. They discussed whether the recruit's family might accept $100,000, which is what they allegedly had paid Bowen's family for Louisville. Code said he wasn't sure if the family would take much less, but he'd try to reduce the offer by $25,000. Code warned Gatto that if they waited until January 2018, the recruit's asking price might be $200,000.

These conversations revealed a marketplace in which families negotiated prices for their sons' commitments, much like agents negotiating contracts. The only difference was that everything was happening underground, in violation of NCAA rules and, as federal prosecutors argued, in violation of federal fraud statutes.

The investigation implicated numerous programs beyond those with coaches who were arrested. Louisville wasn't named directly in initial court documents, but references to a "public research university located in Kentucky" with an Adidas sponsorship quickly confirmed the Cardinals' involvement. The school was already facing NCAA sanctions from a previous sex scandal involving an escort service for recruits, and this FBI investigation would ultimately seal the fate of Hall of Fame coach Rick Pitino.

Let's reflect on the details. The Katina Powell allegations, first published in her 2015 book *Breaking Cardinal Rules*, had described a culture of recruiting corruption that seemed to belong to a different era.

Powell, a self-described escort service provider, alleged that former Louisville basketball staff member Andre McGee had paid her thousands of dollars between 2010 and 2014 to arrange parties with strippers and prostitutes for recruits and players. The parties allegedly occurred in Billy Minardi Hall, the on-campus dormitory that housed basketball players. McGee allegedly paid dancers to have sex with recruits in an effort to secure their commitments to Louisville.

The allegations were lurid and specific. Powell provided photographs, receipts, and detailed accounts of dozens of parties. She named specific recruits who had attended. She described payments, locations, and participants with such precision that dismissal was difficult.

Louisville's response followed a familiar pattern. The university denied institutional knowledge of the activities. Head coach Rick Pitino denied any involvement or awareness of it. The basketball program was placed under NCAA investigation while continuing to compete at the highest levels. Louisville won the 2013 national championship, defeating Michigan in Atlanta, even as the NCAA investigated whether the program had committed major violations.

In June 2017, the NCAA announced its findings. The violations were severe: failure to monitor, lack of institutional control, and impermissible benefits involving sex acts provided to recruits. The penalties included vacating all wins from the 2010-11 through 2014-15 seasons, a self-imposed postseason ban, scholarship reductions, and recruiting restrictions.

Most significantly, Louisville was required to vacate its 2013 national championship. The banner came down. The championship trophy was returned. Louisville became the first Division I men's basketball program to have a national championship vacated by the NCAA.

The escort scandal would have been devastating enough on its own. But it was merely the first act of Louisville's destruction. The FBI investigation revealed Adidas' payments to Brian Bowen's family, leading to Pitino's termination in October 2017 and additional NCAA penalties. A program that had been among college basketball's elite found itself facing consecutive major infractions cases, each more damaging than the last.

Pitino's fall was particularly stark. He had won national championships at two schools, Kentucky and Louisville, establishing himself as one of the greatest coaches in college basketball history. He was a master recruiter, a brilliant tactician, and a larger-than-life personality who had built Louisville into a national power. His annual compensation exceeded $7 million.

Yet Pitino's programs at multiple schools had faced major NCAA investigations. Kentucky vacated its 1996 Final Four appearance due to violations that occurred during his tenure. UMass vacated its 1996 Final Four appearance after Marcus Camby was found to have received improper benefits. And now Louisville had vacated a national championship and been engulfed in dual scandals.

The pattern suggested either extraordinarily bad luck in hiring assistant coaches who violated rules without the head coach's knowledge or a culture of permissiveness that enabled violations while maintaining plausible deniability at the top. Pitino maintained his innocence, insisting he did not know of either the escort parties or the Adidas payments. The NCAA and Louisville's board of trustees concluded otherwise, or at least concluded that he bore responsibility for failing to monitor his program effectively.

What struck me about the Louisville situation was how easily the escort scandal had been absorbed. A program provided prostitutes to teenage recruits for years, violated fundamental principles of appropriate conduct with minors, and the consequence was vacated wins and a self-imposed postseason ban. Pitino remained employed for two years after the allegations became public, continuing to coach and recruit while the NCAA investigated.

Only when the FBI arrests created undeniable evidence of additional violations did Louisville finally act. And even then, Pitino received millions in a settlement rather than being terminated for cause. The financial consequences for the coach at the center of two major scandals were minimal.

Why do I provide all of this detail? This was the unfortunate reality of the NCAA enforcement and infractions system that critics had long noted. Programs could absorb penalties, vacate wins, and continue competing at the highest levels. Coaches who presided over violations could deny knowledge, accept settlements, and find new positions. The system seemed to punish nobody with sufficient severity to deter future misconduct. Still, I recognize that whether these outcomes reflected appropriate proportionality or a serious failure of deterrence is a question that reasonable people answer differently.

Louisville's basketball program eventually recovered under Chris Mack and then Kenny Payne, though it remained under the cloud of its past violations. The vacated championship banner left a gap in the rafters at the KFC Yum! Center, a reminder of what had been lost. But the competitive enterprise continued, generating revenue and attention as if the scandals had never occurred.

On November 8, 2017, the Southern District unsealed new indictments that directly linked Pitino to the alleged scheme to pay Bowen's family. Documents alleged that Pitino met with Christian Dawkins in July 2017, who asked Pitino to call Gatto and request the $100,000 payment to Bowen's family. Pitino reportedly agreed to make the call. FBI phone records indicated that Pitino called Gatto three times before Bowen committed to Louisville.

On April 10, 2018, Southern District prosecutors added criminal counts specifically naming Kansas and North Carolina State, as well as Louisville and Miami. The Kansas allegations involved payments to secure commitments from recruits Silvio De Sousa and Billy Preston. The NC State allegations centered on payments to Dennis Smith Jr.'s family.

Prior to the additional counts in the superseding indictment, on February 23, 2018, Yahoo! Sports published a report that expanded the scope of the scandal dramatically. Based on hundreds of pages of documents obtained by the FBI from two agents and an agency implicated in the investigation, the Yahoo report named more than a dozen additional schools and over twenty-five current and former players as potentially implicated. This brought major programs like Duke, Kentucky, Michigan State, and North Carolina into the conversation, suggesting the corruption extended far beyond the schools whose coaches had been arrested.

The investigation also exposed how apparel companies' influence operated through multiple channels. I'd seen it on a much smaller scale. Adidas, Nike, and Under Armour each funded grassroots basketball circuits, the web of AAU teams and summer tournaments where elite players develop and showcase their talents. These companies poured money into these circuits and then invested heavily in college programs themselves through sponsorship deals worth hundreds of millions over decades.

Multiple media reports indicated that Nike's Elite Youth Basketball League (EYBL) was served with a subpoena by federal investigators, suggesting that alleged corruption extended beyond Adidas. However, Nike was never formally charged. The sneaker companies created complex webs of relationships and financial dependencies through direct sponsorship of college programs, funding grassroots basketball circuits that served as feeder systems, and employing former college coaches and players as consultants and liaisons. This infrastructure facilitated the corruption schemes the FBI documented.

As the legal cases proceeded through the criminal justice system, the outcomes varied. In late 2017, Blazer pleaded guilty to securities fraud, wire fraud, aggravated identity theft, and making false statements and documents. The combined charges could have carried a 67-year sentence. But because he cooperated in the investigation, Blazer received an extraordinarily lenient sentence in February 2020. He was sentenced to one year of probation and ordered to pay approximately $1.56 million in restitution to the clients he defrauded. He avoided prison entirely.

Blazer had testified in multiple trials, and his cooperation had helped secure ten convictions. He was also immensely helpful to the NCAA. In a letter to the sentencing judge, Jon Duncan noted that Blazer had "numerous interviews" with NCAA enforcement staff and that "the information provided by Mr. Blazer materially assisted the NCAA and member institutions in investigating potential rules violations."

Tragically, Marty Blazer died in January 2024 at age fifty-three of natural causes at his home near Pittsburgh. He had hoped his role in the scandal would be turned into a movie. Indeed, he claimed George Clooney had purchased the rights to the story. But he never got to see that project come to fruition.

In 2019, all four Division I assistants were sentenced after pleading guilty to reduced charges. Emanuel Richardson and Lamont Evans were each sentenced to three months in prison. Tony Bland and Chuck Person received probation and community service, avoiding incarceration entirely.

Christian Dawkins, Merl Code, and James Gatto faced more serious consequences. In October 2018, Dawkins, Code, and Gatto were convicted of paying bribes to parents and handlers of high-profile recruits to steer players to schools sponsored by Adidas. In a separate trial in May 2019, Dawkins and Code were convicted of having bribed assistant coaches to steer their players toward Dawkins' agency. They appealed those convictions.

But something haunted me as the legal proceedings concluded and the long-term aftermath unfolded. Despite all this evidence, despite federal prosecutors and FBI agents exposing widespread corruption with tools we could never deploy, nothing materially changed in college basketball.

Consider where the major figures ended up. Rick Pitino was fired from Louisville amid scandal in October 2017. Yet by 2023, he was coaching at St. John's, which was predicted to make a run to the Final Four. The shame, apparently, had an expiration date.

Sean Miller left Arizona in 2021 after wiretapped conversations suggested he knew about payments to players, though he consistently denied wrong-doing and was never charged criminally or sanctioned by the NCAA. He's now the head coach at Texas, earning millions annually.

The NCAA suspended Bruce Pearl at Auburn for two games for failing to monitor Chuck Person. That was the extent of his punishment. Auburn made the Final Four in 2019, and Pearl remained one of the highest-paid coaches in college basketball with a contract that could pay him over $50 million, until he retired before the 2025-26 season.

Bill Self at Kansas received a two-game suspension from the NCAA but maintains a lifetime contract worth tens of millions of dollars. Kansas won the national championship in 2022, during the period when the school was supposedly under NCAA investigation for Level I violations.

Will Wade left LSU in 2022 and was immediately hired by McNeese State, taking the program to back-to-back NCAA tournaments and earning national coach of the year honors. He then went to NC State, before returning to LSU on a seven-year deal. This despite being captured on FBI wiretaps discussing a "strong-ass offer" for a recruit, a phrase that became infamous in college basketball circles.

The system punished nobody permanently. Coaches served brief suspensions or probationary periods and then returned to lucrative positions at other schools. Programs faced scholarship reductions and probation but continued to operate and compete. The underground economy the FBI exposed continued to function because the structural incentives that created it remained unchanged.

And the ultimate absurdity that I can't stop thinking about is that many of the behaviors that led to federal prosecutions and NCAA investigations are now broadly legal under current NCAA policies and the *House* settlement framework. Player compensation? Legal through NIL deals and revenue sharing. Agents working with high school players? Legal through certified agent programs. Shoe companies funneling money to recruits through marketing deals? Essentially legal through NIL collectives funded by apparel sponsors.

> The underground economy that justified federal prosecution has become the above-ground economy we now embrace. We criminalized conduct in 2017 that we celebrate as entrepreneurial in 2026.

What did the FBI investigation actually prove? Not that college basketball was corrupt in ways we didn't know. Everyone involved in the sport knew payments were happening. The FBI simply documented, through wiretaps and financial records, what had been whispered about for decades.

The investigation revealed the extent to which the gap between the formal framework and the economic realities of elite basketball had created an environment where enforcement alone could not address structural pressures. When select players help generate tens of millions in value for schools, conferences, coaches, and apparel companies while receiving only scholarships in return, underground markets can develop. Coaches become middlemen connecting players to money. Financial advisers become recruiters. Shoe companies become the actual funders of talent acquisition.

And no one in the give-me-my-latest-college-sports-fix environment cares. Not then, and certainly not now.

The FBI documented the system as it actually functioned beneath the surface of the rules we maintained. The gap between the formal regulatory framework and the operational reality had grown so large that federal prosecutors could build criminal cases inside it. And the response wasn't to change the system. The response was to wait until courts and legislatures forced change, and then to claim credit for reluctantly accepting what market forces and legal pressure had made inevitable.

Sitting in my office watching that September 2017 press conference, I felt a mix of vindication and despair. Vindication because the FBI had documented what we'd been unable to prove through traditional enforcement, some of which I had seen with my own eyes as a youth coach. Despair because I knew even this may not change the fundamentals of the game within the game.

As Sweeney said at the opening press conference, "[the] arrests should serve as a warning to anyone considering this kind of business in college athletics: we have your playbook." Indeed, the FBI had college basketball's playbook. They knew every scheme, every payment, every corrupt relationship. They had wiretaps, financial records, and cooperating witnesses. They secured convictions of coaches, agents, and shoe company executives.

And none of it mattered.

Because the problem wasn't individual bad actors. The problem was a system built on an errant assumption about amateurism that anyone with eyes could now see through. College basketball operated with the intensity, financial stakes, and organizational complexity of a professional enterprise, while maintaining a compensation structure rooted in the amateur model. That contradiction was what the FBI investigation ultimately documented and exposed as reality.

The subsequent Rice Commission would try to reform the system. The Independent Accountability Resolution Process would promise better enforcement. Independent board members would provide external oversight.

But as I reflect, I think deep down, maybe I knew how this story would end. Not with meaningful reform but with the inevitable evolution toward Collegiate Capitalism, where we would finally acknowledge what September 26, 2017, had made undeniable: college basketball, like college football, was becoming a professional enterprise that could no longer suggest otherwise.

The FBI arrested college basketball that day. Perhaps they didn't realize they were arresting a system already in distress due to internal contradictions. The question wasn't whether it would change. The question was how long we could maintain the pretense before reality forced our hand.

Chapter 17
College Basketball Corruption
Secretary of State Solutions

The morning after the FBI arrests, I walked into a crisis meeting with President Emmert and our senior leadership team. Everyone was asking the same question: What do we do now?

We could launch our own enforcement investigation, but that felt inadequate given what the FBI had just exposed. We could issue statements and wait for the criminal proceedings to conclude, but that felt passive. We needed a response that would demonstrate we took the crisis seriously while also creating space for meaningful examination of the structural problems the FBI had revealed.

We needed an *independent* commission. Not an internal task force. Not an NCAA committee. An independent commission. Something that signaled gravitas and autonomy. I recall Emmert making clear it must be led by someone whose credibility was unimpeachable.

Within days, we had our answer. Former Secretary of State Condoleezza Rice agreed to chair an independent Commission on College Basketball tasked with examining the fundamental structures exposed by the FBI investigation and recommending comprehensive reforms.

The appointment made perfect sense. Rice had served as the National Security Advisor and Secretary of State under President George W. Bush, bringing extensive government experience at the highest levels. As a former Stanford provost, she understood academic institutions and the balance between athletics and education. She chaired the College Football Playoff selection committee, demonstrating sports knowledge and judgment. She had personal connections to basketball through her family's involvement in grassroots programs. If anyone could lend credibility to reform efforts while navigating the political complexities of NCAA governance, it was Condoleezza Rice.

As we assembled the commission, I was hopeful that we would not create an elaborate exercise in institutional theater. Blue-ribbon panels had a long history in college athletics of producing impressive reports that gathered dust on shelves while underlying problems persisted. Would this be different? Could it be different when the commission's mandate was to save and fix what some believed was an irreparably broken system, rather than structurally transform it? This limitation was not a flaw in the commission members' philosophies, who were eager for radical change; rather, it was a product of the legal environment the NCAA was navigating at the time.

With the backing of the Board of Governors, the commission assembled was deliberately formidable, designed to bring diverse perspectives and unimpeachable credentials. Mary Sue Coleman, President of the Association of American Universities and former president of Michigan and Iowa, would provide an academic leadership perspective. Retired General Martin Dempsey, Chairman of USA Basketball, brought military leadership and basketball governance experience. Jeremy Foley, former Florida Athletics Director, understood the operational realities of major college athletics. Grant Hill, Naismith Hall of Famer, Atlanta Hawks co-owner, and broadcaster, possessed intimate knowledge of the student-athlete experience while maintaining business sophistication beyond his playing achievements. Notre Dame President Rev. John Jenkins provided the voice of a major private university navigating athletics and academic mission. Mike Montgomery, retired college basketball coach, knew the recruiting trenches and coaching culture. David Robinson, a two-time Naismith Hall of Famer and Naval Academy graduate, combined elite basketball experience with military discipline. Kathryn Ruemmler, former White House Counsel under President Obama, brought legal expertise, governmental experience, operational excellence, and wise counsel. Ohio State Athletics Director Gene Smith represented current athletics administrators as the universally recognized leader among ADs. Georgetown coach John Thompson III, son of legendary coach John Thompson Jr., served as chair of the National Association of Basketball Coaches board.

President Emmert and the President of the Georgia Institute of Technology, Board of Governors Chair Bud Peterson, were ex officio members but were excluded from executive sessions when proposals were being formulated. This separation was deliberate, designed to preserve independence and credibility.

The message, I believed, was unmistakable. We would bring the biggest guns available to tackle corruption in college basketball. The commission represented academic leadership, military leadership, athletics administration, coaching experience, player perspective, legal expertise, and business acumen. If this group couldn't develop sound solutions, perhaps no group could.

The Commission was assigned three primary duties. First, examining the relationship of the NCAA national office, member institutions, student-athletes, and coaches with outside entities including agents, financial advisers, and apparel companies. Second, reviewing the NCAA's relationship with the NBA and the challenging effect of the NBA's one-and-done rule on college basketball. And third, creating the proper relationship between universities, colleges, and the NCAA national office to promote transparency and accountability.

Yet as the Commission commenced work, members were often reminded that college sports is a game of power brokers including athletics directors, sports network hosts, coaches, players, agents, commercial interests, attorneys, compliance personnel, conference commissioners, and others. This interplay creates winners and losers and sometimes invites government intervention, like the prosecutions that prompted its creation. Accordingly, during meetings establishing the Commission, Secretary Rice and members were encouraged to aim beyond the status quo and to offer bold proposals to address the problems highlighted by the criminal cases.

The commission's work process was extensive and deliberate. They consulted with stakeholders across college basketball, from players to coaches to administrators to agents to the NBA to apparel companies. They operated for approximately six months, conducting interviews, reviewing evidence from the FBI investigation, and analyzing structural issues that had enabled widespread corruption.

Importantly, the commission spent the vast majority of its time in executive sessions, away from NCAA influence, maintaining relative secrecy until its final reveal. This independence was crucial for credibility. The group's deliberations were intentionally conducted without direct NCAA control or involvement, though the mandate came from us, and recommendations would require our approval for implementation.

On April 25, 2018, Secretary Rice released the commission's comprehensive sixty-page report. The media were eager to get their hands on it and hear from the members. University presidents, especially those who attended the 2011 retreat, were acutely attuned to the recommendations. The anticipation was palpable. Many were asking whether the commission would propose genuinely transformative change, or would this be another exercise in preservation?

"The members of this commission come from a wide variety of backgrounds," Rice began, "but the one thing that they share in common is that they believe the college basketball enterprise is worth saving."

Many thought that sentence was revealing. The commission was tasked with saving the existing system, not fundamentally transforming it. Embracing reform within boundaries rather than revolutionary reimagining.

Rice continued, describing the crisis as "first and foremost a problem of failed accountability and lax responsibility." The commission had identified what Rice called "a toxic mix of perverse incentives to cheat," with responsibility going all the way up to university presidents. The overarching message was clear. One must take responsibility for the problems one has created.

The recommendations fell into several key categories: some bold, some cautious, some within NCAA control, and some requiring external cooperation that might never materialize.

Ending One-and-Done was the commission's first and most prominent recommendation. The commission called for the NBA and NBPA to eliminate the rule requiring players to be at least 19 years old and out of high school for at least 1 year to be draft-eligible. The one-and-done rule, implemented in 2006 despite the success of straight-out-of-high-school stars like LeBron James, Kobe Bryant, Dwight Howard, and Kevin Garnett, had created, many believed, artificial incentives for corruption by forcing elite players into college basketball for brief periods, even when they might prefer to go directly to professional careers.

But the commission went further with an implicit threat. If the NBA and NBPA refused to change their rules in time for the next basketball season, the commission said it would reconvene and consider other options for the NCAA, including making freshmen ineligible or locking scholarships for three or four years if recipients left programs after a single season. "One-and-done has to go one way or another," Rice told the Associated Press.

The threat was real, but harbored unfair consequences. Making freshmen ineligible would punish players for the NBA's policy decisions. It would also damage the NCAA's product by preventing fans from watching young elite talent. The commission was essentially threatening to hold college basketball hostage to force the NBA's hand, a strategy that ultimately would not work.

Agent Certification and Access represented one of the commission's better proposals. The recommendation called for allowing certified agents to work with high school and college players much earlier in the process with proper oversight and regulation, replacing the underground network of handlers and street agents with transparent, regulated systems. "Players should be able to receive meaningful assessment of professional prospects earlier with assistance from certified agents," Rice explained in the report. "If NCAA rules do not allow them to receive that advice openly, they will often seek it illicitly."

This recognition that prohibition creates black markets was refreshing. If players needed professional advice on NBA prospects and financial management, why force them to seek it through underground channels? Certifying agents and allowing regulated contact could bring that activity into the open, where it could be monitored.

Enhanced Penalties aimed at increasing deterrence through harsher consequences. Serious Level I rules violations would be punishable with up to five-year postseason bans and forfeiture of all postseason revenue for the duration of the ban. Such penalties could cost tens of millions to major conference schools. The commission also called for lifetime bans for coaches who committed serious violations, replacing the show-cause penalty system that allowed banned coaches to eventually return to college athletics.

The theory was straightforward. If consequences were severe enough, rational actors would choose compliance over rule-breaking. But this assumed the corruption was driven by individual bad actors rather than structural incentives. As long as the fundamental contradictions in the system persisted, severe penalties would simply drive corruption further underground rather than eliminating it.

Independent Enforcement became one of the commission's signature recommendations, ultimately leading to the creation of the Independent Accountability Resolution Process. The commission recommended establishing an independent body to investigate NCAA violations, removing enforcement from direct NCAA control to increase independence, credibility, and effectiveness. The idea was that independent investigators and adjudicators would be more trusted than NCAA staff who might be perceived as protecting the organization's interests.

This reform would prove to be among the commission's most spectacular failures, but in April 2018, it seemed promising. Perhaps independent oversight could restore confidence in enforcement processes that had been criticized for inconsistency and ineffectiveness.

Grassroots Basketball Reform targeted one of the root causes of corruption. The commission proposed that the NCAA take short and long-term actions to reform non-scholastic basketball in partnership with the NBA and USA Basketball, disassociating itself and member institutions from aspects of non-scholastic basketball where transparency and ethical behavior couldn't be assured. It is time that the money flowing from apparel companies and other third parties into non-scholastic basketball be disclosed and accounted for in order to address the corruption we see in the sport, Rice offered.

The commission recognized that corruption in college basketball had its roots in youth basketball, which they described as "ungoverned space." There were good programs, but too many condoned illicit behaviors. The recommendation called for rigorous criteria for certifying non-scholastic basketball events that coaches could attend, with owners, event operators, sponsors, and coaches required to agree to financial transparency for certification.

Having personally lived in this space for many years, I was excited to see these proposals. But the commission's power to reform grassroots basketball was limited. These were private enterprises operating in commercial markets largely beyond NCAA jurisdiction. Without regulatory authority to compel disclosure or cooperation, transparency recommendations remained aspirational.

Return-to-School Provisions allowed players who went undrafted in the NBA to return to college basketball, providing safety nets that might reduce incentives for corruption. This was among the commission's most successful recommendations, ultimately implemented with relatively few complications.

Apparel Company Transparency called for greater financial disclosure from shoe and apparel companies whose sponsorship deals and grassroots basketball funding had been central to FBI corruption schemes. However, the commission acknowledged the NCAA's questionable power to enforce such requirements. Adidas, Nike, and Under Armour were private companies pursuing commercial interests. They had no obligation to disclose their financial relationships with grassroots programs, coaches, or athletes unless compelled to do so by law or contract.

But there was one thing the commission did not recommend, which it explicitly rejected despite this being the elephant in the room. Any proposal to pay athletes or allow them to profit from their names, images, and likenesses was not touched. The commission's report stated plainly: "Paying modest salaries to Division I basketball players will not address the particular corruption the Commission confronts, nor will providing student-athletes a modest post-graduation trust fund based on licensing of names, images and likeness."

The report continued that such payments would not reduce the corrupt incentives of third parties who pay in the hope of securing future professional relationships. Only a professional model would

> potentially offset corruption, but the commission was charged with revitalizing the college model, not replacing it.
>
> "Our focus has been to strengthen the collegiate model," Rice emphasized at the press conference, "not to move toward one that brings aspects of professionalism into the game."

This was the biggest challenge in the entire exercise, given the legal environment. The commission acknowledged extensive corruption driven by commercial forces, while declining to address the commercial inequities that created the incentives for corruption. They recognized that elite players generated enormous value but noted that they should continue to receive only scholarships. They documented how financial incentives drove coaches, agents, and shoe companies to break rules, but proposed no mechanism to address those incentives beyond enhanced punishment.

The commission had correctly diagnosed the disease but declined to prescribe the cure, perhaps because the cure would require admitting that college basketball was already a commercial enterprise in which the primary producers deserved compensation. And that would have assuredly impacted the federal court litigation and NCAA policymaking underway at the time.

Immediately upon release of the report, the NCAA Board of Governors and Division I Board of Directors held a joint meeting at NCAA headquarters. Secretary Rice presented the commission's conclusions and recommendations in person. President Emmert and I walked the Boards through their options, explaining which recommendations were within our control and which required third party cooperation or membership approval.

The discussion was robust. Some board members questioned whether we had the authority to implement specific reforms. Others worried about unintended consequences. Still others pushed for even more aggressive action. But ultimately, the Boards recognized they needed to present a united front. The FBI investigation had exposed college basketball to devastating criticism. Rejecting the Rice Commission's recommendations would compound the reputational damage.

Accordingly, the Boards unanimously endorsed all the commission's recommendations. Every single one. It was a powerful statement of institutional commitment to reform.

However, endorsement differed significantly from implementation. Unanimous approval in a boardroom didn't automatically translate to meaningful change in practice. Actual operationalization would vary considerably across different recommendations, with some implemented quickly and others languishing or failing entirely.

We moved relatively quickly on recommendations within our direct control. We modified the agent access rules to allow certain players to work with certified agents while maintaining eligibility under specific circumstances. Access could now begin in high school rather than after college enrollment, though agents were prohibited from dispersing payments or other benefits. Players were given more opportunities to test the professional waters through pre-draft processes, while maintaining the option to return to college if they went undrafted. However, various restrictions were in place to preserve competitive balance.

We began working on enhanced penalty structures, though implementation proved complex and time-consuming. Defining Level I violations, establishing procedures for postseason bans and revenue forfeiture, and creating lifetime-ban mechanisms for coaches required extensive rule-writing and approval processes through various NCAA committees and councils.

We implemented return-to-school provisions relatively smoothly, creating pathways for undrafted players to reclaim college eligibility. This reform was among the commission's clearest successes.

But many of the commission's most significant recommendations required outsider support that proved impossible to secure. The NBA's response to ending one-and-done was cautious and deliberate. The league and the NBPA changed the draft eligibility rule in 2006, with the stated intent of getting NBA personnel out of high school gyms. Team scouts and executives had been accused of pressuring high school players, creating uncomfortable dynamics with teenage athletes.

Despite the commission's arguments that one-and-done created corruption incentives in college basketball, the NBA was reluctant to quickly reverse the policy. The informal understanding was that, following the termination of the league's collective bargaining agreement with the National Basketball Players Association at the end of the 2023-24 season, the elimination of the age limit could be expected.

But as of 2025, high school players still cannot declare directly for the NBA draft. The fundamental structural problem the commission identified, of having elite players being forced into unpaid college programs when they might prefer professional careers, remains unresolved. The NBA and NBPA have their own interests and priorities that don't necessarily align with NCAA preferences. College basketball's corruption problems aren't the NBA's responsibility to solve.

As much as we lobbied for the NBA to abolish its age minimum, such a change would likely have a more minor impact on illicit payments than many hoped. If high school players could go directly to the NBA, colleges' competition for elite talent would intensify, potentially increasing schools' need to offer financial inducements to compete with professional opportunities.

This reality put enormous pressure on the system and, in some respects, can be credited with helping create the "compensation system" that now exists in college sports. Without the option to go pro from high school, basketball athletes are becoming pro in college through NIL deals and revenue-sharing arrangements.

Our attempts to require financial transparency and accountability from shoe companies and grassroots basketball event operators remained similarly elusive. These entities operated in commercial markets largely beyond our jurisdiction. We had no regulatory power to compel disclosure. Sponsorship contracts between universities and apparel companies were private commercial agreements. Funding relationships between shoe companies and grassroots programs were private business arrangements.

We could refuse to certify events that don't provide transparency, preventing coaches from attending them for recruiting purposes. But this created its own problems. If we decertified major grassroots tournaments where the best players competed, we would push recruiting activity even further underground. Coaches would find ways to evaluate players through other channels. The corruption would simply migrate rather than disappear.

One Rice Commission recommendation deserves special attention. It would prove crucial to the Association in a time of crisis. The appointment of independent members to the NCAA Board of Governors was a critical advancement to our governance structure.

Indeed, adding independent board members to the NCAA's highest governing body was not merely administrative housekeeping. It represented a calculated attempt to inject unconstrained accountability into a system that had repeatedly failed to police itself effectively. The rationale was elegantly straightforward yet profoundly revolutionary for an organization built on shared governance.

Inherent conflicts of interest had plagued traditional NCAA governance. No matter how well intentioned, board members representing universities and conferences faced pressure to protect their institutions' competitive and financial interests rather than prioritizing the broader welfare of student-athletes and college sports generally. When enforcement decisions or policy reforms might disadvantage their own conferences or schools, board members had strong incentives to oppose such measures regardless of merit.

Independent directors would provide objective oversight, free from the parochial concerns that had compromised decision-making for decades. They could evaluate proposals based on what was best for college athletics rather than what was best for particular conferences or institutions. They could support necessary but politically difficult reforms without facing pressure from athletics directors, coaches, or alumni.

The commission was firm in its recommendation that strong, objective, and independent leadership must be brought to the table at the most senior level of governance to help restore trust in college sports. This wasn't just about optics or public relations. It was about shifting the power dynamics within NCAA governance to enable changes that the existing structure had proven incapable of producing.

Following the Rice Commission's recommendation and the Board's unanimous endorsement, we proceeded to implement this historic change. In

2019, we announced the selection of five distinguished independent members to the Board of Governors, each bringing diverse expertise and unimpeachable character to the Board. As the primary liaison for the governance system, I engaged well-known connector Billy Dexter and his partner, Lyndon Taylor, at Heidrick & Struggles to filter and vet more than 250 candidates, receiving 150 nominations directly from members and the public. President Emmert personally reached out to the finalists to secure their commitments to serve. Every single one of them embraced the role with excitement, recognizing the significance of the moment.

The five individuals selected represented extraordinary accomplishments across business, government, medicine, academia, and athletics. Kenneth Chenault, chairman and managing director of General Catalyst and former chairman and CEO of American Express, brought more than sixteen years of experience leading a global financial services company through complex challenges, including the 2008 financial crisis. He was also one of the most prominent Black executives in corporate America and provided an essential perspective on racial equity issues that permeated college athletics. Mary Sue Coleman, president of the Association of American Universities and former president of Michigan and Iowa, understood firsthand the tensions between big-time athletics and academic values and had served on the Rice Commission itself, helping ensure continuity between reform recommendations and their implementation. Grant Hill, the former Duke basketball star, two-time national champion, and nineteen-year NBA veteran, brought credibility with current players that no administrator could match, along with business experience as co-owner of the Atlanta Hawks and media sophistication as a broadcaster for CBS and Turner Sports. He, too, had served on the Rice Commission. Denis McDonough, former chief of staff to President Obama, brought governmental crisis management experience at the highest levels, an ability to build coalitions across competing interests, and the bonus of having been a college football standout for the Division III St. John's Johnnies. McDonough understood how to operate in environments where competing interests required delicate consensus-building and strategic compromise. Vivek Murthy, the nineteenth Surgeon General under President Obama and later the twenty-first under President Biden, provided medical expertise and a crucial public health perspective as the NCAA confronted issues around concussion protocols, mental health resources, and overall student-athlete well-being. His experience would prove crucial when the NCAA faced its own unprecedented health crisis in 2020.

These were not symbolic appointments. The independent members immediately began contributing to meaningful governance discussions on principles of amateurism, enforcement procedures, health and safety protocols, and strategic planning. They asked tough questions that institutional board members might be uncomfortable asking. When policies were proposed that served conference interests but might harm student-athletes, independent members could raise objections without worrying about political repercussions at home institutions. When enforcement policy required difficult choices between institutional interests and fair process, they could support the right decision rather than the politically expedient one.

I watched these dynamics play out in board meetings throughout 2019 and early 2020. Chenault would ask probing questions about financial arrangements that other board members might gloss over. Coleman would remind the board and leadership of academic primacy concerns that could be lost amid athletics-dominated discussions. Hill would speak about the student-athlete experience in ways that resonated differently from those of administrators. McDonough would identify political dynamics and stakeholder interests that needed to be managed. Murthy would raise health and safety issues before they became crises. Their presence elevated the quality of governance in tangible ways: decisions were more thoughtful, deliberations more comprehensive, outcomes more defensible.

This would prove essential when COVID-19 hit in March 2020. Murthy's medical expertise and McDonough's crisis management experience, combined with Chenault's business judgment, Coleman's academic perspective, and Hill's athlete advocacy, provided the Board with capabilities it would not have possessed under the traditional governance structure.

But I'm getting ahead of the story. We'll return to COVID in Chapter 21. For now, what matters is understanding that the independent board members represented one of the Rice Commission's most significant governance reforms, emerging from the ashes of scandal and corruption that had threatened the very foundation of collegiate athletics.

However, the independent board members' influence was ultimately constrained by broader institutional forces beyond their control and beyond even their own remarkable capabilities. The most significant challenges facing college sports required solutions that individual board members, regardless of their qualifications, could not independently provide.

The reality was realized in 2022, when the NCAA adopted a revolutionary new constitution that dramatically restructured the organization's governance. McDonough had departed the board to join the Notre Dame faculty and was replaced by Robert M. Gates in August 2020. Gates had served as the 22nd Secretary of Defense under Presidents George W. Bush and Barack Obama, previously served as Director of Central Intelligence under President George H.W. Bush, and held various senior positions at the National Security Council and CIA across multiple administrations. Gates also served as president of Texas A&M University. His reputation as a pragmatic, bipartisan leader made him a natural choice for leadership roles in complex institutional settings like the NCAA.

In the summer of 2021, the Board tapped Gates to chair a 28-member Constitution Committee charged with overhauling the Association's foundational governing document in the wake of the Supreme Court's landmark decision in *Alston*. Gates framed the urgency plainly, arguing that until the NCAA could better align its mission with its authority, it would be unable to play the role it should in governing college sports. Operating on a compressed timeline that moved from initial feedback gathering in late August 2021 through a Special Convention in November, multiple comment periods, and a final vote at the January 2022 Convention. Gates, as an independent member and the architect of the very document that eliminated three of the five independent seats, essentially wrote himself off the board. In the end, this diminished the role of independent members in ways that revealed institutional resistance to unaffiliated oversight once the immediate crisis had passed.

The number of members on the Board of Governors was reduced from twenty-one to nine. The new board structure included nine voting members: four from Division I, with at least one school president and one conference commissioner; one from the Division II Presidents Council;

one from the Division III Presidents Council; two independent members; and one graduate student-athlete.

The reduction from five independent members to merely two represented a significant retreat from the original Rice Commission vision. The commission had advocated for independent directors ultimately comprising majorities of NCAA governing bodies, recognizing that meaningful accountability required substantial independent representation. Five independent members on a 21-person board was already a minority, but they could form coalitions and influence outcomes. Two independent members on a nine-person board, while roughly the same percentage, could be easily marginalized. Proof that there is no perfectly viable solution so powerful that it can't be diminished by the desire to maintain the status quo.

Many institutional leaders and conference commissioners had never fully embraced autonomous oversight. They viewed independent board members as necessary political responses to a crisis rather than permanent governance improvements. Indeed, it was widely believed that outsiders could not truly understand the system. The FBI investigation had created urgency for reform. The Rice Commission had provided cover for changes that demonstrated responsiveness. But as the immediate crisis receded and attention shifted to other priorities, internal constituencies successfully advocated for restoring more traditional institutional control over NCAA governance, this time with greater direct influence for the conference commissioners.

The new constitutional structure retained Grant Hill and added Nadja West, the former U.S. Army Surgeon General who had replaced Vivek Murthy upon his return to government. Like Gates for McDonough, West a 30+ year veteran was a perfect substitution for Murthy, having served as the 44th Surgeon General of the United States Army and Commanding General of the U.S. Army Medical Command, the first African American to hold the position, the first African American woman three-star general in Army history, and the highest-ranking woman to graduate from the United States Military Academy at West Point.

Nonetheless, the departures of Kenneth Chenault, Mary Sue Coleman, Bob Gates, and, previously, Denis McDonough, and Vivek Murthy represented losses beyond mere numbers. While Hill and West are phenomenal leaders, the independent voice on the board was unquestionably weaker. They lacked the collective influence needed to drive transformative change in the face of institutional resistance. The constitutional restructuring effectively restored the old institutional control while maintaining minimal independent representation for political legitimacy. The godfathers were back in control.

This evolution reflects deeper tensions within college sports governance between reformist aspirations and institutional self-interest. The Rice Commission's recommendations emerged from a genuine crisis. But implementing lasting change proved more challenging than initially anticipated.

> Years later, looking back on the Rice Commission's work and the subsequent implementation of its recommendations, I realized it was an exercise in futility clothed in good intentions. In college sports, the more things changed, the more they stayed the same.

The commission's ultimate conclusions made clear that NCAA membership self-governance was nearly impossible. A reality that Secretary Rice recognized early on when she mused to me and Presidents Emmert and Peterson about that very concern. When your governance structure is composed of the very institutions benefiting from the status quo, meaningful reform becomes nearly impossible. Institutional leaders and conference commissioners have strong incentives to preserve existing arrangements even when those arrangements are demonstrably problematic.

Moreover, many key recommendations required cooperation from entities outside NCAA control, particularly the NBA, the agent community, and the sports apparel industry. As much as we lobbied for changes to NBA policies or greater transparency from shoe companies, we had no authority to compel them to do so. We could make recommendations and issue public appeals, but ultimately those entities would act in their own interests rather than in line with the NCAA's preferences.

I learned that in the face of scandal, everyone wants reform, but no one wants change.

The scandal's limited long-term impact on grassroots basketball demonstrates the resilience of existing commercial structures and the difficulty of reforming complex, multi-stakeholder systems through regulatory responses alone. The shoe company funded circuits that were central to corruption schemes continue to operate with minimal changes. The money still flows through those channels. The relationships among shoe companies, grassroots programs, and college coaches still exist. The incentives that drove corruption in 2017 persist in 2026, just operating through different mechanisms that are now nominally legal.

The Rice Commission's work demonstrated both the possibilities and limitations of reform within existing structures. They identified problems correctly, proposed thoughtful solutions, and generated institutional commitment to change. But they couldn't overcome the structural contradictions at the heart of college basketball. The tension between commercial reality and amateur pretense is real.

As I watched Secretary Rice chair this commission and present its findings, I felt a familiar mix of admiration and resignation. Admiration because the work was serious, thoughtful, and well-intentioned. Resignation because I worried even these distinguished leaders couldn't solve problems that the system itself was designed to perpetuate.

The FBI had exposed what everyone suspected. The Rice Commission documented the structural issues. Independent board members provided external accountability. Enhanced enforcement promised better deterrence. But none of it would change the fundamental economic reality. College basketball was a commercial enterprise generating billions while the primary producers received minimal compensation.

Until that contradiction was resolved, no commission recommendations or governance reforms would eliminate corruption. They would simply drive it into different channels, create new workarounds, and perpetuate the cycle of scandal, reform, and eventual reversion.

The Rice Commission's work didn't prevent Collegiate Capitalism's emergence. It accelerated it. The system struggled to fix itself because the institutions that composed it had strong incentives to preserve arrangements that benefited them, even when those arrangements were demonstrably failing.

Secretary Rice and her distinguished colleagues offered thoughtful solutions within the boundaries they were given. But the most fundamental question, whether the commercial scale of college basketball was compatible with the existing compensation framework, lay outside those boundaries. They had diagnosed symptoms while being limited in their ability to address the disease. And in doing so, they had inadvertently demonstrated why intervention through courts and legislatures would eventually prove necessary to force the transformation that internal governance could never produce.

The commission's final report would sit on the shelves, gathering dust, while the real changes would come from judges, politicians, and market forces. Whether that represents a failure of governance or simply the natural evolution of a complex system is a question I continue to wrestle with. But that's how it worked in college athletics. The committees, task forces, and blue-ribbon panels generated press releases. The courts and legislatures generated actual change.

Chapter 18
A "Strong Ass Offer" You Can Refuse
The Illusion of Independent Accountability

The Independent Accountability Resolution Process was supposed to be the crown jewel of the Rice Commission's reforms. After the FBI exposed systemic corruption in college basketball and traditional NCAA enforcement proved inadequate, the IARP promised something better. We would provide independent investigators and adjudicators free from NCAA institutional biases, bringing fresh perspectives and credibility to infractions cases.

It was created with the best intentions. The Rice Commission had recognized that NCAA enforcement suffered from execution and perception problems. When the organization investigated its own member institutions, accused schools and their coaches questioned whether fair hearings were possible. Conference commissioners sat on committees that judged cases involving their own conference members. University presidents evaluated allegations against peer institutions they competed with for recruits, rankings, and revenue.

The Commission offered that the IARP would solve these problems through independence. Hell, we believed it too! Oliver Luck, the executive vice president for regulatory affairs and I endorsed and even advocated for the creation of an independent system. A panel of 15 members with legal, higher education, or sports backgrounds, but with no current ties to NCAA Division I athletics, would review select complex infractions cases. Once the IARP accepted a case, a public disclosure would be made, and a hearing panel of five IARP members and one alternate would be appointed. Crucially, decisions issued by the Independent Resolution Panel would be final and not subject to appeal or further review.

This finality was intended as a feature, not a bug. Appeals had lengthened traditional infractions cases, sometimes adding years to already protracted processes. The IARP would deliver swift, decisive justice. Schools would get fair hearings from neutral parties. The NCAA would avoid accusations of institutional bias. Everyone would benefit from independent accountability.

That was the theory. The reality proved spectacularly different.

From the outset, the IARP struggled with fundamental problems that would ultimately doom it. The most basic issue was the investigators' perceived competence. The independent investigators hired to work IARP cases were talented lawyers and investigative professionals, but they weren't familiar with NCAA rules or fact-finding protocols. They faced steep learning curves as they tried to understand the Byzantine NCAA bylaws and complex evidentiary standards.

Many investigators from the IARP's Complex Case Unit conducted their own interviews of involved coaches, administrators, and players, duplicating effort already completed by NCAA enforcement staff or, in the context of basketball cases, the FBI. This redundancy further lengthened processes already moving at a glacial pace. Schools found themselves answering the same questions multiple times as different investigators covered the same ground.

The process became prohibitively expensive for schools defending themselves. Kansas spent approximately $10 million on legal fees to fight IARP allegations over six years and with multiple law firms. Louisville, Arizona, and LSU each spent significant amounts. Schools had to hire outside counsel with expertise in navigating this new system. They had to prepare witnesses for multiple rounds of interviews. They had to compile extensive documentation responding to allegations that kept evolving as IARP investigators learned NCAA rules.

Cases dragged on for years. In April 2021, we announced that final rulings in all six initial IARP cases were expected within the next twelve months. But just one case, North Carolina State, reached a resolution during that timeframe. Kansas, Arizona, LSU, Louisville, and Memphis remained in limbo as years passed without decisions.

I left the NCAA for government as we were readying the system for these cases in early 2021, but by August 2022, the NCAA had seen enough. It voted to discontinue the IARP, announcing that no new cases would be sent to the process and that the program would be shuttered once its remaining cases concluded. The experiment in independent accountability had lasted barely three years before being abandoned as a failure.

But the IARP's most damaging legacy wasn't delay or expense. It was the pattern of light penalties issued by the Independent Resolution Panel that made a mockery of enforcement.

Consider the Kansas case, arguably the most high-profile investigation stemming from the FBI probe. Kansas was charged with five Level I violations, which are the most severe breaches of NCAA bylaws, including lack of institutional control and head coach responsibility violations against Bill Self. The FBI had documented that Adidas consultants paid thousands of dollars to the families of recruits Silvio De Sousa and Billy Preston. Phone records and wiretapped conversations established that the coaches knew about, or should have known about, these payments.

On September 26, 2019, when the NCAA issued its Notice of Allegations, Kansas faced potentially devastating sanctions: multi-year postseason bans, massive scholarship reductions, and show-cause orders that could end coaching careers.

Kansas fought back aggressively, defending itself vigorously while awarding Self a "lifetime contract" worth tens of millions as a show of institutional support. The school argued that Adidas representatives weren't acting on Kansas' behalf, that coaches didn't know about payments, and that Kansas was a victim of Adidas' crimes rather than a knowing participant.

On October 11, 2023, more than six years after the FBI investigation began and four years after the initial allegations, the IARP finally issued its ruling. The decision stunned observers who expected serious consequences.

The IARP downgraded all five Level I violations to Level II or Level III violations. Kansas received three years' probation but no postseason ban. Bill Self's violations, originally Level I, were reclassified to Level III, with no additional penalties beyond the four-game self-imposed suspension he'd already served. Assistant coach Kurtis Townsend had his charges similarly reduced with no further sanctions. Neither coach faced show-cause orders.

Kansas had to vacate 15 wins from the 2017-18 season, including their Final Four appearance, which cost them their status as the winningest program in NCAA history. But they avoided other sanctions that may have hurt more. Postseason bans that would cost millions in revenue and recruiting restrictions that would damage competitiveness were off the table.

Most remarkably, Kansas won the 2022 national championship while this investigation was ongoing. I watched them cut down the nets in my family's hometown of New Orleans as champions despite facing allegations that could have destroyed the program. The ultimate penalty? Vacation of wins from a different season and probation that carried no meaningful restrictions.

"The hearing panel was intentional in not prescribing penalties that would have a negative impact on current student-athletes," the IARP stated in explaining its ruling.

This rationale would become standard across IARP decisions: avoid punishing current athletes for past violations by coaches and administrators. It sounded principled. In practice, it meant that schools could regularly cheat, fire or reassign responsible parties, and face minimal consequences because "current athletes" shouldn't suffer.

The Louisville case proved even more shocking. The FBI investigation exposed that Adidas agreed to pay recruit Brian Bowen's family $100,000 to secure his commitment to Louisville. Federal prosecutors presented evidence at trial documenting these payments and the scheme to funnel them through Adidas channels. New indictments alleged that head coach Rick Pitino knew about and approved the payments, even calling Adidas executive James Gatto to request the money.

Louisville fired Pitino in October 2017, along with athletics director Tom Jurich and assistant coaches Jordan Fair and Kenny Johnson. The firings acknowledged institutional recognition that serious violations had occurred. Louisville was also a repeat offender, having recently been sanctioned for the Katina Powell sex scandal involving escorts entertaining recruits described in Chapter 17.

Everything about the case suggested severe sanctions were warranted: documented payments to recruits, head coach involvement, repeat offender status, and institutional failure to monitor. If any case merited postseason bans and significant penalties, this was it.

On November 3, 2022, the IARP issued its ruling. Louisville received two years' probation, a $5,000 fine, and light recruiting restrictions. No postseason ban. Pitino and subsequent coach Chris Mack avoided punishment entirely. The panel determined that Adidas was not a representative of Louisville's athletics interests and that payments made by Adidas representatives weren't Louisville's responsibility.

"Based on the facts presented in the case, the hearing panel concluded that the case record did not provide sufficient or credible information to conclude that the apparel company was a representative of athletics interests," the IARP stated.

This finding defied common sense. Adidas had a multimillion-dollar sponsorship deal with Louisville. Adidas consultants steered recruits to Adidas schools as part of the company's business strategy. The FBI had documented this relationship. But the IARP concluded that Adidas' payments to secure Louisville recruits weren't made on Louisville's behalf. They were made for Adidas' own commercial interests.

The panel did not find that Pitino was personally involved in the violations or that he violated head coach responsibility rules in this case. The same coach who had been fired amid scandal for the second time in his Louisville tenure was unscathed by independent reviewers.

And then there was LSU. The case at my alma mater involved perhaps the most damning evidence of the FBI investigation. LSU head coach Will Wade was captured on FBI wiretaps discussing a "strong-ass offer" for recruit Javonte Smart. When those wiretaps became public in March 2019, Wade was indefinitely suspended after refusing to meet with LSU officials. The audio was eventually played publicly in the HBO documentary "The Scheme," allowing everyone to hear Wade's recorded voice discussing payments.

The NCAA alleged that Wade arranged for, offered, or provided impermissible payments, including cash, to at least 11 men's basketball prospective student-athletes, their family members, or individuals associated with prospects, in exchange for their enrollment at LSU. The case originated from FBI wiretaps capturing Wade in compromising conversations about recruiting inducements.

Yet when the IARP finally ruled, Wade received only a ten-game suspension and a two-year show-cause order. LSU was given three years' probation, ending in 2026. Most importantly, LSU avoided a postseason ban and lack of institutional control charges. The NCAA accepted the university's self-imposed penalties, including scholarship reductions, as sufficient.

Wade left LSU in 2022, but I question how much duress was actually present. He coached two more seasons after the wiretaps became public, leading the Tigers to the NCAA Tournament. He then took the head coaching job at McNeese State, led them to back-to-back NCAA tournament appearances, earned national coach of the year honors, and was hired as head coach at NC State. He is now back as the head coach of the LSU Tigers men's basketball team. The "strong-ass offer" that should have ended his career barely interrupted it.

The pattern was unmistakable. Traditional NCAA enforcement imposed harsher penalties than the IARP for similar or less-serious violations. Oklahoma State received a one-year postseason ban for violations involving assistant Lamont Evans. Auburn received four years' probation and a suspension of the head coach for violations involving Chuck Person. Yet Kansas, Louisville, Arizona, and LSU, cases involving more severe documented violations and higher-profile programs, received lighter penalties when adjudicated through the IARP.

The IARP consistently found ways to excuse, minimize, or redefine violations to avoid imposing meaningful sanctions. Adidas wasn't a representative. Coaches didn't know about payments they should have known about. Current athletes shouldn't be punished. The evidence wasn't credible or sufficient. Every case produced creative reasoning for why serious violations didn't warrant serious consequences.

By the time the NCAA discontinued the IARP in August 2022, the result was unavoidable. The independent process had become an escape hatch for major programs willing to spend large sums to contest allegations. Ironically, schools accused of serious violations fought to have their cases heard by the IARP because they believed the outcome would likely be favorable, or at least less harsh. The process intended to restore credibility to NCAA enforcement instead destroyed what little remained.

I watched this unfold with a mix of frustration and resignation that had become familiar by now. The IARP was supposed to be different. Independent investigators. Neutral adjudicators. Freedom from institutional bias. The Rice Commission had carefully designed it, and we had implemented it with the genuine hope that external oversight might succeed where internal enforcement had failed.

But the IARP's failure taught us something more fundamental than the Rice Commission had perhaps understood. The problem wasn't that NCAA enforcement was biased toward institutional interests. The problem was that no one, not NCAA staff, not independent investigators, not neutral adjudicators, could make a broken system work through better processes.

The IARP investigators struggled to learn NCAA rules, not because they lacked competence but because the rules themselves were increasingly incoherent. How do you enforce amateur restrictions when billions of dollars flow through the system? How do you punish schools for paying players when many believe the players should be paid? How do you maintain competitive equity when the entire premise of amateurism has been undermined?

The independent adjudicators consistently found creative reasons to avoid imposing severe sanctions, not because they were corrupt or incompetent, but perhaps because they recognized that the underlying rules no longer made sense. When they examined cases without institutional pressure to protect NCAA authority, they simply couldn't bring themselves to impose draconian penalties for violations of restrictions that seemed arbitrary or outdated.

Kansas spent millions of dollars defending itself and received probation without postseason bans. Was that justice? Or was it recognition that punishing Kansas severely for alleged Adidas payments when almost every major program had similar shoe company relationships would be arbitrary enforcement rather than fair adjudication?

Louisville was exonerated because Adidas wasn't deemed a representative of the university's interests. That finding seemed absurd given the multi-million-dollar sponsorship relationship. But was it wrong? Adidas was in fact pursuing its own commercial interests, trying to build relationships with future NBA players who would wear Adidas shoes professionally. Why should Louisville be responsible for what a commercial partner did in pursuit of that partner's own business objectives?

The question wasn't whether the IARP got these cases right or wrong. The question was whether the cases themselves made sense in a world where college basketball had become a commercial enterprise generating billions while maintaining the pretense of amateurism.

> The IARP's great revelation wasn't that independent oversight failed. It was that enforcement itself had become almost impossible because you cannot successfully police a system whose foundational rules have been overtaken by economic reality when almost every participant in the system understands that reality and operates accordingly. The gap between the formal rules and actual practice had grown so wide that enforcement became an exercise in selective prosecution rather than enhanced accountability.

I'm evaluating this with the benefit of time and distance. I understand that we had been asking the wrong question all along. We kept asking: how can we make enforcement more effective, more credible, more fair? The right question was: should we be enforcing these rules at all when the rules themselves perpetuate an unsustainable notion of years gone by?

The Rice Commission had tried to save the system through better governance and independent accountability. The IARP had tried to restore credibility through neutral processes and impartial oversight. Both efforts failed not because of poor execution but because they were attempting to preserve something that had retreated into the world of myth decades earlier and was already on life support.

In fact, the amateur model in college basketball was fundamentally challenged between the FBI arrests in September 2017 and the IARP's final rulings in October 2023

The coaches who were supposed to be punished found new jobs. The programs that were supposed to be deterred continued to recruit and compete at the highest levels. The system that was supposed to be reformed simply waited for external forces, such as courts, legislatures, and public pressure, to finally acknowledge what everyone inside already knew.

And by the time the IARP issued its most embarrassing rulings, I had seen enough to know where this was heading. The independent accountability was indeed an illusion, but not because the IARP was captured by institutional interests or biased toward major programs. The illusion was in thinking that any enforcement process could maintain amateur restrictions in a commercial enterprise of this size and magnitude.

The real accountability would come not from independent investigators or neutral adjudicators but from judges deciding antitrust cases, legislators passing NIL laws, and ultimately from a settlement that would force revenue sharing resembling professional employees or independent contractors.

Penn State had shown us that legal and political pressure could force the NCAA to retreat from sanctions. Miami had shown us that enforcement failures could make sanctions impossible to impose. The FBI investigation had shown us the depth of corruption that amateur restrictions produced. The Rice Commission showed us that internal reform was insufficient. And now the IARP had shown us that even unbiased stewardship couldn't salvage a system whose fundamental premise had expired.

These weren't separate failures. They were stages in a transformation that was inevitable once the commercial value of college athletics exceeded the plausibility of amateur restrictions.

Each failure moved us closer to acknowledging what we should have decades earlier. College athletics at the highest levels operate with the financial complexity and commercial scale of a major business enterprise, and the athletes who help generate its value have increasingly been recognized by courts, legislatures, and the market itself as participants entitled to share in the enterprise's economics.

The IARP's dissolution marked the end of the last serious attempt to preserve amateur athletics through better enforcement. What came after wasn't reform within the existing system. What came after is Collegiate Capitalism. The reluctant, belated, and incomplete acknowledgment that the old model was gone and that whatever came next would need to be built on economic reality rather than nostalgia.

The independent accountability revealed that accountability itself was impossible under rules that no one honestly believed in anymore. That revelation, more than any specific ruling or penalty, was the IARP's lasting contribution to the next phase of college athletics. Sometimes you have to try to fix something to prove it's unfixable. The IARP was that proof.

And many wondered what would come next. Next up was an equally troubling dilemma. The Michigan sign-stealing scandal that erupted in October 2023 demonstrated that enforcement challenges would persist long after the IARP's demise, and that new forms of competitive misconduct would test whatever system replaced it.

I followed this story with the fascination of someone who had grappled with enforcement complexities throughout his tenure. Connor Stalions, an analyst on Jim Harbaugh's staff, had allegedly orchestrated one of the most elaborate schemes to gain a competitive advantage in college football history.

The scope was remarkable. According to NCAA investigators, Stalions purchased tickets for more than 30 games over three years at 11 different Big Ten schools. He referred to his network as the "KGB," individuals who would attend games and film opposing teams' sideline signals. They scouted at least 13 future Michigan opponents across 52 games. Stalions personally appeared on the Central Michigan sideline in disguise to scout Michigan State during a September 2023 game.

Sign-stealing itself is not prohibited by NCAA rules. Teams have always tried to decode opponents' signals through film study and in-game observation. But off-campus, in-person scouting of future opponents within the same season had been banned since 1994, oddly as a cost-cutting measure. Stalions' operation repeatedly and deliberately crossed that line.

The scandal unfolded during what would become Michigan's national championship season. The Big Ten suspended Harbaugh for three games in November 2023, just as the Wolverines were making their championship push. Stalions resigned. Other staff members were terminated. Michigan went on to win the national championship anyway, defeating Washington in January 2024.

Harbaugh then left for the NFL, taking the head coaching job with the Los Angeles Chargers. He departed with a national championship and a legal cloud that would take years to resolve. The NCAA investigation continued, complicated by the departure of key figures and allegations of destroyed evidence.

In August 2025, the NCAA finally announced its penalties. The financial penalty was among the largest in college football history, reportedly exceeding $20 million when postseason revenue losses were factored in. Jim Harbaugh received a 10-year show-cause order, though he was already coaching in the NFL and would lead his team to an NFL playoff appearance four months later. The penalty would only affect any future return to college coaching. Connor Stalions received an eight-year show cause order. Sherrone Moore, who had been an assistant during the scheme, received a two-year show-cause order and a total three-game suspension, two self-imposed by Michigan and one added by the NCAA, for deleting his text thread with Stalions after the investigation became public. Moore would later be fired for his own personal misdeeds that did not involve NCAA rules nor athletics investigations.

The NCAA explicitly considered but rejected a multi-year postseason ban. The Committee on Infractions noted that such a penalty "would unfairly penalize student-athletes for the actions of coaches and staff who are no longer associated with the Michigan football program." This reasoning echoed the IARP decisions that had troubled me, but that I keenly understood. The principle of protecting current athletes from past misconduct has become a mechanism for ensuring that cheating produced lasting benefits, sometimes with minimal consequences.

Michigan had won a national championship while under investigation. The coaches responsible had moved on to other positions. The penalties would be paid by a wealthy athletics department for which $20 million, while significant, represented a manageable cost of doing business. The competitive advantage gained, three consecutive Big Ten championships and a national title, could never be taken away.

The Michigan case illustrated several enduring problems with NCAA enforcement. First, investigations take years while competitive advantages are gained immediately. By the time penalties are imposed, the landscape has shifted, key personnel have departed, and the connection between misconduct and consequences has become attenuated.

Second, the desire to protect current athletes from past violations creates perverse incentives. If schools can cheat, succeed, and face meaningful penalties only after the responsible parties have moved on, the deterrent effect is minimal. The rational calculation for a win-at-all-costs program is that cheating might produce championships that can never be vacated, while penalties will fall on future teams and administrators.

Third, financial penalties in the era of Collegiate Capitalism are simply a cost of doing business. Michigan's athletics department reportedly generated over $200 million in 2023. A $20 million fine, spread over multiple years, is manageable. The schools that have the resources to break the rules most effectively are also the ones that can most easily absorb financial penalties.

The Michigan situation also revealed the ongoing tension between conferences and the NCAA in enforcement matters. Big Ten Commissioner Tony Petitti wrote to the NCAA arguing that Michigan should receive no further punishment because the conference had already addressed the matter through Harbaugh's suspension. This argument, that conference discipline should preclude or limit NCAA enforcement, challenged previously unquestioned assumptions about the NCAA's authority.

Michigan itself fought the allegations aggressively, submitting a 137-page response that disputed nearly every finding and refused to negotiate a settlement. The school argued that the sign-stealing scheme offered "minimal relevance to competition" and should be treated as a minor violation. Whether this aggressive posture reflected genuine belief in innocence or a calculated strategy to minimize penalties, it demonstrated that major programs now approached NCAA enforcement as adversarial litigation rather than cooperative self-regulation.

I thought back to my years defending the NCAA's enforcement authority. We consistently argued that member institutions accepted NCAA governance voluntarily and should cooperate with investigations as a condition of membership. The Michigan response suggested that major programs no longer viewed themselves as bound by that compact. They would fight enforcement actions with the same resources and determination they would bring to any high-stakes litigation.

The Michigan case will not be the last enforcement controversy, nor will it resolve the fundamental tensions that make enforcement so difficult. As long as winning produces enormous financial and reputational rewards, some programs will push boundaries and break rules. As long as investigations take years, penalties will arrive too late to undo competitive advantages. As long as we protect current athletes from past misconduct, we will ensure that cheating produces lasting benefits.

What the Michigan case demonstrated most clearly was that enforcement in the era of Collegiate Capitalism would be unlike anything that had come before. With athletes receiving direct compensation, with billions of dollars flowing through the system, and with programs operating more like professional franchises than educational institutions, the old enforcement model is becoming obsolete. The NCAA has not yet figured out what would replace it. But, as 2026 begins, the NCAA is once again planning to review infractions and enforcement. Good luck with that.

Chapter 19
Will Smith Is Playing Who?
Let's Do the Right Thing

I led the NCAA to the initial settlement in the Arrington v. NCAA litigation in July 2014, and I owe that result in large part to the steady work of two valued colleagues: veteran NCAA leader, my trusted and able Deputy General Counsel Scott Bearby, and Mark Mester of Latham & Watkins. The terms were simple. Seventy million dollars to establish a medical monitoring fund to evaluate and diagnose current and former college athletes who suffered head injuries. An additional $5 million was later allocated for concussion research. No damages. No compensation for injuries already sustained. But proper medical care for players.

It was the right outcome for the right reasons, but only the beginning of what had to be done to deal with athlete head trauma.

A few months later, one of my staff members called with news about a movie in development. Hollywood was making a film about concussions in football. Will Smith and Alec Baldwin would star.

"Who is Will Smith playing?" I asked, only mildly curious.

"Dr. Bennet Omalu," she said. "One of the leading experts in head trauma."

I felt my stomach tense. "This is going to be interesting," I said, which was a considerable understatement for what I was actually thinking.

The movie is called "Concussion," and it would be directed by Peter Landesman, released in December 2015, just as we were implementing the *Arrington* settlement, litigating individual concussion cases, and facing mounting criticism about our handling of athlete safety. Will Smith would portray Dr. Omalu, the forensic pathologist who claims to have discovered chronic traumatic encephalopathy (CTE) in former NFL players and whose research had become the scientific foundation for lawsuits against both the NFL and NCAA.

When I finally watched the film, I saw our challenge dramatized in two hours of Hollywood storytelling. The movie portrayed the NFL as a monolithic institution wielding enormous cultural and economic power, mobilizing resources to discredit independent scientific findings that threatened its business model. League executives were shown funding their own research while attacking Dr. Omalu's credibility, demonstrating how powerful organizations investigate themselves and allegedly compromise scientific objectivity to protect financial interests.

The parallels to the NCAA's situation were uncomfortably obvious. While the film focused primarily on professional football, it implicated the entire football ecosystem from youth leagues through college to the NFL. The clear intended message was that universities were complicit in a system prioritizing athletic performance and revenue generation over player safety, sending young athletes into professional football already damaged by years of repeated head trauma.

Watching Will Smith's portrayal of Dr. Omalu, I thought about how this same doctor may testify in our litigation. I thought about Adrian Arrington's claims. I thought about all the defensive arguments we'd made and would continue making in courtrooms across America. And I thought about how the movie's narrative, powerful institutions denying science to protect profits, would shape public perception of every position we took.

This was different from Penn State, Miami, or the FBI basketball investigation. Those were scandals about rule-breaking within the system. This was about whether the system itself was causing irreparable harm to young people, and whether we'd known about that harm for decades while doing nothing meaningful to prevent it.

We'd learned that political pressure could force NCAA retreat and enforcement failures made accountability nearly impossible. The concussion litigation would teach us something more fundamental. Defending the system required honest engagement with the evolving science of concussion while implementing the best protections available at any given time. The challenge was that both the science and the protections were developing in real time, and sport cannot be made 100% injury-proof.

The legal landscape shifted on September 12, 2011, when Adrian Arrington filed his class action lawsuit in federal court in Illinois. He was twenty-five years old, a former safety and team captain at Eastern Illinois University who had sustained what he described as numerous and repeated concussions during his playing career from 2007 to 2009.

Arrington's complaint alleged that he was never coached on safer playing techniques, that the NCAA had engaged in a long-established pattern of negligence regarding concussions, and that the NCAA had "failed its student-athletes—choosing instead to sacrifice them on an altar of money and profits" by neglecting to adopt stricter standards for the kinds of play most likely to cause head injuries.

The language was inflammatory and the allegations were serious. Central to Arrington's case was the claim that the NCAA possessed knowledge of concussion risks decades before implementing meaningful protections. The complaint cited studies dating back to the 1930s that documented neurological damage in boxers, suggesting we should have known that collision football posed similar dangers.

The timing was significant. This came just weeks before Ed O'Bannon's case challenging amateurism restrictions began to gain momentum. The concussion litigation and compensation litigation were parallel attacks on different aspects of the same system. One argued that athletes deserved compensation for their commercial value, the other argued that they deserved compensation for the physical damage the system inflicted.

Both challenges shared a common premise. The NCAA utilized athletes for institutional benefit while denying them fair treatment in return.

The case eventually expanded beyond football to include "all persons who played an NCAA-sanctioned sport at an NCAA member school on or prior to July 15, 2016," potentially encompassing hundreds of thousands of former student-athletes across multiple sports, including lacrosse, wrestling, ice hockey, field hockey, soccer, and basketball. This expansion reflected recognition that concussion risks extended far beyond football to any sport involving physical contact or collision.

As the Arrington litigation proceeded, I found myself in an impossible position that would become increasingly familiar over my years at the NCAA. On one hand, I genuinely believed the NCAA had not acted with deliberate indifference to athlete safety. The science of concussions has evolved dramatically over recent decades. What we understood about chronic traumatic encephalopathy in 2011 was vastly different from what was known about head trauma in 1980 or 1950.

On the other hand, I was reading complaints from former athletes whose lives had been devastated by neurological damage. Adrian Arrington suffered seizures that left him unable to maintain employment. He experienced memory loss, depression, and near-daily migraines. Whether the NCAA bore legal responsibility, this young man's suffering was real and potentially connected to playing football, whether as a youth or in our system.

The legal strategy was clear. We would vigorously defend against allegations that the NCAA owed legal duties to athletes, recognize that member institutions, rather than the national organization, bore proximate responsibility for implementing safety protocols, and emphasize that science evolved over time and that standards from previous eras cannot be judged by current knowledge.

But the human calculus was more complex. The science was evolving, the injuries were real, and the responsibility to respond thoughtfully was taken seriously by the leadership team. President Emmert frequently emphasized the importance of meeting whatever obligations the science revealed, regardless of litigation posture.

In 2014, we negotiated what we thought was an appropriate and reasonable settlement. We agreed to spend $70 million to establish a medical monitoring program. Judge John Lee rejected it, among other concerns, he found the proposed deal insufficient to help everyone who suffered concussions playing college sports. His ruling noted that our statistical models didn't adequately account for athletes in non-contact sports who may also be at risk of head injuries.

The rejection forced us back to negotiations. This time we focused more on creating a genuinely comprehensive program. The scales of justice, as I saw it, needed to weigh more heavily toward caring for the athletes.

The revised settlement, ultimately approved in August 2019 with an effective date of November 18, 2019, clarified that non-contact sport athletes could benefit and established a $70 million medical monitoring program that allows former NCAA athletes to receive free neurological and neuropsychological assessments twice, until November 18, 2069. We also added $ 5 million for concussion research. Fifty years of medical monitoring. It was one of the longest-running court-ordered medical monitoring programs in legal history.

The settlement also imposed specific obligations on NCAA member institutions, requiring compliance with detailed concussion management protocols, including preseason baseline testing, same-day concussion management procedures, return-to-play clearance protocols, and the presence of medical personnel at contact sports competitions and availability at practices. Schools that certified compliance would receive partial legal protection from certain concussion-related claims.

It was, I believed, a reasonable settlement that would actually help people. Medical monitoring would provide diagnostic services that many former athletes couldn't otherwise afford. The institutional protocols would improve safety going forward. The fifty-year duration ensured benefits would continue for generations of athletes not yet born.

But Adrian Arrington hated it.

In June 2015, Arrington issued a statement through the National College Players Association (I'll discuss that group in Chapter 20), declaring the revised settlement "unacceptable" and asserting that he had never approved it. "I feel that I have been misinformed and the preliminary settlement doesn't address the reasons I filed the lawsuit in the first place," Arrington stated. "I would like the judge to reject the preliminary settlement. I plan to secure new legal representation to continue this fight to protect future players in NCAA sports."

The lead plaintiff was publicly repudiating the settlement his own attorney had negotiated. The optics were terrible.

Arrington's attorney was Joseph Siprut, a Chicago class action lawyer who had built his reputation on aggressive consumer litigation. The relationship between Arrington and Siprut deteriorated dramatically, playing out like a legal thriller in which the hero and his lawyer have a falling-out over principles versus pragmatism.

In June 2015, Arrington fired Siprut, alleging that his attorney "didn't keep him informed and didn't keep his best interests in mind." Arrington claimed, "the first time I learned about [the settlement] was in the media," and that he felt "misinformed" about the terms.

Siprut responded defensively: "I'm disappointed that one of the class representatives has decided to withdraw support for our settlement, having apparently adopted some of the misguided and inaccurate views of the settlement expressed in corners of the media and legal filings by other third-parties." He emphasized that "over 20 current class representative plaintiffs remain wholly supportive of the settlement" and that it had "the full support of two retired federal judges who helped us structure the deal."

Despite Arrington's dramatic public opposition and announcement that he would secure new representation, the class action continued under Siprut's leadership with the remaining plaintiffs. The settlement was eventually approved in 2019, four years after Arrington's opposition.

Arrington's situation highlighted a fundamental tension in class action litigation that I'd seen before and would see again. A tension that exposed the disconnect between individual plaintiffs' interests and the broader class they represent. This same dynamic would play out years later when some athletes objected to the *House* settlement for various reasons.

Arrington, suffering seizures and unable to work, sought direct compensation for injuries already sustained. He wanted money for medical expenses, lost wages, and diminished quality of life. Instead, he got access to medical monitoring that might help him understand his condition, but wouldn't pay his bills or restore his health.

His criticism raised troubling questions about attorney-client communication and the adequacy of representation in complex class actions. Had Siprut adequately explained the settlement terms and realistic options? Had he prioritized settling the case over fighting for his individual client's interests? Or had Arrington simply rejected the legal reality that proving causation and damages in concussion cases was extraordinarily difficult, making a settlement focused on medical monitoring the best achievable outcome?

I didn't know the answers. What I did know was that a young man who believed his brain had been damaged playing football felt betrayed by both his attorney and the settlement that was supposed to help him and others.

Ramogi Huma, the longtime athletes' rights advocate who had been pushing for reforms since his days as a UCLA linebacker, supported Arrington's opposition. Huma argued that the settlement "does not provide what is needed by former and future athletes because it does not mandate rules to help minimize traumatic brain injury and does not provide players suffering from brain damage direct financial support."

These criticisms misapprehended the settlement's purpose and impact, at least as I saw it. The settlement did mandate specific rules through the member obligations, requiring institutional compliance with detailed protocols. It did provide medical support for fifty years of monitoring. What it didn't provide was cash compensation to individual plaintiffs, because proving individual causation and damages in concussion cases was legally complex and uncertain.

But I also understood why Arrington and Huma felt the settlement was inadequate. If you're suffering daily seizures and you believe it is from head trauma sustained playing college football, being told you can get free neurological assessments doesn't solve your immediate problems. You probably need money for medical treatment. You may need compensation for lost earning capacity. You want and need acknowledgment that the system you believe damaged you owes you redress.

The settlement couldn't provide that, not in the context of a class action where proving individual causation for hundreds of thousands of potential class members was impossible.

This was the tragic compromise at the heart of the *Arrington* settlement. We would provide forward-looking medical monitoring and institutional reform, but we wouldn't compensate those already injured without individual litigation proving causation and damages in each specific case.

The aftermath of the *Arrington* settlement reinforced a decision we had made earlier that looked increasingly prescient: hiring Dr. Brian Hainline as the NCAA's first Chief Medical Officer in 2013.

Brian's appointment came amid the Arrington litigation, and the timing was only partly coincidental. We needed credible medical expertise at a moment when the organization faced existential criticism for prioritizing competitive and commercial interests over athlete welfare. Brian, a board-certified neurologist with extensive experience in sports medicine, brought exactly the kind of credibility we desperately needed.

I worked with Emmert and Isch from almost day one to identify the need for medical expertise within the NCAA National Office. We knew the concussion issue wasn't going away, but the position was not simply about head trauma. We recognized we needed someone who could speak authoritatively about medical science, lead research initiatives, and develop evidence-based policies that would withstand both scientific and legal scrutiny.

Brian was perfect for the role. But more than his credentials, what made him effective was his genuine commitment to athlete welfare. He wasn't a hired gun brought in to provide cover for predetermined positions. He was a scientist and physician who took the responsibility of protecting young athletes' health seriously.

CBS Sports noted in 2015, "Since the lawsuit was filed in September 2011, the NCAA has hired a chief medical officer (Brian Hainline) whose main duty at the moment is addressing concussion/brain trauma issue." The phrasing suggested skepticism about our motives, implying that Hainline's appointment was primarily a defensive move. The truth was that having Brian lead our medical initiatives made us better at protecting athletes regardless of litigation strategy.

Brian reported directly to me in my role as Chief Legal Officer and Chief Operating Officer. This organizational structure later drew criticism from those who argued that it created inappropriate incentives, implying that medical decisions were driven by legal considerations rather than athlete welfare. The criticism misunderstood how medical and legal priorities in this context were inextricably bound.

Understanding the legal arguments being made in courtrooms across America allowed us to identify knowledge gaps and make better decisions to protect athletes. If plaintiffs' attorneys were arguing we should have known about concussion dangers decades ago, we needed to understand the historical scientific literature and determine whether those arguments had merit. If experts were testifying about specific protocols that would reduce injury risk, we needed to evaluate whether adopting those protocols made medical and practical sense.

The relationship between legal defense and medical policy wasn't corrupting. It was necessary. We couldn't develop appropriate policies without understanding the scientific and legal landscape. We couldn't defend our actions without being able to explain the medical reasoning behind our decisions.

But I'd be lying if I said the arrangement wasn't sometimes uncomfortable. There were moments when legal considerations and medical recommendations may have pointed in different directions, and navigating those tensions required careful judgment about priorities. Judgement that both Brian and I had as we remained steadfastly focused on doing the right thing. And when we needed to sequester from one another, we did.

Under Brian's leadership, we launched the most ambitious concussion research initiative in sports medicine history, the NCAA-DoD Grand Alliance, with two main arms: the Mind Matters Challenge (mental health and concussion awareness for athletes) and the Concussion Assessment, Research and Education (CARE) Consortium. This was a partnership with the Department of Defense to conduct, as Brian described, the largest prospective clinical study ever conducted in the history of concussion.

The Grand Alliance, including the CARE Consortium, eventually received over $105 million in funding across multiple phases. The initial investment came in 2014, followed by $22.5 million in additional funding for CARE 2.0 in 2018, and then a $42.65 million in October 2021 for CARE-SALTOS Integrated. I remember the satisfaction I felt working in government at the time, knowing that my Army and DOD colleagues were committing substantial resources to research whose importance I understood firsthand.

The study examined approximately 50,000 athletes, investigated over 5,500 concussions, and operated across 30 participating institutions, including 26 civilian universities and 4 military service academies. It was led by Indiana University School of Medicine, the University of Michigan, the Medical College of Wisconsin, and the Uniformed Services University. With the funding going directly to the research institutions rather than the NCAA, IU School of Medicine served as the quarterback for the Consortium, managing administrative and fiduciary matters for the effort.

The scope was extraordinary. This was the first major concussion study to methodically assess both male and female athletes across twenty-four different sports, dramatically expanding the evidence base beyond the football-centric research that had previously dominated the field. The study employed advanced neuroimaging protocols, blood biomarker analysis, cognitive testing, balance assessments, and detailed impact monitoring using helmet-mounted sensors.

The consortium's research identified specific blood proteins that showed elevated levels following acute concussion and correlated with injury severity, a breakthrough that promised to move concussion diagnosis beyond subjective symptom reporting toward objective, measurable indicators.

Perhaps most importantly for policy purposes, CARE research demonstrated that widespread implementation of modern concussion management practices, including symptom-free waiting periods and graded exertion protocols, was associated with reduced risk of repeat concussion. This finding validated current management approaches and supported arguments that proper protocol implementation could enhance athlete safety.

The Grand Alliance and its CARE Consortium research served multiple strategic purposes beyond its scientific merit. The massive scale and federal funding provided powerful evidence of the NCAA's commitment to athlete safety and scientific inquiry. The partnership with the Department of Defense lent additional credibility and demonstrated alignment with national security interests in understanding traumatic brain injury.

But the research also had inherent limitations in the study design, which were openly acknowledged in the peer-reviewed literature. The consortium's emphasis on diagnosed concussions might underestimate the cumulative effects of sub concussive impacts, which growing evidence suggested could contribute significantly to long-term brain health problems. Although the attempt was to be comprehensive, the study's design meant it would likely not provide definitive causal evidence linking college-level exposure to repetitive head impacts to late-life neurodegenerative disease.

This was the gap between what the research could demonstrate and what plaintiffs' attorneys needed to prove their cases. CARE could demonstrate that modern protocols reduced the risk of repeat injuries. It couldn't prove that college football in the 1970s or 1980s caused specific former players to develop dementia in the 2010s.

That distinction became crucial as we shifted from defending the Arrington class action to confronting individual lawsuits brought by former athletes or their survivors alleging that college football had destroyed their brains.

The individual cases presented different challenges from the class action. In *Arrington*, we'd been negotiating with attorneys representing hundreds of thousands of potential class members, most of whom had no documented injuries. The settlement could focus on forward-looking medical monitoring because proving individual causation for such a large, diverse class was impossible.

But individual cases require different calculations. Each plaintiff may have had documented neurological damage. Each had a specific playing history. Each presented a jury with a sympathetic story about a young athlete who claimed the sport destroyed his life. And each required us to argue that this particular plaintiff's injuries weren't our responsibility, even if the circumstances seemed tragic.

The case of Greg Ploetz tested our resolve to defend individual cases rather than settle routinely. Ploetz had been a defensive end for the University of Texas Longhorns' 1969 national championship team. He exemplified the warrior mentality that college football celebrates: tough, physical, relentless.

Ploetz's life after football unraveled in devastating fashion. Around 2009, he began to experience serious cognitive decline that forced him to give up his work as a teacher and coach. In the years that followed, his condition steadily deteriorated, marked by worsening memory loss, confusion, and an increasing inability to function independently. By the time he died in 2015 at age 66, the damage was unmistakable. An autopsy later indicated that he had Stage 4 chronic traumatic encephalopathy (CTE), the most advanced and severe form of the disease.

His widow, Debra Hardin-Ploetz, filed suit in January 2017 seeking more than $1 million in damages, alleging the NCAA knew about concussion dangers dating back to the 1930s but failed to warn or protect her husband. The case became the first individual CTE lawsuit against the NCAA to reach a jury trial.

The trial began in June 2018 in Texas. I remember the calls from our outside counsel at Reed Smith, led by Ricky Raven, describing the environment we faced. The judge was making rulings that seemed unfavorable to our case. Public sentiment clearly wasn't on our side. The plaintiff's attorneys had spent several days presenting testimony in support of their case, and we hadn't yet had the opportunity to present our defense.

This was reminiscent of Penn State, where we'd faced a judge seemingly hostile to our positions and a public atmosphere demanding accountability regardless of legal technicalities and sound arguments. I was hesitant to settle given the precedent it would set. This was the first NCAA individual concussion case to go to trial, and I believed we had a strong defense to mount. Our medical experts were prepared to testify. Our causation arguments were solid. Our historical evidence about the evolution of concussion science was compelling.

But I'm a pragmatic litigator. I understand when circumstances dictate strategic retreat, even when you believe your legal position is strong. I held my nose and we agreed to settle.

The settlement was reached after three days of trial for undisclosed terms. My public statement said a lot in what it didn't say: "The settlement gives all parties the opportunity to resolve the case outside of a lengthy trial. The NCAA does not admit liability as part of the settlement. We will continue to defend the association vigorously in all jurisdictions where similar unwarranted individual cases are pursued."

That final sentence was important. We were settling this case, but we weren't establishing a pattern of settling every case. We would defend vigorously when circumstances dictated.

The Ploetz settlement taught us essential lessons about venue, judge selection, and the challenges of defending concussion cases in state courts where procedural rules and evidentiary standards might differ from those in federal courts. It also reinforced that each case required individual assessment rather than blanket strategies.

And the case of Matthew Gee would allow us to demonstrate that we could win these cases when we had the right facts, the right forum, and the right trial team.

Gee was a linebacker for USC from 1988 to 1992, playing on the 1990 Rose Bowl winning team. According to his attorneys, he absorbed an estimated six thousand hits during his college career. Teammates remembered him as someone who "hit like a truck" but was often left dazed after particularly hard collisions.

His post-football life initially appeared successful. He married his college sweetheart, Alana, built a thriving insurance business, and raised three children. But around 2013, Gee began experiencing dramatic personality changes. He became angry, confused, and depressed. He began drinking heavily and experienced memory blackouts lasting days. When Gee died on New Year's Eve 2018 at age forty-nine, doctors diagnosed Stage 4 CTE in his brain.

The case seemed particularly compelling because Gee was one of five linebackers from USC's 1989 squad who died before age fifty, all showing signs of mental deterioration associated with head trauma. The pattern suggested a familiar risk profile for these players.

When the case went to trial in October 2022 in the Los Angeles Superior Court, it represented the first CTE lawsuit against the NCAA to reach a jury verdict. By this time, I had left the NCAA and was working with America's Veterans, but I'd been instrumental in hiring the trial team that would defend the case, led by one of the country's best trial attorneys, Will

Stute, who was then at Orrick, and still represents the NCAA from King & Spalding.

The trial lasted four weeks and featured extensive medical testimony. Dr. Bennet Omalu, the neuropathologist portrayed by Will Smith in "Concussion," testified for the plaintiff, lending star power and credibility to their case. Historical experts presented evidence they believed showed the NCAA had been aware of concussion dangers since the 1930s, including references to "punch-drunk" symptoms in the NCAA's own 1933 medical handbook.

But our defense strategy proved effective. Rather than denying that Gee had CTE, we appropriately argued that his death resulted from multiple other health problems, including substance abuse, cardiovascular disease, liver cirrhosis, and obesity. The causation question wasn't whether Gee had brain damage, but whether that brain damage caused his death and whether the NCAA bore responsibility for that damage decades after he played.

Stute argued brilliantly that "you can't hold the NCAA responsible for something 40 years later that nobody ever reported" and that the plaintiff's attorneys wanted the jury to use a "time travel machine" to apply current knowledge to past circumstances. This framing resonated. The judge excluded evidence about Gee's deceased USC teammates, a crucial evidentiary ruling that prevented the plaintiff from suggesting a pattern of harm.

On November 22, 2022, the jury voted eleven to one and ten to two on key liability questions, finding that the NCAA was not responsible for Gee's death. The verdict represented a dramatic victory and a devastating blow to individual concussion litigation plaintiffs nationwide.

Sports law professor Gabe Feldman captured the significance: "Even with the NCAA being as unpopular as it is, and even with a very sympathetic plaintiff, the jury still ruled against the plaintiff. That's fairly telling."

The Gee verdict, upheld on appeal, demonstrated that compelling individual cases can face substantial challenges in proving institutional liability for concussion-related injuries sustained decades ago. Our ability to argue that current knowledge cannot be retroactively applied to past conduct, combined with the complex causation issues inherent in CTE cases, provided formidable defenses.

The NCAA had not lost an individual concussion case tried by Stute and his colleagues. That success rate mattered not just for the specific cases but for the broader deterrent effect on future litigation in this industry and others. However, the armor is weakening. The first crack came in October 2025, when a South Carolina jury, in a case tried by Bakari Sellers, found the NCAA negligent and awarded former South Carolina State defensive end Robert Geathers and his wife $18 million. Then in April 2026, a Dallas County jury in *Davis v. NCAA*, defended by lead counsel Victor Vital of Haynes and Boone, returned a $30 million compensatory verdict against the NCAA and followed it with $110 million in punitive damages on behalf of the family of former SMU lineman J.T. Davis, for a total of $140 million. While in *Riggs v. NCAA*, the Indiana Court of Appeals affirmed summary judgment for the NCAA, holding that the association owed no general duty of protection as a matter of law to a former Texas A&M player later diagnosed with CTE, the association's exposed flank created by credibility weakness seems to be taking a toll.

Standing in my office in 2014 finalizing the settlement in *Arrington*, or later watching "Concussion" in a darkened theater, or reading about Matthew Gee's tragic decline, I couldn't escape a fundamental question that transcended legal liability. Was this system sustainable?

We had proven the system could be defended in courtrooms. But the question that lingered was whether legal defensibility was sufficient when the human costs were so visible, and the science was moving so quickly. That tension between what the law required and what fairness demanded was something I carried with me throughout this chapter of my career and beyond.

The *Arrington* settlement's fifty-year medical monitoring program implicitly acknowledged that we had ongoing moral responsibilities to athletes long after their playing careers ended. But medical monitoring without compensation could leave some without an adequate remedy. We would help former athletes understand their neurological conditions, but we wouldn't be required to pay for the treatment those conditions required, or compensate for the pain and suffering they may have endured, or for the earning capacity those conditions may have destroyed. This was a product of the legal system, not a suggestion that the NCAA was dispassionate.

Individual litigation allowed athletes to seek that compensation, but proving causation and damages in CTE cases was extraordinarily difficult. The *Gee* verdict demonstrated that even sympathetic plaintiffs with documented brain damage faced substantial barriers to recovery.

This dynamic created a system in which some athletes received medical monitoring, a few received settlements, and most received nothing beyond the scholarships they'd already been awarded. Meanwhile, the institutions and conferences that profited from their play continued generating billions.

The movie "Concussion" had dramatized this dynamic in the NFL context, showing a powerful institution denying science to protect profits. The NCAA's situation was similar but more complex. We weren't just protecting profits. We were protecting the entire amateur model that made college athletics financially viable for institutions. Admitting that college football caused long-term brain damage and that we bore responsibility for compensating injured players would threaten the economic model of college sports.

This was the impossible calculation at the heart of the concussion litigation. Legal liability required proving specific causation in individual cases, which was difficult in most cases. But moral responsibility suggested that we should find a way to help, even if proving legal causation was impossible. And we did with medical monitoring and research.

But the gap between legal liability and moral responsibility was where the amateur model was slowly colliding and collapsing. Courts might not impose liability absent specific proof of causation. But public opinion, legislative pressure, and the athletes themselves were increasingly demanding accountability that transcended legal details.

The concussion cases joined the compensation cases in creating external pressure for transformation. *O'Bannon*, *Jenkins*, and eventually *Alston* and *House* would challenge amateurism restrictions from one direction, arguing that athletes deserved compensation for the commercial value they generated. *Arrington*, *Ploetz*, *Gee*, and others challenged from another direction, arguing that athletes deserved compensation for physical damage they sustained generating that value.

Both challenges shared a premise. The amateur model failed athletes by denying them fair treatment in return for the value and risk they contributed to a commercial enterprise.

These weren't separate challenges. They were interconnected manifestations of a fundamental tension between the commercial reality of college athletics and the amateur restrictions we strived to maintain. The concussion cases, like the compensation cases, forced uncomfortable questions about what we owed athletes.

And both challenges demonstrated that voluntary reform within existing structures was impossible. We'd tried settling *Arrington* with medical monitoring instead of compensation. We'd hired Dr. Hainline and funded CARE Consortium research. We'd implemented concussion protocols and return-to-play standards. These were genuine improvements that helped current and future athletes.

But they didn't address the fundamental question. In a system generating billions, why were athletes bearing potentially catastrophic risks without corresponding compensation?

The answer many feared was that compensating athletes for their value and their risks would transform college athletics from amateur sports into professional enterprises. And that transformation would threaten the entire model that made college sports profitable for institutions and special for generations of fans and athletes.

So we defended individual cases, settled when necessary, and hoped that incremental reforms would be sufficient to maintain the system's viability.

They weren't. You couldn't indefinitely maintain a system where young people potentially suffered brain damage, helped to generate billions in value, and received only scholarships in return.

Will Smith's portrayal of Dr. Bennet Omalu in "Concussion" wasn't just entertainment. It was a cultural indictment that the system's defenders were wrong, that the science was real, and that institutions had prioritized profits over people. The movie reached millions of Americans who would never read legal briefs or scientific studies, but who could watch a compelling drama about courage and institutional corruption.

I watched that movie knowing that in some version of the story, I was one of the institutional defenders. Not the villain, I hoped, but certainly not the hero. I was the lawyer trying to balance the impossible competing demands of protecting the organization's legal interests while genuinely trying to improve athlete safety, defending against litigation while implementing reforms, and maintaining the amateur model while acknowledging its growing implausibility. Sitting in that darkened theater, I was reminded that defending institutional interests sometimes requires moral compromises that are legally justifiable but ethically uncomfortable.

The concussion cases taught me what Penn State, Miami, and the basketball investigation had begun to teach. Defending the system required increasingly creative arguments that strained credulity. That compulsion from courts, prosecutors, politicians, and public opinion was forcing changes we couldn't make voluntarily. The amateur model was in peril not as a result of any single blow but from accumulated contradictions that made its preservation impossible.

The system survived these challenges. We had strong legal defenses. We won important cases. We implemented genuine reforms.

Yet, we didn't solve the fundamental problem. Again, that question. In a system generating billions, was it defensible to deny rewards beyond scholarships to athletes helping to create that wealth who potentially bore catastrophic risks with alleged incomplete protections?

The law said yes if you couldn't prove specific causation. Morality suggested otherwise. And the gap between legal defensibility and moral sustainability was where the amateur model was slowly, inexorably dying.

Chapter 20
Who Represents the Student Athletes?
Maybe We Should Make Them Union Members

I was walking the halls at the Sports Lawyers Association conference in Denver in May 2017 when I spotted DeMaurice Smith heading toward me. De and I had been friends since 1997, practicing law together at both the U.S. Department of Justice and Latham & Watkins. With our busy lives, we connected periodically over drinks or meals through the years, catching up on families, careers, and the strange paths our lives had taken.

On this day, notwithstanding our enduring friendship, De had a message for me that wasn't casual conversation.

College players must be unionized to secure the protections they deserve, he said, his tone leaving no room for misinterpretation. The NCAA and its member schools, he continued, were not equipped, too conflicted, or perhaps not sufficiently motivated to do right by the athletes.

Then he said something that stopped me cold: "Maybe we should make them members of the NFLPA."

I believed he was serious. The executive director of the National Football League Players Association was telling me, the NCAA's Chief Legal Officer, that he was considering organizing college athletes into his union. The implications were staggering. If the NFLPA successfully unionized college football players, it would destroy any remaining notion that college athletics was simply amateur competition rather than decidedly professional sports.

“De,” I said, searching for the right words, "you know I respect what you're trying to do for players. But college athletics is different. These are students. Educational institutions. Not professional franchises."

Even as I said it, I understood clearly what he thought of my points. Students who generated billions in revenue. Educational institutions that paid coaches millions of dollars annually. Not professional franchises except in every way that mattered economically.

De just looked at me with an expression that said he'd heard these arguments before and found them unpersuasive. "Then why do they work forty or more hour weeks? Why can't they major in what they want? Why do coaches control every aspect of their lives? That sounds like employment to me."

If I hadn't known before that conversation, it became crystal clear in that Denver Marriott. The union movement was serious, it had serious backing, and it represented yet another externality that would force the transformation of college athletics, whether we wanted that transformation or not.

The concussion litigation had exposed that we were asking athletes to voluntarily accept potential physical injury in an enterprise that had significant commercial impact. The compensation cases from *O'Bannon* through *Alston* and later *House* directly challenged amateurism restrictions and assumptions. And now unionization efforts were attacking from another direction, arguing that the relationship between athletes and institutions was an employment relationship rather than an educational one.

> The struggle to unionize college athletes represents more than labor organizing. It embodies fundamental questions about fairness, economic justice, and the proper relationship between college sports via educational institutions and the athletes contributing to the generation of enormous revenues for them. At its heart are philosophical differences about the nature of college athletics that have reshaped our understanding of what it means to be a student-athlete in twenty-first-century America.

The origins trace back to contextual inequities that have plagued college athletics for decades. While the NCAA, conferences, universities, coaches, and athletics departments reaped enormous financial rewards from television contracts, ticket sales, and merchandise, the athletes themselves remained tethered to scholarship arrangements that some argued failed to cover basic living expenses or provide adequate medical care. These disparities created fertile ground for organized resistance to emerge, challenging the NCAA's amateur model at its very foundations.

The formation of the National College Players Association in 2001 marked a critical moment in the evolution of college athlete advocacy. Founded by former UCLA football player Ramogi Huma, the NCPA became the primary organizational vehicle for advancing the rights of college athletes outside the NCAA's internal structures. Huma, whom I mentioned in Chapter 19 for his role in the *Arrington* case, had become an advocate while playing for UCLA from 1995 to 1998, founding a student group to give college athletes a voice and secure protections. He later stated that he started the organization after witnessing the NCAA suspend his All-American teammate for eating groceries left anonymously on his doorstep when he had no food, and after it was suggested to him that the NCAA prevented colleges from paying medical expenses for injuries occurring during summer workouts.

The NCPA's early years focused primarily on health and safety issues, recognizing these concerns transcended more contentious debates about financial compensation. In 2001, the NCPA raised concerns at a congressional hearing after the deaths of three football players and the denial of home health care to a paralyzed player. The NCAA had already recognized some of the issues raised. The organization was lifting the prohibition on medical oversight of summer workouts, providing home health care benefits for seriously injured players, increasing death benefits from $10,000 to $25,000, and prohibiting consecutive two-a-day practices to help prevent deaths. As I've discussed, however, outside forces have a way of expediting things.

The NCPA's advocacy increasingly moved beyond safety issues toward fundamental questions about athlete compensation and employment status. This evolution culminated at Northwestern in January 2014 with an announcement that would test much of what we believed about college athletics' legal foundations.

But before I discuss the results of the Northwestern football players' petition in detail, I must reflect on how, in the very next football season, a different group of athletes demonstrated their collective power in a much different and incredible way. In November 2015, the University of Missouri football team showed the world exactly how much economic leverage athletes possessed, even without formal union representation.

The context was not athletics but racial justice. Graduate student Jonathan Butler had begun a hunger strike on November 2, 2015, demanding the resignation of University of Missouri System President Tim Wolfe over what protesters described as inadequate responses to racial incidents on campus. A series of racist episodes had created a climate that many Black students found intolerable, and university leadership's response had been widely criticized as insufficient and tone-deaf.

Butler's hunger strike and ongoing campus protests generated national attention but no immediate action from university leadership. Then, on November 7, the Missouri football team changed everything.

Dozens of Black players announced they would refuse to participate in team activities until Wolfe resigned. They released a photograph showing them standing together in solidarity, arms linked, announcing that they would not practice or play games until their demands were met. Head coach Gary Pinkel initially supported his players, posting on social media that the Mizzou family would stand as one, united, and behind the players.

The economic implications were immediate and devastating. Missouri was scheduled to play Brigham Young University on November 14. Under the terms of their contract, if Missouri failed to play the game, the university would owe BYU a $1 million forfeit fee. Additional games would trigger additional penalties. Beyond direct contract costs, the revenue from game day, ticket sales, concessions, merchandise, and television revenue would all be lost.

University leaders quickly did the math. The football team generated approximately $35 million in annual revenue. A prolonged boycott would cost tens of millions of dollars. The players had discovered what economists had long understood: their labor was the essential input for a commercial enterprise potentially worth hundreds of millions of dollars. Without their participation, the enterprise had no product to sell.

Tim Wolfe resigned on November 9, 2015, two days after the players announced their boycott. Chancellor R. Bowen Loftin announced his resignation the same day. The football players had accomplished in 48 hours what weeks of student protests had failed to achieve.

I remember watching these events unfold with a mixture of admiration and concern. The players demonstrated moral courage by standing with their fellow students against racial injustice. They had shown solidarity across a team, maintaining unity when external pressures must have been enormous. And they had revealed something about the economics of college athletics and athlete power.

My concern stemmed from the implications for the amateur model we were trying to preserve. If athletes could leverage their economic value to force institutional change on racial justice issues, what would prevent them from doing the same for compensation, benefits, or working conditions? The Missouri players had provided a proof of concept for labor organizing that formal union efforts had not yet achieved.

Critics accused the players of using athletics inappropriately for political purposes. They argued that scholarship athletes had obligations to their universities that precluded such activism. Some pointed out that the players' leverage existed only because they generated commercial value, which seemed to undercut arguments that college athletics was, at its core, educational rather than commercial.

Supporters celebrated the players for using the only leverage they had to advance justice. They noted that Black athletes at predominantly white institutions often felt voiceless despite generating enormous value for those institutions. The Missouri protest showed that athletes could demand to be heard and could force accountability from administrators who might otherwise ignore their concerns.

For me, the Missouri situation crystallized something I had been thinking about for years. We must address whether the relationship between athletes and institutions is, in fact, the educational relationship we described in our bylaws and public statements. Or was it an economic relationship in which athletes provided enormous value in exchange for scholarships that did not reflect the market's value? Or both? The athletes understand this conflict, even if others are reluctant to acknowledge it.

Missouri football suffered in the years following the protest. Enrollment declined. Attendance dropped. The program struggled competitively. Some attributed these struggles to the protest and its aftereffects, arguing that the controversy had damaged Missouri's brand. Others pointed to coaching changes and competitive dynamics unrelated to the events of November 2015.

What could not be disputed was that the Missouri players had demonstrated that college athletes possessed economic power that could force institutional change if they chose to use it collectively. The amateur model depended on athletes not recognizing or exercising that power. Missouri showed that this assumption was fragile.

When Northwestern players filed their union petition, they were attempting to formalize through legal processes what the Missouri players would later demonstrate through direct action. The ability to withhold labor, to refuse to generate the revenues on which athletic departments depended, gave athletes leverage that no rule or regulation could eliminate. The only question was whether and when they would use it.

So, let's go back to that precedential petition. On January 28, 2014, Northwestern University football players, led by quarterback Kain Colter, announced they had signed union cards and were seeking representation through the newly formed College Athletes Players Association. CAPA was created by Huma, Colter, and Luke Bonner, a former UMass basketball player, with technical support from the United Steelworkers.

I remember the moment I heard about the Northwestern petition. I was on my way to New York, planning to watch the NFL Super Bowl XLVIII that weekend between the Seattle Seahawks and Denver Broncos at MetLife Stadium in East Rutherford, NJ. My first thought about the effort was that this was what the Steelworkers and others were looking to achieve, though it had come from a different direction. My second thought was more troubling. If this succeeded, the entire amateur model may collapse overnight. It stayed on my mind all weekend, which was not difficult since the NFL game was a blowout.

Kain Colter brought both athletics credibility and leadership experience to the movement. At twenty-one, he'd been Northwestern's starting quarterback for two seasons, sometimes sharing snaps with Trevor Siemian. He was the team captain and piloted the Wildcats to a New Year's Day Gator Bowl victory (the 2012 season), Northwestern's first bowl win in sixty-four years. His decision to risk future NFL prospects to lead unionization efforts demonstrated personal sacrifice that lent moral authority to the cause.

The organizing effort required extraordinary discretion, given the potential consequences for participating athletes. I suspect that Colter had to spread the word among teammates slowly without alerting coaches. Some players had questions about employee status. Would they be able to play against teams of non-employees? But most shared Colter's grievances and agreed that, as Big Ten school athletes, they were uniquely positioned to pressure the system.

I believed their legal arguments were weak. The foundation rested on fundamental principles of labor law governing employer-employee relationships. And that was not this. But Colter testified that he considered the forty-plus-hour weekly commitment to the team to be work, albeit work he enjoyed, as any employee who likes his job would. He said a football commitment required academic sacrifices, including the inability to pursue his preferred major, pre-med. While other prominent program football athletes were, in fact, successfully pursuing pre-med, Colter's testimony proved crucial in establishing that relationships between athletes and universities possessed characteristics of employment rather than merely educational participation.

As the case proceeded, I found myself wrestling with uncomfortable contradictions. Legally, I knew our position was sound. College athletes received scholarships, not wages. They were students participating in extracurricular activities, not employees performing services for compensation. The educational benefits they received, the degrees they earned, and the opportunities athletics provided each distinguished college sports from professional employment.

But I also understood why Colter's argument resonated. The time demands, the academic and coaching structure, the revenue context, and the enforcement practices all created a picture that external observers could reasonably interpret in employment terms, even if the legal framework and the educational mission we believed in pointed to a different conclusion.

The regional National Labor Relations Board decision in March 2014 sent shockwaves through college athletics. The regional director ruled that Northwestern football players were employees under federal labor law and had the right to form a union. The decision focused on the degree of control Northwestern exercised over players' time and activities, concluding that these athletes functioned more like employees than students in their relationship with the university.

I was in meetings with membership committees when the decision came down. The anxiety was palpable. If Northwestern players could unionize, every private school's athletes could follow. And if athletes at private schools were unionized and negotiated better terms, public school athletes would demand similar treatment even though state labor laws might not grant them the right to unionize. The competitive and practical implications alone could rip apart college athletics as we knew it.

Our legal strategy became obvious. We needed to appeal to the national NLRB and argue that allowing unionization at one private school would create impossible competitive imbalances. Northwestern led the way. The argument focused on jurisdiction rather than employment status. A pure employment argument may not resonate after the regional director's detailed analysis. We believed the NLRB shouldn't assert jurisdiction over college athletics because of the unique characteristics that made uniform labor relations impossible across Division I.

We also mobilized politically. Emmert testified before Congress that unionization would "throw away the entire collegiate model for athletics." He characterized the excitement of March Madness and the College Football Playoffs as primarily driven by the fact that competitors were student-athletes, not professional athletes or unionized employees. And while critics dismissed this as romantic nonsense, there was truth to it. The appeal of college sports derives partly from its connection to educational institutions and the idealistic perception that athletes are students rather than hired professionals. It was a position many in the industry fully endorsed and truly believed.

I passionately believed in the educational model we were defending. But I also recognized that the economic evolution of college athletics was creating real tensions with the framework we described in our bylaws and public statements.

Critics posed pointed questions similar to De Smith's: If these athletes weren't employees, why did coaches exercise such extensive control over them? If they were primarily students, why did some find their academic choices constrained? We had answers grounded in the educational mission and the voluntary nature of participation, but the questions resonated publicly.

Indeed, some would suggest our good answers were based on faulty factual predicates, and the national NLRB's decision in August 2015 provided temporary relief but no lasting resolution. In a unanimous ruling, the Board declined to assert jurisdiction over the Northwestern case. Crucially, the Board did not rule that college athletes were not employees. Instead, it determined that allowing unionization at one private school would create competitive imbalances since most Division I schools were public institutions not subject to NLRB jurisdiction.

The Northwestern players never got to form their union. The ballots from their election were sealed and destroyed. Kain Colter risked his final season of eligibility and likely damaged his NFL prospects for nothing. Or so it seemed at the time.

But the Northwestern experience taught valuable lessons beyond the immediate legal outcome. It demonstrated that college athletes could organize effectively despite institutional opposition. It provided that at least one labor board had found them to be employees under federal law. It created a roadmap for future organizing efforts. And it exposed contradictions in our amateur model that would continue driving legal and political pressure for transformation.

The movement didn't end with Northwestern. It evolved, adapted, and waited for more favorable political conditions.

While Northwestern remained in legal limbo, other challenges to athlete employment status emerged through different legal frameworks. In November 2019, former Villanova football player Ralph "Trey" Johnson and other former and current collegiate athletes sued the NCAA and twenty-five Division I member institutions in federal court in Pennsylvania. They claimed Division I college athletes should be recognized as employees under the Fair Labor Standards Act. Unlike Northwestern's focus on unionization rights under labor law, *Johnson* specifically targeted minimum wage and overtime protections.

The case represented the culmination of earlier unsuccessful attempts. In *Berger v. NCAA*, filed in the U.S. District Court for the Northern District of Indiana, similar FLSA claims were dismissed, and the U.S. Court of Appeals for the Seventh Circuit affirmed the dismissal. In *Dawson v. NCAA*, brought in California federal court, another FLSA claim met the same fate. Attorney Paul McDonald made another attempt in 2017 with former Villanova player Poppy Livers. In that case, a judge initially decided that the NCAA should not be exempt from an employment test, but the *Livers* case was clearly outside the statute of limitations. Recognizing as much, McDonald voluntarily dismissed the case, though it had established a crucial procedural precedent.

Our legal defenses in these cases, though standard, were sometimes used to mischaracterize our intentions. In *Livers*, our legal briefs cited *Vanskike v. Peters*, a 1992 case involving prison labor and the Thirteenth Amendment's exception for forced labor as punishment for crimes. Critics seized on this citation to suggest we were likening college athletes to prisoners. Nothing could be further from the truth. A point that I, along with our lead labor lawyer, Donald Prophete, the named partner at the acclaimed labor firm Constangy Prophete, attempted to make clear in public appearances and statements. The reality was that we were merely citing relevant legal precedent and the test for determining whether normal labor laws apply. But as I'd learned from Elsa Cole's advice and many of the matters discussed in this book, almost everything the NCAA says and does is viewed through a different microscope. Technical legal arguments can become public relations disasters.

The Third Circuit's July 2024 ruling in *Johnson* fashioned another new legal paradigm. The court rejected the NCAA position that college players cannot be employees and student-athletes simultaneously. It established a four-part test requiring that athletes perform services for another party, necessarily and primarily for that party's benefit, under that party's control or right of control, and in return for express or implied compensation or in-kind benefits.

Judge David Porter's concurring opinion emphasized that assessing the employment of college athletes is "intensely fact-bound" and that one-size-fits-all solutions won't work. Porter observed that if *Johnson* were certified as a class action, courts would need to determine whether nearly 200,000 Division I athletes playing on nearly 6,700 teams qualified as FLSA employees. The distinction between revenue-generating and non-revenue sports became central to legal and policy discussions.

Strategic research partnerships between advocates and academic experts provided crucial empirical support for the movement's arguments. Studies demonstrated significant gaps between the value athletes generate and the benefits they receive. One study by Huma, Ellen Staurowsky, and L. Montgomery estimated that the fair market value of FBS football and men's basketball players is approximately $208,000 and $370,000, respectively, suggesting that these athletes contribute roughly $10 billion in fair market value over four years. These studies stood in stark contrast to the value of the scholarships we advanced for years to support the amateur model.

Yet this view, based on a professional model, does not adequately account for the fact that college athletics operates under a fundamentally different paradigm from professional sports, emphasizing educational benefits and the tradition of amateurism. As President Emmert stated in 2014, the notion of using a union-employee model to address challenges in intercollegiate athletics struck most people as a grossly inappropriate solution. The membership consistently maintained that student-athletes were students first and foremost, and that the excitement of March Madness and the College Football Playoff derived in large part from the fact that competitors were student-athletes, not professional athletes, and not unionized employees of universities.

By the time the Third Circuit ruled in *Johnson*, I had left the NCAA and was working in Washington. Ironically, I ran into Charlie Baker that day of the ruling in July 2024 as we were both traveling to Washington, DC, from Indianapolis on an airplane rerouted due to weather. We spoke briefly, but nothing of the ruling. I read the decision with a mixture of emotions. Resignation because it represented another legal defeat for positions I'd helped craft and defend. Vindication because the court acknowledged what I'd increasingly come to understand. Employment status would vary dramatically across different sports, divisions, and circumstances.

The internal debates I'd had at the NCAA about athlete representation continued haunting me. We had embraced the Student-Athlete Advisory Committee as the internal mechanism for athlete voice in governance. SAAC operated at the campus, conference, and national levels, with NCAA legislation mandating that all member institutions have SAACs. The mission was to enhance the total student-athlete experience by promoting opportunity, protecting welfare, and fostering positive athlete image. But most importantly, to give the athletes a voice in the system, allowing them to review proposed legislation and represent athlete interests in policy discussions.

But SAAC's effectiveness and independence had become subjects of significant debate, particularly regarding employee status. Cody Shimp, chair of the Division I SAAC and a former baseball player and graduate assistant at St. Bonaventure University, had become a prominent voice in opposition to classifying athletes as employees. Critics pointed out that SAAC's composition, however, wasn't representative of the athletes most likely to benefit from employee classification. In 2023, it was reported that Division I SAAC had only three FBS football players, none from Power Five (now Power 4) schools, and only one Power Five men's basketball player. Revenue sport participants who would most benefit from direct compensation were dramatically underrepresented.

Former Duke lacrosse player and past Division I SAAC chair Maddie Salamone observed: "The fundamental problem with SAAC is not only can they not adequately speak for athletes, but they don't have a mechanism to speak with every athlete within the NCAA." Salamone also asserted that NCAA employees were always involved in drafting public communications attributed to SAAC athletes, and that anything released publicly had to undergo extensive review by NCAA legal staff and the media team.

In my experience, this characterization overstated the NCAA's involvement in SAAC activities. The role of national office staff was to serve as a resource for SAAC, not as a censor. I cannot think of a single circumstance in which SAAC wanted to take a position or deliver a message and had its desires and intent not honored. SAAC members were capable, thoughtful students who genuinely represented their perspectives and those of their teammates. The fact that staff helped polish communications or provided legal guidance didn't mean SAAC was a puppet organization. Rather, I thought, it meant we provided professional support to help them communicate their desires and positions effectively.

Despite this role confusion, SAAC achieved meaningful victories for athlete welfare. The committees successfully advocated for improvements in transfer windows, mental health resources, and academic support services. As Kendall Spencer, the first student-athlete to serve on the NCAA Division I Board of Directors and former Division I SAAC Chair, testified before the U.S. Senate, SAAC members were "charged with representing the voice of student-athletes on all issues from time demands to pay for play." Nonetheless, it is inescapable that these successes generally occurred in areas where athletes' interests aligned with institutional preferences for maintaining the current economic structure of college athletics.

At the Division II and III levels, SAAC opposition to employee status appeared more grounded in genuine athlete concerns about program viability. Division II SAAC members made clear that while employment classification might be workable for the wealthiest Division I programs, smaller schools simply lacked the resources to compensate athletes for their practice and game time. The national SAAC mobilized around this concern, organizing athletes to contact members of Congress directly and urge them to preserve the student-athlete model rather than impose an employment framework that would strain or eliminate programs at lower-division schools.

I consistently defended SAAC's role. But I also recognized the criticism had merit. SAAC represented institutional athletes who had bought into the current system. It didn't necessarily represent those who felt exploited by that system or those who would benefit most from fundamental transformation. Remember the position SAAC took on multi-year scholarships, which I discussed in Chapter 12.

The gap between SAAC positions and broader athlete sentiment became apparent through independent polling. In 2023, results from an email survey of 1,086 college athletes showed that 73% favored becoming employees and that more than half were interested in joining a union. This contrasted sharply with NCAA President Charlie Baker's congressional testimony in October 2023 to the Senate Judiciary Committee that he had "talked to probably a thousand student-athletes since I got this job, and [he hadn't] talked to one yet who wants to be an employee." It also significantly differed from the positions that Baker's predecessors, especially Mark Emmert, consistently advocated.

The disparity perhaps reflected selection bias. Baker spoke with athletes at official NCAA events who were invested in the current system. Just as Emmert had during my time at the NCAA. Independent surveys reached out to athletes with diverse perspectives and experiences. The truth was that athletes' opinions varied dramatically by sport, division, scholarship status, and individual circumstances.

Many athletes worried that employee classification could threaten the existence of certain programs entirely. Division III athletes, like SAAC executive committee member University of Wisconsin-La Crosse tennis player Brady Horstmann, worried publicly that "Division III athletics could cease to exist' under employment classification."

The fear extended beyond financial concerns to fundamental changes in athletics experience. Some athletes worried that employee status could mean they could gain the right to unionize as well as be fired for inadequate performance. This concern reflected deeper anxiety about the transformation of college athletics from an educational experience into a purely commercial enterprise. Many athletes valued educational opportunities, the tradition of amateurism, and the distinct culture of college sports that they believed could be compromised by professionalization.

Conversely, many athletes in revenue-generating sports increasingly viewed employee classification as essential for basic protection and fair compensation. These athletes pointed to significant time commitments, institutional control over their lives, and substantial revenue they helped generate as evidence that relationships with universities were more employment-based, than educationally focused. Football and men's basketball players are more likely to support employee status. In contrast, athletes in Olympic sports, women's programs, and lower divisions expressed greater concerns about potential negative consequences.

When President Biden was elected on November 3, 2020, at the NCAA, we began preparing for a different approach to college athlete union issues than we had experienced under the Trump administration's NLRB. And the expectations were realized quickly after the Biden administration took office. I left the NCAA in July 2021 and joined the Biden administration, and I had no contact with the NLRB, but I could not help wondering what my colleagues at the board might do with these issues. By September 2021, NLRB General Counsel Jennifer Abruzzo answered my lingering angst. She issued a memo deeming that some college athletes are employees under the National Labor Relations Act. While her memo was only guidance to NLRB field offices, it was a thundering message. The agency's lead lawyer was inviting athletes from private colleges to bring forth petitions to unionize as employees.

This guidance represented a dramatic departure from previous NLRB approaches and created new opportunities for athletes to pursue unionization through federal labor law. And, it led directly to the most successful unionization effort since Northwestern.

On February 5, 2024, following Abruzzo's guidance, the NLRB's Region 1 issued a groundbreaking decision in *Trustees of Dartmouth College*, finding that Dartmouth's men's basketball team was an appropriate unit under the NLRA and directing that an election be held. The decision marked the first time college athletes had been granted the right to vote on unionization since Northwestern a decade earlier.

The Dartmouth players voted in favor of unionization in March 2024, making them the first college athletes to successfully form a union. We never learned how Northwestern players voted because their ballots were sealed and destroyed after the national Board declined jurisdiction.

But the Dartmouth victory proved short-lived. On December 31, 2024, the Dartmouth men's basketball team, represented by Service Employees International Union Local 560, requested to withdraw its petition to unionize. The timing was strategic: Donald Trump had been elected president in November 2024, and his administration would soon appoint NLRB members likely hostile to athlete unionization. Withdrawing the petition avoided review by a Trump-appointed Board of the regional director's declaration that athletes are employees. A board that might reverse that finding.

The withdrawal highlighted how political considerations increasingly influenced strategy around college athletics. Unionization efforts required not just legal arguments and organizing capacity but favorable political conditions and sympathetic administrative agencies. The movement was subject to electoral cycles and presidential appointments in ways that made progress uneven and uncertain. Indeed, on February 14, 2025, the NLRB's acting general counsel, William B. Cowen, rescinded Abruzzo's memo.

Meanwhile, other fronts opened in the litigation campaign. The NLRB's Los Angeles Region filed unfair labor practice charges against USC, the Pac-12, and the NCAA, alleging that they are joint employers of FBS football players and Division I basketball players. The joint employer theory represented a potentially powerful legal approach that could extend NLRB jurisdiction to public universities through their relationships with private entities, such as conferences and the NCAA. However, I believed the factual basis was flawed. Neither the NCAA nor the conferences exercised the type of day-to-day control over athletes that genuine joint employer relationships require.

The legal landscape by early 2025 was complex and unsettled. The Seventh Circuit held that student-athletes are not employees under the FLSA. The Third Circuit established that some college athletes could be employees under a multi-factor test. The NLRB had found Dartmouth basketball players were employees under labor law, though that finding was now withdrawn to avoid adverse review. Multiple matters remained pending in various fora, each testing different aspects of employee status under different legal frameworks.

And then came the *House* settlement, which we will explore in detail later, reluctantly embracing the commercial nature of college athletics. Judge Wilken's June 2025 approval order cleared the way for schools to pay

Division I athletes directly for the first time, bringing the NCAA's long-standing amateurism model to a formal close.

But the settlement did not resolve the fundamental question of employee status. Schools could pay athletes through revenue-sharing arrangements while still claiming those athletes weren't employees. The legal gymnastics required to maintain this position were becoming increasingly difficult to land, but the financial stakes were enormous. Treating athletes as employees would trigger workers' compensation requirements, unemployment insurance obligations, and potential union organizing rights, which could cost institutions far more than the $20 million in revenue sharing.

Sitting in my Washington, DC office at the Department of Veterans Affairs and then from my firm back in Indianapolis, watching these developments unfold, I reflected on my conversation with DeMaurice Smith years earlier. Perhaps he was right that the system was unsustainable.

But I'd been right that college athletics presented unique complexities. Division III athletes playing for schools with no athletics revenue genuinely were students participating in extracurricular activities. Women's soccer players at mid-major programs weren't employees in any meaningful sense. Even within Division I, the vast majority of athletes in non-revenue sports didn't generate commercial value that would justify employment classification.

The challenge was that one-size-fits-all legal frameworks struggled to accommodate these distinctions. Either all college athletes were employees, or none were. Courts and agencies couldn't easily adopt rules that would have made football and men's basketball players at Power Five schools employees while field hockey players at Division III schools weren't, even though that distinction may have reflected economic reality.

Significant obstacles remain to the full implementation of collective bargaining. The mixed jurisdiction between private and public institutions complicates uniform organizing efforts, while institutional resistance from universities, conferences, and the NCAA continues to shape both legal strategy and political dynamics. The potential financial implications of treating college athletes as employees including workers' compensation, unemployment insurance, payroll taxes, and other employment-related costs, are creating additional incentives to resist unionization efforts.

The question of whether collective bargaining can occur without formal employee status is among the most challenging legal and policy questions facing the movement. Current federal labor law generally ties enforceable collective bargaining rights to workers who qualify as "employees" under statutes like the NLRA, meaning employers are typically only obligated to bargain with representatives of their employees, but the requirement is about legal classification, not merely the existence of a formal employment relationship. In February 2024, I discussed this very issue on a panel at Bucknell University with John Feinstein and Congressman Dan Meuser. Some members of Congress have discussed creating special statutory frameworks allowing athlete representation without employment, but Republican leaders remain adamantly opposed, making legislative solutions unlikely in the near term.

State-level approaches have demonstrated divergent pathways. California's pioneering name, image, and likeness legislation created a model that other states followed, suggesting meaningful reform can occur through state regulation rather than federal labor law. However, the interstate nature of college athletics and the need for uniform rules impose practical limitations on state-by-state approaches to fundamental issues such as working conditions and compensation.

It is also clear that the divide over unionization falls largely along sport lines. Athletes in revenue-generating sports increasingly view employee classification as essential for basic protection and fair compensation. They point to significant time commitments, institutional control over their lives, and substantial revenue they generate as evidence that their relationships with universities are more employment-based. Meanwhile, athletes in non-revenue sports express greater concerns about potential negative consequences.

Many smaller colleges worry they will be forced to eliminate athletics programs entirely if required to treat athletes as employees. Some athletes fear that employee status could mean they "could be fired for inadequate performance," transforming college athletics from an educational experience into a purely commercial enterprise. These concerns reflect genuine anxieties among athletes who value the educational opportunities and distinct culture of college athletics.

Yet the current legal landscape suggests forms of collective bargaining will emerge through combinations of court decisions, administrative actions, and legislative compromises. Successful unionization efforts may ultimately force institutional adaptation rather than program elimination, as retaliation against unionization may violate established labor law principles. The NLRB could issue complaints against schools attempting to eliminate teams in response to unionization.

What's clear is that traditional models treating high-revenue college athletes as purely amateur students are difficult to maintain in the face of mounting legal challenges and changing social expectations. The transformation is already visible in the *House* settlement revenue-sharing provisions, the expansion of NIL opportunities, and the growing sophistication of athlete advocacy efforts.

I had defended the amateur model because I believed in the paradigm of athletics tethered to education and that the system could be reformed from within. Yet subsequent years proved otherwise. The convergent pressures were all demonstrating the same fundamental truth. College athletics at the highest levels had evolved into an enterprise whose commercial dimensions created tensions with the traditional educational framework, tensions that the legal system was increasingly being asked to resolve through the lens of the athlete.

Ramogi Huma and Kain Colter provide both inspiration and practical lessons for future organizing efforts. Huma built the NCPA from a student organization into a sophisticated advocacy operation that repositioned the conversation about athletes' rights. Colter sacrificed his final season of eligibility and likely damaged his NFL prospects to lead the first serious unionization attempt in college sports history. Their willingness to challenge entrenched interests and risk personal consequences for broader principles has created possibilities for future generations that seemed impossible two decades ago.

They failed to form unions at Northwestern or to maintain the Dartmouth victory across changing political administrations. But they succeeded in forcing the questions that the system couldn't answer: Why aren't these workers treated like workers? Why can't these employees organize like employees? Why should commercial enterprises generating billions be exempt from labor laws?

The amateur model has no good answers to those questions. It only has increasingly desperate arguments about educational traditions that ring hollow when confronted with the reality of athletics time demands, coaches routinely earning eight-figure salaries and more upon being fired, and television contracts worth billions.

I believe the evolution toward collective representation is inevitable, driven by legal precedents, economic pressures, and generational changes in attitudes toward athlete rights. Whether this takes the form of traditional labor unions, unique representative structures, or hybrid arrangements remains uncertain. The distinction between revenue-generating and non-revenue sports will likely play a crucial role in determining which athletes ultimately gain employee status and collective bargaining rights.

The unionization movement represents more than labor organizing. It embodies fundamental questions about fairness, economic justice, and proper relationships between educational institutions and athletes helping to generate enormous revenues. The persistence and sophistication of organizing efforts, combined with supportive legal developments and changing public attitudes, suggest that some form of collective representation will eventually emerge, even if its exact structure remains subject to ongoing negotiation.

Many argue that college athletes need the protections that only employment status and collective representation could provide. I defended the amateur model. After all, I believed in it because I thought it could be reformed from within, and because the financial implications of abandoning it seemed catastrophic. But defending a model doesn't make it defensible when the facts demonstrate its foundational premises are misplaced.

Critics argue that college athletes at the highest levels work like employees, are controlled like employees, and generate value like employees. They suggest that calling them amateurs doesn't change those facts. It just perpetuates the fiction while claiming educational nobility. Labeling them as amateurs appropriately addressed the regulatory and institutional framework, but unfortunately did not resolve the underlying tensions that courts, agencies, and athletes themselves were increasingly identifying.

In the end, the restructuring we are witnessing isn't motivated by any single lawsuit or organizing campaign. It's being driven by accumulated tensions, demonstrating that you cannot indefinitely maintain a system in which young people dedicate countless hours to their sport vis-à-vis their studies, help generate billions in revenue, accept potentially catastrophic physical risks, and receive only scholarships in return. All the while being told they're amateur students.

Standing in that Denver corridor listening to DeMaurice, I had defended the system I worked for. But I also knew he was right. The question wasn't whether college athletes would eventually gain employment status and collective representation. The question was how long we could delay the inevitable, and how much damage we would do to our credibility and to athletes' welfare by continuing to defend the somewhat indefensible.

The answer, it turned out, was . . . not much longer. The unionization movement would continue pressing forward. And eventually, through some combination of court decisions, administrative rulings, legislative action, or institutional surrender, college athletes would gain the employment status and collective representation that the facts of their working conditions had always justified.

That transformation would mark not the death of college athletics but its evolution into something more honest, more just, and more aligned with economic reality. The amateur model was already dead. The unionization movement was just helping bury it and build something better from its remains.

Chapter 21
COVID-19 Forces Final Four Cancellation
A Case Study in Crisis Management

The unionization battles had taught us that external pressures could force changes we'd never make voluntarily. Each challenge over the previous decade had tested the NCAA's ability to adapt and respond to rapidly changing circumstances. But nothing in our organizational history prepared us for what would happen when a global pandemic forced us to make decisions at speeds we'd never contemplated and with stakes that extended far beyond college athletics.

On the morning of March 12, 2020, I sat in an emergency hybrid videoconference meeting with President Emmert, members of our Board of Governors, and senior staff, about to make a decision that seemed unthinkable just days earlier. We were going to cancel March Madness. The NCAA tournament that had run seamlessly through world wars, assassinations, terrorist attacks, and national tragedies would not be played in 2020.

Not because of war or violence or catastrophe in any traditional sense. Because of COVID-19, a novel coronavirus that was spreading rapidly across the globe and had been declared a pandemic by the World Health Organization hours earlier.

The decision could cost us over $800 million in revenue and force us to cut distributions to member schools by hundreds of millions. It would devastate seniors whose careers would end without final opportunities to compete for championships. It would upend the entire college sports calendar and force the cancellation of dozens of spring championships across multiple sports.

But as I listened to our Chief Medical Officer Dr. Brian Hainline walk through the latest epidemiological data, and as I heard independent board members Chenault and Murthy argue passionately for health and safety above all else, I realized this decision, while painful, was the right one.

We have to do this, I thought. Not just because it's the medically right decision, though it clearly is. We have to do this because protecting the health and safety of student-athletes, staff, and fans is a fundamental responsibility. If we compromise on that, nothing else matters. Moreover, I contemplated, if we don't, and people get sick or die, we'll have that blood on our hands, and the organization can't survive that.

The vote was unanimous. March Madness 2020 was canceled.

And in that moment, I felt both the weight of what we were giving up and the conviction that we were making a principled decision that reflected our values even at enormous cost. I also understood something that all the litigation and political pressure and reform efforts had been teaching us. The amateur model we'd defended so vigorously was far more fragile than anyone had acknowledged. One event generated the vast majority of our revenue. And when circumstances made that event impossible, the entire financial structure of college athletics was under stress.

This is the story of how college athletics responded to an unprecedented global health crisis, demonstrating both the challenges and the leadership necessary to navigate extraordinary circumstances while maintaining our fundamental commitment to the welfare of humanity.

The warning signs had come first, and unlike many organizations that would later be caught off guard by the pandemic's rapid spread, we began taking proactive measures relatively early. Most organizations dismissed those early warnings about what seemed like a distant problem. We didn't. In mid-January 2020, Dr. Hainline sent a message to the membership to raise awareness of reports about a novel respiratory virus in Wuhan, China. By February, President Emmert, Dr. Hainline, and I were reaching out to public health experts, including Dr. Anthony Fauci, Surgeon General Dr. Jerome Adams, Dr. Sylvie Briand from the WHO, and Professor George Gao to understand the progression of what would soon become a global pandemic.

In late January, the WHO declared COVID-19 a Public Health Emergency of International Concern. By early March, we had assembled a COVID-19

Advisory Panel, drawing on prominent medical experts, including Dr. Vivek Murthy, who served on our Board of Governors; Dr. Leon McDougle of the National Medical Association; Dr. Carlos del Rio of Emory; and Dr. Amesh Adalja of Johns Hopkins.

As I stated when creating the group: "The NCAA will make decisions that are first and foremost reflective of medical best practices and keep the health and safety of student-athletes, administrators and fans as the number one priority." I believed that when I said it, and the decisions we would make over the coming weeks and months proved that commitment was genuine even when the costs were staggering.

The advisory panel initially focused on monitoring the rapidly evolving situation and providing guidance to member institutions. We recognized the fluidity of COVID-19 and its impact on hosting events in public spaces. They worked to understand transmission patterns and risk factors associated with the new virus. Dr. Hainline coordinated our medical response, established communication protocols with the CDC, and maintained regular contact with state and federal health authorities. This early formation of an expert advisory group, combined with our proactive outreach to leading public health officials, positioned us to make informed decisions as events rapidly accelerated throughout March 2020.

The first test of our commitment to health-based decision-making came from an unexpected source. A Division III basketball tournament game involving Yeshiva University, which represented the first domino to fall, was the proverbial canary in the coal mine.

In early March 2020, the hotel where Yeshiva's men's basketball team was scheduled to stay during the tournament canceled the team's reservation over fears of COVID-19 after one student at the university, not on the basketball team, tested positive for coronavirus, and the school closed its main campus.

Fear was beginning to cripple the country.

Information was inconsistent and recommended preparation and response plans were sometimes contradictory. The hotel cancellation illustrated how anxiety and uncertainty were already rippling through the broader ecosystem surrounding college sports, affecting not just games themselves but the entire infrastructure supporting them.

We faced the billion-dollar question. Could fans, officials, media, and most importantly the athletes be safe if the game were played? This wasn't just any game; it was part of the NCAA Division III men's basketball championship tournament. After much deliberation, while our Advisory Panel did not recommend cancellation or public spacing at that time, Johns Hopkins University, where the game was to be played, determined it was prudent to hold the tournament without spectators, based on Maryland's COVID-19 numbers and CDC guidance.

On March 6, 2020, the game between Yeshiva University and Worcester Polytechnic Institute at Johns Hopkins became historically significant as the first U.S. sporting event played without fans in attendance. The New York Post reported: "The game was delayed by more than an hour after a Yeshiva rabbi tested positive and the school needed to provide documentation to ensure it was safe to play. WPI waited at its hotel while that was completed, and three players decided not to take the court because of fears about the virus."

Our unprecedented decision to exclude spectators from a college basketball tournament game represented a watershed moment, demonstrating our willingness to adapt traditional competition formats to protect health and safety. The virus was beginning to impact the fundamental nature of college sports competition. In an empty gym, Yeshiva went on to win its first NCAA tournament game 102-78 and advanced to the Sweet 16 before the rest of the tournament was canceled.

Six days. That's all the time between that empty-gym game and the decision that would test everything we believed about leadership and values.

Things moved with terrifying speed. On the morning of Wednesday, March 11, we still believed we could salvage the tournaments by conducting them without fans. Our Advisory Panel met. Our Board of Governors convened. Our independent board members, led by Chenault and Murthy, were instrumental in changing the typical NCAA decision-making process from slow and deliberate to light speed. Their leadership during this crisis exemplified effective governance under pressure.

I was in constant communication with Emmert and key board members throughout the day. The consensus was building that we couldn't safely host tournaments with large crowds, but maybe we could conduct them with only essential staff and limited family attendance. That morning, Emmert announced the decision to play all championship events, including the Division I men's and women's basketball tournaments, with only essential staff and limited family attendance.

Conferences followed suit. Big Ten Commissioner Warren announced his conference would move forward without fans. Other Power Five conferences began planning for limited or no fan attendance at their tournaments.

For a few hours that Wednesday afternoon, I thought we'd found a path forward. Restricted access. Enhanced protocols. Medical monitoring. We could salvage some version of March Madness, preserve the revenue stream that funded most of college athletics, give athletes their championship opportunities, and maintain our commitment to health and safety.

Then, around 12:30 pm. Eastern time, mere hours after Emmert's announcement, the WHO officially declared COVID-19 a pandemic after more than 118,000 cases in 114 countries and 4,291 deaths. At approximately 9:30 p.m., the NBA suspended its regular season after learning that Utah Jazz player Rudy Gobert had tested positive for COVID-19 before a game scheduled in Oklahoma City.

Mark and I jumped on the phone with Dr. Hainline when we learned of the NBA season suspension. I recall Brian reflecting on the significant development and the need to seriously reconsider whether we can do this safely.

As Dr. Hainline later reflected, Gobert's positive test "reinforced where we were going, but [as the day of March 11 unfolded] we were going there anyway. It already was a given that there was absolutely no way March Madness could exist. Wednesday night, we came to that realization."

I spent most of that night on calls with Emmert, senior staff, and board members. Dan Gavitt, our senior vice president of basketball, and like his dad, Dave Gavitt, the most creative mind in college basketball, worked feverishly to explore contingency options. If there were a way we could logistically conduct the tournament safely, Dan would make it happen. He proposed holding a shortened sixteen-team tournament in Atlanta, split between State Farm Arena and Mercedes-Benz Stadium, with all participants chosen by the selection committee.

"We can do this," Dan argued on one call late Wednesday night. "Controlled environment. Single city. Limited teams. We can test everyone, control access, make it work."

I wanted to believe him. The impact on student-athletes would be devastating. The financial implications of cancellation were catastrophic. We were looking at the possibility of losing almost a billion dollars in tournament revenue. We'd have to slash distributions to member schools by hundreds of millions. Programs may eliminate sports. Jobs would be lost. The economic devastation would cascade throughout college athletics.

But as I listened to Dan's ideas, I kept thinking about what Dr. Hainline and our medical advisors were telling us. The virus was spreading exponentially. We didn't have adequate testing capacity. Contact tracing was virtually impossible. Bringing teams from across the country to a single location might concentrate and accelerate transmission rather than containing it.

I appreciated Dan's creativity and determination to find solutions. But as we contemplated the proposals and consulted with our medical advisors, the challenges seemed insurmountable.

I remember saying something to Dan like, “I love that you're trying to find a way. Your commitment to the student-athletes and the tournament is exactly what we need. But based on what our medical experts are telling us, I’m beginning to become convinced we can’t do this safely right now."

The calls continued into Thursday morning, March 12. Our emergency planning efforts demonstrated our commitment to finding solutions and our desperation to salvage some form of tournament for America. Still, the rapidly evolving situation made any new and creative format impractical, given our legitimate health and safety concerns.

The announcement came in a stark statement that would send shockwaves through American sports and society: "Today, NCAA President Mark Emmert and the Board of Governors canceled the Division I men's and women's 2020 basketball tournaments, as well as all remaining winter and spring NCAA championships. This decision is based on the evolving

COVID-19 public health threat, our ability to ensure the events do not contribute to the spread of the pandemic, and the impracticality of hosting such events at any time during this academic year given ongoing decisions by other entities."

The tournament, which had been held without interruption since 1939, was canceled. Not halted for World War II, the Korean War, Vietnam, or the Gulf War. Not interrupted because of assassinations, including President Kennedy and Martin Luther King Jr., or attempts on Presidents Truman and Reagan. And, not canceled after tragic events like the Challenger explosion or the Oklahoma City bombing.

It was the right decision. And it was one of the hardest decisions we'd ever made. COVID-19 had accomplished what wars and tragedies never had.

The decision's impact extended far beyond basketball. Twenty-seven different sports would not host championship events for the 2019-20 academic year. For many student-athletes, particularly seniors, this represented the abrupt end of competitive careers without the opportunity to play for national championships they'd spent years working toward.

As Dan Gavitt aptly stated: "The disappointment and heartbreak we all feel for student-athletes unable to compete is significant, yet nothing is ever more important than the health and safety of student-athletes, coaches and fans."

Dan also made a courageous decision not to release any brackets showing teams that might have competed. "...[A]nything less than a credible process is inconsistent with the tradition of the NCAA basketball championships," he stated. "Brackets based on hypotheticals can't substitute for a complete selection, seeding and bracketing process. …There is not an authentic way to produce tournament fields and brackets at this point without speculating, and that isn't fair to the teams that would be positively or negatively impacted by manufacturing March Madness."

We will never know who would have played in or won the 2020 men's and women's basketball tournaments. In the end, COVID-19 won. But we know we made the decision that protected health and reflected our values.

The decision to cancel was not easy, but one thing was clear in every discussion of our COVID-19 Advisory Panel, Board of Governors, and staff. The health and safety of all involved stood as the paramount priority. While we were keenly aware of the financial situation, we focused on doing what was right.

But the financial reality was devastating. The Division I men's basketball tournament generates the vast majority of the NCAA's annual revenue, with the organization earning more than $1 billion, primarily from television rights deals with CBS and Turner, valued at around $827 million. The cancellation triggered an immediate financial crisis that would test our crisis management planning and organizational resilience. Few enterprises can potentially lose almost one billion dollars and remain steadfastly focused on the bigger picture. We did.

Here's where the advance planning we'd done proved crucial. Under President Emmert's leadership, our Chief Financial Officer Kathleen McNeely, Isch, Mark Lewis, Dan Gavitt, Bearby, and other senior leaders had put in place a multi-tier plan designed to mitigate the financial impact of an unthinkable tournament cancellation.

We'd been called paranoid for maintaining such extensive contingency planning. Purchasing pandemic insurance seemed like wasteful spending to some. Building substantial reserves was criticized as hoarding resources that should be distributed to members. But now that planning proved essential and validated our approach to risk management.

As Kathleen later stated: "We had a plan. We've implemented the plan. And the plan is working."

The plan involved using millions from our reserve fund, receiving millions in guaranteed payments from media partners, drawing millions down on our line of credit, and using millions in event cancellation insurance to pay off that line of credit. Through this approach we could provide the greatest monetary distribution possible to our membership during an unprecedented crisis.

Importantly, we were among the few enterprises with event cancellation and business interruption insurance against a pandemic. Insurance covered $270 million of the over $800 million in tournament revenue we would lose. Our contracts with Turner, CBS, and ESPN provided additional protection. While we couldn't prevent all financial pain, our planning significantly mitigated the impact.

We had projected distributing $600 million to more than 300 Division I schools from April to June. With the tournament canceled, we were able to distribute $225 million in June. While this was $375 million below budget, it was far better than many feared possible when the cancellation was first announced.

The financial challenges, however, cascaded throughout college athletics. Dozens of schools eliminated sports, with Stanford shocking the college world by cutting eleven. Sports Illustrated reported that eighty-six Division I sports teams were eliminated in the 2020-21 academic year. Employee furloughs and layoffs became common across athletics departments nationwide.

At the NCAA, we worked mightily to avoid layoffs. As part of that effort, at the end of March, President Emmert, I, and the other eight members of senior management agreed to a 20% salary cut. The rest of our president's cabinet agreed to a 10% pay cut.

This was a generous act by a highly functioning and cohesive leadership team demonstrating organizational commitment to shared sacrifice during crisis. As Emmert stated, the action "frees up needed resources and highlights our commitment to weather the current economic challenges we face while continuing to provide opportunities to college athletes."

I remember the conversation when we made this decision. It was a video conference, all of us in our home offices during the early days of lockdown. Someone on the call suggested we should cut salaries to avoid staff layoffs and show solidarity with member institutions facing their own financial crises.

There was no debate. Every senior leader immediately agreed. The money we saved wouldn't solve the financial crisis, but it sent an important message about organizational values and leadership responsibility.

Ultimately, our revenue fell to $521 million between September 1, 2019, and August 31, 2020, compared to more than $1 billion in the previous fiscal year. Yet through careful planning, disciplined financial management, and collective sacrifice, we navigated this crisis while maintaining our commitment to supporting member institutions and student-athletes.

The loss of revenue and cancellation of tournaments were only the beginning of operating within the new pandemic paradigm. As we worked to safely resume sports activities, we collaborated with professional sports to model how to conduct competitions during a pandemic.

The NBA's successful implementation of a bubble environment in Orlando, Florida provided both inspiration and a blueprint for potential college sports adaptations. The bubble was a $190 million investment by the NBA to protect its 2019-20 season, which was initially suspended on March 11, 2020. The bubble recouped an estimated $1.5 billion in revenue.

The NBA's bubble strategy proved remarkably effective. From the resumed season until the end of the NBA Finals, the league recorded zero COVID-19 cases for teams participating in the bubble. This success was achieved through stringent protocols governing almost every aspect of players' lives. Participants quarantined before departure and upon arrival, remained in the bubble, tested regularly, maintained physical distance, wore masks, and practiced rigorous hand hygiene.

Under the leadership of Dan Gavitt and Dr. Hainline, our Basketball Committee explored whether a bubble approach could work for the 2021 NCAA tournament. As Emmert noted, the scalability challenges: "Starting with sixty-four teams is tough. Thirty-two, okay, maybe that's a manageable number. Sixteen, certainly manageable. But you've got to figure out those logistics."

Implementing a bubble strategy for college athletics presented unique challenges. For example, it would potentially violate NCAA rules on athlete-only residence halls, which were banned in the 1990s. While professional athletes could be sequestered for months, college student-athletes had academic responsibilities and different legal and regulatory frameworks governing their participation. We needed to find approaches that worked within the college athletics environment while constantly focused on health and safety.

While basketball captured initial attention due to the March tournament cancellation, college football faced perhaps even more complex challenges as the pandemic extended into fall 2020. The sport's importance to university finances and cultural significance in American higher education made decisions about the football season particularly consequential.

But here's where the structure of college athletics created additional problems. Since the Supreme Court's *Board of Regents* decision in 1984, the NCAA's national organization has controlled neither the economics nor the competition of Division I FBS football. Decisions around football would need to be made by individual conferences. The absence of national leadership quickly became apparent as conferences jockeyed for competitive advantages.

The Power Five conferences took varying approaches. On August 11, 2020, the Big Ten made the courageous announcement that presidents and chancellors voted to postpone all fall sports, including football, amid the pandemic, with hopes of playing in the spring. Later that same day, the Pac-12 announced the CEO group had reached the same conclusion.

Michael Schill, chair of the Pac-12 CEO group, stated: "We feel good about our decision. We would have made it independent of the Big Ten. We respect the institutions in the Big Ten, many of them have the same values that we have, and we're happy they're joining us."

The SEC and ACC made clear they were not postponing their seasons. The Big 12 remained undecided. The decentralized decision-making reflected both the structure of college football governance and the distinct circumstances facing conferences across different regions of the country. This was developing in a way that would make holding a College Football Playoff exceedingly difficult, if not impossible.

However, the Big Ten reversed its decision on September 16, 2020, reinstating play with an eight-game shortened season after implementing enhanced safety protocols. This turnaround demonstrated intense pressure from every angle, including influencers, boosters, parents, media, and even President Trump, who called the Big Ten Commissioner. The message was clear: conferences must maintain football programs despite health concerns.

The challenges facing football were different from those facing basketball. Football's longer season, larger rosters, and physical nature created unique safety considerations. Outdoor venues offered advantages for crowd management and ventilation, but extended player contact during games and practices posed ongoing transmission risks.

Once we were past spring sports and football season, we turned our full attention back to basketball. The 2021 NCAA men's basketball tournament represented a crucial test of our ability to safely conduct championships during the ongoing pandemic.

While an NBA-style bubble wasn't practical for the college tournament, we decided in January 2021 that all tournament games would be held in Indiana rather than at sites across the country. This extraordinary decision to centralize the entire tournament in one state was driven by the need to create a controlled environment and minimize the risk of virus transmission.

It wouldn't be a strict bubble, but we would host the tournament in what we called a "controlled environment." Through this centralized approach, we hoped to limit exposure to the coronavirus and prevent outbreaks while providing student-athletes with championship opportunities they deserved.

Our decision to allow limited fan attendance marked a significant step toward normal operations. Dr. Hainline and I had several meetings with Dr. Virginia Caine, Director and Chief Medical Officer of the Marion County Public Health Department, who was coordinating the COVID-19 response for Indianapolis. Eventually, the decision to allow up to twenty-five percent capacity with physical distancing was made in conjunction with state and local health authorities.

The Indianapolis-centered tournament required extensive coordination and planning. Everyone was ushered out between games, and crews had at least ninety minutes to wipe down everything and prepare for the next game. Because many existing locker rooms weren't big enough, we created makeshift locker rooms, in some cases using large spaces far removed from playing areas to accommodate social distancing requirements. Those of us attending events were tested in a separate designated area daily, sometimes twice daily, before entering the arenas.

The tournament's execution proved largely successful from a health and safety perspective, with minimal COVID-19 disruptions. Sadly, VCU's men's tournament hopes ended prematurely due to COVID. But the controlled environment approach validated our strategy for conducting large-scale events during the pandemic while maintaining competitive authenticity and providing meaningful opportunities for student-athletes. We replicated this approach in San Antonio for the 2021 Women's Basketball Tournament.

These successful tournaments demonstrated that with proper planning, medical guidance, and commitment to protocols, we could conduct championships safely even during a pandemic. The experience provided valuable lessons for future event management and crisis response.

In the end, the pandemic's impact extended far beyond the immediate crisis period. Perhaps most significantly, the Division I Board of Directors granted an additional year of eligibility to fall, winter, and spring sport athletes whose 2020 seasons were affected, recognizing these athletes had been denied the opportunity to complete competitive seasons through no fault of their own. The eligibility extensions created convoluted situations as programs accommodated additional years while maintaining scholarship limits and roster caps, but it was the right thing to do for athletes who had lost competitive opportunities.

For players, the question was not abstract. "For me and my parents, one of the things we're focusing on is eligibility," Stanford defensive back Joshua Drayden, a member of the players' rights group We Are United, told the Associated Press days before the vote. "We're just trying to weigh all of our options. Same for a lot of athletes around the Pac-12 and the nation." Shane Lyons, chair of the Football Oversight Committee, heard the same concern from across the country. "Not having a normal season, not having that normal 20 games in soccer, or 28 matches in volleyball, and even football not sure what that season's going to look like, that was the No. 1 concern that the student-athletes had, was the eligibility piece," he said after the vote. Lyons conceded administrators and coaches would spend years working through inflated rosters and scholarship math on the back end, but he was unequivocal about the trade: "The eligibility piece, without question in my mind, this is a win for them. The pandemic also reshaped daily operations in ways that became permanent: regular testing requirements, enhanced medical monitoring, detailed contact tracing procedures extended recruiting dead periods, and the adoption of virtual recruiting technologies that proved to have lasting value.

Sitting in my home office in April 2020, I reflected on everything we had been through over the previous decade: self-governance innovation failures, Penn State's political crisis, Miami's enforcement failures, the FBI investigation, concussion litigation, unionization efforts, and now COVID revealing the ultimate fragility of the amateur model's economics. These were not separate challenges. They were convergent pressures all demonstrating that the model's contradictions were becoming unsustainable. The pandemic just made those contradictions impossible to ignore.

Yet the NCAA's response to COVID-19 represented a positive watershed moment in college athletics history, demonstrating our ability to make difficult decisions rapidly while maintaining core values, even at enormous cost.

> Perhaps most importantly, the pandemic highlighted the central role that college athletics plays in American culture and higher education. The widespread disappointment over canceled seasons and tournaments demonstrated the deep emotional and cultural significance of college sports, while our response showed that values and principles matter even when tested by extraordinary circumstances.

Our response, while imperfect, demonstrated leadership and values that college athletics can celebrate. We made good decisions under extraordinary pressure. We prioritized health over revenue when the costs were staggering. We found ways to conduct championships safely when circumstances allowed, and we protected student-athlete eligibility when seasons were stripped away through no fault of their own. I was overwhelmed with emotion as I went through this process. We were doing the right thing. Why could we not replicate this process in other circumstances?

But pride in our crisis response should not obscure what the crisis revealed about the underlying structure. The financial concentration we experienced in March 2020 was not an accident of the pandemic. It highlighted questions about revenue diversification and organizational resilience that had been building for years.

The litigation, the legislation, the political pressure, and the reform debates I have described throughout this book were all expressions of a deeper tension between commercial reality and the governance framework designed to manage it. The pandemic did not create those contradictions. It compressed the timeline in which they demanded attention, making undeniable in a single fiscal year what had been building across a decade.

The question college athletics has been slowly answering, through court decisions and settlement agreements and rule changes rather than through voluntary leadership, is how to reconcile what the enterprise has become with the principles it was built on. COVID forced that question into sharp relief not through legal liability but through economic reality. The answers that follow will define whether college athletics can build a model that is financially sustainable, genuinely fair to the people at its center, and honest about what it actually is.

Chapter 22
Unequal Courts
Gender Equity in Basketball and Beyond

I was at the men's Final Four in Indianapolis when my phone started blowing up with messages about the women's basketball tournament in San Antonio. On April 5, 2021, Baylor demolished undefeated Gonzaga 86-70 to claim its first men's basketball national championship. The Bears were dominant from the opening tip, building a 19-point first-half lead and never allowing the Bulldogs to find their characteristic rhythm. Gonzaga had entered the game seeking to become the first undefeated national champion since Indiana in 1976. They left having suffered their lone defeat of the season, losing by 16 points.

The game was anticlimactic. What surrounded it was anything but.

By the time Baylor and Gonzaga tipped off in Indianapolis, we were engulfed in a crisis that revealed concerns about the treatment of women athletes in ways no external audit ever had. I watched the championship game that night knowing that whatever happened on the court had already been overshadowed by what happened in faraway hotel ballrooms and convention centers. Jared Butler scored 22 points. Davion Mitchell added 15. The Bears shot 43.5 percent from three. None of it mattered as much as a smartphone video from a twenty-year-old forward.

The timing also created another brutal irony. The men's championship represented exactly what March Madness was supposed to be: two elite programs with contrasting styles, a potential perfect season on the line, and genuinely transcendent basketball. Baylor's defense was among the best I had ever seen at the collegiate level. Scott Drew became one of five active coaches at the time to win an NCAA title. His program won its first championship and, in fact, had only ever played in a championship game in 1948. But Baylor's championship would be remembered not for the basketball, but for what it obscured. The coverage focused on

Emmert's apology for the women's tournament failures and the announcement that the law firm Kaplan Hecker and Fink would conduct an independent review of gender equity across all NCAA championships.

In mid-March 2021, we began both tournaments in controlled environments. Indianapolis for the men. San Antonio for the women. Same protocols. Same commitment to health and safety. Everything under control.

Or so I thought.

Ali Kershner, a performance coach with Stanford's women's basketball team, had posted photos on social media showing the weight room facilities at the women's tournament. A single dumbbell tree. Some yoga mats. That was it. Next to those photos, she'd included images of the men's tournament weight room near where I was in Indianapolis. It was an expansive, meticulously designed facility with every piece of equipment athletes could need.

Based upon what I was hearing internally, my first reaction was defensive. There must be more to this story. Space constraints in San Antonio. Logistical challenges with the controlled environment. Were COVID protocols limiting what we could provide? The explanation would make sense once people understood the full context, I thought.

Then, University of Oregon player Sedona Prince posted a TikTok video that went viral within hours. She showed the simple women's facilities, then panned her camera to reveal large empty spaces around the minimal equipment, directly refuting claims about space limitations. "If you aren't upset about this problem, then you're a part of it," she said.

I watched that video in my home just north of Indianapolis, and something shifted. The defensive explanations died in my throat. Although there was a more complicated explanation than the public had patience for or than the media would tolerate, Prince was on to something. This wasn't about space constraints or COVID protocols. This was about a historical primary focus on men's basketball and treating almost everything else, including women's basketball, as an afterthought. And some would argue, rightfully so, given that men's basketball was and is the economic engine of the NCAA. I am not addressing football here. Ever since the *Board of Regents* decision, College Football Playoff money does not flow through the NCAA.

It appeared that the COVID-controlled environments we'd implemented to conduct the 2021 tournaments safely had inadvertently created something else. We were living through a natural experiment that exposed gender inequities that may have existed, but had been less noticeable when tournaments were held at different sites across the country. By centralizing everything, by putting men's and women's tournaments in controlled environments where direct comparisons were unavoidable, we'd inadvertently revealed the different treatment of women's sports embedded in NCAA structure and culture.

The disparities extended far beyond weight rooms, and as details emerged over the following days, each revelation was more damaging than the last. The Kaplan report later exposed that the NCAA had spent about $125 per player on initial gifts for men's teams, compared to around $60 per player for women's teams, and had spent over $70,000 on personal hygiene kits for men, even though women weren't provided with them. Men received buffet meals with steak and lobster mac and cheese, while women received box meals. Perhaps most concerning from a health perspective, men's teams received highly accurate PCR-based coronavirus tests, while women's teams received less accurate antigen-based tests.

Our immediate response needed to be swift and transparent. Bob Williams, an Air Force veteran with extraordinary judgment in communications, laid out the plan. Dan Gavitt, head of men's basketball was first up. He was clear and unequivocal. Apologizing for the significant disparities between men's and women's basketball facilities, he acknowledged that the NCAA fell short in providing equal access to weight-training facilities. Dan credibly expressed a commitment to improving communication and collaboration between the men's and women's basketball committees and stated that the disparities highlighted would lead to better practices in the future. And, as true leaders do, Gavitt emphasized that the buck stopped with him. He was clear that it was his responsibility to ensure consistency across both tournaments, and he would.

Next was Lynn Holzman, vice president of women's basketball, providing an interview from San Antonio. Taking over for Northwestern University

Hall of Fame basketball athlete Anucha Browne, Holzman was appointed to the role in February 2018 after impressive leadership roles throughout her college athletics journey. Three years later, this crisis would require all her skills to be put to use. She laid out the concerns and the path forward in a straightforward manner. While Holzman was criticized for not taking enough personal responsibility and her earlier comment suggesting limited space, she was passionate about leading through the quagmire to achieve gender equality. And she did.

Emmert's comments, like Gavitt's, represented an explicit acceptance of responsibility and accountability. A minor attempt at an explanation was misplaced and drew fire from the media. Still, in the end, he made clear that we were taking gender equity issues in championships and elsewhere seriously.

Emmert, Williams, and I, along with the men's and women's basketball leadership, discussed matters as the crisis was exploding on social media. We again believed an external review was most appropriate. It was simple. This couldn't be an internal investigation. We lacked sufficient credibility to investigate ourselves.

There was some resistance within the membership due to prior experience with external examinations. External reviews are expensive. They're unpredictable. You lose control of the narrative. And those not enmeshed in college sports can face a steep learning curve. But the viral spread of those images had created a public accountability moment that traditional NCAA processes couldn't handle. Social media had accelerated institutional scrutiny in ways that decades of advocacy and litigation never had.

I knew exactly who we needed. I had professional experience with Roberta Kaplan, one of the nation's leading civil rights attorneys. She had argued *United States v. Windsor* before the Supreme Court, the landmark case that struck down the Defense of Marriage Act. Her work on gender equity issues was exceptional, and her reputation for thorough, fearless investigation was precisely what this moment required. We needed someone who would find the truth regardless of how uncomfortable that truth might be for the NCAA.

We retained Kaplan Hecker & Fink LLP to conduct a comprehensive external review of gender equity issues, initially focusing on basketball tournaments and subsequently examining all 84 NCAA championships. Emmert insisted that the investigation be completely independent. No limitations on scope. Full access to staff, documents, and decision-makers. Let them find whatever they find, and we'll deal with the results.

The firm's investigation was, in fact, exhaustive, involving interviews with hundreds of NCAA staff, committee members, and external stakeholders, including commissioners, coaches, and student-athletes. What they found was devastating in its clarity.

The Phase I report, delivered on August 2, 2021, concluded that "the NCAA has not lived up to its stated commitment to diversity, inclusion and gender equity among its student-athletes, coaches and administrators." But the key finding went deeper. The gender equity issues were not new in 2021, but were "the inevitable result of the current structure of the NCAA itself, which is designed to maximize the value of and support to the Division I Men's Basketball Championship as the primary source of funding for the NCAA and its membership."

There it was in black and white. The NCAA had evolved a structure centered on men's basketball as its economic engine. The Kaplan report confirmed what many had suspected: this structural priority had implications for gender equity across all other championships.

At the time, women's basketball operated in organizational silos with little strategic coordination. Resources were allocated disproportionately, even when accounting for differences in tournament size. The media rights structure may have systemically undervalued women's basketball. And we lacked comprehensive oversight mechanisms for gender equity that might have caught and corrected these problems before they became public scandals.

The review identified specific failures in the planning process. The six-person women's tournament staff was half the size of the men's staff. The NCAA announced the men's tournament location on January 4 and began immediately planning, but the women's staff didn't visit San Antonio until January 25. One women's staffer told investigators that March 13, just two days before Selection Monday, was the first time she learned men would have a full weight room for the entire tournament, leaving little time to plan for equivalent women's facilities.

That seemed incongruous to me. The people planning the women's tournament didn't know until two days before the event that there would be differences in basic facilities. Not because anyone was deliberately hiding information, but because the organizational structure was so siloed and so focused on men's basketball as the priority that inequities were built into the processes. Although the two staffs should have been working in lockstep with Gavitt and Holzman leading the way, the information did not seem to flow efficiently through their organizations.

The silos were part of a system that developed through economic imperatives. College athletics at the highest levels is a commercial enterprise structured around maximizing revenue not just from CFP football, which the NCAA did not control, but also from men's basketball. That structure perpetuated multiple forms of manipulation or favoritism, which could persist only as long as external accountability mechanisms remained weak. A structure that may have been adequate to govern intercollegiate athletics in the past appeared not to have adjusted adequately to changes in the product itself, perhaps because doing so would have exposed a crumbling cornerstone of the enterprise and an underlying behavioral tendency toward chauvinism.

To understand how we got here, we need to go back to an interesting start to women's college athletics. It had been deliberately structured to avoid the competitive, revenue-focused model that characterized men's sports. Beginning with Senda Berenson's modified basketball rules at Smith College in 1893, women's physical education leaders embraced a "sports for all" philosophy that emphasized participation over winning and explicitly rejected intercollegiate competition.

Fast forward to 1972, when Representative Patsy Takemoto Mink of Hawaii championed thirty-seven words that would transform American education. Mink, the first Japanese American woman elected to Congress, had been rejected by more than a dozen medical schools because of her gender. After graduating from the University of Chicago Law School, she couldn't find legal work as a married woman. Her personal experience with institutional barriers drove her to ensure future generations wouldn't face the same obstacles.

Working with Representative Edith Green of Oregon and Senator Birch Bayh of Indiana (the NCAA's home state), Mink pushed through Title IX. It read, "No person in the United States shall, on the basis of sex, be excluded from participation in, be denied the benefits of, or be subjected to discrimination under any education program or activity receiving Federal financial assistance." President Nixon signed it into law on June 23, 1972.

The NCAA's response was immediate and oppositional. The NCAA filed a lawsuit in 1976 challenging Title IX's legality, though it was dismissed in 1978. Senator John Tower later tried to exempt revenue-producing sports from Title IX compliance. These early challenges reflected anxiety about the financial and structural implications of gender equity requirements. The NCAA represented member institution concerns about financial demands and implementation challenges, arguing that proposed interpretations imposed excessive financial obligations and lacked specific compliance standards.

Think about the pattern. The NCAA challenged Title IX implementation in the 1970s, as it would later resist athlete compensation reforms, recognition of employment status, and other improvements. The playbook was always the same. Defend the existing structure, argue that proposed changes would destroy college athletics, resist until external pressure became overwhelming, then make reforms while fighting further accountability.

Title IX's implementation was gradual. Federal regulations weren't issued until 1975, giving high schools and colleges three years to comply. The Office for Civil Rights initially showed limited enforcement, with very few complaints investigated and resolved under Presidents Reagan and Bush.

Critical legal developments shaped Title IX's evolution. In 1984, the Supreme Court's decision in *Grove City v. Bell* held that Title IX applied only to programs that directly receive federal funds, effectively exempting athletics departments. However, Congress passed the Civil Rights Restoration Act of 1987 over President Reagan's veto, nullifying the *Grove City* ruling and establishing that gender-based barriers were prohibited throughout entire educational institutions if any part of the institution received federal funding.

This was another example of the Supreme Court making social policy through its decisions, and of active U.S. Presidential involvement in matters of college sports. Courts and political leaders kept getting drawn into college athletics because the NCAA's governance structure and the amateur model's contradictions created legal and social problems that demanded intervention.

In 1992, the Supreme Court's decision in *Franklin v. Gwinnett County Public Schools* was crucial in establishing monetary damages for Title IX violations, giving the law significant enforcement power. This decision allowed victims to seek financial compensation and made institutions more responsive to compliance, as they now faced financial consequences for violations. Things began to improve as women's college sports gained momentum and attention.

Yet this revealed a paradoxical outcome. While Title IX dramatically increased women's participation in athletics, it also had unintended consequences for women in leadership positions. Before Title IX, more than ninety percent of women's athletics departments were run by women. This dominance eroded as separate women's athletics organizations, such as the Association for Intercollegiate Athletics for Women, were absorbed into the NCAA structure in 1981, following years of debate and legal concerns about operating men's and women's programs under different organizational rules.

A decade later, a 1992 NCAA gender equity study of Division I institutions found significant discrepancies in participation rates and funding between men's and women's programs, with fewer than fifty percent of women's teams having female head coaches and substantial salary disparities. Despite significant progress in women's participation in athletics, the percentage of women in athletics department leadership positions actually decreased over Title IX's first fifty years. More female athletes, fewer female leaders. More opportunities to play, less power to shape how sports were organized and valued.

While educational institutions are subject to Title IX as recipients of federal financial assistance, the NCAA has historically avoided direct compliance. In the 1999 Supreme Court case *NCAA v. Smith*, the Court ruled that the NCAA's receipt of membership dues from educational institutions did not constitute direct receipt of federal aid, effectively exempting the organization from Title IX requirements.

This exemption had profound implications. Without legal accountability under Title IX, the NCAA's organizational culture and resource allocation could miss gender inequities. Indeed, the issues that exploded into public view in 2021 might have roots in the Title IX exemption. To be clear, the NCAA has many programs and policies dedicated to advancing women's sports. And I personally witnessed an organization committed to the principles of gender equity, despite Title IX not being applicable. Yet, I recognize that the public and female athletes experienced the association quite differently. Gender inequity revealed that the financial architecture of amateurism we had defended so vigorously was built around revenue from male athletes in a couple of high-profile sports, while female athletes' competitive and commercial potential remained underinvested and undervalued.

The vast majority of NCAA revenue comes from its media rights agreement with CBS and TNT Sports, which provides $8.8 billion from 2016 to 2032, exceeding $1 billion annually during the contract's current lifespan. This revenue had historically been distributed to conferences based solely on men's basketball tournament performance, creating financial incentives that for decades had no parallel in women's sports. As the Knight Commission pointed out in April 2024, the NCAA had distributed more than $340 million through the men's basketball performance unit system without ever creating an equivalent formula for women's tournament success. Between 1991, when the unit system was established, and 2024, conferences whose women's teams reached Final Fours and won national championships received nothing extra from the NCAA for those achievements.

The inequity was so deeply embedded in the distribution model that it took a public reckoning, record-shattering viewership, and sustained advocacy from coaches like Dawn Staley to force a structural change. In January 2025, Division I membership unanimously approved the creation of women's basketball performance and equal conference funds, beginning with the 2025 tournament. The initial pool of $15 million, growing to $25 million by 2027-28, represented progress, but also highlighted the remaining gap: a women's tournament unit in its first year was worth roughly $113,000, a fraction of the value of a men's unit built on more than three decades of compounding revenue.

The Kaplan report prompted both immediate and longer-term reforms that I worked on directly before leaving the NCAA. By the 2022 tournaments, several key recommendations had been implemented. We adopted "March Madness" branding for the women's tournament, expanded the tournament to a 68-team bracket to match the men's format, implemented budget oversight to ensure equity, and provided identical gifts and perks.

The Kaplan review recommended holding joint men's and women's Final Fours at the same site in the future and conducting annual gender equity assessments. Additional recommendations included eliminating gender modifiers in tournament branding and improving overall gender equity oversight. The women's sports community embraced some of these reforms; others were rejected.

What happened after the 2021 crisis accelerated in ways nobody predicted. The reforms we implemented significantly improved tournament equity, and the belated creation of women's performance units in 2025 addressed the most glaring financial disparity. But the unit values themselves revealed a deeper truth that echoed the Kaplan review's key finding: the NCAA and ESPN decision to bundle women's basketball with other championship media rights, rather than selling those rights separately, undervalued women's basketball at a moment when the market was signaling its enormous and rapidly growing worth.

In the 2023-24 season, University of Iowa guard Caitlin Clark and LSU forward Angel Reese became cultural phenomena. Their extraordinary talent, competitive fire, and amazing performances drew massive audiences. The 2023 women's national championship game between LSU and Iowa attracted a record 9.9 million viewers, only to be surpassed by the following year's Elite Eight between the same teams, which drew 12.3 million. The 2024 semifinal between Iowa and UConn drew 14.2 million viewers, becoming the most-watched women's college basketball game ever on any network. Then, on April 7, 2024, South Carolina's undefeated championship victory over Iowa drew an average television audience of

18.9 million viewers. This was more than any basketball game of any kind since 2019. It exceeded the men's championship viewership. It surpassed every NBA Finals game over the preceding 5 years. It was, by any measure, the most watched basketball broadcast in modern history.

These weren't niche audiences for a secondary sport. These were mainstream, prime-time viewership numbers that rivaled and sometimes exceeded men's tournament games. Women's basketball attendance exploded. NIL opportunities for female athletes expanded dramatically. The conventional wisdom that women's sports couldn't generate significant revenue was being demolished by actual market performance. The 2024 Championship game was played at Rocket Mortgage FieldHouse in Cleveland, a venue with around 19,500 seats. The men's championship would be played at the 63,400-seat State Farm Stadium in Arizona. The women's Final Four had sold out in minutes, with average ticket prices exceeding $1000. Demand had overwhelmed supply because the sports world had never imagined that women's basketball could generate this level of interest.

A media expert hired by Kaplan estimated that rights to the women's basketball tournament alone could be worth $81 to $112 million by 2025, compared with the $34 million ESPN was paying for the women's tournament plus 28 other sports combined. By 2024, those estimates looked conservative as networks competed for women's basketball content and viewership data demonstrated massive untapped commercial value.

The undervaluation had not only been based on actual market performance. It was also based on decades of organizational structure and culture that treated women's basketball as subordinate, invested fewer resources in promotion and development, and created self-fulfilling prophecies about commercial viability.

Attending a Caitlin Clark versus Angel Reese battle in person, observing the fan excitement, and then learning the television viewership numbers made me think about the opportunities we'd missed. Not just at the NCAA, but across college athletics. The NCAA had built an entire economic model around male athletes in revenue sports while lacking a clear picture of the value of female athletes' performances. And then we'd use the revenue disparities that model created to justify continued inequitable resource allocation.

The circular logic was apparent. Men's basketball receives more resources, which leads to better products and marketing, which generates more revenue, which then justifies giving it more resources. Women's basketball never got the chance to prove what it could do.

The 2021 crisis, as well as the individual and collective Caitlin Clark and Angel Reese phenomenon, broke that cycle by forcing acknowledgment that revenue disparities weren't natural or inevitable but were the result of organizational choices about resource allocation and marketing investment. When women's basketball received even modest increases in promotional support and media exposure, audiences responded enthusiastically.

And now college women’s basketball had star power typically seen only in professional sports. Reese, affectionately known as the Bayou Barbie, set NCAA single-season records in double-doubles and rebounds. Clark, a genuine cultural phenomenon, transcended her sport in ways that women's basketball had never achieved. Her regular season game against Ohio State, in which she broke Pete Maravich's all-time scoring record, drew 3.39 million viewers, the most watched women's regular season game on any network since 1999.

The championship against South Carolina was Clark's final college game. She finished with 30 points but was overwhelmed by the Gamecocks' depth and defensive intensity. South Carolina completed a 38-0 season with a 12-point victory. Dawn Staley, who built South Carolina into a dynasty through sheer force of will, vision, and competitive brilliance, claimed her third national championship that night, cementing her place among the greatest coaches in the history of American sport. None of the basketball mattered as much as those starring in the event and the audience watching it.

The Kaplan report recommended that the NCAA sell women's tournament rights separately and invest in marketing comparable to that of men's basketball. The market had responded.

In January 2024, the NCAA announced a new eight-year, $920 million media rights deal with ESPN covering 40 championships, including the women's basketball tournament. The deal represented a more than 300 percent increase over the previous agreement, which had paid just $34 million annually for 29 championships bundled together. The NCAA's own media consultants estimated that roughly 57 percent of the new deal's value, approximately $65 million per year, was attributable to the women's basketball tournament alone. That was a significant step forward, but it also confirmed the Kaplan report's central insight: the women's tournament had been dramatically undervalued for years, bundled with dozens of other properties in a package that obscured its true market worth. The Desser Sports Media analysis commissioned for the Kaplan review had projected the women's tournament could command $81 to $112 million annually beginning in 2025. The NCAA chose not to test that projection. Rather than unbundling the women's tournament and bringing it to open competitive bidding as Kaplan recommended, the NCAA negotiated the new deal within ESPN's exclusive negotiating window, never formally putting the rights on the open market.

The result was a deal that tripled the overall price but still left money on the table for women's basketball. At $65 million per year, the women's tournament was valued well below the lower bound of the Desser estimate, and the deal was struck without competitive bidding from other networks. The NCAA defended the approach, arguing that the bundle created efficiencies and that the media landscape had shifted in ways that made open-market negotiations riskier. Critics, including many in the women's basketball coaching community, saw it differently: the NCAA had once again prioritized institutional convenience over maximizing the value of its fastest-growing property. When both the men's and women's media rights deals expire in 2032, the women's tournament will get its first real opportunity to have its standalone value tested in the marketplace, at a moment when the market may finally be ready to pay what the product is actually worth.

This connected to the broader Collegiate Capitalism transformation in revealing ways. The amateur model we'd defended for decades was vulnerable not only because of revenue concentration and compensation questions, but also because it produced gender disparities that were increasingly difficult to justify, as the Kaplan review vividly exposed.

The transformation continues today with new battlegrounds emerging around revenue sharing. The *House* settlement allows schools to share up to $20.5 million annually with athletes, with that figure set to increase 4% annually over the next ten years. It also includes $2.8 billion in back payments to athletes who competed between 2016 and 2024 for missed NIL opportunities. The question of how this money should be distributed has reignited the gender equity debate with even higher stakes.

Just days before leaving office in January 2025, the Biden administration's Department of Education issued guidance stating that Title IX rules would apply to future revenue generated by schools sharing with college athletes. The fact sheet declared that schools must provide equal athletic opportunities including benefits, opportunities, publicity, and recruitment, and that in the new NIL environment, these same principles apply. The guidance suggested that NIL payments from schools would be treated as "athletic financial assistance" and that this would require a distribution between male and female athletes in a manner consistent with the law.

The response was swift and predictable. On February 12, 2025, the Trump administration's Department of Education rescinded the Biden guidance. Acting Assistant Secretary Craig Trainor stated bluntly that the claim that Title IX forces schools and colleges to distribute student-athlete revenues proportionately based on gender equity considerations is sweeping and would require clear legal authority to support it. That does not exist. The bureaucratic reversal represented a different vision of what college athletics should become. Biden's assistant secretary for the Office for Civil Rights, Catherine Lhamon, promptly responded, "I think it's appalling for an administration that performatively and repeatedly claims to be intent on protecting women and girls' equal access to sports, then disavows a legal interpretation that protects women and girls' ability to benefit financially from their athletic talents."

Interestingly, President Trump himself had issued an executive order on July 24, 2025, titled "Saving College Sports," which stated that collegiate athletic departments with significant revenue should maintain or increase scholarship opportunities for non-revenue sports and that any revenue-sharing should be implemented in a way that protects women's and non-revenue-generating sports. The mixed messages from the same administration reflect the deep tensions between market forces and equity principles that define the new era. That tension only deepened on April 3, 2026, when the President issued a second, more sweeping executive order, "Urgent National Action to Save College Sports," which again directed that revenue-sharing models preserve or expand opportunities in women's and Olympic sports and avoid reallocating resources in ways that reduce scholarships or participation. Yet the same administration had, just over a year earlier, rescinded the Biden guidance that would have made such protection enforceable under Title IX, leaving the gender-equity commitments in both orders dependent on voluntary institutional compliance rather than federal civil-rights law. I return to the 2026 order in the Epilogue.

The courts will ultimately decide. An appeal to the Ninth Circuit by objectors argues that the *House* settlement's damages and injunctive relief provisions violate Title IX, contending that they allow schools to compensate male athletes disproportionately compared to female athletes. Female athletes who feel the system unfairly burdens them are preparing additional challenges. As Michael LeRoy, a University of Illinois labor and sports law professor noted, the recent surge in women's sports popularity couldn't have been better timed. The question is whether they'll be stuck with a compensation model for the next 10 years that reflects the past, not the future.

Making matters more complex, the U.S. General Accounting Office reported in 2024 that 93% of colleges still don't give women proportional opportunities to play sports, one of the goals of Title IX, and the Department of Education has been falling down on enforcing compliance. The revenue-sharing pressures could either accelerate progress toward equity or entrench existing disparities.

Legal scholars continue to argue that the NCAA should voluntarily comply with Title IX, even without legal mandates, upholding the organization's stated commitment to gender equity. Congressional efforts to address the NCAA exemption included a 2021 concurrent resolution stipulating that Title IX applies to the NCAA and the reintroduction of the

College Athletes Bill of Rights, which mandates that athletics associations not discriminate based on gender.

Yet data reveal ongoing disparities despite decades of Title IX implementation and gender equity practices. While women constitute approximately 60% of college students, they receive significantly fewer athletics opportunities, scholarship funding, and coaching positions. The Kaplan review found that the NCAA spent $4,285 per men's tournament participant, compared with $2,588 per women's participant, with even greater disparities in single-gender sports.

The persistence of these disparities fifty years after Title IX's passage demonstrates the complexity of achieving substantive equity beyond formal compliance in an environment based on capitalism. History reveals that formal equality does not automatically produce substantive equity, and that meaningful change often requires sustained external pressure combined with internal institutional commitment.

The journey from Title IX's passage to the 2021 tournament crisis to the current explosion of attention to women's sports illuminates both the transformative power of federal civil rights legislation and the persistence of institutional resistance to genuine equity. Patsy Mink's declaration that "what you endure is who you are" and her commitment to helping future generations avoid the barriers she faced established a legal framework that has dramatically expanded opportunities for women in education and athletics.

Yet gender equity extends beyond financial considerations to encompass institutional messaging about the value and worth of female athletes. As Prince noted after achieving immediate changes to the 2021 tournament facilities, the goal must be to "make our NCAA experience what we all hoped it would be." That aspiration demands continued vigilance, advocacy, and institutional commitment to equity principles embedded in Title IX's foundational promise.

The structural revenue challenges persist, but incremental progress is occurring. The NCAA's distribution system now includes some recognition of both men's and women's tournaments. Advocates argue that any future increases in media rights revenue must be distributed in ways that incentivize schools to invest more in women's basketball and reward success in both men's and women's basketball.

> And here's what gives me hope about future progress. The explosive growth in women's basketball viewership proved that commercial success isn't limited to men's sports when resources and promotional support are provided. The market will reward quality products regardless of athlete gender.

The seven-year WNBA collective bargaining agreement ratified in March 2026 turned that market validation into structural progress, quadrupling minimum salaries, raising the league's salary cap from $1.5 million to $7 million, and establishing the first comprehensive revenue-sharing model in women's professional sports history. It is the clearest proof yet that when women athletes are given both the platform and the leverage, the commercial case for equity becomes undeniable.

The undervaluation appeared to be a choice, not an economic necessity.

But the deeper question is whether the transformation can extend beyond rule changes to cultural transformation. Setting aside our discussion of the football phenomenon that drives all college sports, the unique NCAA financial structure was grounded in men's basketball. Everything else was an afterthought. Changing rules and resource allocation have been necessary, but will prove insufficient if the underlying culture continues treating women's sports as subordinate to men's basketball rather than as equally valuable components of college athletics. The fundamental question is whether participation in intercollegiate athletics equally benefits men and women? If the answer is yes, and it obviously is, then higher education has no choice but to support the two genders equally.

It has become increasingly apparent to me that this is how transformation happens in college athletics. It was not through voluntary reform or gradual evolution, but through pressures that forced acknowledgment of problems the system would prefer to ignore. Gender inequity joined the list of forces driving transformation: legal challenges to compensation restrictions, criminal investigations of corruption, litigation over catastrophic injuries, workers demanding union representation, pandemic exposing financial fragility, and now social media accountability forcing gender equity.

As I reflect on what happened and subsequent developments, I recognize my own evolution. I'd defended institutional priorities and organizational structure without fully appreciating how those priorities and that structure devalued women's sports. The defensive reaction I felt in Indianapolis when I saw those weight room photos reflected institutional blindness that social media accountability forced me to confront.

But I also take pride in the response once we acknowledged the problem. We hired Kaplan and gave her team complete independence to investigate. We implemented reforms rapidly rather than dragging out the process. And we worked to ensure the 2022 tournaments reflected a genuine commitment to equity rather than just public relations damage control.

Sometimes it takes balls to be a woman in college athletics. To compete despite significant resource disadvantages. To advocate for equity despite institutional resistance. To post photos on social media that expose differences that powerful institutions would prefer to hide. To demand that your NCAA experience be what you hoped it would be, rather than accepting subordination as inevitable. And because of courageous pioneers uncovering disparities, future generations of female athletes will inherit systems that move closer to the equality that Title IX promised and that genuine equity demands.

Chapter 23
Don't Bet on It
Gambling Doesn't Pay

On October 23, 2025, FBI Director Kash Patel stood before cameras in New York and offered: "This is the insider-trading saga for the NBA." Bordered by New York Police Commissioner Jessica Tisch, U.S. Attorney Joseph Nocella Jr. for the Eastern District of New York, and officials from other agencies, federal prosecutors announced indictments of more than thirty people in a sweeping case that read like a crime novel. The charges detailed insider bets on NBA basketball games and high-stakes poker games rigged by organized crime families. Current and former NBA players Terry Rozier and Chauncey Billups were among those named in the investigation. While allegations against Billups focused on poker games, Rozier was accused of participating in illegal gambling rings that exploited confidential information about player injuries and game plans. The scheme involved a network of bettors who received inside information from players, coaches, and team personnel, then placed massive wagers with illegal bookmakers, some of whom were connected to organized crime families.

The investigation revealed how the operation worked. Players and team insiders would tip off gamblers about injuries that hadn't been publicly disclosed, late scratches from lineups, or strategic decisions that could affect game outcomes. The gamblers would then place huge bets on games where they had information the public lacked. In the poker component, the scheme involved rigged games at underground casinos where marked cards and collusion among players ensured that confederates won large sums from unsuspecting wealthy participants.

The sophisticated nature of the operation, the involvement of current professional athletes, and the connection to organized crime made clear gambling's threat to sports.

And on that same day, the NCAA announced a ridiculously ill-timed potential policy change that would have been unthinkable just years earlier. College athletes, coaches, and athletics staff would now be permitted to bet on professional sports. Seriously?!

I read the news from my home office, feeling vindication and despair in equal measure. Vindication because the indictments proved we'd been right all along. Despair because the NCAA's announcement, released as federal prosecutors were describing organized crime's infiltration of sports gambling, represented a significant departure from the position we'd fought for decades to defend.

But events would soon overtake that initial despair. The gambling scandals would multiply, the NCAA would reverse course, and in January 2026, the largest college basketball point-shaving scandal since 1951 would validate every warning we had issued for decades. This chapter tells that story.

The FBI sting and initial NCAA announcement weren't simply bad timing. They epitomized a masterclass in how external pressures force institutions to adopt positions that contradict everything they'd previously stood for. Courts stripped away legal prohibitions. States legalized for the sake of tax revenue. Commercial operators made gambling ubiquitous. And now the NCAA membership was preparing to permit the very activity it had spent a century warning would destroy college athletics.

Let me explain how we got here, because the journey from principled opposition to reluctant accommodation, even if short-lived, reveals everything about what's happened to college athletics and why the amateur model couldn't survive contact with economic and political realities.

Seventy-four years before Joseph Nocella Jr. proclaimed this "one of the most brazen sports corruptions since online sports betting became widely legalized in the United States," and sixty-six years before Southern District of New York U.S. Attorney Joon Kim stood at a podium in 2017 to describe modern corruption in college basketball, another New York prosecutor, Manhattan District Attorney Frank Hogan was busy busting up gambling and game-fixing rings threatening to destroy NCAA hoops. The City College of New York point-shaving scandal, involving bribery and game fixing at Madison Square Garden and beyond, captured the most attention.

The 1950 Final Four and NIT Champion CCNY Beavers had seven players, all banned from the NBA, charged with accepting bribes to curb scoring against weaker opponents. But CCNY was just one example of gambling issues plaguing sports and involving organized crime, players, coaches, and referees. The 1919 Chicago White Sox throwing the World Series remains the most notorious.

The relationship between gambling and college athletics represents one of the most contentious aspects of American sports history. From clandestine betting operations in the late nineteenth century to today's regulated sportsbooks, the intersection of wagering and collegiate competition has generated scandals, legislative battles, and ongoing debates about integrity, amateurism, and commercialization.

This is fundamentally a story of prohibition meeting persistent demand, regulatory failure confronting commercial opportunity, and the traditional amateur paradigm clashing with modern entertainment economics. The growth of college football as a mass spectator sport in the 1920s significantly expanded betting activity. More games drew substantial wagering interest, and the development of point spread betting systems made mismatched games attractive to bettors. Organized bookmaking operations specifically targeted college sports and participants, laying the groundwork for future corruption.

Between the 1940s and the 60s, several major point-shaving scandals rocked college basketball and football. Yet, the 1951 basketball scandal remains the most significant in college sports history. Players from City College of New York, Long Island University, Kentucky, and others accepted payments to ensure their teams won by fewer points than betting spreads predicted. The scandal implicated over 30 players from seven schools, resulting in criminal prosecutions, the expulsion of students, and permanently damaged reputations.

The scope shocked America. Organized crime figures targeted college players from modest economic backgrounds who were vulnerable to financial inducements. The revelation that some of the nation's most celebrated amateur athletes had been compromising games for money challenged historic assumptions about college sports and amateurism.

Subsequent 1960s scandals, including additional basketball point-shaving cases, reinforced concerns about gambling's corrosive influence and prompted universities to implement stricter monitoring, increased law enforcement cooperation, and enhanced education programs.

For decades, the NCAA, NBA, NFL, NHL, MLB, and other leagues worried that spreading casinos and gambling would further invade sports. Congress stepped in with the Professional and Amateur Sports Protection Act (PASPA) in 1992. Legislators were concerned that widespread legal sports betting would increase corruption risks, particularly in college athletics, where amateur athletes might be more susceptible to inducements. The law's title explicitly included "Amateur" sports, reflecting congressional intent to protect college athletics from gambling-related corruption.

The "Bradley Act," named after former Princeton and NBA player and New Jersey Senator Bill Bradley, outlawed sports betting nationwide, with limited exceptions for lotteries in Oregon, Delaware, and Montana, and licensed sports betting in Nevada.

The legislation enjoyed strong support from major professional sports leagues and the NCAA. Sports leagues argued widespread legal betting would create conflicts of interest, increase corruption risks, and undermine public confidence in competition. For college sports, the NCAA contended that legal betting was incompatible with the principles of amateur athletics and would create unsavory pressures on student-athletes.

PASPA created a unique legal environment where sports betting remained popular but largely illegal. Underground betting operations flourished, particularly around March Madness and college football bowl games. Through education and PASPA enforcement, leagues reduced but didn't eliminate known inappropriate gambling influence.

New Jersey, however, which missed the one-year window to offer sports wagering, decided in 2012 to reverse course. Big money beckoned as Atlantic City was losing its luster. Jerseyans approved a Constitutional amendment authorizing sports gambling in Atlantic City and at horse racing tracks. The legislature quickly passed a statute.

Watching this unfold disturbed me. At the NCAA, we believed Congress had spoken clearly in 1992. Potential revenue from gambling wasn't worth inviting the attendant risks of widespread wagering back into sport. We met with lawyers and officials from the NFL, NBA, NHL, and MLB, and determined that New Jersey's action had to be stopped. We sued Governor Chris Christie, seeking to enjoin the law on PASPA grounds.

Our position was strong. Even the U.S. Department of Justice joined us. The sports leagues won in the trial court and on appeal. The Supreme Court declined review. Interestingly, Christie didn't deny his statute violated PASPA. He argued PASPA violated the U.S. Constitution's Tenth Amendment. Under that Amendment, the federal government cannot require a State to use its personnel or resources for federal purposes. While courts rejected this argument, the Third Circuit left the door open, offering "we do not read PASPA to prohibit New Jersey from repealing its ban on sports wagering."

Jersey wasn't done. In 2014, its legislature enacted a new law that was an end run around PASPA, repealing state law provisions that prohibited gambling schemes. Interestingly, the new law excluded wagering on sporting events involving a New Jersey college team or collegiate event in the state. Apparently, someone in Jersey recognized the potential negative impact of sports wagering and didn't want it to harm their own schools. How revealing. And more than a little hypocritical.

Initially, Christie thought this trick play was too much even for his state and vetoed the bill. But all politics are local, and often driven by ambition. As Christie geared up for his 2015 Presidential campaign, he changed his mind and signed it into law.

We gathered again to develop a strategy to respond to New Jersey's imaginative approach. We determined that defending the constitutionality and purpose of PASPA was important. The professional leagues and the NCAA presented a united front, arguing that this almost quarter-century-old Congressional prohibition was vital to sport, and Jersey's creativity was dangerous. We won in District Court, and the Third Circuit, *en banc*, affirmed, holding that the 2014 law violated PASPA just as the 2012 law did. Furthermore, PASPA did not violate the Tenth Amendment's "anti-commandeering" clause because it did not direct New Jersey to do anything.

Armed with strong language from the Third Circuit and U.S. support as *amici*, we responded to Jersey's petition before the Supreme Court. I felt confident. We'd won at every level. Multiple federal courts had upheld PASPA for over twenty years. The law successfully protected the rules of sport by limiting the spread of legal gambling. Policy arguments were on our side.

But this time we were dueling over what "authorize" meant in PASPA. The December 2017 oral arguments didn't go well. As I sat in the Court listening to the battle between appellate advocate titans Ted Olson for Jersey and Paul Clement for us, I grew concerned. The Justices seemed skeptical of our position, focusing on the balance of power between the federal government and the states, rather than the institutional principles that had motivated PASPA's passage.

On May 14, 2018, Justice Alito delivered the Opinion of the Court striking down PASPA as violating the Constitution's anti-commandeering doctrine. The Court held that PASPA directly dictated state legislatures' actions by prohibiting them from authorizing sports wagering. A law upheld by several District and Circuit Courts, operating for over twenty years to protect sports from gambling vagaries, was gone.

I was in my office at NCAA headquarters when the decision came down. I remember the sinking feeling as I read Alito's opinion. We'd lost. After winning at every level, after decades of PASPA successfully limiting gambling's spread, the Supreme Court invalidated the entire framework in a federalism decision that seemed to ignore or minimize the real-world consequences.

This was yet another example of the Court wandering into issues with apparent disregard for practical impact. In a postscript to Alito's Opinion, the Court recognized the important public policy consequence of its decision, yet offered that the "important public policy choice is not ours to make."

That line infuriated me. The Court had just made an enormously important public policy choice by invalidating PASPA. They'd chosen federalism principles of State's rights over the protection of integrity, abstract constitutional interpretation over practical consequences for college athletics. And then claimed they weren't making policy choices.

Not all Justices agreed. Ginsburg filed the dissent, joined by Sotomayor, and partially by Breyer, who also concurred in part. They sought to salvage portions of PASPA and preserve some existing protections. But dissents don't create law. The majority opinion did, and in May 2018, the floodgates opened.

> Driving home that evening, I reflected on how this connected to everything else we'd faced. Everyday burdens were becoming too heavy for amateur athletes' shoulders to carry.

The *Murphy* decision (the name of the case automatically changed when Phil Murphy was elected New Jersey Governor in January 2018) represented judicial intervention forcing change. Another instance wherein forces beyond our control reshaped college athletics regardless of what we thought was right.

While court battles proceeded, many in the sports betting world planned for the day they could advance full speed ahead. FanDuel was created in 2009 and DraftKings in 2012, each to facilitate fantasy sports. Modern fantasy sports leagues in baseball, football, and basketball had become nationwide phenomena, and the internet and access to data and statistics made them an undeniable part of the professional and college sports ecosystem.

Whether they were gambling was debatable. Some argued fantasy sports contests were games of skill exempt from gambling laws, while others, like Nevada, where gambling was legal and taxed, opined they were sports betting requiring licensing.

The arguments may have mattered to state Attorneys General but not to consumers, media companies, advertisers, and sports leagues. I recall in 2015 you couldn't walk down a city street anywhere in America without seeing a bus or bus stop with DraftKings or FanDuel signage. The companies reportedly spent $33.6 million on advertising over seven days leading up to the start of the NFL season that year, signing up more than 1 million new customers through that strategy.

Fantasy sports were wildly popular. Professional baseball, hockey, soccer, and football used DraftKings and FanDuel to drive fan engagement. But at the NCAA, we viewed the activities as gambling and wanted nothing to do with it. As with things like alcohol, tobacco, and adult entertainment, the NCAA had rules prohibiting gambling and gambling advertising at all championship events, including the Final Four.

DraftKings and FanDuel wanted to extend their advertising blitz to our events. They were gaining traction with universities and conferences, which could extend to the college football playoffs. But it wasn't simply advertising. They promised to make gamblers millionaires by having them compete on their sites, especially when customers could choose player lineups and win substantial sums based on points earned in a single day.

We sent cease-and-desist letters on August 27, 2015, regarding their contests, arguing that they were inconsistent with the values and rules of college sports. At the companies' requests, we went on a field trip to visit both at month's end.

Emmert, Mark Lewis, and I listened to the companies' positions. The meetings were fascinating exercises in competing worldviews. The companies insisted they weren't gambling operations but skill-based gaming platforms. They argued their products increased fan engagement, and prohibiting them from NCAA events left money on the table for no good reason.

I recall telling DraftKings leaders: "Sure, if it's not gambling, your product might be legal... until it's not." The legal landscape was shifting rapidly. State attorneys general were investigating. Federal authorities were examining whether fantasy sports violated gambling laws. The regulatory environment was uncertain and evolving.

Notwithstanding varying views about fantasy sports and investigations, we reached our own conclusion. We believed fantasy games met the definition of wagering, presented real risks in the college environment, and decided to ban all advertising, on-site and on television, during championship events. This was potentially a big hit for two companies that were major advertisers and a major missed financial opportunity for the NCAA.

Sure, significant additional revenue could be gained by taking their money, but our core values weren't aligned with their business model. In our broadcasting agreements, we endorsed prohibitions against accepting advertising from sports wagering companies. And we would not compromise our beliefs nor violate our contracts.

We held firm to our values and concerns about the critical importance of honest game outcomes, notwithstanding tremendous pressure to allow wagering and to accept those significant revenue opportunities. We reminded schools of the rules, regulations, and potential penalties for anyone participating in DraftKings or FanDuel contests. We told all referees and game officials they couldn't participate in paid fantasy games, and we required companies to verify that our officials weren't compromised.

As with the COVID-19 decision we'd make later in 2020, this was one of those many moments when I was proud of the NCAA national office for choosing principles over profit. Revenue from fantasy sports advertising would have been substantial. Commercial pressure to accommodate these companies was intense. But we believed maintaining the integrity of our competition was more important than generating additional revenue.

We understood the risks. Long before the 2018 Supreme Court ruling in *Murphy*, the NCAA had been examining the impact of betting on college sports. Could confidence in the games be preserved? Could the enterprise prevent betting schemes, point shaving, game fixing, and other ills that accompany sports betting? The answers were never promising.

But this internal debate wasn't limited to college sports. In 2014, while we were litigating against New Jersey, NBA Commissioner Adam Silver wrote a New York Times op-ed supporting the regulation and legalization of sports betting. In "Legalize and Regulate Sports Betting," Silver recognized the problems posed by the illegal sports betting market, advocated for regulation to control the environment, and reflected on the country's appetite for sports betting.

Once betting was legal, Silver proposed levying "integrity fees" on sports wagering revenue. That didn't seem right to us. Profiting from or taxing gambling when we didn't believe it should be part of our system was against our values. How can you argue that you are fundamentally opposed to a particular behavior and then say that you will accept revenue from taxing that behavior?

The NCAA, conversely, focused on education and consistent national guidelines. Over the years, we'd committed our own resources to policy, research, and education with student-athlete wellbeing at the core. And that, we would continue. Would that be enough? Not even close.

Since PASPA's repeal, sports betting has exploded. Total legal wagers reached about $148 billion in 2024. Bettors won approximately $130 billion. Bookmakers kept about $13.5 billion. States collected around $3 billion in tax revenue. Legal betting is available in thirty-eight states and D.C. The hold rate – the percentage of money wagered that the sportsbook expects to keep as profit – is 9.3 percent per dollar bet. New York, New Jersey, Illinois, Nevada, and Colorado represent the biggest markets. Eighty to ninety percent of bets are on mobile devices. FanDuel and DraftKings dominate, with ESPN BET playing catch-up.

We're only eight years out since legalization. Analysts believe this will continue to grow, with a dozen states contemplating legalization, eyeing New York's whopping 51% tax rate and $2 billion in gross revenue. AI solutions will improve odds-setting accuracy and enhance customer experience through personalization. The industry is shifting its focus from market share to profitability, with reduced marketing spend.

Yet as predicted, with additional access and money come greater problems. Of course, regulatory compliance costs rise, and an increased focus on responsible gambling is necessary. The NCAA focus, however, has consistently been on integrity. Not simply the "integrity of the games," because as we have explored, that notion has been used as both a shield and a sword. But I am talking about integrity in the college athletics model, which would be further eroded by the foray into gambling.

Shortly before I arrived at the NCAA, they and professional leagues were fighting Delaware's efforts to expand sports betting. In *Office of the Commissioner of MLB et al v. Jack Markell*, attorney Kenneth J. Nachbar wrote: "Sports lotteries involving single-game betting threaten the integrity of professional and amateur sports and are fundamentally at odds with the principle that the outcomes of professional and collegiate athletic contests must be perceived by the public as being determined solely on the basis of honest athletic competition."

The NCAA won that case in August 2009. But then, in May 2018, the Supreme Court invalidated PASPA in *Murphy*. Eight years later, what we'd worried most about is happening.

Despite enhanced measures and protections for legal sports betting expansion, several significant college sports gambling scandals have occurred since *Murphy*, demonstrating ongoing vulnerabilities. Concerns from years ago have been thrust into the spotlight, exacerbated by technology and mobile betting, the demand for the illegal market, and nuanced rules for players.

Scandals began immediately after PASPA's repeal in 2018, with an NBA investigation into several incidents in which referees and players placed bets, some of whom were implicated in providing insider information on game outcomes. During the 2019 college basketball season, several investigations examined allegations that Division I players engaged in point-shaving and match-fixing. And again in 2021, suspicious betting patterns prompted investigations of match-fixing or insider betting in college hoops.

In 2022, Ohio lawmakers investigated potential corruption and illegal sports betting after reports emerged that athletes were being targeted for match-fixing, with a focus on Ohio State football games.

That same year, Calvin Ridley, a wide receiver for the Atlanta Falcons, was suspended for the entire 2022 NFL season after revelations he'd placed bets on NFL games during a period when he was away from the team focusing on mental health. Ridley placed multiple bets on games, including his own team's, though there was no evidence of game-fixing.

Detroit Lions' Jameson Williams was among several players suspended for violating the NFL's gambling policy in 2023. Williams was suspended for six games after placing bets on non-NFL games while on team premises.

Other players suspended that year included Lions Quintez Cephus, Ifeatu Melifonwu, and Colts Isaiah Rodgers.

In April 2024, Toronto Raptors player Jontay Porter was banned for life from the NBA after an investigation revealed he had placed bets on NBA games and shared confidential information about his own playing status with gamblers. It was alleged that Porter deliberately limited his participation in certain games to help bettors who wagered on his underperformance. This represented one of the most serious violations in modern professional sports, demonstrating how even well-paid professional athletes could be compromised by gambling temptations.

The Porter scandal was particularly alarming because it involved active manipulation of game outcomes based on insider information. It validated almost every concern that sports leagues and the NCAA had raised about the corruption risks of widespread legal gambling. The NBA's lifetime ban sent a clear message about the severity of gambling violations. Still, the incident proved existing monitoring systems and education programs weren't sufficient to prevent determined athletes from compromising.

The University of Alabama baseball scandal in 2023 involved multiple players allegedly sharing inside information with bettors and potentially influencing game outcomes, resulting in player suspensions, and highlighting how even sophisticated monitoring systems might miss corruption activities that don't create obvious betting pattern anomalies.

During the 2024 men's basketball season, controversy arose when several regular season, conference, and early-round NCAA tournament games were linked to unusual betting activity, with large sums wagered on games involving underdog teams. Investigators speculated that point-shaving and game-fixing might have been involved. Hardly a year has passed without a major sports gambling scandal since the Court's *Murphy* decision in 2018.

And then came the October 2025 announcement I mentioned to open the Chapter about the sweeping case involving insider bets on NBA games and poker games rigged by Mafia families. The indictments detailed how the operation worked. According to prosecutors, the scheme involved creating a "betting marketplace" where information from NBA insiders was commodified and sold to high-stakes gamblers. Some bets reportedly reached six and seven figures based on inside information about which players would be rested, how coaches planned to rotate lineups, and other strategic decisions not yet public. The poker game rigging involved organized crime families using marked cards, collusion among players, and other techniques to ensure predetermined outcomes. These high-stakes games, held at underground locations across New York and New Jersey, attracted wealthy businesspeople, athletes, and celebrities who had no idea the games were rigged. The Mafia families allegedly netted millions from the fixed poker games alone.

Organized crime hadn't disappeared from sports gambling. They'd adapted to the legal market, finding new ways to exploit betting opportunities. The surveillance and monitoring systems designed to protect the games weren't smarter than the sophisticated operations that used encrypted communications and obscured obvious betting patterns.

The NCAA's policy change announced on that same day appeared to represent complete capitulation to external pressures. State legalization had made gambling ubiquitous. Commercial operators had made betting socially acceptable. Athletes were being bombarded with gambling advertisements and promotions. Enforcing absolute prohibitions had become increasingly difficult as betting became normalized throughout society.

But I wondered if this decision reflected something deeper than practical enforcement complexities Did it demonstrate how external pressures, commercial temptations, and legal constraints could force institutions to abandon principles they'd defended for a century, even when recent events proved those principles were justified?

Then something remarkable happened. The membership revolted, and this time with a good outcome.

The proposal to allow athletes and coaches to bet on professional sports had been adopted by a Division I Committee in early October and subsequently approved by Divisions II and III. It was set to take effect on November 1, 2025. But under an updated override process to the one I discussed in Chapter 12 (which was used to invalidate the $2000 miscellaneous expense allowance from the Presidential retreat in 2011), Division I member schools have thirty days to vote on whether to rescind the rule change if it had received less than 75% support from the Division I legislative body. The vote had fallen short of that threshold, opening the door for schools to reject the change.

Greg Sankey sent a letter to Charlie Baker requesting that the rule change be rescinded. Pittsburgh football head coach Pat Narduzzi publicly opposed the change. Athletics directors and compliance officers across the country voiced concerns. The October gambling indictments had provided a stark reminder of exactly why prohibitions existed in the first place.

On November 21, 2025, just 30 minutes before the deadline, the NCAA announced that two-thirds of Division I member schools had voted to rescind the proposed rule change. Sounds like somebody was whipping votes again. The ban on all forms of betting on sports in which the NCAA sponsors a championship would remain in place for all three NCAA divisions. The longstanding prohibition on sports wagering by student-athletes, coaches, officials, and staff was preserved.

I read that news with profound relief. The membership had recognized what the Committee had momentarily forgotten: that the October indictments weren't abstractions and that corruption risks weren't theoretical. That the principles we'd defended for decades existed for good reasons. In a rare display of institutional self-correction, the schools themselves had rejected the capitulation initially embraced.

But even as I celebrated the membership's wisdom, I suspected the underlying pressures hadn't disappeared. The forces that had led to the October proposal, including the ubiquity of legal gambling, the difficulty of enforcement, and the normalization of betting throughout society, remained powerful. The reprieve was welcome, but the war wasn't over.

And now here we are, and some of the worst fears I had harbored for decades materialized in a devastating fashion.

On January 15, 2026, fewer than three months after the October NBA gambling indictments, and less than two months after the NCAA membership had voted to preserve its gambling prohibitions, another U.S. Attorney, this time David Metcalf from the Eastern District of Pennsylvania, stood before cameras and announced what he called "a massive scheme that enveloped the world of college basketball." Federal prosecutors unsealed a 70-page indictment that initially charged 26 people (20 current or former college basketball players) in connection with a point-shaving operation that had corrupted more than 29 Division I men's basketball games over the 2023-24 and 2024-25 seasons. The scheme involved more than 39 players across 17 NCAA programs.

"This was a significant and rampant corruption of college athletics," Metcalf declared. "We allege an extensive international criminal conspiracy of NCAA players, alumni, and professional bettors who fixed games across the country and poisoned the American spirit of competition for monetary gain."

The scheme began not in American college basketball but in the Chinese Basketball Association. According to the indictment, professional sports bettors Shane Hennen and Marves Fairley, coincidentally the same individuals named in the October 2025 NBA gambling case, recruited former LSU star and NBA player Antonio Blakeney to fix games while he was playing overseas for the Jiangsu Dragons. "The only things certain in life," Hennen allegedly texted a co-conspirator, "are death, taxes, and Chinese basketball."

The conspirators then brought their operation to American soil, targeting the one population we feared was most vulnerable: college athletes at mid-major and lower-tier Division I programs who were not benefiting substantially from NIL opportunities. Players who were struggling financially while watching others profit. Players for whom bribes of $10,000 to $30,000 represented meaningful money. Indeed, as prosecutors noted, it exceeded what many of these athletes could earn through legitimate name, image, and likeness deals.

The fixers targeted players at programs like Abilene Christian, Alabama State, Buffalo, Coppin State, DePaul, Eastern Michigan, Fordham, Kennesaw State, La Salle, UNO, Nicholls State, North Carolina A&T, Northwestern State, Robert Morris, Saint Louis, Southern Miss, and Tulane. They recruited players to ensure their teams failed to cover point spreads, particularly first-half lines where manipulation was easier to accomplish and harder to detect.

The betting amounts were staggering. According to the indictment, the conspirators wagered approximately $458,000 on Towson to beat North Carolina A&T. They bet $424,000 on Kent State to cover the first-half spread against Buffalo. They placed $275,000 on South Alabama to cover against Southern Miss. They wagered $256,000 on Robert Morris to fail in the first half against Northern Kentucky. These were massive sums placed on games that ordinarily attracted little attention. This was exactly the kind of vulnerability we had warned about for years.

The scheme was remarkably successful. In game after game, the fixes worked. Players underperformed on command. Teams failed to cover spreads as promised. The gamblers collected millions while corrupting college basketball at its very foundation.

Not every fix succeeded. In one instance detailed in the indictment, a Fordham player, Elijah Gray, was allegedly paid to help ensure his team failed to cover a 3.5-point spread against Duquesne. Gray scored only three points that day, well below his 8.4 season average. But his teammates played too well, and Fordham pulled off a 79-67 upset. "I tried," Gray allegedly texted one of the alleged ringleaders. "You did your job for sure," came the reply. As U.S. Attorney Metcalf observed at the press conference announcing the indictment, "there's nine other players on the court, there's coaches and there's referees."

Four players charged in the indictment had played for their current college teams within the previous week: Kennesaw State's Simeon Cottle, the preseason Conference USA Player of the Year, averaging 20.2 points per game; Eastern Michigan's Carlos Hart; Delaware State's Camian Shell; and Texas Southern's Oumar Koureissi. They were immediately suspended from their teams. Their seasons, and likely their basketball careers, are over.

NCAA President Baker responded to the indictments with a strong statement that simultaneously acknowledged the organization's awareness and the limitations we learned during previous scandals: "Protecting competition integrity is of the utmost importance for the NCAA. The pattern of college basketball game integrity conduct revealed by law enforcement today is not entirely new information to the NCAA. Through helpful collaboration and with industry regulators, we have finished or have open investigations into almost all of the teams in today's indictment."

Baker revealed that the NCAA enforcement staff had opened sports betting investigations into approximately forty student-athletes from twenty schools over the past year. Eleven had been found to have bet on their own performances, shared information with known bettors, or engaged in game manipulation. All eleven lost their NCAA eligibility permanently. Another thirteen failed to cooperate with investigations and also lost their eligibility.

But here was the most damning admission: despite all the monitoring, despite all the protections, despite the millions or maybe billions spent on surveillance systems, this massive scheme had operated for over two years before law enforcement intervened. Although one of the best, the NCAA's "layered integrity monitoring program that covers over 22,000 contests" didn't catch the depths of it. The sophisticated detection systems that were supposed to flag suspicious betting patterns hadn't stopped the conspirators from fixing at least twenty-nine games.

The timing could not have been more brutal. Just one day before the indictments were announced, Baker delivered his State of College Sports address from the Gaylord National Resort and Convention Center near Washington, D.C. In that speech, he also called on the Commodity Futures Trading Commission to halt prediction market contracts involving college sports. He warned about the proliferation of betting platforms operating outside traditional regulatory oversight. He pleaded for stronger protections.

Then the next morning, federal prosecutors revealed that college basketball had already been thoroughly corrupted, again.

The January 2026 indictments connected directly to the October 2025 NBA gambling case. Hennen and Fairley had exploited professional basketball overseas, then professional basketball in America, then college basketball. They showed how gambling corruption spreads across borders and levels of competition. The same organized gambling networks that had compromised NBA players and rigged poker games were now actively corrupting amateur athletics.

This was the nightmare scenario we had warned about since 1951. This was why we had fought to preserve PASPA. This was why we had resisted the gambling industry's encroachment at every turn. And now it continues to clobber college sports in devastating fashion.

AI, social media, and digital communication have created new vectors for potential corruption that existing monitoring systems struggle to detect. Athletes can communicate with bettors through encrypted messaging platforms, social media direct messages, or other channels, leaving limited evidence for investigators.

For many fans and gamblers, the most critical concern for the future of sports remains what it's always been. The concern over the ethical operation of sport is no different from what it was in 1919, after the Black Sox threw the World Series, or fifteen years ago, when lawyers raised it in the fight over Delaware sports betting.

As sports business expert Leigh Steinberg notes: "Bad behavior by athletes doesn't kill sports. There's been plenty of that. The only thing that could [hamper the popularity of sports] is the perception by fans that they [are] watching [professional wrestling]. That it is somehow scripted or predetermined or there were actions or facts going on the public wasn't aware of, and we have seen that happen."

> That's the existential threat. Not that individual athletes might occasionally place bets or share information. But that corruption could lead fans to believe outcomes are predetermined. That games are fixed. That what they're watching isn't honest athletics competition, but scripted entertainment designed to benefit gamblers.

The NCAA continues advocating for comprehensive restrictions on college sports betting, including prohibitions on proposition bets involving individual performances and enhanced penalties for violations. As we asserted when I was there, the unique characteristics of college athletics require stronger protections than those afforded to professional sports. Athletes are on campus or in classrooms regularly with those betting on their performance. Nothing good can come of that.

The membership's decision to rescind the October policy change was the right call, even if it arrived almost too late. How could the NCAA credibly argue for restrictions on betting on college sports while simultaneously allowing athletes and coaches to bet on professional sports? The position would have been internally contradictory. By preserving the prohibition, the membership maintained the coherence of the NCAA's historical advocacy, even as the January indictments demonstrated how badly that advocacy was needed.

Technology companies, artificial intelligence platforms, social media monitoring, and enhanced data integration may provide advanced solutions. The development of increasingly sophisticated integrity monitoring systems promises improved detection capabilities. But technological solutions alone cannot eliminate corruption risks, and human judgment remains essential. More importantly, monitoring systems apparently didn't catch the October 2025 NBA player/mafia operation or the January 2026 college basketball scheme until they had been running for extended periods.

The relationship between legal sports betting and college sports will likely continue to evolve as stakeholders gain experience with current systems and identify areas for improvement. But current developments suggest that evolution may be moving in the wrong direction. Corruption risks are materializing, and protections remain under pressure. And institutions must continue defending principles against commercial and social forces that would undermine them.

The *Murphy* decision replaced the old legal construct, but it did not resolve underlying tensions about gambling's appropriate role in college athletics. Current protection measures represent significant improvements over historical approaches, but cannot eliminate all corruption risks. Sophisticated monitoring systems and legal frameworks require continuous refinement and vigilant enforcement, which all involved continue to refine and perfect.

Moving forward, the success of integrating legal sports betting with college athletics will depend on continued stakeholder cooperation, adequate resource allocation, and adaptive regulatory approaches that respond to emerging risks. The stakes remain high, as public confidence in college sports integrity affects not only athletics competitions but also the broader educational missions of American universities.

I'm increasingly skeptical that these conditions can be met without greater restrictions or even a return to prohibition.

Commercial pressures and social normalization continue to challenge confidence in the game. Forces keep pushing policy in directions that contradict decades of experience and recent evidence about corruption risks. The November membership override vote bought time, but the underlying dynamics haven't changed.

The evolution from underground betting operations to regulated markets represents change, though whether it constitutes progress in addressing gambling's relationship with college sports remains debatable. Ongoing vigilance and continuous improvement remain essential for protecting the unique character that distinguishes collegiate athletics.

When the Supreme Court struck down PASPA, reversing decades of lower-court rulings, we were forced to consider adjusting sports wagering and championship policies. It's abundantly clear we're dealing with big business. Collegiate Capitalism is more significant than ever. The traditional amateur framework, as it existed for most of the twentieth century, has been overtaken by market realities. The absence of a comprehensive federal framework has created an environment with uneven outcomes for institutions and athletes alike.

We couldn't maintain prohibitions once courts stripped away legal frameworks. We couldn't resist commercial temptations once betting became ubiquitous. We struggle to adhere to core principles when outside influences make them costly to maintain. Yet the November NCAA membership vote showed that schools themselves remain ultimately committed to those principles.

This is the pattern throughout the metamorphosis of college athletics. Gambling, combined with other challenges in this book, has proved that needed protections face constant assault when courts remove legal frameworks, states legalize for revenue, commercial operators create massive markets, and social pressure makes prohibitions seem antiquated.

I wanted to start this chapter by discussing the college basketball scandal Joon Kim prosecuted in 2017, but was interrupted by the breaking news of the October 2025 Nocella indictments and the outrage of the January 2026 Metcalf disclosures. And, I'm worried the breaking news will continue.

Yet I will end where expected: reflecting on what happens when the Supreme Court makes major policy decisions while claiming "important public policy choices are not ours to make." When federal prosecutors indict dozens. When organized crime infiltrates sports gambling. When new prosecutors return three months later to charge twenty-six in the most significant college basketball corruption scandal in seventy-five years. When college sports committees propose allowing athletes and coaches to bet, only to reverse course after the membership revolts.

I'll tell you what happens! The integrity of sports faces constant challenges. Corruption risks materialize. Institutions must fight to maintain principles they've defended for decades, as everything around them makes that increasingly difficult.

The present restructuring of college sports isn't just about athlete compensation or revenue sharing or employment status or gender equity. It's about how commercial pressures and other foreign stresses can overwhelm institutional principles, lead to the abandonment of longstanding values, and create systems that contradict almost everything institutions previously stood for.

These developments crystallize this transformation.

We were right to fight gambling expansion. We were right about corruption risks. We were right that legalization would create problems that monitoring systems couldn't solve. Being right matters, and the membership's decision to preserve gambling prohibitions suggests that at least some within college athletics understand that. But the external forces remain powerful. Legal frameworks have been stripped away. Social normalization makes enforcement difficult.

And now we're living with the consequences. Organized crime is infiltrating legal gambling markets. Monitoring systems aren't catching sophisticated operations. The amateur model, or what remains of it, will face constant challenges in an era of Collegiate Capitalism.

Gambling's integration into college sports represents another milestone in the evolution from amateur athletics to commercial entertainment. The balance has shifted from integrity to commercial accommodation, from principled resistance to practical adaptation, and from amateur ideals to the realities of Collegiate Capitalism.

There may yet be a path back. But it will require vigilance, courage, and an unwavering commitment to the principles that once defined college athletics. The January 2026 indictments should serve as a permanent marker, a warning to everyone in college sports about what happens when game protections fail.

The warnings we issued were correct. The protections we built were insufficient. The principles we defended remain under assault. And college basketball, the sport that gives us March Madness, Cinderella stories, and the mythology of amateur competition, continues to be corrupted by the very forces we spent decades trying to keep at bay.

Ironically, one of the greatest threats to all collegiate games is success. The more successful they become, the more inviting they are to infiltrate, corrupt those involved, and then manage the outcomes. How do you embrace success and protect yourself from its corruptive fellow travelers?

This is Collegiate Capitalism in its purest and most troubling form. The question now is whether we have the will to fight back.

Chapter 24
Fake Classes...
In the Name of Athletics

I was travelling to Baton Rouge, via New Orleans, to visit family and watch the LSU homecoming game against Ole Miss in October 2014. Yes, we won the game. That's when the Wainstein report hit the airwaves. Former federal prosecutor Ken Wainstein completed his examination of academic fraud at the University of North Carolina at Chapel Hill. I'd seen the executive summary earlier that morning before my flight, but now I had the full 120-page-plus report.

I started reading. And I couldn't stop.

Eighteen years. Nearly 3,100 students. Approximately 200 fake classes. An entire shadow curriculum designed to keep athletes eligible while providing zero education. Classes that required no attendance, no instruction, often just a single paper that an administrator with no teaching credentials would cursorily review. Athletes steered into these fraudulent courses by academic counselors who knew exactly what they were doing.

As I read, I kept thinking about all the courtroom, boardroom, and barbershop arguments I'd crafted to defend the amateur model. "Education has tremendous value," I had told everyone who would listen, and our lawyers told judges and juries. "Scholarships provide fair compensation because a college degree transforms lives. The system works because athletes receive invaluable educational opportunities in exchange for their athletic participation."

And here was comprehensive evidence that for thousands of student-athletes at one of America's most prestigious public universities, the educational experience promised to athletes had been compromised for nearly two decades. For years, the NCAA's defense of amateurism rested on the premise that scholarships provided genuine educational value that led to a lifetime of opportunity. The Wainstein report provided the most comprehensive evidence yet that this premise could be corrupted, not by athletes, but by institutions themselves, under the commercial pressures the system created.

Indeed, the educational mission and value we claimed justified denying athletes compensation was being manipulated to maintain eligibility, while athletes were devoted to their sports and hoping for a leg up through learning. On this day, the amateur model's central justification, that athletes were students first, was exposed as fraudulent when the education itself was fake.

I picked up the phone to call Mark. He had just finished reading and reflected that it was worse than we thought. He had no words for it.

I think we both understood that it appeared to be an institutional betrayal of educational mission in service of athletics success.

Yeah. That about covers it. We needed to figure out quickly how to respond. It struck at the heart of everything we claim college athletics is about.

What neither of us fully realized at that moment was how completely the NCAA system would fail to hold UNC accountable, and what that failure would reveal about the organization's inability to maintain even the pretense of educational integrity.

The roots of UNC's elaborate deception traced back to 1993, when the African and Afro-American Studies ("AFAM") department, under the newly appointed leadership of Julius Nyang'oro and execution of Deborah Crowder, began offering what would become known as "paper classes." They required no attendance and no faculty instruction. They frequently demanded only a single research paper that was cursorily reviewed by department administrator Deborah Crowder, who possessed neither an advanced degree nor teaching credentials.

Students enrolled in these phantom courses consistently received artificially inflated grades, typically A's and B's, regardless of work quality. What started as an ostensible accommodation for struggling students gradually evolved into a structured operation that would eventually ensnare over 3,100 students, roughly half of whom were student-athletes.

The scheme's alleged mechanics were elegantly simple yet profoundly corrupt. Academic counselors within UNC's athletics department maintained close relationships with Crowder, who effectively controlled course enrollment and grading. When star athletes faced academic difficulties that threatened their eligibility, counselors would strategically steer them into these bogus classes.

The first cracks in this carefully constructed facade appeared in 2010, when our enforcement staff investigators arrived in Chapel Hill to examine allegations of improper contact between agents and football players. What seemed like a routine athletics violation investigation soon uncovered deeper academic irregularities that would ultimately expose the entire fraudulent enterprise.

Enforcement staff investigators assiduously documented the academic anomalies they'd discovered. They were seeing patterns that didn't make sense. Players with known academic struggles were suddenly getting high grades in courses they apparently never attended.

How is that possible?

The scandal gained national attention beyond the walls of the NCAA when investigative reporter Dan Kane of the Raleigh News & Observer began scrutinizing player transcripts and uncovered glaring academic anomalies. Kane and his colleagues' dogged reporting revealed that football players with remedial academic skills were somehow receiving high grades in advanced courses they had never attended.

Among the most compelling and controversial figures to emerge was Rashad McCants, the former basketball star who helped lead North Carolina to the 2005 NCAA Final Four men's basketball championship. McCants' eventual public testimony would prove particularly damaging to the university's efforts to minimize the scope of the scandal.

In a bombshell 2014 interview with ESPN's "Outside the Lines," McCants detailed that tutors routinely authored his papers, that he rarely attended classes for substantial portions of his academic career, and that he remained eligible to play basketball primarily through enrollment in these phantom courses.

McCants revealed that he had earned placement on the Dean's List during the spring 2005 semester despite never attending any of his four enrolled classes. Coincidentally, this was the same period when North Carolina captured the national championship. His transcript showed a stark dichotomy. While he struggled mightily in legitimate courses, earning multiple C's, D's, and F's, he consistently received A's in AFAM classes.

McCants went further, alleging that head coach Roy Williams was "100 percent" aware of the paper class system and had assured him that academic problems would be "figured out" to maintain his eligibility. These explosive accusations directly contradicted Williams' repeated denials of knowledge about the fraudulent scheme.

The testimony proved particularly damaging because McCants represented precisely the type of high-profile athlete whose success was built upon this academic fraud. His allegations suggested that North Carolina's 2005 national championship, one of the program's most celebrated achievements and Roy Williams' first, was potentially tainted by deliberate academic dishonesty.

McCants faced credibility challenges, including a disappointing professional career, prior controversial statements about his college experience, and questions about his motives for coming forward a decade after graduation. Nevertheless, his detailed, specific knowledge of the scheme's operations carried weight, particularly given the contemporaneous documentary evidence that would later emerge.

While McCants provided the scandal's most prominent whistleblower testimony from the player side, Mary Willingham emerged as perhaps the most significant and persistent voice demanding accountability. Willingham, who served as a learning specialist in UNC's academic support program from 2003 to 2014, possessed intimate knowledge of how academically underprepared athletes were managed within the university system.

Her evolution from loyal employee to determined whistleblower would ultimately prove instrumental in exposing the full scope of the fraud. Through her work providing tutoring and academic support, she discovered that numerous basketball and football players had reading skills far below the college level, with some functioning at the elementary school level. Although UNC disputed the methodology, her research suggested that approximately 60% of UNC football and basketball players between 2004 and 2012 were reading at fourth- to eighth-grade levels, while 10% read below the third-grade level.

Willingham observed how academic counselors routinely steered struggling athletes into AFAM courses as a solution to eligibility problems. Willingham's decision to go public proved costly on a personal level but crucial for exposing the scandal's actual dimensions. In early 2014, she began speaking with national media outlets, sharing her research findings and insider observations with CNN and other news organizations. University officials responded aggressively, launching what Willingham's supporters characterized as a coordinated retaliatory campaign to discredit her research methodology and question her motives.

Willingham filed a lawsuit against the university alleging retaliation and a hostile work environment. The case eventually settled in 2015 for $335,000, with the university agreeing to payment without admitting wrongdoing.

Watching Willingham's treatment reminded me of Mike McQueary at Penn State. Another whistleblower. Another person trying to expose institutional wrongdoing. Another person was punished for telling the truth, while the institutions they challenged escaped meaningful accountability.

The mounting pressure from media coverage, coupled with Willingham's detailed allegations and McCants' explosive testimony, eventually forced UNC to commission a comprehensive independent investigation. In February 2014, the university retained Wainstein, who, as I discussed in Chapter 14, conducted an independent investigation for the NCAA regarding the handling of the University of Miami matter, giving him specific expertise in collegiate enforcement cases. UNC's decision to hire Wainstein signaled that the university was prepared to conduct a genuinely comprehensive examination of the scandal. Skeptics, however, questioned whether institutional self-interest would ultimately limit the investigation's scope.

Unlike previous internal reviews criticized as limited and defensive, Wainstein's team at Cadwalader was granted broad access to university records, personnel, and witnesses. They reviewed more than a million emails and documents, interviewed scores of witnesses, and analyzed thousands of student transcripts dating back decades. Crucially, they secured the cooperation of both Nyang'oro and Crowder for the first time. These two central figures had previously declined to participate in university and NCAA investigations.

When the report was released in October 2014, its findings exceeded even the most pessimistic expectations about the scandal's scope and duration. The investigation confirmed that fraudulent courses had been offered for eighteen years, from 1993 to 2011, affecting at least 3,100 students. The report detailed how Crowder had assumed de facto control over course offerings, grading, and enrollment, despite lacking any formal teaching authority.

Perhaps most damaging, the report directly contradicted years of university claims that the fraud was limited to a single rogue professor acting independently. Instead, the investigation revealed a coordinated effort involving multiple athletics personnel who viewed the paper classes as essential tools for maintaining player eligibility.

Looking back on that report, I can't help but ask a critical question: Is this what the amateur model produces? The structural tensions between athletic time demands and academic requirements, combined with the competitive and financial pressures on institutions, created an environment where the risk of academic shortcuts was significant. The UNC case demonstrated what can happen when those pressures go unchecked.

This wasn't about a few bad actors. This was about pressures inherent in the amateur model, making academic fraud a rational institutional response to impossible demands. And it proved that the educational justification we offered for denying athletes compensation was, in some cases, complete fiction. A fiction paid for most dearly by the thousands of students who had been promised an education and received the credential without the substance instead.

At the time I thought: What the hell is going on? How many more scandals before we realize that the system itself was fundamentally broken and take drastic steps to repair or replace it?

The report's release triggered immediate consequences within the university administration. Chancellor Carol Folt announced the terminations and disciplinary actions against several employees. Folt publicly acknowledged the investigation's findings and accepted institutional responsibility for the academic fraud, marking the first time UNC had fully admitted the extent of wrongdoing.

However, critics noted that most individuals facing consequences were lower-level employees, while senior administrators who should have provided oversight escaped meaningful accountability. This pattern would repeat in the NCAA's response: punish the small players, protect the powerful institutions.

The NCAA's infractions system's reaction to the report and mounting evidence of academic fraud would ultimately prove to be one of the most controversial aspects of the entire scandal. Initially, our enforcement staff seemed poised to pursue severe penalties against UNC, issuing multiple notices of allegations that included the most serious charge of "lack of institutional control." The charges alleged that the university had failed to maintain adequate oversight of its academic and athletics programs, potentially warranting severe sanctions, including postseason bans and scholarship reductions.

Some commentators argued for the harshest possible penalties. Eighteen years of systematic fraud, after all, is as clear a case of lack of institutional control as we'll ever see. But the courses were theoretically available to all students, not exclusively to athletes. Some wondered whether the NCAA had authority over academic matters that affect the general student body.

I found myself increasingly troubled by both positions. Perhaps we could hold UNC accountable for actions that made a mockery of the educational justification for amateurism. But the jurisdictional questions were real, not mere technicalities, and UNC's legal team was already preparing aggressive challenges to our authority.

However, the NCAA's investigation became mired in procedural disputes and legal challenges that would stretch for years. UNC's legal team, led by experienced NCAA defense attorneys, mounted an aggressive challenge to the association's jurisdiction over academic matters. They argued that, since the fraudulent courses were theoretically available to all students, not exclusively to athletes, the scheme fell outside the NCAA's purview.

This argument would prove crucial to the university's ultimate escape from meaningful penalties. And it exposed a fundamental problem with the NCAA enforcement and infractions system. We could punish athletes for accepting meals or selling memorabilia, but apparently, we couldn't punish institutions for academic fraud that lasted eighteen years and affected thousands of students.

The case was assigned to a Committee on Infractions panel led by Greg Sankey. When I first learned that Sankey would chair the panel, I was pleased knowing how knowledgeable and effective he was on the Committee. Yet, the potential conflict-of-interest question was immediate. The SEC competed directly against UNC in multiple sports. While Sankey had deep experience with NCAA enforcement matters, the perceived conflict of interest might become a thing.

But the Committee on Infractions regularly included conference commissioners and Sankey's experience was valuable. In the back of my mind, I recognized that we were already facing criticism about the credibility of NCAA enforcement, and that having a conference commissioner with potential competitive interests deciding a case involving a direct rival could be problematic at best. Some questioned whether he faced inherent conflicts of interest that should have required his recusal from the case. However, Sankey denied a formal request for his removal and appropriately defended his participation throughout the process.

The lengthy investigation process became increasingly contentious as UNC's legal strategy evolved. Initially, university officials had publicly acknowledged the academic fraud and promised comprehensive reforms. However, as the NCAA enforcement process progressed, UNC's position shifted dramatically. The university began arguing that, while the courses may have been academically deficient, they did not violate NCAA rules because they were open to all students and provided legitimate academic credit.

This strategic pivot frustrated NCAA investigators and would later draw sharp criticism from the Committee on Infractions. The panel noted in its final report that it was "troubled by the university's shifting positions about whether academic fraud occurred on its campus." However, these concerns would not translate into meaningful sanctions.

From time to time, I attended COI hearings, and this was one that I observed personally. What struck me as unusual was the number of official attendees and lawyers present. Not that they needed all the space the Gaylord Opryland offered, but this Army of defenders was effective.

The Committee on Infractions' final decision, announced in October 2017, represented a stunning victory for UNC and a devastating blow to those who had demanded accountability. Despite acknowledging that student-athletes had "likely benefited" from the fraudulent courses, the panel concluded that it could not definitively prove that the scheme was designed exclusively to benefit athletes. The legal gymnastics UNC deployed had worked.

And the COI had just decided it couldn't punish an institution for 18 years of academic chicanery because the fake classes were available to non-athletes as well. The decision essentially said that if you're going to run an academic scheme to keep athletes eligible, just make sure non-athletes can also enroll in the fake classes, and you may escape punishment.

Sankey's statement accompanying the decision carefully noted that while the evidence suggested academic fraud had occurred, the NCAA's rules and procedures prevented the COI from imposing penalties. The decision sparked immediate controversy and widespread criticism from reform advocates, rival schools, and media commentators, who viewed it as a complete abdication of the NCAA's responsibility.

Critics argued that the ruling essentially provided a roadmap for future academic fraud by suggesting that universities could avoid penalties simply by making fraudulent courses theoretically available to non-athletes. To many observers, the decision represented the triumph of legal technicalities over substantive accountability.

The Committee on Infractions' written report revealed deep frustration with the constraints of NCAA enforcement procedures. The panel's language suggested that while they believed academic fraud had occurred, they felt bound by procedural limitations that prevented the imposition of appropriate sanctions. This tension highlighted fundamental problems with the NCAA's enforcement and infractions structure and its ability to address academic misconduct that fell outside traditional violations, such as improper benefits or recruiting violations.

Emmert recognized the case's significance for the Association's credibility. In the immediate wake of the Wainstein report's release, he appropriately described the findings as "troubling," "disturbing," and "shocking."

But Mark's concerns and public statements grew increasingly cautious as the process dragged on and legal maneuvering cast doubt on the strength of the case. By the time of the final decision, he found himself in the uncomfortable position of defending an outcome that many viewed as a complete failure of the NCAA enforcement system.

Of course, while not involved directly in enforcement matters, Mark was aware of how it unfolded. I believe he genuinely was troubled by what had happened at UNC and frustrated by the jurisdictional limitations that ultimately prevented meaningful penalties. In the end, we would not have to fight a case in court brought by UNC because the COI did not rule against them. Raleigh attorney Elliott Abrams and his team, who represented Crowder, proved to be formidable, and the jurisdictional questions raised by UNC lawyers led by then–Attorney General Roy Cooper and outside counsel at Womble Carlyle were genuine legal issues rather than mere technicalities.

The end result was that we had failed to hold accountable an institution that had run an academic fraud scheme for almost two decades. Another enforcement failure. Another powerful institution escaping consequences. Another example of the pattern we had seen at Penn State and Miami. When grave institutional misconduct was exposed, our system couldn't or wouldn't deliver accountability.

The UNC case became emblematic of broader criticisms of Emmert's tenure, which was characterized by numerous high-profile enforcement failures and a perceived inability to maintain the association's credibility. Whether you believe those criticisms of Emmert were fair or unfair, in the eyes of many, the system was not working.

At one point, when speaking about a case brought by UNC women's basketball player Rashanda McCants (Rashad McCants' sister) and former football player Devon Ramsay about the same academic fraud, I offered, "this case is troubling for a number of reasons, not the least of which is that the law does not and has never required the NCAA to ensure that every student-athlete is actually taking full advantage of the academic and athletic opportunities provided to them." This prompted critics to argue that the association's narrow interpretation of its jurisdiction essentially abandoned any meaningful oversight of the educational component of the student-athlete experience.

The scandal also underscored the vulnerability of whistleblowers within collegiate athletics systems. Both Willingham and McCants faced significant personal costs for their willingness to expose institutional wrongdoing, including professional retaliation, public attacks on their credibility, and social ostracism. Their experiences illustrated the powerful institutional interests that can be mobilized to protect the status quo and silence critics of big-time college athletics.

The broader implications extended far beyond Chapel Hill, raising fundamental questions about the sustainability and integrity of big-time college athletics. The case highlighted the inherent tensions between athletics success and academic integrity at major universities, where enormous financial pressures and competitive demands create incentives to cut academic corners.

Perhaps most importantly, the scandal illustrated the human cost of prioritizing athletics success over educational integrity. Thousands of students, many from disadvantaged backgrounds, were denied the educational opportunities they had been promised in exchange for their athletics talents. While some received degrees from a prestigious university, others were functionally illiterate and unprepared for life after athletics. The tragedy was not simply the corruption of institutional processes but the betrayal of individual dreams and the perpetuation of educational inequality under the guise of opportunity.

I'm struck by what this scandal revealed about the system I believed in. I'd argued that the amateur model worked because it provided athletes with a valuable education. In boardrooms, I'd watched as we contracted for billions in revenue that ultimately flowed to coaches, administrators, conferences, and broadcast partners, but not directly to the athletes whose performances made it possible. And now we had comprehensive evidence that the educational justification was, at least in this instance, a fallacy.

By the time UNC's scandal concluded, I had witnessed almost a decade of fractures accumulating in the amateur model's foundation. Political forces had overwhelmed us at Penn State, proving that external pressure could override NCAA autonomy whenever the stakes grew high enough. Our own enforcement failures at Miami had made a mockery of institutional accountability. Federal prosecutors investigating college basketball had succeeded where we could not, exposing corruption that voluntary reform had failed to address. Athletes were potentially suffering brain injuries in service of our commercial enterprise, and courts were forcing us to acknowledge risks we had long minimized. At Northwestern, the NLRB had examined what we called "student-athletes" and seen something that looked remarkably like employees. A pandemic had revealed just how fragile our financial model truly was. Women's basketball players had posted photos of weight room disparities that went viral, exposing festering inequities. And gambling, the threat we had fought for decades to keep at bay, had flooded into college sports the moment the Supreme Court opened the gates.

Now, UNC delivered the cruelest blow of all: proof that the educational justification we had invoked to deny athletes compensation was, in at least one prominent case, an eighteen-year fraud. The enforcement system we had built to protect institutional integrity couldn't, or wouldn't, hold one of America's most prestigious universities accountable for making a mockery of the very principles we claimed were sacred.

The traditional model was facing convergent challenges: each episode revealed questions that the existing governance framework was not designed to address. And the journey to a new form of college sports became not just inevitable but necessary, because the old system's foundational premises had been broken.

The University of North Carolina academic fraud scandal stands as one of the most comprehensive and damaging cases of institutional misconduct in the history of American higher education. Its duration, systematic nature, and ultimate lack of meaningful consequences created a precedent that continues to influence college athletics today.

While UNC implemented reforms and moved forward institutionally, the scandal's legacy serves as a permanent reminder of how easily educational missions can be subordinated to athletics ambitions, and how difficult it remains to hold powerful institutions accountable for blatant wrongdoing. The case continues to resonate as both a cautionary tale about institutional corruption and a sobering example of how legal technicalities can triumph over substantive justice in the complex world of college athletics governance.

Yet the case also represents something more. The scheduling and time demands of high-level athletic competition (travel, practice, games, film study, conditioning) left little room for meaningful academic engagement. The system created structural conflicts between athletic participation and academic achievement, conflicts that the UNC scandal made impossible to ignore. Yet another demonstration that when the house of cards the system built on falls, Collegiate Capitalism is just around the corner. All the while this dilemma was unfolding, athletes were successfully arguing in court that they deserved more for their efforts. And those legal challenges would culminate in a case that would transform college athletics in ways the UNC scandal never could.

Make room for the *House* case.

Chapter 25
A House of Cards
It All Falls Down

On June 21, 2021, I was eagerly awaiting my confirmation to become the 9th Deputy Secretary of the Department of Veterans Affairs when the Supreme Court delivered its unanimous decision in *NCAA v. Alston*. I've mentioned the case a few times given its critical role and importance in defining where we are today. On that day, I read Justice Neil Gorsuch's majority opinion first, then Justice Brett Kavanaugh's concurring opinion. To put it in perspective, against my reserved hope, it seemed clear now the amateur model I and many others revered, was gone.

Gorsuch's majority opinion was devastating enough. It was narrow, but rejected almost every NCAA argument and held that restrictions on education-related benefits violated antitrust law. Kavanaugh's concurrence went further, dismantling the entire philosophical foundation of amateurism in language that would make future defenses nearly impossible.

"The NCAA's business model would be flatly illegal in almost any other industry in America," Kavanaugh wrote. He called our arguments "circular," noting that we were essentially claiming that paying athletes would destroy college sports because we'd repeatedly said paying athletes would destroy college sports. "That reasoning," he observed acidly, "is not enough to justify the NCAA's restraints on student-athlete compensation."

Then came the paragraph that would haunt every future NCAA legal defense: "Nowhere else in America can businesses get away with agreeing not to pay their workers a fair market rate on the theory that their product is defined by not paying their workers a fair market rate. The NCAA is not above the law."

Some background on Alston is necessary to appreciate the gravity of what I was reading. The case began in 2014 as a consolidation of two parallel antitrust actions. Shawne Alston, a former West Virginia running back, had filed suit alongside other athletes challenging the NCAA's caps on the value of athletic scholarships. Around the same time, Jeffrey Kessler, the Winston and Strawn antitrust lawyer who had spent a career representing professional athletes against league compensation restrictions, filed *Jenkins v. NCAA*. Kessler's theory was more aggressive and transparent than anything we had previously confronted. Where Michael Hausfeld had built *O'Bannon* around the narrower question of name, image, and likeness rights, and Steve Berman focused on educationally related benefits, Kessler sought to enjoin all NCAA compensation restrictions outright as a Section 1 Sherman Act violation. *Jenkins* was eventually consolidated with *Alston*, and Kessler became co-lead class counsel alongside Berman.

The *O'Bannon* district court judge, Claudia Wilken, ruled against the NCAA in 2019, holding that restrictions on education-related benefits failed rule of reason scrutiny. The Ninth Circuit affirmed. We then sought Supreme Court review, hoping for the kind of definitive ruling that had eluded us when the Court denied *certiorari* in *O'Bannon*. We got our hearing. On March 31, 2021, Kessler argued the case for the athletes, and Waxman for the NCAA. From the questions at oral argument, it was clear our position was in serious trouble. The justices were skeptical of almost every theory we offered for why college athletics should be treated differently. Eighty-two days later, they unanimously confirmed that skepticism in writing. Kessler had taken the doctrinal opening that *O'Bannon* had cracked and pried it the rest of the way open. By the time he stood before the Court, he was a generation into a legal strategy aimed at compensation restrictions across professional sports, and college athletics was the last frontier.

Kavanaugh concluded his concurrence by noting that colleges and student-athletes could compete in an ecosystem in which they negotiate their compensation like ordinary Americans, and intimated that student-athletes seeking compensation would likely qualify for large salaries and endorsement deals.

I sat in my home office reading that language and thought: This is over. Not just this case, but the entire amateur model. Kavanaugh had just written the roadmap for every future plaintiff challenging compensation restrictions. Untold millions were available in a free market, and the analysis led one to question why antitrust law should prevent access to that. Kavanaugh's concurrence articulated a legal critique that will define the years ahead, regardless of whether one agrees with every premise or the fact that it was not the majority opinion.

I chatted with several attorneys who had been following the case. "Have you read Kavanaugh's concurrence?" I would ask.

"It's only a concurrence not joined by any other Justice, but it's bad," is a response I uniformly received.

Or something like, "it's worse than bad. He just told every plaintiff's attorney in America exactly how to bring compensation cases against the NCAA."

Sometimes, on the other side of the line, it was quiet for a moment. Then came some form of, "This may change everything."

What we all quickly appreciated was that one of those cases was already pending. Grant House, an Arizona State swimmer, alongside women's basketball player Sedona Prince—yes, the same Sedona Prince whose TikTok video had exposed gender inequity at the 2021 tournaments—had filed an antitrust lawsuit in June 2020 challenging the NCAA's prohibition on revenue sharing.

The case was assigned to Judge Claudia Wilken. The same district court judge who'd decided *O'Bannon* and *Alston*. The same judge who'd been dismantling amateurism restrictions for over a decade. The same judge who'd watched the NCAA lose or partially lose appeal after appeal, watched us defend positions that higher courts found insufficient, watched us argue that compensation restrictions were necessary for competitive balance while generating billions in TV revenue. Now, with the Supreme Court's endorsement in *Alston,* she would preside over what came next. And Kessler was back, with Berman, as co-lead counsel in *House*.

Ironically, on the shiny side of the house, the championships continued while the noise around us, not from the fans but the courts, was deafening. The final out of the 2021 College World Series came shortly before midnight on June 30. Mississippi State pitcher Landon Sims threw three shutout innings and closer Preston Johnson struck out the final Vanderbilt batter to complete a 9-0 championship shutout, and for a few hours, social media filled with celebrations of the Bulldogs' first national championship in any team sport. Dallas Cowboys quarterback Dak Prescott, a former Mississippi State star, was captured on video screaming in the stands. The crowds were so large, it appeared that the state of Mississippi had sent roughly one percent of its population to Omaha.

What struck me most about that night was not just the baseball. It was the calendar. In a matter of hours, the entire economic framework of college athletics would change. July 1, 2021, would be the first day college athletes could legally profit from their name, image, and likeness.

The timing had a quality of divine coordination that no human planner could have orchestrated. The *Alston* ruling was just nine days old. Kavanaugh's words were still reverberating.

So as Mississippi State celebrated in Omaha, the old order was quite literally living its final hours. The Bulldogs who won that championship did so under rules that would be obsolete by breakfast. Will Bednar, who threw six scoreless innings in the title game and was named Most Outstanding Player, could not have signed an endorsement deal on June 30. On July 1, he could.

The juxtaposition was not lost on industry observers. Here was college sports in its purest and most romantic form: a state flagship university with no prior national titles, fans who had traveled from farming communities devastated by flooding, a team of unheralded players who simply wanted it more. And here also was the machinery of transformation grinding forward, indifferent to sentiment or tradition. NIL was coming whether Mississippi State won or lost.

Before I raised my hand to join the Biden Administration, we had spent weeks preparing NCAA member institutions for the transition. Truthfully, the July 1 deadline had been forced by state laws, not by the NCAA's preference nor the *Alston* decision. Florida, Alabama, Georgia, Mississippi, Texas, and New Mexico had passed legislation that would take effect that day, with Kentucky and Ohio acting by executive order, and more than a dozen additional states with laws queued to take effect in the months and years following. The NCAA had been coerced into adopting an interim policy rather than see its membership fractured by a patchwork of state rules. We were implementing change under duress, not from conviction.

The College World Series championship provided one last glimpse of what college sports had been. The championship parade through downtown Starkville on July 2 was a celebration of community and belonging that no NIL deal could replicate. But it was also a farewell. The athletes who would arrive on campus that fall would inhabit a different world than the ones who had left Omaha as champions.

Mississippi State's Will Bednar would be drafted 14th overall by the San Francisco Giants three weeks later. He was not offered NIL. But the freshmen who would fill roster spots on future teams would have opportunities he never had without the restrictions he faced. The championship he won marked an ending as much as a beginning.

Looking back on what brought us here prompted a myriad of emotions for me. While we were busy making slow incremental change through the complicated NCAA membership governance system States were passing laws and athletes were in court, successfully arguing they deserved compensation for helping to generate billions in revenue. And they were winning.

I think now about the full weight of what we had faced over the previous decade, and the cumulative force of it takes my breath away.

Ed O'Bannon had discovered his likeness in a video game and asked a simple question: Why can't I be paid for this? That question had metastasized into an existential challenge. Penn State had shown us that when political pressure reached sufficient intensity, NCAA autonomy meant nothing. Governors, senators, and an outraged public could force outcomes our bylaws never contemplated. Miami had exposed our enforcement apparatus as faltering, incapable of delivering accountability when our own investigators compromised the process. The FBI had arrested college basketball and revealed a shadow economy of cash payments, shoe company bribes, and systematic corruption that our voluntary compliance model had utterly failed to prevent. Former athletes were suing us over brain injuries, forcing acknowledgment that we had asked young people to absorb thousands of head impacts in service of a billion-dollar entertainment product. Northwestern football players had petitioned to form a union, and an NLRB regional director had examined their athletics demands, institutional control, and lack of meaningful choice and concluded that they were employees, regardless of what we chose to call them. A global pandemic had canceled March Madness and revealed that our entire financial model depended on a single tournament, a single month, a a shaky foundation that could collapse overnight. An athlete had posted a TikTok video comparing weight rooms, and the world had seen what we had allowed: underinvestment in women's sports that Title IX was supposed to have ended decades ago. The Supreme Court had struck down PASPA, and gambling, the corruption threat we had fought for a generation to contain, had flooded into every corner of college sports. And UNC had proved that the educational justification for amateurism, the very foundation of our argument that athletes shouldn't be paid, was sometimes nothing more than an elaborate, institutional lie.

Each of these pressures had seemed manageable in isolation. But *House* would force us to acknowledge what all those pressures had been revealing from their different angles: the vulnerabilities weren't separate problems requiring separate solutions. They stemmed from a single source: the fundamental unfairness of a system that generated billions from athletes' efforts while denying them rational remuneration.

By July 2021, the *House* litigation was accelerating. I watched from outside the NCAA bubble as the case I would have been defending proceeded without me. And I felt a strange mixture of emotions. On the one hand, relief that I wasn't trying to fashion new arguments out of what was left after *Alston*. On the other hand, sadness about the transformation I'd helped resist or even facilitate for years, combined with a growing conviction that what was happening was both inevitable and necessary.

The *House* case consolidated three separate lawsuits(*House v. NCAA*, *Carter v. NCAA*, and *Hubbard v. NCAA)* representing approximately 390,000 current and former college athletes who had been denied the opportunity to receive compensation for their name, image, and likeness rights, as well as their share of massive television and media revenues.

The legal theory was straightforward after *Alston*. If restrictions on education-related benefits violated antitrust law, why wouldn't restrictions on revenue sharing? The *House* plaintiffs simply asked courts to apply the Supreme Court's logic to the next category of compensation.

The NCAA's defense faced an impossible challenge. How do you defend compensation restrictions when the Court has just held that the specific restrictions before it could not survive rule of reason scrutiny, and Justice Kavanaugh's concurrence declared that such restrictions would be "flatly illegal in almost any other industry"? How do you argue that paying athletes would destroy college sports when Kavanaugh called that reasoning "circular"?

You can't. Not effectively. Not after *Alston*.

As the litigation progressed through 2022 and 2023, I watched from Washington as the NCAA tried anyway. Although pleased with my new role, I longed to be in the game and knew the arguments that had to be made. The attorneys argued that some compensation restrictions were necessary for competitive balance, that unlimited payments would concentrate talent at wealthy schools, and that maintaining distinctions between college and professional sports served essential purposes.

Judge Wilken wasn't buying it. She'd heard these arguments in *O'Bannon*. She'd watched the Ninth Circuit partially reverse her, only to see the Supreme Court essentially vindicate her approach in *Alston*. She'd presided over the gradual erosion of amateurism restrictions for over a decade, watching the NCAA lose ground in case after case while insisting that each defeat was unique and limited.

By early 2024, facing potential damages exceeding $20 billion and the real possibility that Wilken would completely eliminate compensation restrictions, the NCAA and power conferences began serious settlement negotiations. I heard from former colleagues in the membership that internal discussions were contentious. Some wanted to fight to the bitter end, arguing that settling would abandon amateurism entirely. Others recognized that *Alston* had already done that, and settling offered at least some control over the transformation rather than risking total defeat.

The settlement framework that emerged reflected that tension between inevitable transformation and institutional attempts to preserve control. Rakesh Kilaru, a partner at Wilkinson Stekloff and former clerk to

Supreme Court Justice Elena Kagan, led the NCAA's defense and served as the principal architect of that framework. Where successive NCAA leaders had struggled for years to reconcile the association's legal exposure with its institutional resistance to change, Kilaru accomplished in months of intensive negotiation what had eluded the organization's own leadership: a structured surrender on compensation restrictions that preserved at least some institutional control over the transformation. He navigated contentious talks involving the NCAA president, power conference commissioners, and opposing counsel Jeffrey Kessler and Steve Berman, ultimately securing the $2.8 billion deal that introduced direct revenue sharing for the first time in NCAA history while establishing a decade of antitrust peace.

As discussed many times in this book, the NCAA and conferences would pay $2.8 billion in damages over ten years. More significantly, schools would be permitted to directly compensate athletes through revenue sharing of up to approximately $20.5 million annually, representing about 22 percent of the average Power Five school's athletics revenue.

But the settlement also attempted to impose new restrictions. Roster limits would replace scholarship limits. Restrictions on third-party NIL payments to control collectives and restore some semblance of normalcy.

Judge Wilken immediately expressed skepticism about these restrictions during preliminary approval hearings in September 2024. Indeed, she questioned whether limiting NIL payments from boosters would actually harm athletes by restricting earning potential rather than protecting competitive balance. When Judge Wilken pushed back during the approval process, including her insistence on grandfathering current athletes into roster limits, Kilaru held firm on provisions the defense team considered structurally essential to the deal while making targeted concessions to address the court's concerns. Her concerns forced multiple rounds of renegotiation before she indicated willingness to approve the settlement.

On Friday, June 6, 2025, Judge Wilken wielded her judicial pen to paint a new horizon of American college athletics that may last forever. The NCAA and Power 5 conferences had agreed to a settlement that, whatever its terms, of course, carried no admission that prior rules violated the law. With her final approval, she officially terminated the NCAA's historic commitment to amateurism, ushering in an unprecedented era where universities can directly compensate student-athletes for their athletic contributions. This monumental settlement represents far more than a legal resolution; it constitutes a fundamental reimagining of the relationship between higher education institutions and the athletes whose performances are the engine behind the success of the enterprise. Through settlement, the organization founded in 1906 to bring order and safety to college football had just formally abandoned the principle that athletes shouldn't be compensated beyond scholarships.

I often contemplate the journey that led us here. Many chapters in this book, and countless more that remain unwritten, represent pressures that have exposed the amateur model's vulnerabilities and forced incremental transformation. Each pressure had attacked different aspects. Each had exposed different contradictions. Each had forced incremental changes. But all of them had been resisted, minimized, or deflected through legal arguments, procedural defenses, and institutional intransigence.

The *House* settlement establishes several key frameworks that will govern this new era. On July 1, 2025, institutions began distributing up to $20.5 million annually to athletes, with the cap set to increase by at least 4% annually. Industry experts project the cap could exceed $33 million per school within a decade. The procompetitive rationale for this structure is that it preserves competitive balance, sustains non-revenue sports, and prevents a race to the bottom that would eliminate smaller programs. Laudable, but time will tell if that is enough.

The distribution of these funds reflects data-driven disparities in revenue generation across sports. Early projections suggest roughly 75 percent will flow to football players, 15 percent to men's basketball, 5 percent to women's basketball, and the remaining 5 percent distributed among all other sports. Star quarterbacks and basketball players at major programs will earn millions annually when combining direct institutional payments with permitted NIL deals.

For athletes in non-revenue sports, the reality has been far different. While all athletes theoretically gain access to revenue sharing, in practice funding has been concentrated heavily in revenue-generating sports. The settlement's treatment of women's sports represents one of its most controversial aspects. Multiple objections challenged the distribution of damages, arguing that it violated Title IX's mandate for gender equity in athletics financial aid. The settlement's market-value methodology produced an outcome in which over 90 percent of damages flowed to male athletes in football and men's basketball, which Title IX objectors argued contradicted principles requiring substantially proportionate distribution of athletics financial assistance. I discussed this in Chapter 22, and the appeals are ongoing. In August 2025, eight female student-athletes filed an appeal challenging the back damages distribution as discriminatory. But the real litigation will come against individual schools over their revenue-sharing distribution plans. Multiple Title IX experts have said it's not a question of whether schools will be sued, but which schools will be sued first and how courts will rule.

"We are waiting to see which school or schools are the first ones sued, not whether or not colleges will be sued, over their revenue sharing plans," explained Alexis Trumble, an attorney focused on Title IX issues in college athletics. Schools directing 90 percent of revenue sharing to male athletes while claiming Title IX compliance seems legally risky, but competitive pressures make a more equitable distribution practically difficult.

The solutions for the settlement's enforcement mechanisms represent perhaps its most innovative and potentially problematic elements. Rather than relying on the NCAA's historically ineffective enforcement apparatus, the settlement creates an entirely new entity, the College Sports Commission, governed by the power conferences and led by MLB executive Bryan Seeley as CEO.

This organization assumes responsibility for monitoring revenue-sharing compliance and evaluating third-party NIL deals exceeding $600 through a clearinghouse system operated by Deloitte called NIL Go. All deals above $600 must be submitted for review to determine whether they reflect "fair market value" and serve "valid business purposes" rather than functioning as recruiting inducements or pay-for-play arrangements.

The result is profound. A settlement designed to resolve antitrust claims could create new antitrust challenges by imposing artificial market restrictions. The NCAA argued for years that it needed to restrict athletes' compensation to maintain competitive balance. Courts rejected those arguments. Now, the settlement implementation attempts to restrict compensation through a clearinghouse system that is being challenged under antitrust law.

With respect to the roster limits to replace scholarship limits, the settlement presents different concerns. Football rosters will shrink to 105 players, with all rostered athletes eligible for full scholarships. Similar dynamics affect sports like baseball, which transitions from 11.7 scholarships across unlimited rosters to 34 full scholarships for 34 roster spots. Fall sports began the 2025 season already subject to the new limits, with "grandfathering" provisions that protect some current athletes but create administrative nightmares for athletics departments trying to determine who qualifies for exemptions. Winter and spring sports met their roster limit deadline on December 1, 2025.

Walk-on programs in football have been virtually eliminated. The tradition of non-scholarship athletes earning roster spots through determination, like Georgia's Stetson Bennett, who went from walk-on to national championship quarterback, is largely gone. Every roster spot now requires scholarship funding, changing the culture and opportunity structure of college athletics.

And then there is the financial hit. For schools and conferences, the impacts vary dramatically based on resources and competitive aspirations. Power conference institutions with robust television revenues can absorb the $20 million revenue-sharing commitment while maintaining existing program levels. For example, Ohio State, which generated $336 million (FY2025), can comfortably accommodate the new expense.

Conversely, the Group of Five conferences and smaller institutions face existential challenges. More than 50 percent of Group of Five schools generate less than $40 million in total athletics revenue annually. The settlement's financial pressures threaten to accelerate program elimination and competitive stratification, perhaps rendering the NCAA's traditional model of broad-based athletics participation obsolete.

To be sure, the financial architecture of the settlement reveals staggering economic stakes. The NCAA is responsible for approximately 40 percent through its reserve funds and reduced operating expenses. The remaining

60 percent comes from conferences, but the distribution methodology exposes significant inequities. Power conference schools shoulder 40 percent of the conference portion, while non-power conference institutions bear the remainder. This structure effectively forces smaller conferences to subsidize compensation for predominantly Power Four athletes who generated the vast majority of revenue at issue.

At the end of 2025, four months into the revenue-sharing era, the implementation revealed exactly the challenges and complications that critics predicted, along with some new problems nobody fully anticipated.

On July 1, 2025, the transformation officially began. Schools started making direct payments to athletes. The NIL Go clearinghouse launched on June 11. The College Sports Commission is operational. And the reality of Collegiate Capitalism hit athletics departments across the country.

All Big Ten and SEC schools committed to the full $20.5 million in revenue sharing, as expected. Most other Power Five schools followed suit or came close. But the Mid-American Conference schools, which generate roughly $1 million annually from their media deals, faced an impossible equation. How do you find $20 million for athlete compensation when your entire athletics budget struggles to reach $40 million, and you're already operating at a deficit?

The answer, for many smaller schools, has been painful choices about program elimination, reduced participation opportunities, and accepting that they simply cannot compete with Power Conference schools for talent in the revenue-sharing era. The competitive stratification we warned about is accelerating faster than even the most pessimistic predicted.

The distribution patterns within schools have largely followed projections. Most Power Four schools are directing approximately 75 percent to football, 15 percent to men's basketball, 5 percent to women's basketball, and 5 percent to all other sports combined. Early data suggest that power conference players receive between 5 and 60 times as much as non-power conference players, depending on sport and position.

Star quarterbacks at major programs are reportedly earning seven figures when combining institutional revenue sharing with NIL deals. Meanwhile, athletes in Olympic sports at Group of Five schools are receiving minimal or no revenue-sharing payments. The gap between haves and have-nots has widened dramatically.

But it's the NIL clearinghouse that has created the most immediate controversy. Deloitte initially indicated that roughly 70 percent of historical payments from booster collectives would be denied under the "fair market value" standard. In comparison, over 90 percent of payments from public companies would be approved. This threatened to gut the collective system that had developed since 2021.

The Power Conferences pushed back hard. Within weeks of the July 1 implementation, the College Sports Commission reversed or substantially modified its initial guidance on evaluating collective deals. Whether this reversal represents healthy flexibility as the new entity finds its footing or demonstrates that the CSC will simply do whatever the conferences demand remains an open question.

Continued legal challenges to NIL seem inevitable. Commentators like Kristi Dosh and Lexi Trumble have suggested that viable arguments exist that this system violates antitrust laws, especially since it does not apply to other influencers on campus. But the NCAA and CSC have defended the clearinghouse's monitoring function as the best minimally restrictive means of preventing sham NIL deals that would effectively constitute under-the-table payment for athletic performance.

The technology and compliance challenges have also proven more burdensome than anticipated. Schools are implementing new software systems costing anywhere from $5,000 to $500,000 to manage multiple payment streams, track compliance with revenue-sharing caps, and integrate with the NIL Go clearinghouse. Compliance officers are managing scholarships, cost of attendance payments, *Alston* educational benefits, revenue-sharing payments, and third-party NIL deals simultaneously. Administrative complexity is overwhelming for smaller athletics departments.

International athletes face particular complications. Questions about whether revenue-sharing payments constitute "royalties" or "self-employment income" for tax and visa purposes have created uncertainty that could affect athletes' legal status in the United States. Some international athletes are consulting immigration attorneys before accepting revenue-sharing payments to ensure they don't jeopardize their student visas.

The *House* settlement didn’t resolve the employment status question, as we predicted it could not. The *Johnson* lawsuit in Pennsylvania continues challenging the classification of athletes as non-employees under the Fair Labor Standards Act. The NLRB cases at Dartmouth and USC proceed independently. Direct institutional payments of potentially millions of dollars make it harder to sustain the argument that athletes aren't employees with each passing month.

And new eligibility litigation has emerged. In September 2025, athletes challenged the "four-and-five rule" limiting the number of years of competition, arguing that these restrictions violate antitrust law. Courts are split on whether junior college eligibility counts against NCAA eligibility limits. These new movements against the NCAA will likely be resolved soon, further adding chaos to the mayhem.

Early on, Congress was absent from the discussion. And still, despite continued NCAA lobbying for federal antitrust exemption legislation, no bill has become law. The SCORE Act twice reached the House floor and was pulled both times before any recorded vote, as I detail in the Epilogue. Creating further uncertainty, the Trump administration reversed the Department of Education guidance on Title IX compliance and revenue sharing. The hoped-for federal intervention to provide legal certainty hasn't materialized except in one material and confusing way.

As I mentioned in Chapter 22, in July 2025, President Trump's Executive Order "Saving College Sports" was issued. Shortly after the implementation of the *House* settlement, it represented another watershed moment executive branch involvement in college athletics governance.

The order's stated purpose is to “protect student-athletes and collegiate athletic scholarships and opportunities, including in Olympic and non-revenue programs, and the unique American institution of college sports.” Its provisions reveal an administration attempting to slow a transformation that has already occurred.

The order establishes tiered requirements based on athletic department revenue. Schools with revenues exceeding $125 million, essentially the Power conference universities, must provide more scholarship opportunities in non-revenue sports than the previous year and maximize roster spots. Schools with revenues between $50 million and $125 million must maintain current scholarship levels. Smaller schools face fewer specific requirements but cannot disproportionately cut non-revenue sports based on revenue generation.

Perhaps most significantly, the order directs the Secretary of Labor and the National Labor Relations Board to clarify that student-athletes are not employees. This directive aims to close the path that Dartmouth basketball players and USC athletes pursued through the NLRB.

The order also prohibits third-party "pay-for-play" payments while preserving legitimate NIL deals offering fair market value. This distinction, which the NCAA and College Sports Commission have struggled to enforce, becomes federal policy. The Attorney General and the Federal Trade Commission received instructions to develop litigation strategies to protect the NCAA from antitrust challenges that "unreasonably" threaten athletic opportunities.

On April 3, 2026, the President escalated Executive Branch involvement by issuing a second order, "Urgent National Action to Save College Sports." Where the July 2025 order largely urged federal agencies to study and recommend, the 2026 order directed them to act, conditioning federal grants and contracts on institutional compliance with national standards for eligibility, transfers, and NIL compensation. I take up that order more fully in the Epilogue. The executive orders' practical impact remains uncertain. Executive orders direct agency action but do not themselves create enforceable law. The agencies tasked with implementation may take years to develop regulations. Courts may ultimately determine that the orders exceed executive authority or conflict with judicial precedents.

What the orders demonstrate most clearly is that Collegiate Capitalism has become a federal policy concern. Congress had not yet provided a statutory framework, and the executive was filling the vacuum, though by the time I finished this book a bipartisan Senate effort had finally taken shape, as I describe in the Epilogue. A U.S. President felt compelled to issue emergency directives about college sports governance. Members of his cabinet received assignments to develop enforcement mechanisms.

When I arrived at the NCAA in 2011, college athletics sought to operate below the radar of federal policy. U.S. Presidents might attend championship games and host winning teams, but they did not issue executive orders attempting to restructure the industry. That a president now considers college athletics worthy of emergency intervention reflects how seriously the landscape has changed.

I spent years defending a system I now understand lacked some of the core tenets of fairness. I made arguments that contradict my present-day private convictions. I defended principles that scandals kept proving were either impossible to maintain or actively corrupted by the commercial pressures inherent in big-time college athletics. And now, here we are.

> The transformation wasn't voluntary. It was about accumulated evidence showing that the evolution of the amateur model was built on manipulation, maintained through hypocrisy, and sustained by denying fundamental rights to athletes who helped generate billions in revenue while receiving scholarships that sometimes came with fake education.

And we are neither done nor settled. Schools are making revenue-sharing payments. Athletes are navigating new financial realities. The College Sports Commission is adjusting its enforcement approaches. Title IX litigation looms. Employment status cases proceed. And everyone involved recognizes that the frameworks established by *House* will face continued challenges and modifications.

The *House* settlement doesn't eliminate competitive imbalances, guarantee gender equity, address employment status questions, or prevent future litigation challenging its restrictions.

But it does officially end the pretense that college athletics at the highest levels is purely amateur competition. It acknowledges that athletes deserve a greater share of the pie. It does represent institutional acceptance that the old model became legally vulnerable and morally bankrupt.

The House of Cards has fallen. We now have a system where Power schools can afford to pay athletes millions while smaller schools struggle to compete, where football and men's basketball dominate compensation while Olympic sports receive minimal benefits, where Title IX compliance creates legal exposure, where employment questions remain unresolved, and where new restrictions on NIL payments face antitrust challenges that may prove fatal. The question now is not whether college athletics will continue transforming, but how that transformation will proceed and whether the framework established by the *House* settlement can maintain any meaningful distinction between college and professional sports.

I suspect it cannot. And we're all living in the new world that its collapse revealed.

Chapter 26
Fairness Matters
In Perspective

After spending most of this book examining how external pressures transformed college athletics from amateur competition to competition based on Collegiate Capitalism, we need to confront the underlying issue that made the system vulnerable to all those pressures in the first place: fundamental unfairness.

The gambling scandals, the antitrust lawsuits, the concussion litigation, the unionization efforts, the COVID financial crisis, the enforcement fumbles, fake classes, and the gender equity failures. All of these events and more exposed the same vulnerability. The amateur model did not collapse because it was conceived in bad faith. Indeed, it was quite the opposite as the design by well-intentioned people was to protect the participants and the ideals of higher education. It fell apart because its original design could not absorb the weight of what college athletics had become. Look closely enough, and you will see a multi-billion-dollar commercial enterprise that the rules and assumptions of an earlier era were never built to govern.

Fairness isn't just an abstract ideal; it's the foundation of justice in American society. Yet our system of college athletics had deliberately denied fundamental fairness to the very athletes who made the system function. This contradiction between our democratic values and institutional practices demands urgent examination and reform.

I didn't fully grasp this contradiction until I found myself confronting antithetical arguments in different contexts. In 2014, I was in a courtroom coaching outside counsel to defend the NCAA's amateurism principles, arguing that athletes received tremendous value through scholarships and shouldn't be compensated beyond educational benefits. Doing more would upset the financial underpinning of broad-based athletics offerings, I thought.

In 2016, I was in a boardroom with senior NCAA leadership discussing revenue projections from the television contract renewal, which would run through 2032. I recall that Mark Lewis, in particular, reflected that the tournament generates extraordinary value, given the over $1 billion in anticipated annual revenue from the CBS/Turner deal. Momentarily, that afternoon, I thought about the arguments I'd been advancing in and out of court for years. Athletes receive fair value. Education is invaluable compensation. The system works. I believed then and still believe in the promise of higher education, but as I pondered billion-dollar revenue projections generated in part by athletes' performances, the contradictions floated in and out of my mind.

That night at dinner, I was debating college sports with some friends. They pushed me: "How do you defend a system in courtrooms that you are having a hard time defending here in an honest conversation? How do you tell athletes to their faces that they're fairly rewarded when the NCAA is generating billions from their contributions? How do you argue this is about education when you are really running a commercial entertainment business?"

I did not have fully satisfying answers, and the transformation that has since occurred suggests the system needed to evolve. But the legal arguments we made were not frivolous; they reflected a genuine interpretation of existing law that the Supreme Court had not yet addressed.

Simply put, I didn't have good answers then. I still don't.

Critics often point to our Supreme Court loss in *Alston*, which I've mentioned several times and detailed in the previous chapter, asking, "Doesn't a 9-0 defeat prove you were wrong?" From a purely legal perspective, absolutely. The Supreme Court defines the law of the land and interprets legislative intent. My jurisprudential philosophy and legal education compel me to accept the Court's rulings and new precedents. Being "wrong" in this context simply means I had a different interpretation, lacking the authority of those who disagreed and ruled otherwise. It is what it is.

But let me explain why being legally "wrong" at the Supreme Court doesn't mean the fundamental issue is settled. Courts can change their minds when society's values evolve.

And the Court's decision in *Alston* demonstrates something profound about how legal interpretations shift and evolve as society's values change and our understanding of justice develops. The Court was influenced not just by a strict interpretation of antitrust laws but also by the societal context at the time. Every decision, every ruling, is more than just an impartial assessment of the law's text; the Court also, at a minimum, is aware of the broader impact of its verdict on society.

This pattern repeats throughout American legal history, and understanding these precedents helps explain why today's "settled law" often becomes tomorrow's embarrassing relic. Consider the Court's most dramatic transformations, each reflecting profound shifts in societal understanding of justice and human dignity.

In 1896, *Plessy v. Ferguson* established the "separate but equal" doctrine, with Justice Henry Brown writing that enforced racial separation did not "stamp the colored race with a badge of inferiority" unless they chose to interpret it that way. For nearly sixty years, this decision institutionalized Jim Crow laws and legitimized state-sponsored segregation across American society. The legal reasoning seemed sound to the Justices at the time. Separate facilities could theoretically be equal. The Constitution, they argued, didn't require social integration.

Yet by 1954, in *Brown v. Board of Education*, Chief Justice Earl Warren explicitly rejected Plessy's reasoning, writing that "we cannot turn the clock back to 1868, when the Amendment was adopted, or even to 1896, when *Plessy v. Ferguson* was written. We must consider public education in the light of its full development and its present place in American life." The Court unanimously declared that "separate educational facilities are inherently unequal" and violated the Equal Protection Clause. This wasn't merely a legal technicality; it represented society's evolving recognition that racial segregation was incompatible with human dignity and democratic principles.

What changed between 1896 and 1954? Not the Constitution's text. Not the Fourteenth Amendment's language. What changed was society's understanding of equality and human dignity. The Court adapted because American values evolved.

Similarly, the Court's treatment of sexual privacy demonstrates how legal interpretations respond to changing social understanding. In 1986, *Bowers v. Hardwick* upheld Georgia's sodomy law, with the majority dismissing claims that the Constitution protected private consensual conduct between same-sex adults. The decision "reflected prevailing societal attitudes of the time but failed to anticipate the evolution of legal and social norms." Justice White wrote that to claim constitutional protection for such conduct would be "facetious."

Seventeen years later, in 2003, the same Supreme Court explicitly overruled *Bowers* in *Lawrence v. Texas*. In remarkably strong terms, Justice Anthony Kennedy wrote that "liberty protects the person from unwarranted government intrusions" and "presumes an autonomy of self that includes freedom of thought, belief, expression, and certain intimate conduct." The decision was described by legal scholars as "the LGBT *Brown v. Board of Education*" because it markedly recast how American law viewed individual privacy and dignity. What changed? Society's understanding of equality, privacy, and the proper role of government in regulating private life.

Seventeen years. That's how long it took for "settled law" to become indefensible precedent. What seemed obviously correct to one generation of Justices became obviously wrong to the next.

The winds, of course, do not always blow toward greater protection of individual rights, and the Court's recent decision in *Louisiana v. Callais* illustrates the point as clearly as any case in modern memory. In 2023, in *Allen v. Milligan*, the Court reaffirmed that Section 2 of the Voting Rights Act required Alabama to draw a second majority-Black congressional district, a ruling that appeared to settle the constitutional ground beneath the most consequential civil rights statute of the twentieth century. Louisiana, following that mandate, redrew its map to include a second majority-Black district, only to be hauled back before the Court to defend what the same Court had told it to do. On April 29, 2026, by a six to three vote, the Justices struck down the Louisiana map as an unconstitutional racial gerrymander and, in the same stroke, rewrote the *Thornburg v.*

Gingles framework that had governed Section 2 cases for forty years. Plaintiffs must now show present-day intentional discrimination, must draw illustrative maps without using race as a criterion, and must satisfy a tightened set of conditions that Justice Kagan in dissent observed renders Section 2 all but a dead letter. What the Court blessed in 2023 it condemned in 2026, and the states that had complied in good faith were left to redraw their districts under rules that did not exist when they drew them the first time. The lesson is sobering. Precedent yields to the prevailing currents of judicial philosophy, and those currents can carry the law toward greater fairness or away from it, depending on who is rowing.

The Court has also reversed precedent in response to economic and technological evolution. In 2018, *South Dakota v. Wayfair* overturned decades-old precedent that prevented states from collecting sales tax from online retailers without physical presence in the state. The Court noted that the economy had changed drastically, with a marked increase in the prevalence and power of internet commerce, and that states had argued in their supporting materials that revenue shortfalls could reach as much as $33 billion per year due to the limitations imposed by the Court's prior decisions. When economic reality made the *physical presence* rule unworkable, the Court adapted its legal precedent.

Labor rights provide another telling example. In *Hammer v. Dagenhart*, the Court struck down federal child labor laws, ruling that states should determine their own child labor policies. But by 1941, in *United States v. Darby*, the Court openly questioned the rationale of the 1918 Court, with Justice Harlan Fiske Stone writing that the earlier distinction was "novel when made and unsupported by any provision of the Constitution" and had "long since been abandoned." The economic and social changes of the Great Depression and the New Deal era had reshaped the American understanding of federal power and worker protection.

Most tellingly for our discussion, in 1984, the Supreme Court included language in *Board of Regents* that, while the NCAA had violated antitrust laws by restricting access to media rights, it supported the notion that student-athletes should not be paid and that amateurism remained an appropriate principle underlying college sport. Yet thirty-seven years later, in 2021, the Court articulated something entirely different in *Alston*. Why this dramatic change? It appears that "society" developed a different view of the preferred outcome. Because the contradictions in the amateur model became impossible to defend as college athletics generated billions while athletes received little. Because Americans' understanding of fairness has evolved.

We're witnessing the collision between institutional agendas and evolving societal norms about fairness and individual rights. And I predict that just as *Brown* overruled *Plessy*, just as *Lawrence* overruled *Bowers*, just as *Alston* gutted the precedential weight of *Board of Regents*, future Courts will look back at decisions upholding amateurism restrictions and wonder how we ever thought denying athletes compensation while they were helping to generate billions was consistent with American values or maybe future Courts will wonder how we opened the floodgates to Collegiate Capitalism into higher education.

This evolution forces us to confront uncomfortable truths about the systems we've created. And here's where my personal contradiction became impossible to ignore. Because over the years, depending on the audience, I found myself making vastly different arguments about the same system.

In courtrooms, I've successfully led arguments. I still believe that college athletics provides tremendous value to participants. Student-athletes receive free education worth hundreds of thousands of dollars, world-class training, nutrition, and comprehensive healthcare. An individual's earning power increases dramatically over a lifetime for someone with a college degree compared to someone without one. What NCAA colleges and universities provide isn't just valuable; it's priceless in many ways.

These young athletes gain access to resources they couldn't obtain elsewhere: professional-grade athletics training, nutritional guidance, medical care, and educational opportunities that can transform their lives. They learn how to care for their bodies with tools they can use for the rest of their lives. This comprehensive support system represents significant in-kind compensation for their athletics participation. From this perspective, the current system appears not just fair but generous. James Heckman, who received the Noel Prize in Economics, testified as much in *O'Bannon*.

Yet in meeting rooms and boardrooms, away from legal proceedings, I now embrace the uncomfortable truth that reveals the system's fundamental unfairness. College athletes represent the only Americans systematically denied the right to fully capitalize on their peak market value. Nowhere else in this nation do we maintain a system in which someone at their highest earning potential is deliberately forbidden from self-actualization. We've created a uniquely un-American arrangement in which citizens, at their athletic and marketable prime, cannot fully benefit from their own talents and hard work.

Think about Ed O'Bannon, whose likeness helped popularize the EA video game, while he received nothing until he sued. Think about Shabazz Napier, the national championship point guard who claimed to go to bed hungry because NCAA rules prevented him from receiving adequate food. Think about the football players who may have suffered brain injuries while their school's system did not adequately protect them. Think about the female athletes who trained in inferior facilities while men's teams had state-of-the-art everything. Think about athletes who were told they couldn't bet on professional sports while organized crime infiltrated gambling markets, exploiting inside information about the very games these athletes played. The incidents we've examined in this book ultimately stemmed from this fundamental unfairness.

The analytical model I've used applies with particular force. Fundamental unfairness creates profound vulnerability. External pressures exploited that vulnerability. The system failed to address the underlying injustice. Transformation became inevitable.

Amateurism in big-time college sports collapsed not because any single lawsuit, politician, or scandal destroyed it, but because a system built on fundamental unfairness couldn't withstand sustained examination of its contradictions.

This contradiction strikes at the heart of American democratic principles. We pride ourselves on individual liberty, free market economics, and equal opportunity for all citizens. Yet college athletics carved out an exception for college athletes, essentially arguing that their citizenship rights should be suspended during their prime competitive years. The system tells these young people what should be "enough" for them rather than allowing them to determine their own path forward.

The challenge I've consistently faced is the argument that the current system is infinitely fair to participating athletes. Defenders claim that free education, combined with athletics training and support services, provides more value than any monetary payment these athletes could receive during their playing days. They argue that we enhance the futures of these young athletes through the education we provide, offering them tools for lifelong success that transcend their temporary athletics careers. Indeed, I've argued as much!

This perspective contains truth but misses the larger point about fairness and self-determination. True fairness requires more than providing valuable benefits while denying fundamental rights. It demands treating college athletes as equal American citizens with the same opportunities as everyone else. We cannot simultaneously celebrate the American values of individual liberty and free-market participation while creating institutional barriers that prevent these young people from fully participating in those same systems.

The democratic solution requires giving these athletes a meaningful voice in the systems that govern their lives. Democracy isn't just about voting; it's about ensuring that affected parties participate in decisions that impact them. Historically, college athletes have been subject to rules and restrictions imposed by administrators, coaches, and governing bodies, without meaningful input into those processes. They're told what's best for them rather than being invited to help determine their own futures.

This paternalistic approach contradicts fundamental American principles. We don't tell other citizens what career choices they should make or how they should monetize their talents. We don't restrict other college students from earning money from their skills, whether those involve tutoring, performing, writing, or any other marketable ability. Only in athletics do we maintain that institutional concerns override individual rights.

I entered the NCAA as a skeptic, questioning whether the organization truly served athletes' interests rather than institutional ones. My experiences over more than a decade both dispelled that predisposition and reinforced the skepticism. But knowledge since I left the NCAA, watching from outside the bubble of college athletics, seeing how other sectors treat young workers, understanding how American labor law applies in places beyond college sports, has reinforced my growing conviction that we'd created and defended an unfair system.

That skepticism has proven essential because genuine fairness only emerges when we critically examine entrenched systems and challenge comfortable assumptions. Skepticism forces us to look beyond traditional justifications and examine whether our systems actually serve the people they claim to protect.

The pursuit of perfect fairness may indeed be an attempt to attain an impossible goal, but abandoning the effort represents a logical fallacy, a caving to futility that conveniently preserves unjust systems. This reasoning suggests that because we cannot achieve perfect fairness, we shouldn't strive for greater fairness at all. Such thinking protects existing power structures while dismissing legitimate concerns about equity and justice.

Instead, we must continue working toward greater fairness, especially when powerful interests benefit from maintaining the status quo. The billions of dollars college athletics help generate create strong incentives to preserve current arrangements or even revert to "the old ways," regardless of their impact on individual athletes. These financial pressures make it easy to rationalize restrictions on athlete compensation by emphasizing the benefits they do receive while ignoring the rights they're denied. A fundamental argument behind the American experiment of democracy is that nothing is an adequate reward or compensation for giving up freedom to fully self-actualize.

The path forward doesn't require abandoning college athletics' educational mission or destroying the traditions that make college sports meaningful. We can preserve the collegiate atmosphere, academic integration for those who want it, and community connections that define college athletics while treating athletes fairly. The choice isn't as simple as one between pure amateurism and unrestricted commercialization; it's between perpetuating a system that denies fundamental rights and creating one that honors both educational goals and individual liberty.

This issue extends far beyond college sports into fundamental questions about American democracy and equal treatment under law. When we allow powerful institutions to restrict individual rights for their own benefit, we undermine the principles that define our society. When we tell citizens that their concerns about fairness don't matter because they receive other benefits, we establish dangerous precedents that could extend to other areas of American life.

The athletes at the center of this debate deserve nothing less than the same rights we guarantee every other American citizen. They deserve the opportunity to benefit from their talents, to participate in decisions that affect their lives, and to determine their own definition of fair compensation. They deserve to be treated as full citizens rather than institutional assets, as individuals with rights rather than resources to be managed.

Having defended an unfair system for years, I find the hypocrisy surrounding the "ideals" of amateurism that much more despicable. And I need to be honest about my own role in perpetuating that hypocrisy.

For years, I stood in courtrooms and conference rooms defending amateurism principles. The legal arguments I advanced were sincere in the sense that lawyers are paid to make the best case available, and there was a real case to be made. Education has genuine value. Scholarships are real compensation. Athletes do gain from the support systems universities provide. But as the commercial scale of college athletics grew, I found myself increasingly unable to answer the harder question: whether the best available legal argument was also a just one? Those are different questions, and conflating them is where institutional advocacy and personal integrity can quietly diverge.

We demand integrity from athletes while operating a system that sometimes fails to uphold the same values. We celebrate the educational mission while tolerating, and in some cases failing to prevent, academic accommodations that prioritize eligibility over learning. We preach about amateurism's purity while generating billions in commercial revenue. We claim to protect athletes while denying them basic rights that other American citizens enjoy.

We must demand integrity. Demanding that, while allowing rampant rule violations or permitting "fake" education to occur, is unforgivable. It matters to the lives of the athletes involved. It matters as part of a greater, overarching principle.

Fairness matters ultimately because it reflects our commitment to treating all Americans equally, regardless of their circumstances or the institutions they encounter. It matters because it reflects our dedication to individual liberty and democratic participation. Most importantly, it matters because these young athletes, like all citizens, deserve the chance to pursue their dreams on the same terms as everyone else. Only when we extend these fundamental rights to college athletes can we claim to have created a truly fair system that honors both athletics excellence and American values.

As I have said before, a lone episode didn't drive the shift toward a fully commercial model. It was driven by the accumulated weight of an imperfect system that couldn't withstand sustained examination of its contradictions. Courts, prosecutors, politicians, public opinion, pandemics, and social movements all attacked different aspects of the amateur model. But they were all ultimately attacking the same underlying vulnerability: a system built on denying fundamental fairness to the athletes who made it possible.

Fairness matters because without it, no system can long survive. And college athletics' journey from amateur ideal to commercial reality proves that unfair systems eventually collapse under the weight of their own contradictions, regardless of how vigorously we defend them in courtrooms or how much money flows through them in boardrooms.

Chapter 27
Collegiate Capitalism Has Arrived
Accepting Reality is Hard

Ohio State's 34-23 victory over Notre Dame in the 2025 CFP National Championship was, on its face, a familiar outcome. The Buckeyes claimed their ninth national title and first since 2014. Will Howard threw for 231 yards and two touchdowns. Quinshon Judkins rushed for 100 yards. The storylines were classic college football: redemption after a devastating loss to Michigan, a transfer portal quarterback finding his moment, a freshman receiver named Jeremiah Smith making the championship's defining catch.

But nothing around the game was really familiar. The expanded 12-team playoff that allowed Ohio State to reach the championship as an eighth seed was brand new. The revenue sharing framework that would take effect in five months was unprecedented. The enforcement body that would police NIL transactions, the College Sports Commission, would kick off a few months after the game. Grant House, the Arizona State swimmer whose name adorned the litigation that had transformed everything, was watching his settlement move toward final approval.

The symbolism of the matchup was almost too obvious. Notre Dame, the most tradition-bound program in college football, fiercely independent and perpetually nostalgic for a purer era. Ohio State, the prototype of the modern athletic department, generates more than $336 million (FY2025) in annual revenue and operates with the sophistication of a professional franchise. The game was played in Mercedes-Benz Stadium, a monument to corporate naming rights and luxury suites, while commissioners discussed revenue sharing and roster limits in nearby hotel conference rooms.

Ohio State's championship roster was a product of the new marketplace. Howard had transferred from Kansas State. Judkins had transferred from

Ole Miss. The Buckeyes had assembled their championship team through a combination of traditional recruiting and portal acquisitions that would have been impossible five years earlier. Their NIL infrastructure, built on a foundation of institutional support and booster collectives, was among the most robust in college athletics.

Big Ten commissioner Tony Petitti watched from the sidelines, contemplating a conference whose schools would soon begin directly compensating athletes. The SEC, which had dominated the playoff era, had no representative in the championship game for the second consecutive year. The balance of power had shifted, and money was the mechanism.

What struck me most about that January night in Atlanta was the conversation happening around the game rather than within it. Between plays, television analysts discussed the *House* settlement's implications. Commissioners gave interviews about enforcement mechanisms and roster limits. Notre Dame athletic director Pete Bevacqua speculated about whether the seeding system needed adjustment. The football was excellent, but it was almost incidental to the transformation unfolding in real time.

Ryan Day's championship vindicated his program's approach to the new era. Ohio State had embraced NIL, invested in transfer portal evaluation, and built the infrastructure necessary to compete in a marketplace that rewarded spending. The Buckeyes had been criticized for years as underperformers in January. Now they were champions precisely because they had adapted faster than their competitors.

The first payments under the *House* settlement would begin on July 1, 2025, fewer than six months after Howard took a knee to run out the clock. The championship that Ohio State celebrated would be among the last won under the pre-revenue-sharing framework. The athletes who hoisted the trophy would be among the last for whom NIL deals represented the primary mechanism of direct compensation. By the following season, schools could pay athletes directly.

The 2025 championship was a bookend. It closed the "old" NIL era, distinct from the present revenue-sharing era. It demonstrated that the sport could survive transformation and still produce compelling competition. And it suggested that the future would belong to programs willing to spend whatever it took to win. Ohio State had shown the way. How many can afford to follow is the question that will define the next decade. Indiana and Miami both proved they could en route to the 2026 National Championship.

So here we are, several months into that revenue-sharing era, and I need to acknowledge an uncomfortable truth. The transformation I resisted, the change I defended against in courtrooms and conference rooms, the evolution I argued was neither necessary nor inevitable, has been realized. Collegiate Capitalism isn't coming. It's here.

As I complete this project, I'm watching schools make their first direct payments to athletes, watching the College Sports Commission navigate enforcement of the new regime, watching Title IX litigation materialize exactly as predicted, watching employment status cases advance, and watching the amateur model's final remnants dissolve in real time.

It didn't happen the way I thought it would when I first conceived the Collegiate Capitalism framework several years ago. I imagined it might already involve private equity ownership, intellectual property licensing, facility leasing arrangements, unionized players, and completely professionalized operations. Some of that will still come. But what's actually arrived is something more organic and messier. We are in the midst of a hybrid system in which universities directly pay athletes millions while trying to maintain some distinction from professional sports, where new enforcement entities attempt to regulate compensation while facing inevitable antitrust challenges, and where the word "student-athlete" remains in use even as the concept it represents has been abandoned.

The *House* settlement didn't create Collegiate Capitalism so much as it formalized what had already occurred. When Judge Wilken approved that settlement on June 6, 2025, she didn't transform college athletics. She acknowledged a transformation that external pressures, including hers, had already forced over the preceding decade.

Let me trace how we arrived here because the journey matters as much as the destination. Almost every chapter of this book represented a moment of friction that exposed the amateur model's vulnerabilities and pushed the system toward this inevitable endpoint.

Penn State showed that political pressure could override NCAA autonomy. When the scandal broke in 2011, I learned that external forces could propel institutional action faster than any internal process. The consent decree and its unwinding demonstrated that power, accountability, and public outrage could reshape college athletics regardless of what we wanted or what our bylaws required. The amateur model's first lesson: external pressure trumps institutional control.

Miami proved that our enforcement system couldn't hold powerful institutions accountable if mistakes are made. Despite comprehensive evidence of pervasive rule violations, we couldn't deliver meaningful penalties. Our investigation became a scandal itself. I watched as enforcement failures made clear that the system designed to maintain integrity was overwhelmed by contradiction. The amateur model's second lesson: when enforcement fails, voluntary compliance becomes impossible.

The FBI basketball investigation exposed corruption we'd been unable or unwilling to address internally. Federal prosecutors succeeded where NCAA investigators had failed, revealing that shoe companies and agents had infiltrated college basketball at the highest levels. We heard testimony coming out of that New York courtroom in 2018 about cash payments and wondered what the hell we'd been doing while organized corruption operated openly. The amateur model's third lesson: systemic problems require intervention because internal reform is insufficient.

Concussion litigation forced acknowledgment of catastrophic risks we'd asked athletes to accept without incomplete protection and inadequate compensation. The *Arrington* case and other individual cases demonstrated that treating athletes as students rather than employees created liability exposure that could prove problematic. We were asking young people to sacrifice their long-term health for our commercial entertainment without providing the protections or compensation that professional athletes appeared to receive. The amateur model's fourth lesson: you cannot ask people to accept professional-level risks under amateur-level protections.

The Northwestern unionization effort proved that some athlete relationships looked like employment regardless of what we called them. When the NLRB regional director ruled that scholarship football players were employees under federal labor law, I suspected the legal foundation for amateurism was fragmenting. Even though the Board ultimately declined jurisdiction, the analysis was clear: these were akin to employment relationships. The amateur model's fifth lesson: legal fictions eventually collide with factual realities.

COVID exposed financial fragility and forced us to confront uncomfortable truths about who bore risks in our system. When we canceled tournaments in March 2020, I watched as revenue disappeared and schools contemplated cutting sports, while coaches kept multi-million-dollar salaries and administrators maintained their positions. Athletes bore the health risks and opportunity costs while lacking the compensation or collectively bargained protections that professional athletes would have received. The amateur model's sixth lesson: when crisis hits, institutional interests are protected while athletes' interests are sacrificed.

Gender equity failures demonstrated inequities enabled by the amateur model's lack of accountability. Sedona Prince's TikTok video in March 2021 exposed what internal processes had ignored: organized underfunding and, some argued, a lack of respect for women's sports. The inequities weren't accidental. They were structural features of a system that prioritized revenue generation over equity and relied on athletes' lack of bargaining power to perpetuate marginalization. The amateur model's seventh lesson: without accountability mechanisms, discrimination becomes institutionalized.

Gambling scandals proved that integrity protections failed when commercial pressures overwhelmed amateur principles. The October 2025 indictments involving NBA players and organized crime validated every concern we'd raised about legalization creating corruption opportunities. Yet the NCAA simultaneously contemplated allowing athletes and coaches to bet on professional sports. The amateur model's eighth lesson: commercial pressures eventually overwhelm integrity principles that conflict with financial interests.

UNC's fake classes exposed that educational justifications were sometimes fraudulent. For 18 years, one of America's most prestigious universities engaged in academic fraud to maintain athletes' eligibility. And when exposed, our enforcement system couldn't deliver accountability because of jurisdictional technicalities. The amateur model's ninth lesson: the educational foundation justifying denial of compensation was sometimes a complete fiction.

Alston eliminated the legal arguments. When Justice Kavanaugh wrote in his concurrence that the NCAA's business model would be "flatly illegal in almost any other industry in America" and called our reasoning "circular," he destroyed the intellectual foundation for compensation restrictions. You cannot defend a system when the Supreme Court has unanimously declared it violates antitrust law, and one Justice questions why athletes shouldn't earn "large salaries" in a free market. The amateur model's tenth lesson: legal arguments eventually fail when they are based on preserving a business model rather than serving legitimate purposes.

House forced the institutional acknowledgment. Facing $20 billion in potential damages and the real possibility that Judge Wilken would completely eliminate compensation restrictions, the NCAA settled. The decision represented acknowledgment that defending the amateur model was legally impossible and financially catastrophic. The amateur model's eleventh lesson: when all legal arguments fail, and all pressures converge, transformation becomes inevitable, regardless of institutional resistance.

My exploration of fairness forced me to acknowledge that the system was built on fundamental unfairness. I'd made arguments in courtrooms and boardrooms, defending principles I increasingly questioned, arguing that scholarships provided fair and adequate compensation. At the same time, realizing that at their peak market value, athletes were denied rights that every other American citizen enjoyed. The amateur model's final lesson: embedded unfairness eventually becomes indefensible when examined honestly.

Each pressure had seemed manageable in isolation. *O'Bannon* was about the proper application of antitrust law and right of publicity. Penn State was about one scandal. Miami was about enforcement procedures. The FBI investigation was about basketball corruption. Concussions were about health and safety. Unionization was about labor law. COVID was about a financial crisis. Gender equity was about Title IX compliance. Gambling was about integrity protection. UNC was about academic fraud.

Fairness was about philosophical principles. *Alston* was about education benefits. *House* was about revenue sharing.

Altogether, these pressures revealed something more fundamental. We were running commercial entertainment businesses while claiming educational purposes. We were generating billions while paying athletes nothing. We were asking athletes to accept professional-level risks and commitments without professional-level compensation or protections. We were celebrating educational missions while sometimes providing fake education. We were demanding integrity while commercial pressures incentivized corruption. We were preaching fairness while denying fundamental rights.

This is what Collegiate Capitalism actually is now, rather than what I theorized it might be in Chapter 2. It's not yet private-equity ownership of teams or a complete separation of athletics from universities. It's a hybrid system in which universities directly pay athletes while attempting to maintain some distinctions from professional sports. It's the College Sports Commission trying to regulate NIL deals while facing inevitable antitrust challenges. It's Title IX litigation over compensation disparities. It's employment status cases advancing through courts. Its roster limits reduce participation opportunities. It's competitive stratification between wealthy programs and everyone else.

It's messy and complicated and legally uncertain and unsustainable in its current form. The *House* settlement resolved some questions while creating new ones. It established that athletes merit compensation while attempting restrictions that some argue violate the antitrust principles it purports to honor. It acknowledged transformation while trying to preserve institutional control, noting that external pressures will likely continue to erode it.

And make no mistake, Collegiate Capitalism definitely has delivered the formal acknowledgment that college athletics at the highest levels is commercial entertainment, not simply amateur competition. That athletes are professionals helping to generate billions, not merely students playing games. That compensation should reflect market value, not artificial caps based on amateur restrictions. That fairness requires treating athletes as employees with rights, not students with privileges.

The potential gains from this transformation are real. Athletes will finally receive compensation reflecting their contributions. Professional status brings professional protections such as collective bargaining rights, workplace safety standards, and healthcare that extend beyond immediate injuries. The prior structure has ended, at least in its most egregious forms.

Athletes like Sedona Prince, who exposed gender inequity and then became a House plaintiff, now have compensation opportunities that would have been unthinkable under the old model. Athletes who might have suffered catastrophic injuries without adequate long-term protection now have pathways to fair compensation. Athletes who were steered into fake classes to maintain eligibility can now be openly professionals without the pretense that education justifies denial of payment.

But the losses are real too. At the highest levels of college sports, the distinction between college and professional sports has seemingly collapsed in everything but name. The amateur ideal that motivated participation for the love of competition rather than financial gain is gone. The educational integration that supposedly made college sports special has been severely weakened. The broad-based participation model, where non-revenue sports were subsidized by football and basketball revenue, faces existential threats.

Walk-on programs that created opportunities for athletes like Stetson Bennett are largely eliminated. Roster limits reduce participation opportunities for thousands of people. Smaller schools cannot compete financially with Power Four programs. Olympic sports face uncertain futures as football and basketball revenues are redirected to athlete compensation rather than program subsidization. The community connections and regional rivalries that made college sports meaningful to fans may not survive the commercial pressures of Collegiate Capitalism.

I'm not going to pretend these losses don't matter. They do. Something valuable has been lost in this transformation. The amateur ideal, however imperfectly realized in practice, represented genuine values about sport, education, and opportunity. The community connections that made college sports meaningful were real, not just marketing narratives. The educational integration that we claimed as justification for amateurism was well-founded.

What I've learned after spending years defending the amateur model and then watching it give way is that you cannot preserve a system built on mishandling just because transformation involves loss. You cannot maintain a business model that courts have unanimously ruled violates antitrust law just because the alternative is uncertain. You cannot deny people fair compensation just because paying them fairly disrupts traditional arrangements. You cannot sacrifice fairness for nostalgia.

The old amateur model didn't collapse because bad people destroyed it. It collapsed because it was built on contradictions that became unsustainable once examined honestly. Commercial entertainment cannot be amateur. Billion-dollar businesses cannot behave like they're simply educational enterprises. Professional-level performance requires professional-level compensation. Fairness matters more than tradition.

I spent years defending positions I have now come to doubt. I advanced legal arguments about the value of education during a period when some institutions were failing to deliver on that promise. I argued that the traditional compensation model was sufficient even as the commercial scale of college athletics continued to grow. I argued that scholarships provided fair compensation, even as athletes helped generate billions in revenue. I defended amateurism principles while commercial pressures rendered them meaningless. I resisted the transformation, but I have ultimately come to believe it was both necessary and just.

There is one of those positions I can point to precisely, because I put it in writing. In January 2012, the New York Times ran a Joe Nocera column calling college sports a cartel, paired with a magazine piece arguing we should start paying the players. Nocera and I had a history; I had first known him years earlier when he covered Fannie Mae and I was an executive there, and I respected his work. But I thought he was wrong on the facts, wrong on the law, and wrong on the economics, and I said so publicly. I built the antitrust argument, walked through the Supreme Court precedent, and closed with the line I was proudest of: “The distinguishing feature of college sports is that they are played by amateur participants in the collegiate model, a model so successful that it is almost universally accepted in this country despite the absence of any barriers to exit or entry.” I believed every word. Sit a minute with that certainty. The model I called almost universally accepted, the one I said survived precisely because nothing prevented anyone from leaving it, is the model that has now unraveled. Nocera was not entirely right. But on the central point, that the system could not hold, he saw something in 2012 that I, from inside it, would not let myself see for another decade.

That's the personal cost of this transformation for me. I was part of the system that perpetuated unfairness and later truly came to understand that unfairness. I advanced institutional positions in legal proceedings that I found increasingly difficult to reconcile with the realities I observed in operational settings and with my own convictions. And when the transformation I'd resisted finally arrived, I felt both vindication that the unfairness had been acknowledged and sadness that the system I'd devoted years to defending was gone.

The question now is not whether Collegiate Capitalism has arrived. It has. The question is what form it will ultimately take as the current hybrid system evolves toward a more sustainable system.

Private investment will likely increase as sophisticated investors recognize that college athletics represents an underexplored entertainment asset with significant growth potential. Whether that investment takes the form of private equity ownership, facility financing, or corporate partnerships remains uncertain. But the flow of private capital into college sports will accelerate.

Athletes will continue gaining rights and protections through litigation, legislation, and collective action. The employment status question will soon be resolved, potentially bringing unionization, collective bargaining, and professional labor protections. The compensation restrictions that survive the *House* settlement will face additional antitrust challenges. The Title IX implications of revenue-sharing distributions may compel more equitable compensation.

Universities will need to make explicit choices about their athletics ambitions and operations. Some will embrace full professionalization, accepting that they're running entertainment businesses that happen to be housed within educational institutions. Others will retreat from big-time athletics, focusing on genuinely amateur sports with limited budgets and scope. The current pretense that all Division I programs operate under the same model will end.

Conference realignment will continue as schools seek affiliations that maximize the television revenue needed to fund competitive athlete compensation. The geographic conferences that made sense when travel was expensive will be replaced by competitively balanced leagues designed to maximize media revenue. Traditional rivalries may not survive commercial pressures that prioritize national television audiences over regional connections.

The regulatory framework will require complete reconstruction. NCAA rules designed for amateur athletics don't work for professional enterprises. State laws governing NIL rights need to be updated for the new reality. Federal antitrust regulations and labor law must be applied consistently to what are now openly professional operations. Congress may intervene, though whether that intervention helps or hurts depends entirely on its form.

Olympic sports development will need new structures if football and basketball revenue no longer subsidizes non-revenue sports. The United States has achieved remarkable Olympic success through college athletics, which serves as a *de facto* national training ground. If that system disappears, government funding may be necessary to maintain a competitive advantage. Other nations already operate such systems. We may need to as well.

Yet all of this is speculation about the future evolution of Collegiate Capitalism, not a description of what's actually here. What's here is messy, complicated, and uncertain. It's a transformation that's real but incomplete, acknowledged but still evolving, necessary but costly.

What I know for certain is that the amateur model that governed college athletics for over a century is gone. What replaces it remains to be fully determined. But whatever emerges will need to treat athletes fairly, acknowledge commercial realities honestly, and align legal requirements with practical operations.

For athletes, Collegiate Capitalism means compensation, rights, and protections that the amateur model denied. That matters more than tradition or nostalgia or comfortable fictions about amateurism. Fairness matters. Justice matters. Treating people fairly matters more than preserving errant systems.

For universities, it means acknowledging that major athletics programs are commercial entertainment operations and making explicit decisions about whether to embrace that reality or retreat from it. The pretense that big-time college sports serve primarily educational missions can no longer be sustained.

For fans, it means potentially losing some aspects of college sports that made them special while gaining more competitive, entertaining, and professionally operated competitions. Whether that trade is worthwhile depends on what individual fans valued about the amateur model and what they'll value about whatever replaces it.

For me personally, it means acknowledging that the transformation I resisted was both inevitable and necessary. The tensions that accumulated over a decade made the amateur model unsustainable. The unfairness in the treatment of athletes made change morally imperative.

As the NCAA's Chief Legal Officer and Chief Operating Officer, I vigorously defended a system I now know was, at best, stumbling. I made the difficult arguments, even as I worried about a radical change on the horizon. And when that transformation arrived, I recognized that my role in defending the old system was complete.

The *House* settlement approval on June 6, 2025, and implementation beginning July 1, 2025, marked the end of an era for college athletics. For me personally, it also marked the end of a chapter. As Collegiate Capitalism arrived, as the transformation became irreversible, as the system I'd defended for years officially died, I knew my time at the NCAA was in the rearview mirror.

The journey from defending the amateur model to witnessing the arrival of Collegiate Capitalism has been professionally challenging and personally transformative. I entered the NCAA as a skeptic, questioning whether the organization truly served athletes' interests. I left having watched adversities force acknowledgment that the system was unfair and, at times, misaligned with how many courts viewed the law.

Twenty-six chapters documenting how we got here. Eleven distinct external pressures attacking different vulnerabilities. One analytical model explaining how transformation became inevitable. And now, Collegiate Capitalism has arrived, ready or not, wanted or not, acknowledged at last.

The question was never whether this transformation would happen. The question was whether we would guide it thoughtfully or resist it until circumstances forced changes we couldn't control. We chose resistance. The transformation happened anyway, exactly as the accumulated stresses made inevitable.

Collegiate Capitalism is here. The old amateur model has ceased to exist. The 119-year experiment has ended. And for me, as for college athletics itself, it's time for a new chapter.

Chapter 28
Full Circle
The President's Calling, Again

I'm finishing this book as 2025 turns to 2026, watching from outside as Collegiate Capitalism unfolds in ways both predictable and chaotic. Schools are cutting their first checks to athletes. The College Sports Commission is testing the limits of a new enforcement regime. Title IX suits are materializing. Employment status cases are advancing. The last remnants of the old amateur model are dissolving in real time.

And I'm thinking about what it meant to spend a decade defending that model. I left in 2021 just as its collapse became irreversible. The timing, even if coincidental, was almost poetic. Understanding why requires going back to Chapter 8 and 2009, to another presidential nomination, to a door that closed and led me to the NCAA in the first place.

When President Barack Obama nominated me to serve as General Counsel of the Department of the Army, I thought I was finally returning to the kind of service that had always felt most meaningful. Military service is foundational to who I am. My father came home from Vietnam with a Bronze Star and lessons he lived by every day: duty, excellence, and service to something greater than himself. My mother raised and nurtured a family of Army "brats" in her home and in the neighborhood. I'd served as an Army Captain, worked in the Army General Counsel's Office, and been detailed to the Office of the Secretary of Defense. The Meritorious Service Medal and National Defense Service Medal reminded me I'd contributed meaningfully to missions that mattered.

After hanging up my uniform, I'd built a career with real range: Howard Law School, a clerkship with Sixth Circuit Judge Nathaniel R. Jones, O'Melveny & Myers under the legendary William T. Coleman Jr., Deputy Assistant Attorney General in the Clinton Administration, handling cases involving Waco and Ruby Ridge. Then, at Fannie Mae, where I rose through legal and business leadership roles and led post-Katrina housing redevelopment efforts in my home state of Louisiana.

The Obama nomination felt like coming home. But sometimes leadership means stepping aside for the greater good. And that's what I did. I won't pretend it didn't hurt. The door to the public service that felt most authentic to me had closed.

When that door closed, another opened. The NCAA was facing unprecedented challenges to its traditional amateurism model. Emmert offered me the General Counsel position. I was passionate about college sports and higher education, notwithstanding a bit of cynicism about the amateur model. I accepted because it was a chance to lead a major organization through complex challenges, to apply legal and crisis management skills to problems that mattered, and, absolutely, to make a difference.

What I didn't fully appreciate in 2011 was that I was stepping into a decade that would witness a makeover of college athletics at the highest levels, from amateur competition to commercial entertainment. I would spend those years defending the system as external pressures accumulated against it.

And now, five years after leaving the NCAA and more than three years after completing my service as Deputy Secretary of Veterans Affairs, I can see what that decade meant. Not just for college athletics, but for me personally. The cost of defending positions that became weaker and weaker. The lessons about institutions and transformation. And ultimately, the understanding that defending an institution's interests can be fundamentally different from serving people's needs.

Let me be honest about what that decade was like. Every chapter of this book represents a crisis or pressure I helped navigate: the presidential retreat, adverse court rulings, Penn State, UNC's fake classes, and more. Each exposed different vulnerabilities. Each forced incremental change. Each made clearer that the system was unsustainable. Through it all, I was the one making the legal arguments, defending the policies, and explaining the principles before courts, Congress, and the public.

I worked with the Power Conferences and led legal strategies through the District Courts, Circuit Courts, and the Supreme Court. We achieved partial victories, but always suspected broader changes were on the horizon.

Here's what I couldn't fully grasp at the time. The tension between our legal framework and the evolving commercial realities of college athletics grew sharper every year. I defended principles I now question. I represented positions courts kept rejecting and membership actions kept undermining. I did this work professionally, competently, and in good-faith reliance on existing precedent, even as I began to recognize some of the system's fundamental contradictions.

The personal cost was real. Not financial; I was well compensated. The price was intellectual and moral. UNC exposed the gap between educational ideals and institutional realities that enforcement could not fix. Courts began questioning whether scholarships alone adequately reflected the commercial value athletes brought to their institutions. The growing scale of college sports made the amateurism framework harder to reconcile with the market; a tension courts ultimately resolved in ways the NCAA could not prevent.

The NCAA needed strong legal representation. The transformation needed to be managed rather than chaotic. Student-athletes depended on the organization functioning effectively. The work mattered. But, at times, there was a disconnect between what I argued publicly and what I reflected on privately, between the principles I guarded and the realities I witnessed. I defended zealously anyway. That was the job.

And then in early 2021, I got a phone call that would change everything. President Joe Biden, who had been Vice President when Obama nominated me in 2009, wanted to nominate me as Deputy Secretary of Veterans Affairs. The door that had closed twelve years earlier was opening again.

Secretary Denis McDonough talked me through the process and advocated for my nomination. The Senate Veterans' Affairs Committee held my confirmation hearing on May 19, 2021. When Chairman Jon Tester asked about my reasons for wanting to serve, my answer came from the heart: "Mr. Chairman, my motivation is highly personal. I'm a veteran. My father's a veteran. My brother, my uncle, my late father-in-law, many friends, and family have all served this nation in uniform and are now veterans. My family would not be where it is but for the VA."

That was the truth. When your Commander in Chief asks you to serve those who've served the nation, you answer the call. Full stop.

Three weeks after that hearing, on June 21, 2021, the Supreme Court handed down its *Alston* decision. The timing was coincidental. I had already been nominated, already testified, and already decided to leave if confirmed. But the coincidence was almost poetic.

The Court ruled unanimously against the organization I'd spent a decade defending. The intellectual framework I'd been safeguarding collapsed the same month I was waiting for a Senate vote.

Of course, I didn't leave because of *Alston*. But *Alston*, arriving when it did, felt like the universe acknowledging what I'd come to understand: that the transformation was now irreversible, and it was time for a different kind of service.

Senator Marsha Blackburn placed a hold on my nomination, creating a frustrating two-month delay. Chairman Tester defended me passionately, and when the Senate finally voted on July 15, 2021, the 91-8 margin was overwhelming and bipartisan. Being sworn in by Secretary McDonough as the 9th Deputy Secretary of Veterans Affairs, the second Black veteran ever to hold this role, was among the proudest moments of my life.

The contrast with my NCAA work was immediate and profound. At the NCAA, my role was institutional: to defend legal positions and manage legal and operational risk. At VA, the mission was direct human service. At the NCAA, I had developed arguments that courts kept rejecting. At VA, the mission was clear and the purpose unambiguous: implement policies that directly helped veterans and their families, caregivers and survivors, who deserved support.

The scope was massive: day-to-day operations of the federal government's second-largest agency, a budget exceeding $300 billion, more than 450,000 employees, and over 1,300 healthcare facilities. Using the analytical framework I discussed throughout this book, I oversaw the troubled Electronic Health Record Modernization program, with a projected cost exceeding $16 billion and running behind schedule. In congressional testimony, I was candid: "Right now, the bottom line is that the Cerner system is not delivering for veterans in the ways that it should. Not even close." At the NCAA, I'd defended positions even as courts rejected them. At the VA, I acknowledged problems honestly because solving them mattered more than defending them.

We expanded healthcare services, cut appointment wait times, improved benefits claim processing, scaled telehealth, continued the work on veteran unhoused, and strengthened suicide prevention. The passage of the PACT Act, the most significant expansion of veterans' healthcare and benefits in decades, required preparing the VA for millions of newly eligible veterans. The satisfaction came from knowing the work directly helped people who had served the nation.

When I announced my departure effective April 2023 after nearly two years, Secretary McDonough called me a "steadfast public servant who has fought like hell every day for our nation's veterans." That meant more to me than any other professional recognition because it captured what service should be: fighting for people who deserve support.

I didn't start drafting this book immediately after leaving the NCAA, or while still processing the transformation. I started years later with the perspective that only distance provides; I could see the full arc of what had happened and understand what it meant.

Writing has been an exercise in understanding my own journey as much as explaining the transformation of college athletics. For a decade, I professionally and competently defended the amateur model. I never had the chance to fully process what that decade meant until now.

Systems built on fundamental unfairness cannot survive honest examination. Legal arguments defending misaligned values eventually fail when courts question traditional assumptions. Institutional resistance gives way once the forces against it accumulate enough weight. I was part of defending a model destined to collapse, and I can see now both why that defense was necessary at the time and why it was ultimately doomed.

The bookends of my journey are profound. In 2009, Obama nominated me, but the opportunity was denied. In 2021, Biden called, and the Senate confirmed me.

The decade in between taught me that defending an institution's interests is different from serving people's needs. Both can be meaningful. Both demand excellence and integrity. But the latter can be personally rewarding in ways the former cannot.

My personal transformation mirrored the institutional one. I entered the NCAA believing in incremental reform from the inside. I left understanding that systems built on unfairness require fundamental change, not adjustment. That recognition didn't come from disillusionment. It came from watching external pressure after external pressure expose vulnerabilities that internal reforms couldn't address, from making arguments that sounded increasingly hollow, even as I made them professionally, and from witnessing the gap between the principles we espoused and the enterprise that emerged.

Collegiate Capitalism became inevitable once courts began examining the old amateur model honestly. My role was to defend that model during its final decade. When that role was complete, and the President called me to serve veterans, I answered without hesitation or regret.

Looking ahead, I'm committed to continuing service in whatever form opportunity presents. Writing this book allows me to share lessons learned about institutions, transformation, fairness, and the values that guide meaningful work.

The story of my career is ultimately about doors closing and opening, about service across sectors, about defending systems that ultimately couldn't be defended while maintaining integrity throughout. It's about recognizing when transformation is inevitable, when resistance is futile, when it's time to move from one kind of service to another.

In addition, the story of my career is also about understanding that the thread connecting everything, from military service through government, law, finance, sports, and back to government, is commitment to values established early and maintained throughout. Service before self. Excellence and accountability. Integrity and transparency. Fairness over tradition. The belief that creating opportunities for others is the true measure of leadership.

The NCAA decade was difficult, demanding, and ultimately disillusioning in ways I couldn't fully acknowledge while living it. Yet it was also necessary, meaningful, and professionally important. The organization needed strong legal representation during an unprecedented period of challenge. The transformation needed to be managed rather than chaotic. And the experience taught me lessons about institutions, change, and service that I couldn't have learned any other way.

I'm grateful for that decade even as I'm grateful it ended when it did. Grateful for the chance to serve veterans, even as I recognize that the NCAA work mattered. Grateful for the perspective that distance provides, even as I acknowledge the cost of defending positions many around me doubted.

The journey from Fort Lee, Virginia, through Army service, legal practice, government positions, corporate leadership, NCAA battles, VA service, and current work across sectors has been guided by values instilled by parents who understood that service to something greater than yourself is the measure of a meaningful life.

The door that closed in 2009 led me somewhere I didn't expect, taught me things I couldn't have learned otherwise, and reopened in 2021, at precisely the moment the work it had prepared me for was done.

And for me, the journey continues, guided by the same values that have shaped every major decision, committed to the same service that first drew me into uniform and hopeful that this book might help others understand how institutions change, why fairness matters, and how service across sectors makes life worth living.

Epilogue: Congress Attempts a Rescue

Too Little, Too Late?

I left the NCAA in July 2021, but I've been watching the transformation continue from the outside. And in July 2025, when the House of Representatives introduced the SCORE Act (the Student Compensation and Opportunity through Rights and Endorsements Act), I recognized immediately what was happening. After spending a decade defending the amateur model against adversities that ultimately made it unsustainable, I was watching Congress attempt to do what the NCAA never could: impose order on chaos through legislative fiat.

The timing was revealing. Judge Wilken had approved the *House* settlement just five weeks earlier, on June 6, 2025. Schools were weeks away from making their first direct payments to athletes. The transformation to Collegiate Capitalism that all those pressures had forced was becoming an operational reality. And the NCAA, having lost many major legal battles and facing an uncertain future navigating the new regime, was desperately seeking congressional intervention to provide certainty, stability, and most importantly, protection from further litigation.

The SCORE Act represents the NCAA's final attempt to control a transformation it can no longer prevent. If external pressures forced acknowledgment that athletes deserve compensation, perhaps Congress could at least determine how that compensation would be structured, limited, and regulated. If courts dismantled the old amateur model through antitrust law, Congress could provide antitrust immunity to prevent further legal challenges. If the *House* settlement established a framework for revenue sharing, perhaps Congress could codify that framework into federal law and prevent future modifications.

It's a logical strategy. Hell, I advocated quite strongly for congressional intervention in my final years at the organization. But the strategy was almost certainly doomed. Understanding why requires examining both what the SCORE Act would do and how it fits within the broader pattern of outside influences that prompted change I've documented throughout this book.

The SCORE Act's key provisions reveal its dual nature as both progressive reform and defensive reaction. On the surface, it appears to benefit athletes by codifying the *House* settlement's revenue-sharing model, requiring schools with athletic revenue exceeding $20 million to provide benefits, including mental health programs, legal and tax services, career counseling, degree completion assistance, and post-eligibility medical coverage. It would prohibit scholarship rescission based on athletic performance, illness, injury, or mental condition. It would establish federal NIL standards, replacing the current patchwork of state laws. It would require schools to maintain at least sixteen varsity sports, theoretically protecting Olympic sports from elimination.

Many of these provisions sound athlete-friendly and are genuine improvements over the pre-*House* settlement status quo. But the SCORE Act's defensive provisions reveal its alternate purpose. It will protect institutions and the NCAA from the external pressures that forced reform in the first place.

Most significantly, the SCORE Act would provide limited antitrust immunity for the NCAA, its member conferences, and the College Sports Commission, deeming compliance with the Act's provisions lawful and protecting them from the continued antitrust litigation that has driven major reforms over the past decade. At the same time, it would explicitly prohibit athletes from being classified as employees under federal or state law, preempting *Johnson*, the Dartmouth and USC NLRB cases, and any future labor status challenges. It would allow restrictions on third-party NIL payments deemed "prohibited compensation," giving the NCAA authority to limit deals from booster collectives and enforce caps that courts have noted violate antitrust law. It would limit transfer rights that federal courts validated, restricting athletes to one transfer without penalty.

In the analytical framework I've used throughout this book, the pattern is clear. External pressures accumulated through *O'Bannon, Alston, House*,

Northwestern, and the state NIL laws. Courts repeatedly rejected NCAA defenses. Now, rather than adapt, the NCAA seeks congressional intervention to override those decisions and preempt further legal challenges. The SCORE Act is counteraction dressed as reform.

It's the same playbook the NCAA has frequently used. Defend the existing structure. Argue that the proposed changes will destroy college athletics. Resist until pressure becomes overwhelming. Then seek minimal reforms while preventing further accountability. The difference is that now the NCAA is asking Congress to institutionalize that resistance by providing statutory immunity from the circumstances that forced major reforms. Again, I understand the need for clarity and certainty. But the method matters.

I've learned that successful legislation requires genuine consensus about problems and solutions. The SCORE Act has neither.

The opposition reveals fundamental disagreements about what reform should achieve. Senate Democrats, led by Maria Cantwell, Richard Blumenthal, and Cory Booker, have been unequivocal in their rejection. "I can pretty well guarantee the SCORE Act ain't going to make it through the United States Senate," Blumenthal stated bluntly in October 2025. Cantwell was equally direct: "The SCORE Act is really not what we think it is for the athlete." Their alternative, the SAFE Act (Student Athlete Fairness and Enforcement), would amend the Sports Broadcasting Act of 1961 to let conferences pool and negotiate media rights collectively, similar to professional leagues. It would guarantee athletes scholarships for 10 years after eligibility ends, require 5 years of post-eligibility medical coverage, cap agent compensation, and limit athletes to 2 transfers. The SAFE Act takes a different philosophical approach, focusing on athlete protection rather than institutional immunity. This isn't a minor technical adjustment. It's a radical restructuring of how college sports television revenue would be generated and distributed.

The current system concentrates media wealth in two conferences, which negotiated separate deals worth billions, while smaller conferences receive comparative pittances. Senator Cantwell released a report documenting how these "skyrocketing media rights payments have exacerbated a massive financial gap between traditional power conferences, especially the new Power 2—the SEC and Big Ten—and everyone else." In 2023, the average FBS athletic department earned $79 million in revenues but spent $98 million, a financial model Cantwell characterizes as unsustainable for small to mid-sized schools.

The SAFE Act would create a committee within the NCAA, not controlled by the biggest conferences, to negotiate pooled media rights and determine a fair distribution, ensuring that all schools receive more media revenue than they did in 2024-2025. The committee would be chosen by university presidents representing the Division I ecosystem broadly. Crucially, schools would be required to use increased media revenues to maintain the same number of scholarships and roster spots for women's and Olympic sports as existed in 2023-24, directly addressing concerns that revenue sharing will devastate non-revenue sports.

Unlike the SCORE Act, the SAFE Act leaves employment classification open, withholds blanket antitrust immunity, and does not authorize NCAA limits on third-party NIL payments through subjective "fair market value" determinations. Senator Cantwell was explicit about these distinctions: "The SCORE Act is not the solution for the athlete. You can say there's a lot of people scoring. Two big divisions and their commissioners, they're scoring. The NCAA, they're scoring. And now apparently private equity is scoring. Who is not scoring? The athletes."

The SAFE Act garnered immediate support from professional athlete unions. The NFLPA, NBPA, NWSLPA, MLSPA, MLBPA, and NHLPA all endorsed the legislation at an October 2025 video teleconference, warning that the SCORE Act would "roll back hard-fought NIL rights and health protections." Athletes.org, which vehemently opposes the SCORE Act, has been more receptive to the SAFE Act's athlete-centric approach. Even Cody Campbell, the billionaire Republican donor and Trump supporter who has spent considerable money airing television commercials against the SCORE Act, surprisingly expressed support for the SAFE Act's media rights provisions.

But here's the political reality: the SAFE Act faces obstacles that make the SCORE Act's challenges look manageable by comparison. Senator Ted Cruz, a Republican who strongly supports the SCORE Act, chairs the Senate Commerce Committee. As committee Chairman, he controls what legislation receives hearings and moves to the floor. Cruz has shown no indication he'll advance Democratic legislation that power conferences vehemently oppose. Senator Cantwell acknowledged after speaking with Cruz that she hopes for a hearing but admits passage is "possible but uphill."

And "uphill" is generous. The SAFE Act's core provision to pool media rights is a complete non-starter for the SEC and the Big Ten. Why would conferences that negotiated lucrative separate deals giving them massive competitive advantages agree to pool those rights for equitable distribution to schools they're trying to distance themselves from financially? The entire competitive strategy of the Power 2 conferences depends on concentrating media revenue rather than sharing it. They'll fight pooling provisions with every resource at their disposal.

Senator Blumenthal captured the legislative stalemate perfectly: "Nothing will pass if it is purely partisan" before the 2026 midterm elections. The SAFE Act is Democrat-backed legislation opposed by Republicans and power conferences. The SCORE Act is Republican-backed legislation opposed by Democrats and athlete advocates. Neither side has shown willingness to compromise. Conversations between the two sides "haven't gone anywhere so far," according to Senator Cantwell.

The SAFE Act was introduced as Congress was facing a government shutdown, limiting attention and momentum. And critically, the SAFE Act punts on the most fundamental question of whether athletes should be classified as employees with collective bargaining rights. When asked about this, Senator Cantwell responded vaguely: "Collective bargaining certainly would be one way to manage the system, but this is where we are today."

That evasion reveals the political constraints even athlete-friendly Democrats face. Connecticut Senator Chris Murphy, who wasn't among the SAFE Act's co-sponsors, has introduced separate legislation (the College Athlete Right to Organize Act) that would designate athletes as employees and expand NLRB jurisdiction to public universities. Former NLRB General Counsel Jennifer Abruzzo, who forcefully advocated for recognizing athletes as employees during her tenure, argues that taking a passive approach to collective bargaining rights undermines genuine athlete empowerment.

So the SAFE Act represents a middle ground: better for athletes than the SCORE Act, worse for athletes than Murphy's employment-focused legislation, unacceptable to power conferences who control Republican support, and unable to advance through a committee controlled by opponents. Its prospects for passage are worse than the SCORE Act's, which at least made it out of House committees before being pulled from the floor. The SAFE Act can't even get a hearing in the Senate Commerce Committee.

The SAFE Act still serves important purposes even if it does not become law. It provides a framework for what athlete-centric reform could look like, demonstrating that alternatives to the NCAA-friendly SCORE Act exist. It generates media attention and public discussion about revenue distribution inequities. It puts the SEC and Big Ten conferences in the uncomfortable position of explicitly opposing legislation designed to help smaller schools compete. And it establishes Democratic senators' position that any eventual compromise must include genuine athlete protections and revenue-equity provisions, rather than just institutional immunity.

But as practical legislation with realistic prospects for passage, the SAFE Act faces even longer odds than the SCORE Act. Both bills represent partisan attempts to impose preferred visions through legislative fiat rather than finding genuine consensus. Both face opposition too strong to overcome in a narrowly divided Congress. And both demonstrate that congressional intervention, which the NCAA has desperately sought for years, is unlikely to provide the stability, certainty, or resolution that any stakeholder seeks.

Indeed, Athletes.org, with approximately 5000 current and former athlete members, has been even more forceful in its opposition to the SCORE Act. Co-founder Brandon Copeland argued that no other sports model, professional or otherwise, restricts athletes' rights or grants governing bodies the unchecked power the SCORE Act would confer on the NCAA. Co-founder Jim Cavale emphasized the fundamental unfairness: "The legislation in the SCORE Act would provide serial antitrust violators with unprecedented antitrust protection, allowing the hard-fought rights college athletes have been able to claw back through courts and state law to be rolled back. If the NCAA and others want protection from antitrust law, they should agree to engage in the same activity that every other multi-billion-dollar sports business in this country is required to engage in to obtain that protection: collective bargaining." This is a characterization the NCAA disputes, but one that reflects the depth of mistrust athlete advocates bring to the legislative debate.

That critique cuts to the heart of the SCORE Act's constitutional and practical problems. Professional sports leagues receive antitrust exemptions because they engage in collective bargaining with player unions, creating negotiated agreements that balance league and player interests. The SCORE Act would grant the NCAA similar immunity without requiring collective bargaining, ostensibly allowing the organization to unilaterally determine compensation limits, transfer restrictions, and eligibility rules while prohibiting athletes from organizing or seeking employment protections.

Legal scholars have identified the fatal flaw of the private nondelegation doctrine. The SCORE Act would delegate regulatory authority to the NCAA as a private entity to make rules governing compensation, eligibility, and competition without adequate governmental oversight. Several law reviews and symposia have published comprehensive analyses concluding that the Act violates constitutional prohibitions against delegating legislative power to private parties, particularly when those private parties are market competitors regulating other market participants. By contrast, the Horseracing Integrity and Safety Act survived constitutional challenge only because it built in robust FTC oversight, something the SCORE Act lacks.

Even if these constitutional problems could be resolved, the SCORE Act faces insurmountable political obstacles. The bill needs sixty votes to pass the Senate, meaning at least seven Democrats must support it alongside all Republicans. But Democratic opposition is nearly uniform, with key senators characterizing the legislation as favoring institutions over athletes and accelerating competitive stratification between power conferences and everyone else.

And then there's what happened between December 2-4, 2025, when the political reality became impossible to ignore. Speaker Mike Johnson had scheduled a floor vote on the SCORE Act. Some congressional observers described it as their most important bill of the week. Yet it was pulled abruptly hours before the scheduled vote amid opposition from Freedom Caucus Republicans led by Chip Roy, who called the bill "well-intended but falls short and is not ready for prime time."

The procedural vote the previous day had barely squeaked through 210-209, with Freedom Caucus members Byron Donalds, Scott Perry, and Roy initially voting with Democrats to block consideration before Freedom Caucus Chair Andy Harris and Andrew Clyde switched their votes after huddling with House Majority Leader Steve Scalise. The razor-thin margin demonstrated that Johnson lacked the votes for passage, even within his own Republican caucus.

What happened subsequently made the point even more forcefully. On April 3, 2026, four months after the SCORE Act was pulled from the House floor, President Trump signed his second executive order on college athletics, "Urgent National Action to Save College Sports." The Order directs federal agencies to treat violations of NCAA eligibility, transfer, revenue sharing, and improper inducement rules as grounds to question a university's fitness for federal grants and contracts. It calls on the NCAA to install a five-year participation window, structured transfer limits, and NIL guardrails by August 1, 2026. It applies, by its terms, only to schools with athletic revenue above $20 million, which is to say the Power Four and the upper reaches of the Group of Six. Many of the attendees at the white house meeting that promoted the executive order issued statements of support.

I understand the impulse. After a decade of watching courts dismantle the old model and a year of watching Congress fail to replace it, the executive branch offered what looked like a shortcut. But the shortcut runs into the same wall. An executive order is not legislation. It does not bind the NCAA, it does not supersede the *House* settlement, and it does not override the antitrust decisions that drove the transformation in the first place. Many of its provisions, particularly the transfer restrictions and the eligibility cap, conflict directly with federal court rulings that practitioners and athletes assuredly will test the moment enforcement begins. The Order is silent on the one question that matters most for the system's long-term architecture: whether athletes are employees. And its enforcement mechanism, conditioning federal funding on compliance with private association rules, raises private nondelegation concerns that mirror the ones already identified in the SCORE Act. The Order buys time. It does not buy resolution. If anything, layering executive action on top of unresolved litigation and stalled legislation increases the number of fronts on which the next round of conflict will be fought.

Then came May 2026, and the political reality became undeniable. On May 18, hours before a scheduled House floor vote, leadership pulled the SCORE Act for the second time in less than six months. The proximate cause was a remarkable announcement earlier that day. The Congressional Black Caucus, all fifty-four voting members, declared unanimous opposition to the bill. Two CBC members who had been original co-sponsors, Representatives Shomari Figures of Alabama and Janelle Bynum of Oregon, withdrew their support. The CBC's stated rationale was striking because it had little to do with the bill's substance. The Caucus objected that "major athletic institutions continue to remain silent while Black voting rights and Black political power are being systematically dismantled across the South," a reference to the Supreme Court's April 29, 2026 decision in *Louisiana v. Callais,* which I discuss in Chapter 26, and the redistricting waves it set in motion. College sports administrators, the CBC argued, had benefited from Black athletes for generations while staying conspicuously quiet on the political rights of Black communities. That silence had a cost, and the cost was a bill the NCAA had spent years building.

I will not pretend the CBC's reasoning fits neatly within the analytical framework of this book. It does not. But it illustrates a point I think the NCAA has consistently underestimated. When you ask Congress for protection, you are asking individual members to spend political capital. Members spend that capital on their own priorities, not yours. The CBC's vote was not directly about NIL or revenue sharing. It was about whether silence on issues affecting Black voters was a price college sports leaders were willing to keep paying. The answer they received was no. Moreover, the day after, the NAACP joined the Caucus in launching a campaign it called "Out of Bounds," urging Black athletes, families, alumni, and fans to withhold their support from flagship public universities in eight Southern states moving to weaken Black voting representation, a deliberate effort to turn the labor that powers SEC, ACC, Big 12 and American programs into leverage on redistricting.

What is emerging in the SCORE Act's place is also revealing. Senate Commerce Committee Chairman Ted Cruz and Ranking Member Maria Cantwell, who spent years on opposite sides of this debate, have entered active bipartisan negotiations on alternative legislation. More than thirty participants in President Trump's college sports roundtable, including university presidents, athletic directors, and the commissioners of the ACC, Big 12, and American, sent a joint letter endorsing the Cruz-Cantwell effort. Days after the second SCORE Act collapse, a group of Senators delivered their answer. Cruz and Cantwell, joined by Senators Eric Schmitt of Missouri and Chris Coons of Delaware, two Republicans and two Democrats, announced the Protect College Sports Act of 2026 and released its text, with formal introduction expected once the Senate returned to session in June. After years of single-party bills going nowhere, the most serious legislative effort to date arrived with bipartisan authorship and the backing of the President's own roundtable. The Republican-only, NCAA-drafted approach had been definitively rejected, and the framework that would replace it had to be negotiated rather than dictated.

The Protect College Sports Act, as announced and released in draft, is by design a hybrid. It takes the two provisions the NCAA wanted most from the SCORE Act, a limited antitrust exemption for the NCAA and the College Sports Commission and federal preemption of the state NIL patchwork, and trades them for a slate of athlete protections drawn largely from Cantwell's earlier SAFE Act: guaranteed health insurance and scholarship protections, enforceable NIL contract terms, and agent regulation that requires registration and caps agent fees. It limits athletes to a single unrestricted transfer over a career, codifies something close to the five-year eligibility window the NCAA was already preparing to adopt, and reworks the Sports Broadcasting Act to let conferences pool their television rights, with a condition that any league opting in must direct part of the new revenue to women's and Olympic sports. It even reaches the sideline, with a so-called "Lane Kiffin Rule" barring coaches from changing schools midseason. Cruz called it "a stability bill, not just an NIL bill."

Cantwell framed it as protecting "the entire ecosystem," not just the small fraction of athletes bound for professional careers. On the question that sank the SCORE Act for many Democrats, whether athletes are employees, the announced bill takes a deliberately neutral position rather than the SCORE Act's flat prohibition.

I have spent this entire chapter explaining why I doubted Congress could deliver, and I want to be direct about what has changed and what has not. What has changed is genuine. For the first time, the bill carries weight from both parties; it pairs institutional relief with real athlete protections rather than offering immunity alone, and its neutral posture on employment removes the single most radioactive provision in the SCORE Act. That is the consensus I believe successful legislation requires, and it is closer than anything I expected to see while writing this book. What has not changed is the underlying difficulty. The bill still needs sixty votes. It still hands the NCAA and the College Sports Commission antitrust protection, which athlete advocates and some legal scholars will contest on the same grounds they raised against the SCORE Act, and at least one sports lawyer has already observed that an organization given everything it would gain from collective bargaining has little reason ever to bargain at all. The employment and unionization issues loom heavy. The media-rights pooling that smaller schools want remains a likely dealbreaker for the SEC and the Big Ten. As I go to print, the bill has not yet even been formally introduced or amended, only announced, and the SCORE Act's collapse came only days before that announcement, a reminder of how quickly apparent momentum can evaporate. So I will revise my prediction without abandoning my caution. The Protect College Sports Act is the first proposal I have seen that could actually become law. Whether it does will depend on whether its authors can hold a bipartisan center together against the conferences, the advocates, and the clock, and that is a question this book cannot yet answer.

Watching this unfold, I thought about the parallels to my days at the NCAA. Every time we thought we'd achieved stability through incremental reform, a new crisis would expose new vulnerabilities requiring additional changes. Every time we sought to control transformation through institutional processes, courts or legislators or public opinion would force acknowledgment that more fundamental changes were necessary. The SCORE Act represents a similar dynamic.

The opposition from Freedom Caucus Republicans is particularly revealing. These are lawmakers who generally favor reduced government regulation and protection of institutional autonomy. Their opposition suggests concerns about granting the NCAA unprecedented regulatory authority backed by federal antitrust immunity and broader concerns that the SCORE Act attempts to solve complex problems through blunt legislative instruments that will create as many issues as they resolve.

The SCORE Act seeks to address pressures from antitrust litigation, employment status challenges, variations in state NIL laws, and competitive chaos. But it doesn't resolve the fundamental tensions. The *House* settlement created an unstable equilibrium, allowing direct payments while establishing a compensation framework whose long-term legal durability courts and legislators are still assessing. The SCORE Act creates statutory permission to maintain an unsustainable system.

Almost every chapter of this book documents events forcing acknowledgment that the old model was unsustainable. The SCORE Act attempts to halt this trajectory by preventing future external pressures from forcing further change. Candidly, that's not resolution. That's resistance to inevitable evolution.

If it wasn't before, it is clear now, the SCORE Act will not pass in its current form. After two House floor pulls, Freedom Caucus member rejection, and unanimous opposition from the Congressional Black Caucus, even the bill's most committed advocates pivoted to alternative legislation. Senate Democratic opposition is too strong. Constitutional concerns are too serious. Political dynamics are too unfavorable. Even if it somehow passed, it would face immediate legal challenges on private nondelegation grounds and practical challenges implementing restrictions that athletes and their advocates would contest at every opportunity.

But one thing concerns me most about the SCORE Act. It represents the same fundamental mistake that characterized NCAA policy throughout my tenure. The belief that modification can be controlled through intransigence rather than guided through thoughtful adaptation. I spent a decade claiming that restrictions were necessary for competitive balance or educational integration. Arguing that allowing direct payments or employment status would destroy college athletics. Seeking congressional intervention that would validate our positions and prevent courts from continuing to dismantle our defenses.

The things I defended against proved more durable than the defenses themselves. Courts applying increasingly rigorous antitrust scrutiny found them insufficient, and the legal framework evolved in ways that made the old model untenable. Scandals exposed our enforcement failures. Litigation validated some athletes' concerns. Transformation became inevitable despite our resistance.

The SCORE Act represents the NCAA's final attempt to win through legislation what it lost through litigation. But understanding the motivation doesn't make the strategy viable. The influences forcing transformation haven't stopped. If anything, they've accelerated.

Senator Cantwell's August 2025 letter to Division I university leaders captured this fundamental problem. She argued that the SCORE Act "will incentivize a Power 2 conference system and create inequities for other conferences and leave behind small to mid-sized schools." She warned that it "moves us in the wrong direction" regarding Olympic sport development and could embarrass the United States "on the world stage."

These concerns are well-founded. The SCORE Act would accelerate almost every trend that makes big time college athletics less sustainable, including revenue concentration at the top, competitive stratification between haves and have-nots, elimination of non-revenue sports, and reduction of broad-based participation opportunities. By providing statutory immunity for institutional policies rather than requiring genuine negotiation with athlete representatives, it ensures that reforms will serve institutional interests rather than achieve equitable outcomes.

The collective bargaining approach would be more sustainable because it would create negotiated agreements that balance legitimate interests rather than impose restrictions that serve one party's preferences. Professional sports provide the model. Player unions and leagues negotiate compensation structures, revenue-sharing formulas, health and safety protections, and eligibility rules through processes that give both sides meaningful voice. Those negotiated agreements receive antitrust protection because they result from good-faith bargaining, not because Congress grants immunity to allow one party to dictate terms.

But the NCAA consistently has resisted athlete organizing and collective representation. The SCORE Act continues that resistance by explicitly prohibiting employment classifications that would enable or facilitate unionization. This ensures continued asymmetry in which institutions can organize through conferences and the NCAA to advocate collective interests, while athletes must operate as individuals without collective representation. Of course, I understand better than most the difficulties attendant to employment, unionization, and collective bargaining,

So where does this leave college athletics as I finish this book in 2026? The *House* settlement is being implemented with all the complications I detailed in Chapter 26. Schools are making direct payments to athletes. The College Sports Commission is attempting to regulate NIL deals. Title IX litigation is materializing over revenue-sharing disparities. Employment status cases are advancing. Competitive stratification is accelerating. And Congress is weighing a new bill, from the SCORE Act's attempt to freeze this unstable system in place through statutory immunity to the broader, bipartisan Protect College Sports Act, that would pair that immunity with enforceable athlete protections.

Of course, I understand why the NCAA pursued strategy it did. I devoted a decade advancing similar strategies myself. But from outside the organization, with the perspective of distance and experience, I can see what I couldn't appreciate while defending the system: that transformation can't be prevented through legal maneuvers, that external pressures ultimately force change regardless of institutional resistance, and that genuine sustainability requires addressing athlete concerns rather than suppressing them through statutory immunity.

The evolution of college sports will continue whether or not Congress passes the SCORE Act or not. The question is whether that metamorphosis will be managed thoughtfully through negotiation and compromise, or proceed chaotically through continued litigation, executive fiat, or legislative battles.

As I conclude this book, the SCORE Act's looks dead. Perhaps college athletics would be better served by allowing the transformation to continue organically, adapting to outside forces rather than resisting them, negotiating with athletes rather than imposing restrictions, and earning stability through fair treatment rather than seeking immunity through legislation.

That was the lesson I learned too late at the NCAA. The one I hope current leaders will learn before causing more unnecessary conflict. The transformation is happening. External pressures will continue forcing change. Institutional resistance ultimately fails. And genuine sustainability requires addressing athlete concerns rather than suppressing them through legal maneuvers, statutory or otherwise. And based on everything I witnessed during my NCAA decade, and everything I've observed since, that resistance is futile.

The transformation will continue with or without the SCORE Act. Collegiate Capitalism has arrived. The only question is what form it ultimately takes and whether institutions guide that transformation thoughtfully or resist it until they are forced to change by inevitable changes they cannot overcome.

Congress attempted a rescue, and twice failed to deliver one. A third attempt, the most credible yet, will soon be on the table. But you can't rescue a system that's fundamentally broken by providing immunity for the policies that broke it. You can only delay the inevitable reckoning while making the eventual transformation more chaotic, more contentious, and more costly for everyone involved.

I learned that lesson the hard way. I hope Congress learns it more quickly.

Acknowledgments

It was not easy to come to grips with what I have described in this book. Making it particularly difficult was my epiphany on the role I played in it all. For more than a year, I put my thoughts on paper and then revised them incessantly until I came to my truth. In fact, this book started out as a defense of a system and a longing for what it once was. Yet the more I wrote and the more I researched and the more I reflected, the more I realized that I was sharing my story as if I were still in the trenches, rather than from the perspective that distance brings. Writing this book forced me to confront truths I had spent years deflecting. The process was sometimes painful, often clarifying, and ultimately liberating. I don't know if I could have arrived at this destination without the support, honesty, and critical engagement of my family and friends. And so, I need to say thank you.

First and foremost, To My God. I am not a particularly religious man, but I am a spiritual being, and I know that I do all things through you. You guide my pen and my life. I am grateful.

There are so many people to thank, I am afraid I would miss some if I tried to name them all. But I will give a special shout-out to a few.

To My Publisher. Melissa Wilson, and her team, thank you for proposing that I write this book in the first place, and thank you for helping me with the many revisions. This does not happen without you.

To My Family. Mom, Dad, Brother, Sister, In-laws, Nieces, Nephews, Godchildren, and my "Play Cousins." Thank you for helping me reach my truth and for your thoughtful input on my style and substance.

To My Sons. J. Alex & Jason, thank you for your reverse mentorship, your basketball talents, which led me to this dream job, and our experiences that I have now shared with the world. See you at the next Final Four.

To My Bonus Children. Lauryn & Brendan, thank you for inviting me into your lives and joining my journey through my time at the NCAA.

To My Wife, Alicia, you lived through almost every crisis in this book alongside me, tolerated the late nights of writing and the even later nights of second-guessing, and never let me settle for anything less than my best. This book exists because of your patience, your judgment, and your love.

To My Friends. I shared my book ideas with very few of my trusted friends, and each of you delivered. Your collective expertise in law, business, politics, sports, media, higher education, common sense, and who I am brought me closer to each of you and helped me offer my perspectives, grounded in real events and data, in my authentic voice.

To My Colleagues at the NCAA and in the Membership. Several of you will disagree with some of what I have written here. I understand, and I hope you appreciate that I know you serve(d) with dedication and integrity through extraordinary challenges. You know who you are, and I respect your service even where our conclusions may now differ.

To the Student Athletes I encountered during my decade at the NCAA and the decade before in the grassroots world. Your talent, your resilience, and your willingness to challenge a system that did not always serve you as expected inspired this book more than you know.

To My lawyer. I believe in Lincoln's admonition that a lawyer who represents himself has a fool for a client, so I hired Daniel Watkins, who read every word with the eye of a media expert and litigator and the patience of a saint, and who kept me honest about the line between memoir and legal exposure.

And to my brother from another mother. Wally Renfro. Your insight, encyclopedic knowledge of history, thoughtful perspectives, expertise in prose, and tough love helped me bring this book to life. You are the closest I had to a co-author on this journey. WE did it.

Index

Index

Index

Index

Index

Index

Index

Index

Index

Index

O

Index

Index

www.ingramcontent.com/pod-product-compliance
Lightning Source LLC
LaVergne TN
LVHW020412220926
848484LV00016B/2540/J
* 9 7 8 1 9 5 9 9 9 3 7 1 1 *